1987
13th EDITION
THE COMPLETE HANDBOOK OF
PRO FOOTBALL

SPECTATORS SPORTS

☐ **THE COMPLETE HANDBOOK OF BASEBALL: 1987 EDITION edited by Zander Hollander.** The essential book for every baseball fan.. Twenty-six team yearbooks in one, with nearly 300 player and manager profiles, year-by-year stats, all-time records and award winners, and hundreds of photos.   (147618—$4.95)

☐ **SPORTS NOSTALGIA QUIZ BOOK (Revised and Updated Edition) by Zander Hollander and David Schulz.** Packed with entertainment and exciting memories. Great sports figures are recalled and thrilling athletic events recaptured as you dig deep into the old mental bean bag for answers to over 150 tantalizing quizzes.   (140230—$2.50)

☐ **INSTANT REPLAY: THE GREEN BAY DIARY OF JERRY KRAMER edited by Dick Schaap.** From the locker room to the goal line, from the training field to the Super Bowl, this is the inside story of a great pro football team..."The best behind-the-scenes glimpse of pro football ever produced."—*The New York Times*   (146301—$3.95)*

☐ **EVERYTHING YOU ALWAYS WANTED TO KNOW ABOUT SPORTS* *and didn't know where to ask by Mickey Herskowitz and Steve Perkins.** Here is the book that answers every question a sports fan ever had in the back of his mind and tells the truth about the whispered rumors of the sports world.   (124715—$2.75)

1987
13th EDITION
THE COMPLETE HANDBOOK OF
PRO FOOTBALL

EDITED BY ZANDER HOLLANDER

A SIGNET BOOK
NEW AMERICAN LIBRARY

ACKNOWLEDGMENTS

Can Ray Perkins and Vinny Testaverde turn it around in Tampa? Can the champion Giants do it again? (Nobody has since the Steelers of 1978–79.) How will Al Saunders (San Diego) and Frank Gansz (K.C.) fare as first-time head coaches? What is more certain is that instant replay is back for another year's trial and ESPN makes its NFL debut (including eight Sunday night games and the Pro Bowl).

The new season marks the 13th annual edition of *The Complete Handbook of Pro Football*, for which we acknowledge the writers on the facing page, contributing editor Eric Compton, Rich Rossiter, David Kaplan, Steve Wisniewski, Westchester Book Composition, Dot Gordineer and Beri Greenwald of Libra Graphics, Elias Sports Bureau, Pete Abitante, Dick Maxwell, Roger Goodell, Joe Browne, Jim Heffernan and the NFL team publicists.

Zander Hollander

PHOTO CREDITS: Front and back cover—Mitchell Reibel. Inside photos—John Biever, Vernon Biever, Ira Gooden, George Gojkovich, Kevin Reece, Wide World, Candid Productions and the NFL and college team photographers.

First Printing, August 1987

1 2 3 4 5 6 7 8 9

PRINTED IN THE UNITED STATES OF AMERICA

CONTENTS

Herschel Walker:
Special Delivery in Dallas ....By Gary Myers   6

The New Super World
of Phil Simms.....................By Peter King   16

John Elway: Mile High & No Vice...By Dick Connor   24

Lawrence Taylor vs. The Greatest
All-Time Linebackers ....By Ray Didinger   34

Inside the AFC.................By Peter Finney Jr.   44

Buffalo Bills 48   Los Angeles Raiders......113
Cincinnati Bengals.........57   Miami Dolphins...........123
Cleveland Browns 66   New England Patriots.....132
Denver Broncos 75   New York Jets............142
Houston Oilers 85   Pittsburgh Steelers 151
Indianapolis Colts..........94   San Diego Chargers......161
Kansas City Chiefs 104   Seattle Seahawks 171

Inside the NFC.....................By Bill Verigan 182

Atlanta Falcons...........184   New Orleans Saints 248
Chicago Bears 193   New York Giants..........258
Dallas Cowboys 202   Philadelphia Eagles......267
Detroit Lions 212   St. Louis Cardinals 276
Green Bay Packers.......221   San Francisco 49ers......285
Los Angeles Rams 230   Tampa Bay Buccaneers...294
Minnesota Vikings 239   Washington Redskins.....302

NFL Statistics 312
NFL Standings: 1921-1986.............................330
NFL Draft 350
NFL Schedule 364
NFL TV Schedule......................................367

Editor's Note: The material herein includes trades and rosters up to final printing deadline.

HERSCHEL WALKER: SPECIAL DELIVERY IN DALLAS

By GARY MYERS

Herschel Walker was having dinner in a Dallas restaurant with friends in August 1986, just a couple of days after he had signed a $5-million contract with the Cowboys.

Walker was trying to dig into his prime rib but he was having trouble concentrating. Every two minutes, a waiter would come over to wish him luck or a fan would stop by asking for his autograph. Even before he played for the NFL's most visible team, Walker was already one of the world's most recognizable athletes.

Finally, a woman in her mid-20s approached.

"Herschel?" she asked.

"Yes," he said.

"Welcome to Dallas," she said.

"Thank you," he said.

"Do you mind if I give you a kiss on the cheek?"

"No ma'am," he said.

"Thanks," she said after a quick poke. "Now my girlfriend pays for my dinner. She bet me I wouldn't have the nerve to do that."

Walker laughed. "Enjoy your dinner," he said.

Walker went right back to work on the prime rib. Unfazed.

That's because, in some ways, everybody has always wanted a piece of Herschel Walker.

It began with the college recruiter who tried to set up clandestine meetings with him at a cemetery or interrupted his 10:30 accounting class to give him one more reason to attend his school. It continued during his record-breaking days at Georgia,

Herschel Walker sprouts his wings as a Cowboy.

then for his three years with the USFL New Jersey Generals when he was running wild in a league few cared about.

Now, it's the Dallas Cowboys who want a piece of Walker.

The sparkle is missing from the silver star these days in Dallas. That's what results from a 7-9 season, the first time the Cowboys have lost more than they've won since their infancy in 1964. And it was the second time in the last three years the playoffs have started without them, which leads some to believe a trend has developed.

But there is hope. There's always hope as long as the coach is named Tom Landry. He has proven capable of transforming desperate situations into playoff years.

Herschel tries another racquet in TV's "The Superstars."

And he will have to do it again in 1987 if the Cowboys are to assume what they believe to be their rightful place among the league's elite. And this year, Landry will place a tremendous amount of the burden on a running back who stopped by in 1986 and left everybody hungry for more: Herschel Walker.

"I think he's going to have a great year," says Cowboys' president Tex Schramm. "He may be the greatest two-way threat in modern football. I'm not worried about him. He's going to be alright."

Walker signed his 5-year, $5-million contract with the Cowboys on Aug. 13, 1986, two weeks after the USFL was awarded $1 in damages—a few bucks short of the $1.69 billion it was seeking—in its antitrust suit against the NFL.

His arrival caused quite a stir among the Cowboys. There was team-wide jealousy about his contract. But it began to subside very early in the season. Walker scored on a twisting run in the final two minutes of the season opener to beat the Giants, 31-28. He soon displayed a surprising ability to catch the ball. And he was running over people.

"Look at what Herschel did," Schramm said. "And we didn't even figure out how to use him until the middle of the season."

Walker finished his NFL rookie year with 76 catches for 837

Can Herschel lift the Cowboys back into the playoffs?

yards and rushed for another 737. He was the Cowboys' Mr. Versatility: lined up in the backfield, split wide or put in motion. He was a cinch to become just the second player in league history to put together a 1,000-1,000 season until a midyear ankle injury slowed him down for four games.

By the end of the season he was fine. Example: he had 292 yards total offense in the 15th week against the Philadelphia Eagles, which included matching 82-yard touchdowns, one running, the other receiving.

Like the time the woman gave him the kiss in the restaurant, Walker remains unfazed by his accomplishments. He was the first college back to rush for over 5,000 yards in his first three seasons and would have broken Tony Dorsett's NCAA record (6,082) if he had remained at Georgia for his senior year. In his final USFL season, Walker rushed for a professional football-record 2,411 yards.

But ask him what his expectations are for this season and in his typically humble, low-key tone, he'll say: "That's hard to say."

Very rarely does he reveal a glimpse of what goes on inside. He's always friendly, always accommodating, always saying the right things. He has perfected his public presence.

He was a world-class sprinter at Georgia.

Now he must save the Dallas Cowboys.

"I'm not better than anyone else," he said. "I'm a person. People say, 'You've always got a camera on you.' But I have chosen this lifestyle and I want to be the best at it that I can be. I'm fortunate to be able to play football and to be on TV, but I didn't get there by myself. I had a lot of support and a lot of encouragement. The Lord has given me the ability and the way I show my appreciation is to be the best that I can be. You're not going to sneak your way into heaven. You're not going to sneak your way into anything."

Thus, Walker doesn't get angry—and he's had his reasons—when teammates become full of themselves. "An athlete must realize that everyone is important," he said. "Rich, poor, fat, skinny, it doesn't matter. Life is very special and you only live once. When you get an opportunity to do something, you have to give it 110 percent. Otherwise, you may never get that chance again. You may wish you gave it 110 percent, but then it's too late."

The Cowboys feel that not only is Walker a special player, he's a special person. But they are paying him the $5 million to get them back into the Super Bowl. At 6-1, 222, Walker is built more along the lines of a streamlined fullback than the NFL's prototype tailback.

But, in the truest sense, he is a rare player for his size. He has world-class speed with capabilities of a 4.4 for the 40. In "The Superstars" in February, in which he won the overall competition, he defeated Washington cornerback Darrell Green, considered the NFL's fastest player, in the 100-yard dash. Walker, obviously, can run away from most of the NFL's defensive players.

He can also run over them. He doesn't go near the weight cage, but he might be the strongest running back in the NFL. Unlike Dorsett, his teammate with the Cowboys, Walker is not a juke and jive runner. "He's a strong runner, not a very elusive guy," said Dorsett, who is just the opposite. "He has a lot of explosion and power and has the ability to take off and leave you."

The Cowboys are expecting an All-Pro season in 1987 in return for the money Walker is getting.

Money has certainly posed no problem for Walker in the last four years. He left Georgia after his junior year to accept a three-year contract from the Generals for $3.9 million. He later signed a four-year extension for $6 million, which was to have kicked in for the 1986 USFL season that was never played. Still, Walker escaped with a healthy settlement from Generals' owner Donald

Trump, with estimates that he collected about $2 million, with more to come. The Cowboys, fighting a deadline to get Walker signed, negotiated into the night with his agent, Peter Johnson. In a Cowboys' first, they guaranteed every last penny of the $5 million. Schramm told Johnson: structure it any way you want.

Johnson did. Walker's salary for the five years are $400,000, $500,000, $800,000, $900,000 and $1 million. The remaining $1.4 million comes in the form of a signing bonus: $400,000 to be paid this year and $1 million in 1988.

By midseason, Walker was the talk of the NFL. Cowboy fans loved him. The Cowboys were 6-2, scoring 30 points a game, and apparently headed to the playoffs. Johnson said he couldn't answer his phone fast enough. The endorsement offers were flying in. But then the Cowboys suffered a succession of injuries to key people, including Walker, Dorsett and quarterback Danny White. And Dallas had the NFL's worst record over the second half of the season: 1-7.

As a result, many of the companies that were ready to hand over their checkbooks to Walker backed off. Nobody wants to be associated with a 7-9 team, even if the player is Herschel Walker.

"People relate to winners," Johnson said. "We were able to do things right off the bat, but as things turned out, the majority of things he did in the offseason were appearances."

Walker can be seen in Corn Flakes commercials or "Who's Behind Those Foster Grants?" or doing spots for Adidas. He also did an endorsement for a large Dallas supermarket chain. And he gets $10,000 to $15,000 for appearances on the rubber-chicken circuit. But Johnson is counting on a big season from Walker and a playoff season from the Cowboys to really set things in gear.

"You've got to be a merchandiseable personality on a winning team," Johnson said.

Nobody could blame Walker, however, if he wanted out of Dallas before he even got there. The welcome from teammates was less than heart-warming. Cowboy players are annually strung out by management in contract negotiations. And many resented not only the amount of money Walker received, but the ease in which he got it.

The most put-out was Dorsett, who had nothing against Walker personally, but issued the classic "This town's not big enough for the two of us" speech. Dorsett's contract, with a lucrative long-term $6-million annuity, was actually very close to Walker's in current dollars. But Dorsett is a proud man and he couldn't handle constantly hearing about "FIVE YEARS, FIVE MILLION DOLLARS."

"If these figures are correct, Tony Dorsett is unhappy," Dorsett said in the summer of '86. "When they pay this man that kind of money, they're telling me they don't have a need for me . . . If I'm unhappy here, I can be a very disruptive force.

"Herschel hasn't contributed one yard to this team's success and they're going to pay him twice as much? That tells me that this man is their top back, and Tony Dorsett is second to no back on this team."

Dorsett dismissed his annuity and real estate deal that brought his annual salary closer to $700,000 than its $450,000 base. "Real estate and annuities ain't nothing," he insisted. "This is present-day dollars [for Walker] and mine is dollars down the road. A village idiot can figure that one out. Nobody's mad at Herschel but all the players say they can't believe this."

Dorsett was not the only one to protest. Safety Dennis Thurman painted a dollar sign on the towel he wears to practice. Everson Walls painted a dollar sign on his spats. Danny White said, "I'm one of those guys who has been around a long time and after you play 11 or 12 years you feel like you've paid your dues, worked hard, accomplished a lot. Then they bring a guy in who hasn't played a down in the NFL and they pay him twice as much as you get."

Walker's reaction to Dorsett's tirade: "I respect Tony a great deal. There's not too much I can say. He's been a credit to his team and to the game."

With each of the 1,604 total yards Walker gained, with each of the 14 touchdowns he scored, the barriers began to break down. He became one of the Cowboys. He's comfortable enough that he's building a house in Las Colinas, the newest of the many fashionable towns in the Dallas area.

And he's hoping that Landry finds a way to fully utilize his talents. Landry took it slow with Walker, perhaps overemphasizing the difficulty of the Dallas playbook. One month into the season, Walker was already frustrated with his playing time. That didn't change. In 11 of the 16 games, he carried 10 or fewer times.

He went to speak with Landry in midseason, who told him to be patient. To that point, Walker was being used as a changeup to Dorsett, not with Dorsett. Finally, with the Cowboys' playoff hopes crumbling, Landry started Walker and Dorsett together for the first time with four games remaining. The Dream Backfield lives.

"Last year was tough not knowing what I was going to do, because all my life I've sort of known what I was doing in the offense," Walker said. "I'm a runner and I want to run with the ball more."

Landry goes into the season with plans to play Walker and Dorsett together full time. They will have to block for each other occasionally and neither makes his money doing that. But the negatives are far outweighed by the positives. Playing them together puts tremendous pressure on the defense, which can not key on one or the other. They can both run, they can both catch and they both realize the importance the other can play in helping the team's success.

There's no question that Walker is the Cowboys' back of the future. But Dorsett is far from used up, so Walker will have to wait awhile until he is the featured back in the offense.

But Walker has always understood that football is a team game and he's always worked hard at trying not to alienate teammates who might be jealous. Walker has turned off some people in the past because he is hard to get to know. He talks all the time about retiring, how football is fun, not a passion.

While college coaches from around the country had waited for Walker to select a school, he scared them all by suggesting he might join the Marines.

He once wrote a poem about himself, called "They Do Not Know."

I wish they could see,
The real person in me.
Someday I reckon they will know,
I'm not only here for the show.
I have one man upstairs,
They do not know, but they will see one day.

He simply has a different perspective on life. He insisted when the USFL closed up that he might go into real estate with Trump. Or he might go back and run track, his first athletic love. "I'm just weird," he says. "Nobody really knows Herschel."

He once felt so bad about getting stopped for speeding that he called the police officer to apologize. He once ripped the door off a burning car and saved a woman.

He grew up one of seven children in racially torn Wrightsville, Ga., a town of 2,300, in a family that had to make do on $30 a week.

By his senior year in high school, he was a legend. By his junior year at Georgia, he was a natural resource. On the afternoon of Feb. 22, 1983, Lt. Gov. Zell Miller interrupted the proceedings of the Georgia State Senate in Atlanta to announce that Walker was going pro.

Rep. Culver Kidd of Milledgeville suggested that all senators

Herschel and Cincy DeAngelis (now Mrs. Walker) in '82.

should wear black armbands for the rest of the week. Walker was obviously big in Georgia. During the 1980 election, he received three write-in votes for President.

He gave credibility to the Georgia football program. In 1980 the University of Georgia received 7,358 financial contributions totaling $1,069,656. In 1981, the year after Walker's freshman season, the university received 9,395 contributions totaling $2,750,114.56.

Some Georgia fans have not forgiven Walker for taking the money and running. But he built his family a five-bedroom brick home with a built-in swimming pool in Wrightsville. He took care of those who took care of him.

He has a strong sense of responsibility and purpose. He is never out of shape. He spends his free time watching television and doing situps. He often does over 1,000 situps at night. "I do it watching 'Love Connection,'" he said. "I'm usually done by the first date."

The Cowboys hope Walker gets them a date into the playoffs in 1987. They can't do it without him.

"Just getting adopted into the Cowboys' family, I think, was the best thing that ever happened to me," he said.

And he doesn't ponder about what the future holds or what the past has brought. "I never think about a season. I never think about a game when it's over," he said. "I go home and watch TV and forget about everything."

Phil Simms eludes Broncos in the Super Bowl.

THE NEW SUPER WORLD OF PHIL SIMMS

By PETER KING

The marketing of Phil Simms, American Hero, began about 30 seconds after the gun sounded to end the New York Giants' 39-20 victory over Denver in Super Bowl XXI last January. A disheveled Simms, the winning quarterback, turned to a camera and answered a question about his post-Super Bowl plans by saying: "I'm taking my family to Disney World."

Simms, for that one-sentence endorsement, made $75,000. That's $4,000 more than three Giants did in base salary for the entire season.

That's show biz.

Winning the Super Bowl and the MVP award did wonders for Phil Simms, who had been one of the best-kept promotional secrets in professional sports. When he completed 22 of 25 passes (for an NFL postseason record 88 percent completion rate) for 268 yards and three touchdowns, he finally began to show America what Simms the quarterback could do when the professional pressure was on and Simms the person could do when products needed to be pushed.

"Phil Simms," said his Manhattan-based agent, David Fishof, "is an American hero. He's perfect for so many products."

He is perfect because he is a work-ethic, underdog type who made it big. Ain't that America? He earned all his spending money as a kid from two Louisville paper routes, grew up with the nickname of Whitey, received no major-college scholarship offers, played for a perennial NCAA Division I-AA loser, fought his way to a first-round draft choice by the most storied franchise in the NFL, overcame four season-ending injuries in his first five NFL seasons, endured years of home-crowd hatred, and finally —in a year in which he was a Giants Stadium target as late as November—played the greatest game of any quarterback in the 21-year history of the Super Bowl.

When he was named the Super Bowl's Most Valuable Player, NFL commissioner Pete Rozelle sidled up to Simms and told him: "I'm glad you won it. You have the type of image we need in this league."

So in the months following the game of his life, Simms jetted from Los Angeles to Newark to Los Angeles to Newark to Florida to Newark to Kentucky. And back. And to other places. He schmoozed with Justine Bateman of "Family Ties" on the "Tonight Show." He grinned and posed with every Subaru dealer and family west of Tokyo when he received a $17,000 sports car for being the Super Bowl MVP, saying all the right things to all the right people. He told a crowd at his alma mater, Morehead State, that he felt terrifically honored to have his college number—12—retired.

As a pro football writer for Newsday, *Peter King followed Phil Simms' every move in the New York Giants' championship season.*

He urged employees at corporate motivational sessions in New York, New Jersey and Florida to sell, sell, sell, using his blue-collar-to-riches background as inspiration. He earned his picture-perfect wife, Diana, an expensive fur for a short photo session at a New Jersey furrier. He became the corporate image for a New York brokerage house in advertisements. He and teammate Phil McConkey did a book with Dick Schaap. He made a workout video and an instructional video.

Fishof said Simms could have earned $1 million in the off-season following such a Super Bowl showing as his. But the earnings probably were closer to $500,000, to supplement his $650,000 salary in 1986 (with $150,000 deferred until 1990 for tax reasons) and $64,000 playoff earnings. That's about $1.21 million, give or take a few hundred grand.

That's good. It could have been much, much more. "I'm going to make a lot of people mad, especially my agent," Simms said when the corporate jockeying with Fishof was heavy in the late winter. "But I'm going to say no to a lot of things. That's the way it's got to be. I won't let my offseason conditioning be affected by this."

"I could have had him out every day, for two appearances," Fishof said. "But his offseason [workout] program is important, and it's also important that he not change his image to do an ad. Plus, you don't want to overexpose someone like Phil. I did the Monkees' reunion tour last year, and when I brought the Monkees back, I held them off live TV although there were plenty of chances to do TV. We wanted to make sure people came to see them in person. So this is like building the career of an entertainer."

Strange how one season—one game, really—can change how a man is perceived so dramatically.

* * *

When Simms was a white-haired teenager in the Louisville suburb of Okolona, he was one of eight children in the lower-middle-class family of Barbara and William Simms. He had some Huck Finn in him: in the mornings, he'd deliver the *Louisville Courier-Journal*; in the afternoons, it was the *Louisville Times*. He'd walk the narrow streets of Okolona, balancing papers on his head, folding them and throwing them porchward.

Whitey Simms took to lifting weights in the basement of his small frame house, and it appeared the diligent work would pay off. He had a terrific year at Southern High in Louisville, drawing scouts to watch him play quarterback in the fall and pitch in the spring. But as a senior he hurt his shoulder playing football,

MVP Simms basks in the afterglow of his Super performance.

missed a couple of games, and lost the interest of scouts.

Indiana offered him a baseball scholarship, but all he wanted to do was play quarterback. Anywhere. No scholarship came until the Louisville-area recruiter for Morehead State, coerced into watching some late-season high-school game films by the Southern coach, saw enough in Simms to offer him a free ride. The offer was an unenthusiastic one, but who was Simms to bicker? He had his chance. He set school records for passing yardage (5,542) and touchdown passes (32) despite Morehead changing to a running game before his senior year.

(Simms never forgot Morehead, the only school to remember him in high school. He returns there annually to raise money for the football program. He had a clause put in his contract with a football shoe company to outfit every MSU football player with two pairs of cleats—for grass and artificial turf—each year. "Phil Simms has never lost touch with his past," said Morehead assistant coach Jerry Mayes.)

Simms was the cult player of the 1979 draft. In December, a few scouts thought well of him. In January, he began getting quiet raves from some birddogs who flocked to the eastern Kentucky hills to see him throw. By February, everyone knew him.

The 49ers sent passing-game coach Sam Wyche to Morehead, and he thought he could be their quarterback of the future. (When they failed in their attempt to draft Simms, the 49ers waited until the third round and picked someone named Joe Montana from Notre Dame.) Offensive coordinator Joe Gibbs of the San Diego Chargers flew 2,000 miles to watch Simms—who had mononucleosis—throw 10 passes. "I knew he wouldn't last until our pick (late) in the first round," Gibbs said.

In late February and March, the Giants got interested. New general manager George Young, hired on Feb. 14, put Simms with Washington State's Jack Thompson atop his quarterback list. When new coach Ray Perkins came back from a scouting trip, he walked into Young's office and said: "You won't believe the quarterback I like best." Young said he would believe it. "Simms," Perkins said. Young agreed.

The Giants decided to take Simms over running back Ottis Anderson in the draft, which was a difficult pick for a franchise in need of public backing and a drawing card. Anderson was an All-American, a legitimate star. Simms was—ahem—second-team All-Ohio Valley Conference. "I think George and Ray wanted to get some feeling about what I thought," said team president Wellington Mara, reminiscing about the selection of Simms. "I just told them, 'That's fine. But you'd better erect some barricades in the Lincoln Tunnel, because the draftniks will be over here when they hear.'"

When Pete Rozelle stepped to the microphone in New York to announce the Giants' first-round pick, he said: "The New York Giants pick quarterback Phil Simms of . . ."

"BOOOOOOOOOOOOO!!!!!!!!" yelped the gallery of about 300.

They continued to boo for much of seven seasons. They booed because he kept getting hurt; a shoulder sprain, separated shoulder, torn knee ligaments and dislocated thumb finished 1980, '81, '82 and '83 for him. Before the injury in 1983, Simms lost the starting quarterback job to Scott Brunner and asked to be traded. "I was probably lucky," Simms says now. "I wasn't able to play myself out of the position. That's what happened to Scott. He played himself out of the league."

Before the 1984 season, coach Bill Parcells handed him the starting job and medium- to long-range passing offense, both for the first time in his pro quarterbacking life. The result: 4,044 passing yards, a 9-7 Giants' record and a wild-card playoff victory over the Rams.

The fans, and the advertising world, weren't convinced of much. "I hear no one saying, 'I want Phil Simms,'" Manhattan ad executive Al Ries said in July 1985. "In New York, Doug Flutie right now occupies the quarterback position in peoples' minds."

How times change.

Simms threw for 3,829 yards and the Giants went 10-6 in 1985. They won another playoff game. He won the Pro Bowl's MVP award with a three-touchdown day. But Joe Montana stayed the high-gloss quarterback and Jim McMahon became the punky and rebellious one.

It took the strange season of 1986 to propel Simms into America's consciousness. On Nov. 2, when the Giants' offense was introduced before playing Dallas at Giants Stadium, a full 60 percent of the crowd booed. Simms was playing with inexperienced and injured receivers, and struggling. On Nov. 23, Simms willed the Giants to a win in Minnesota, after which Parcells whispered in his ear: "You can play for my team anytime."

He threw for a Giants' playoff-record four touchdowns in the January win over San Francisco, getting knocked senseless and not seeing two of the touchdowns. He played a super Super Bowl. He finished the season with 3,487 passing yards—more than John Elway, more than Dan Fouts—and respect. At last.

"To me," Young said, "the whole credibility factor is moot. I'm not going to defend this guy any more. He doesn't need it."

Looking back, Simms hides any resentment he surely feels. "I came in with a terrible . . . I didn't come in with a very good team," he said. "We were bad, and we even got worse. Players very seldom think the problem is them. I was always the same way. I always thought I was good enough. I know this: For a quarterback to succeed there's got to be some help around him.

"You've got to be lucky. I mean, for me to complete a pass, I've got to have protection, a guy's got to get open, I've got to throw it, he's got to hold it. A lot of things have to happen for me to be good. In those days, I knew it wasn't all my fault. I knew physically I had the chance to be a pretty good player. I never had doubts. I really didn't.

"I've changed as a quarterback. I do a lot of things better than I did before. I get rid of the ball fairly quick. I just understand now more than I did when I was younger. You've got to learn to be a quarterback in this league. I don't know if it's anything specifically you learn. It's not something a coach can teach you. You just learn to do things. You have to."

Simms made himself good. The weightlifting hobby he began in high school continued through college and to today. On the

Friday before last January's NFC championship game, he left the weight room at 8 P.M.—three hours after everyone else had left. Again this offseason, he was a constant participant in the Giants' four-times-weekly workout program at Giants Stadium.

Said teammate Phil McConkey, a former naval officer: "I think I've got a pretty good eye for football and a pretty good eye for people. Let me tell you something about Phil Simms. I've met some POWs, guys who were in camps for six or seven years in Hanoi. God forbid this ever would happen, but if he ever became a POW, he'd be as tough as any of the guys I ever met. He's got guts that just spill out of him."

"The best thing I did was just hang in there and keep fighting," Simms said. "There was a time where I never thought I'd play any more than a year or two, I was getting so beat up. Now I can see how some of these quarterbacks play a while: they're on good teams. They don't get beat up all the time."

And they have good offensive lines. The Giants have an adequate wall to open up daylight for Joe Morris (2,851 rushing yards in the past two years) and to keep the forearm shivers off Simms, who has always liked to hold the ball until the last second before throwing.

"I don't know what else he can do," offensive coordinator Ron Erhardt said.

Except to do it again.

*　*　*

At one offseason awards ceremony, Simms saw Fishof talking to a few reporters, pumping up his image and his talents. "Hey, Fish," Simms called over. "Don't talk about me so much. You're getting me nervous."

He should get used to it. Life could get very soft right about now for Simms. The fame, the money, the absence of boos. Will the head fit into the size 7⅜ helmet this fall?

"I won't change," he said. "I think this is going to be my best season."

There are good reasons to think he has his mental house in order. Here's why:

• He has shared the wealth. Reportedly, Simms didn't want to have a book written by him or about him in the offseason. When Fishof suggested he share a book with McConkey, thereby giving McConkey a good chunk of offseason change, Simms agreed. The book deal brought Simms and McConkey about $65,000 each. According to Fishof, Simms said: "Let's get McConkey in it. Let's split it with McConkey." Simms didn't want any resentment from his teammates.

• He worked. By mid-February, he had already lifted weights six times, something strength and conditioning coach Johnny Parker opposed. Parker told him to rest until March. Simms rested some, spending a week at his parents' six-acre place in suburban Louisville in late February, but he worked out steadily beginning in March.

• He didn't relish being famous. "Phil's not a Broadway jock," said George Young. Simms wanted to cancel his "Tonight Show" appearance in the week after the Super Bowl because of the coast-to-coast grind, but he had to do it because it was a firm date. He'd just as soon play 18 holes of golf or throw the baseball around with five-year-old son Christopher in the front yard of his colonial home in Franklin Lakes, N.J.

• He's realistic about his fate. Simms knows if he starts poorly in 1987 and the team follows, he'll feel the heat again. "I just don't care about that anymore," he said of the fan reaction to him. "I've said enough about that and been asked enough about it." While Diana Simms watched the celebration at Giants Stadium after the Super Bowl, she had a sobering reaction to the wild cheers her husband heard. "They'll find something else [to be critical about] next year," she said. As Ken Anderson has said for years, "Quarterbacks get far too much credit when you win and far too much blame when you lose."

This has been Phil Simms' life in New Jersey since 1979. Mostly blame, but some credit. Finally, some credit.

At one of his offseason appearances, at the Grand Hyatt Hotel in Manhattan, after Simms received the keys to his MVP automobile, he was enveloped. Ten reporters surrounded him, asking him mostly the same questions he had heard countless times since the Super Bowl. Four TV crews waited their turns. A women with a garbage bag filled with 20 official Super Bowl XXI footballs kept handing him the balls in mid-sentence; he didn't skip a syllable, signing his autograph with a magic marker as he talked. At one point, former Giants' coach Allie Sherman walked by and whispered to him: "I just wanted to come by and say you did a wonderful job. Great. Wonderful. Congratulations."

Fishof stood nearby, reveling in the success. "He's an all-American boy," Fishof said.

At last, people know.

JOHN ELWAY: MILE HIGH & NO VICE

By DICK CONNOR

They hurry through the now-empty lobby, two husky young men with their pretty wives, stopping only long enough to buy some popcorn from a suddenly flustered vendor.

Inside, the house lights have gone dark, the previews are running.

John Elway is not late for the movie. Neither are the rest of his party, wife Janet and teammate Keith Bishop and wife Mary.

When you go out with John Elway in Denver these days, late arrivals and early departures are built into the schedule. "We always make sure we get there late. And we leave before the lights go on at the finish, when they are still running the credits," Elway said of a lifestyle strong-armed young millionaires must adapt to in a city that paints orange stripes down principal streets for a parade honoring the Super Bowl losers.

"It's tough to go out," he acknowledged. "The most embarrassing thing for me is when I'm around high-school kids. It's the fact they are loud, and start shouting my name, and all of a sudden heads are turned."

Hard as it may seem to be to believe, Elway remains an essentially private person, and one still not at ease with his fame.

"I figure God's getting back at me," Elway said. "I used to stare at people when I was young. My mom always used to slap me. I figure now He's getting back at me. Now they are staring at

Dick Connor, perennial Colorado Sportswriter of the Year, is sports columnist of The Rocky Mountain News.

Giants frustrate John Elway in the Super Bowl.

me and I'm not comfortable with that."

He'll have to work on that. Fame is as much a part of John Elway's life these days as are blitzing linebackers and gawking hero worshipers.

Unless Denver renegotiated an even healthier figure before the start of the 1987 season, Elway will earn $1 million in the final year of a five-year contract this season. He has quarterbacked Denver to 37 victories, two playoff appearances and the Super Bowl in his last three years, and emerged as one of the legitimate new supernovas in the NFL firmament.

The No. 1 choice of the 1983 collegiate draft is finally living up to all expectations—except his own. "I won't be able to regard myself as a great quarterback until I win the Super Bowl," he said last November.

On a snowy late February day, babysitting his daughter Jessica in their suburban Denver home, nothing has happened to change that for him.

Not the 98-yard march in Cleveland that made him at least president pro tem of the Class of '83; not the gaudy winning marks of the past three seasons; not the club record 11 straight completions against the Raiders in the Los Angeles Coliseum; not the fact he led all NFL quarterbacks in total yards in 1985 (4,144); not even last season's Pro Bowl nomination by his peers has quite convinced Elway he is where he wants to be.

"I have taken big steps, but I don't think just playing [in the Super Bowl] will get it done. I guess that is more in my mind than anything else," he noted.

But it is there. John Elway wants to be the best. Period. Not "one of" or "among" or "near the top of." Until he takes his Denver Broncos to another Super Bowl, and wins, that nagging little unfulfilled chamber will linger for this 26-year-old who came into the league with more fanfare than anyone since Joe Namath almost two decades earlier.

Like Namath, he had to learn to live with it. Like Namath, he also had to learn to live up to it.

It's the story of a likeable, basically unaffected superstar who went through an indoctrination process almost unprecedented in NFL history—and survived it.

Before he threw his first pass in a professional game, he was pictured on the cover of *Sports Illustrated*. He arrived at training camp in Greeley, Colo., an hour's drive northeast of Denver, as the object of an incredible media focus. What he ate for breakfast, what he said, every pass in practice, even where he got his hair cut . . . all were grist for daily tables in both Denver newspapers as part of The Elway Watch.

Just at the time he wanted to be accepted by his teammates, that circus atmosphere set him apart. Even the circumstances of his becoming a Bronco separated him. He had refused to go to Baltimore, the team that drafted him. Steeler quarterback Terry Bradshaw had ripped him as a spoiled brat. "He ought to grow up and pay his dues," Bradshaw snapped. The rich brat image is a characterization that still haunts Elway.

Several factors combined to make his arrival in Denver— where owner Edgar Kaiser had arranged a trade with the Colts' Robert Irsay to obtain Elway's rights in one of the century's great steals—less than ideal. There was the attempt by the Raiders to land him from Baltimore, and claims that the league had somehow prevented it by persuading Chicago not to part with a draft choice that might have cemented the deal.

A newspaper war between the *Rocky Mountain News* and *Denver Post* had created a hotly competitive situation that was duplicated by television, where three Denver stations and three talk shows were in a war of their own. With no major-league baseball to dilute interest and attention, the Broncos have always been the objects of attention unlike that in most other cities.

Elway squirrels for a first-period Super Bowl TD.

And there was Elway himself, tall, blond, blessed with a toothy grin and a dogged willingness to oblige all comers. At times that first summer, public relations man Jim Saccomano would have literally dozens of interview requests after practice.

Elway arrived to find a team that had settled in behind Steve DeBerg the previous season and was unwilling to accept this kid who had led the charmed life and defied the NFL system. There were veterans who resented Elway's immediate projection into the starting job.

When he didn't make it to halftime in Pittsburgh in his opening game (1 of 8, 4 sacks, a fumble and interception), they nodded. When he was yanked in Baltimore amid deafening boos in 100-degree heat the next week, they nodded again. Each time, DeBerg came on to rescue a win.

By the end of the fifth game, Elway was a spectator, DeBerg the starter. Elway was being booed at home and pressing, and Dan Reeves was questioning himself. So were others. Reeves, at the distance of four years, makes no excuses. He mishandled his thoroughbred at the outset, forcing him too far, too quickly.

"Do you think of yourself as a $5-million failure?" television's

Confident now, Elway should be tougher than ever.

Len Berman asked Elway at one point that year.

Elway had never failed—at anything. The son of Jack Elway, now head coach at Stanford, he had grown up in the Los Angeles area, where by the time he was a senior at Granada Hills High, he was the most sought prep in the land.

They still talk of the time he stood at midfield and threw—and hit—another ball thrown up from the goal line. "That was overblown," he said. "I vaguely remember it. I know it was only once."

The hotly competitive Elway household included a twin sister,

Unlike Bo Jackson, Elway chose football over baseball.

Jana, as well as an older sister. "My dad would even time us getting into our pajamas," Elway recalled.

He was a multi-sports star, including a major-league potential in baseball. He was Los Angeles' City Player of the Year for 1979, hitting .491 as an outfielder and coming on in the title game to pitch to Darryl Strawberry. The legend holds he struck him out. Again, the legend exaggerates. "He took me deep to the opposite field, but we got him out." And won, 10-4.

By then, Jack had sat with his wife in the stands one fall evening, watching John throw a 20-yard touchdown pass. It was called back due to holding. The next play, he threw another, this one for 35 yards and this one counting. "I wonder if he's as good as I think he is," Jack asked his wife that evening. He knew the answer, of course.

All the Elways migrated north shortly after, Jack to coach at San Jose State and John to become the new wunderkind at Stanford, in baseball as well as football.

He spent the summer of 1982 as a $140,000 bonus baby at the Yankees' Class A team in Oneonta, N.Y., hitting .318. It gave him the leverage he and agent Marvin Demoff would use the next spring in freeing Elway from the Colts and sending him to Denver.

Neither Elway nor the Mile High City's football followers have been the same since.

"I went through a learning process," he understated. "People in Denver thought I could walk on water. I thought so, too."

Pittsburgh, Baltimore and the bench quickly brought things back into some perspective, but that image of bigger than life still haunts him.

Touchdown pass? Of course. They expected that. They settle for nothing less. Why not four? Five? Isn't this John Elway, Superman?

He came out in the year Dan Marino dazzled as a rookie, and the comparisons were inevitable: Marino was worth more, Elway less. Marino was doing things no rookie is supposed to be able to do. Elway was throwing one touchdown for every two interceptions, and although there were moments, little peeks behind the curtain of the future, he was playing like rookies are supposed to play—inconsistently.

His wife was in Seattle in the fall of 1983. "We were engaged his first year, and I was working in Seattle," Janet said. "I would get his phone calls and he would sound so forlorn. He had no camradery with his teammates. He was not getting along with Dan Reeves that well. He would say that he was not sure he wanted to be doing this. I think he was just licking his wounds, so to speak. And I don't think he was serious."

From the start, it was a tumultuous season lesser talents would not have survived. At one point, against San Diego on the west coast, the frustrated Elway came off after a particularly bad series and he and Reeves engaged in a shouting debate before the startled Broncos.

In that same game, Elway, trying to concentrate on the long, involved Broncos' play-calling nomenclature (he must set the formation, some of the blocking and all the pass routes) and also looking over the defense, the preoccupied rookie walked up to scrimmage . . . and lined up behind a startled left guard, Tom Glassic.

"What are you doing?" Glassic said. Elway, humiliated, recalls thinking to himself, *Boy, you've hit rock bottom.*

Denver finished the year 9-7, and Elway had the worst quarterback proficiency rating of any starter in the league. "Everybody tries to relate John to Marino," said Reeves. "That's so unfair. Marino is picked by a team that just the year before has been to the Super Bowl. John is picked, of course, by Baltimore and winds up with us, and we had gone 2-7. It's difficult to judge two quarterbacks in two totally different situations. Miami had a good football team.

"Also, I think Don Shula was much better prepared to coach Marino than I was to coach John. He had been in the league a lot longer. He had coached quarterbacks. This was the first rookie quarterback I'd ever had to coach. I had coached quarterbacks before, but they never played until like their third or fourth year in the league. It was a totally different situation and I think it was unfair to John."

His numbers gradually improved, and Denver, with Elway eventually restored to starting status, beat both Cleveland and Baltimore before Kansas City demolished them, 48-17, to end the regular season and Seattle won, 31-7, in the wild-card playoffs.

It was a chastened, shaken Elway who fled the Mile High City as soon as possible, going back to Palo Alto and sanctuary. "I was wondering if I was going to be able to make it," he admits now. The calls to Janet had become more frequent and lasted longer. He even thought about giving up playing and joining his dad as an assistant.

"I don't think, deep down, I seriously doubted myself, but there certainly was more of it than I had ever had before that," he said.

Reeves had to talk him into coming back early to Denver in the spring of 1984 to begin conditioning and classroom work. It was a critical spring and summer, but one helped by several factors. One was the hiring of Mike Shanahan out of the University of Florida. He coached wide receivers before becoming offensive coordinator in 1985, but in 1984 he also served as something of a buffer between Elway and Reeves as they gradually smoothed their working relationship.

Reeves and Elway, for their part, adjusted to each other. They discovered they are virtual clones when it comes to competitive zeal. "They'll both have 20 bets going on a golf game," a Bronco staffer said. There were personal bets: who would blow up at the other first? It cost $100 to the loser.

A stronger team, and of course just the fact both Elway and Reeves had a year with each other, were other elements. The Broncos soared to 13-3 and into the playoffs, where Elway, hurt and playing on one leg, was unable to offset a powerful Pittsburgh running game.

In 1985, the Broncos were 11-5, but the record was not good enough to make the playoffs.

Last season, when the Broncos' 11-5 got them into the playoffs, the most dramatic moments came when Elway led the drive from the two that tied Cleveland with 37 seconds left and set up the 23-20 overtime victory that landed Denver in the Super Bowl against the New York Giants.

His scrambling and his arm gave the underdog Broncos a 10-9 halftime lead. But the margin didn't hold up. It was more a condemnation of the Denver defense and MVP Phil Simms' third-quarter brilliance than any criticism of Elway that Denver eventually lost, 39-20.

The confidence is back. And the playoffs and Super Bowl, while enhancing his playing credentials, did something else. "It got me some exposure with the national people that could see what type of person I am really like," Elway said. "It took a lot of the stigma off the Baltimore thing. I think it helped me image-wise, helped show I'm not the spoiled brat everybody has been writing about."

It also demonstrated that Elway has arrived as a major-league quarterback, easily the most dangerous in the league on the run and one that a stronger running game and bigger line would make even better.

"I believe John can carry a team better than any quarterback in the league. And has," said offensive coordinator Shanahan.

"My confidence level is so much higher now, there is no comparison," Elway said. "Even from last year. I'm settled in here now, where the first year I was still on edge, about everything. I didn't know. I have established myself as a good quarterback, as someone who can be respected. That has a lot to do with confidence. Coming out '83, I didn't have any of that. I was wondering if I was going to be able to make it."

Now, he has people like Dallas' Gil Brandt saying, "He made two plays against us [in a 29-14 Denver win] that were just unbelievable." And the Raiders' Al LoCasale: "He throws better running to his left than anybody I've ever seen."

It's not perfect, of course. There was the time two years ago when he gave up five interceptions in the course of beating Kansas City at home. A fan seated behind Janet stood and screamed, "You can get your bleeping wife pregnant, but you can't do anything else." Janet turned and slapped him.

And there is this persistent desire by Elway to be liked. "I don't want anyone not to like me," he admitted. "I don't want to be one of those prima donnas. But I know now that things are going to happen. And I know people who don't know me aren't going to like me. It used to bother me a lot more. I guess that's another way I've grown up."

He can even place success in the proper perspective. "There haven't been a whole lot of endorsement offers since the Super Bowl," he was saying that snowy February day, as daughter Jessica protested in the background. ("Daddy's been baby-sitting all day. She wants her mommy.")

He had turned down a cameo role on "Miami Vice," accepted an award in Seattle, was heading for Hawaii with Shanahan and their wives.

So the Elways and the Bishops sneak off at 1 in the afternoon for the early movie before school is out. Or they go to what Bishop describes as "the one or two restaurants where John can feel comfortable, ones that kind of put him off in a secluded area where people don't bother him. But mostly we'll go to his house, or they'll come over to ours, and we'll just rent a movie."

"The Miami Vice thing, I was supposed to be a bad guy, a biker," said Elway. "I could envision myself having fun doing it, but I figured it wasn't best for the image. So I didn't do it. Besides, it would have meant a week down there, and I'd rather just stay home anyway."

John Elway, veteran quarterback but still rookie babysitter, doesn't have to wait until the house lights go down to feel comfortable there.

LT: Wordless Giant in the jungle.

Lawrence Taylor
vs.
The Greatest
All-Time Linebackers

By RAY DIDINGER

In the modern era of professional football, there have been very few players who could be described accurately as "intimidating."

We are talking about true warriors who played each Sunday in a 100-yard rage. Chicago's Dick Butkus was such a man. So was Philadelphia's Chuck Bednarik and Green Bay's Ray Nitschke. In

Packers' Ray Nitschke made NFL All-50-Year team.

the '70s, it was Pittsburgh's Jack Lambert.

You will notice they are all linebackers. That's not coincidence.

"The linebacker is the King of the Jungle," said Sam Huff, the Hall of Famer who played 13 rough-and-tumble seasons in New York and Washington. "He's the guy nobody messes with. He looks mean, he plays mean and he is mean. You can't be a goody-two shoes and play linebacker in the NFL."

Today, the reigning intimidator is Lawrence Taylor, the New York Giants' All-Pro outside linebacker. At 6-3 and 243 pounds, Taylor embodies the beauty of pro football and also the beast. Last season the Giants rolled to their first NFL championship in 31 years and Taylor became the second defensive player ever to be voted the league's consensus MVP (Minnesota's Alan Page was the first). And the accolades did not stop there.

No less an authority than Miami coach Don Shula was quoted as saying, "Taylor could be the best [linebacker] ever."

Ray Didinger, sports columnist of the Philadelphia Daily News, *has followed the linebackers since 1970.*

Consider that statement for a moment. The best linebacker. Ever. That means better than Butkus, better than Bednarik and Nitschke, better than Huff and Bill George, better than Joe Schmidt and Willie Lanier, better than anybody who ever stuffed a fullback on fourth-and-goal.

That's a pretty sweeping statement. But, remarkably, it has support. Lots of it.

A survey of football experts—mostly ex-players and coaches—found almost 50 percent agreement that Taylor is the best NFL linebacker ever. Several former greats at the position—Huff and Bednarik included—didn't need a moment to think it over.

"Taylor's the best, absolutely," said Bednarik, the man former Redskin coach George Allen rated the all-time No. 1 linebacker in his 1982 book "Pro Football's 100 Greatest Players."

"Taylor has it all: size, speed, tremendous strength," Bednarik noted. "The thing I like about him is his intensity. He plays every game like he's frothing at the mouth. I hated the guys I played against every Sunday. Taylor has that same killer instinct."

"I played the middle but I could not have played outside," Huff said. "And I've seen great outside linebackers who could not have played the middle. Taylor is the only linebacker I can name who would be All-Pro at any of the three or four spots.

"LT led the league in sacks last season [20½]. No other linebacker ever did that. I know I couldn't. He plays almost like a defensive end. Maybe they should just come up with a new name for the position Taylor plays."

Any suggestions?

"Yeah," Huff said. "Call him the monster because that's how he plays. He looks like he came down off a movie screen, the way he tosses people around."

The other half of the experts polled agreed Taylor was a great linebacker, clearly the best today, but they hesitate to rank him No. 1 all-time. As former Giant defensive end Andy Robustelli said, "We always relate to what's current. We assume that what's modern is best. It's not true all the time."

Robustelli prefers to talk about "an elite group" of linebackers that spans a quarter of a century. He puts Butkus, Huff, Nitschke and George in that class. He puts Taylor in there, too, although he notes the defensive scheme of the Giants gives Taylor more freedom to make spectacular plays.

"Taylor is a great athlete with keen instincts," Robustelli said. "He blitzes and free-lances and has the opportunity to make the big play. Does that make him better than Huff and Nitschke, who had to play within a system? I don't know."

Paul Hornung, the former Green Bay star, agrees that group-

Eagles' Chuck Bednarik: Last of the 60-minute men.

ing the great linebackers makes the most sense. Hornung's class includes Nitschke, George, Schmidt, Butkus and, yes, Lawrence Taylor.

"Taylor can dominate a game for one or two key series," Horning said. "He can turn it on and get three tackles, two sacks and a tackle behind the line of scrimmage and change the momentum of a game. That's where he is outstanding. The only [defensive] player in recent years I've seen do that is Alan Page when he was at his peak in Minnesota. He could take over a game pretty much single-handed, but he was a tackle. As a linebacker, Taylor can do a lot more things.

Dick Butkus reigned for nine years as a Bear blitzer.

"Taylor is a helluva talented guy, but if I had to pick a No. 1, I'd have to go with Butkus. I've never been hit by Taylor, but I've been hit by Butkus and I know how it felt. It was like stepping in front of a Greyhound bus."

*   *   *

The 1986 season was a triumph for Lawrence Taylor in more ways than one. Not only did he lead the Giants to a 39-20 rout of Denver in Super Bowl XXI, but he overcame the drug and alcohol problems that threatened to wreck his career.

In February 1986, less than two weeks after the Pro Bowl, Taylor signed himself into a Texas rehabilitation facility, where he underwent treatment for six weeks. He had hoped to keep his stay quiet but, of course, that was impossible.

Within two days, Howard Cosell had the story on ABC radio. Then the New York tabloids took over. A sample of the headlines:

"Booze, Coke Send LT to Rehab Clinic."
"Robustelli, Huff Grieve for Taylor."
"LT's Mom Says She's Shocked."

On March 20, Taylor issued a statement through the Giants admitting he had "left the road I had hoped to follow both as a player and as a public figure . . . I have just completed the first phase in what I know will be a difficult and ongoing battle to overcome these problems."

Taylor refused to discuss the matter beyond that. In fact, he shut himself off from the media all season. Coach Bill Parcells supported Taylor's vow of silence and threatened to bar the press from the locker room if it insisted on pursuing the drug story.

"Why can't you concentrate on football?" Parcells said. "That's what Taylor is doing."

Indeed, he was. The 28-year-old Taylor had his finest season as the Giants rolled over the NFC East. His 20 and one-half sacks was just one short of the NFL record set by the Jets' Mark Gastineau, a defensive end, in 1984.

In a five-game stretch, Oct. 5 through Nov. 2, Taylor had 10 sacks, 32 tackles and 32 quarterback "hurries." And this was against double- and triple-team blocking.

Taylor injured his shoulder in a 27-20 win over Washington and played, in his words, "with one arm." He had three sacks. The next week, he had four sacks and 14 tackles in a 17-14 win over Dallas.

"Lawrence Taylor is the most dominant defensive player I've seen," said CBS-TV analyst John Madden, who broadcast almost half the Giants' 1986 schedule. "He can play at any of four notches and they're all damn good. His first notch is good, his second is very good, his third is All-Pro and his fourth . . . forget it. He's unblockable. When he has it cranked up full, I don't know what you do.

"He played at that level the second game against Washington [Dec. 7]. He was in [quarterback] Jay Schroeder's face all day. He forced four interceptions. The Skins kept trying different things to slow him down, but nothing worked. Washington had [tackle] Joe Jacoby on Taylor for awhile, and Jacoby is a helluva pass-blocker. Strong, big as a billboard [6-6, 310], and he couldn't handle Taylor. I told Pat [Summerall], "I can't believe what I'm seeing. This guy is unbelievable.""

Madden coached a great outside linebacker, Ted Hendricks, in Oakland. Like Taylor, Hendricks was another dimension on defense. Nicknamed "the Mad Stork", Hendricks was 6-7 and 215 pounds, with long, spidery arms. He, too, did a lot of freelancing and specialized in making the big play.

"I've seen Ted turn games around by tipping a pass or blocking a kick," Madden said. "He was great, one of the best ever, but he was more the opportunist. Taylor can take a game over by sheer force. That's the difference."

Taylor can be an opportunist as well. Against San Francisco in the NFC playoffs, Taylor picked off a Joe Montana pass and returned it 34 yards for a touchdown, kicking loose the rocks that became a 49-3 Giant avalanche. It could be argued the play was really made by nose tackle Jim Burt, who delivered the crushing hit on Montana just as he released the ball. Montana suffered a concussion on the play and was through for the afternoon.

That raises the question of how much the Giants' supporting cast contributes to Taylor's success. Former New York Jet middle linebacker Al Atkinson feels Taylor's all-world performances should be "viewed in context."

"Taylor is extremely good, but so are the people around him," said Atkinson, defensive signal-caller for New York's other Super Bowl champion, the 1969 Jets. "Carl Banks is outstanding, Gary Reasons is very good. Harry Carson is older, but he pulls things together out there. That unit is so strong, Taylor is free to take a lot of chances. He can do his thing and not worry about getting burned because he knows guys like Banks and Reasons are backing him up. Taylor does a lot of open-stuff, blitzing and pursuing, that catches the eye.

"I don't want to sound like I'm putting LT down because I'm not. He's a gifted athlete, but I think the media is guilty of hyping these things. You hear it on TV all the time: 'This guy's the best, that guy's the best . . .' It gets ridiculous after awhile. I think Taylor has great ability and plays with a great team. But does that make him THE greatest? Ever? I don't think so."

Atkinson puts Taylor in a group of five outside linebackers he considers a cut above the rest. The other four are: Dave Robinson, formerly of Green Bay; George Webster, formerly of Houston; Bobby Bell, formerly of Kansas City; and Hendricks. Atkinson ranks Hendricks No. 1 in the class.

"Hendricks was the same kind of player as Taylor . . . he came at you from a dozen different directions," Atkinson said. "The difference is Hendricks played at that [All-Pro] level for a longer period of time. Let's see what happens to Taylor in the next few years, then measure him against the other linebackers."

Another factor to be considered is the evolution of the game. Andy Russell played outside linebacker in Pittsburgh from 1963 through 1978. He made the Pro Bowl seven times. Russell contends it is easier to play outside linebacker in the NFL today than it was ten years ago.

"When they put in the rule against crackback blocks, it made the linebackers' job safer and, really, easier," said Russell, now an investment broker in Pittsburgh. "When I played, a linebacker needed a sixth sense to survive. We had those receivers cracking back on us almost every play. Knee injuries were a dime a dozen. The Players' Association found the highest risk position was outside linebacker, not running back.

"That was something the Bobby Bells and George Websters had to contend with that Lawrence Taylor does not. I'm sure there are still crackbacks being thrown in the NFL [illegally], but they aren't part of the offensive game plan anymore. That makes a difference."

In all-around ability, Russell would put Taylor "high" on his list of NFL linebackers but not at the top. Russell puts Bell, a Hall of Famer, ahead of him. The former Chiefs' great not only played linebacker but also snapped for punts and placekicks.

Russell also puts Jack Ham, a former Steeler teammate, ahead of Taylor. Ham covered pass receivers man-to-man in the Pittsburgh scheme. Taylor plays a zone when he is not blitzing the quarterback. And Russell claims Taylor does not "react as well" as Ham against the run. "You didn't see blockers get to Jack very often," Russell said. "He would see the play develop and cut through the traffic to the point of attack. He was ingenious that way.

"Taylor plays more recklessly. I see him crashing through blockers, running over them. He has such faith in his physical ability that he really believes nobody can handle him. I don't know how intelligent that is. Sooner or later, you have to pay for that."

* * *

Bill Bergey was an All-Pro middle linebacker with Cincinnati and Philadelphia in the '70s. He was a throwback to the old days, a tobacco-chewing street fighter scowling through a bristly beard.

Bergey was a punishing hitter. He knocked both Terry Bradshaw and Terry Hanratty out of a game in Pittsburgh one season and needed a police escort to make it through the angry mob afterwards.

"Clean hits, both of 'em," Bergey said of the shots that left the two quarterbacks with broken ribs.

It is still not a good idea to mention Bergey's name in any Pittsburgh taverns. But if he had played for the Steelers, those same fans would have loved him.

Bergey was winding up his NFL career with the Eagles when

Taylor came into the league in 1981. He saw the rookie from North Carolina one time and realized this was something special.

"I saw Taylor take our All-Pro tackle, Stan Walters, drive him into the backfield, then shuck him off and tackle Ron Jaworski," Bergey said. "He did it once and I thought, 'He must be good.' Then he did it again and I thought, 'Wait, this can't be . . .' Then he pursued a play down the line, ran over a blocker and tackled Wilbert Montgomery before he could turn upfield. These are not plays a linebacker normally makes.

"Butkus looked like a real thug on the field, but Taylor can do more things. He plays like all 11 men on defense. He plays havoc with a quarterback's mind. The poor guy has to be thinking, *What's LT gonna do next?*"

He is bigger than George (6-2, 230), Schmidt (6-1, 220), Ham (6-2, 215) and Nick Buoniconti (5-11, 220). With his 4.7 speed in the 40-yard dash, Taylor could run circles around bruisers like Butkus, Bergey, Bednarik and Nitschke.

The linebackers that are most physically comparable to Taylor are Bell (6-4, 228), Webster (6-4, 223) and Robinson (6-3, 245), but they did not dominate games quite the way Taylor does. And they surely didn't have his mystique.

"Lawrence could have excelled in any [NFL] era," Giants' general manager George Young said.

"I met Taylor when he came to town to receive the Maxwell Club Award," said Bednarik, who now works for a corrugated box company in Philadelphia. "I was surprised at how big he is. I congratulated him on the honor [NFL Player of the Year] and I told him, 'You're a great football player.' I don't throw superlatives around as a rule. But how else can you describe Lawrence Taylor?

"You can put most of us [linebackers] in a bag and pick any one out, we're all pretty much the same. I'm talking about Huff, George, Schmidt, Butkus, Nitschke and myself. But Taylor is better than that."

It was Bednarik, you might recall, who delivered the devastating blindside hit on New York's Frank Gifford at Yankee Stadium in 1960. "The greatest tackle I ever saw in my life," Huff said. "I used to stay awake nights, thinking about hitting someone like that."

Bednarik, a 6-3, 235-pounder, hit Gifford, a 6-1, 180-pound halfback, as he came across the middle after catching a pass. Gifford never saw Bednarik until it was too late. The Eagles' linebacker knocked Gifford cold, causing a fumble that preserved a 17-10 Philadelphia victory.

Gifford was hospitalized with a concussion and did not return to the Giants until the 1962 season. Bednarik sent Gifford flowers and left town with a clear conscience.

"It wasn't a cheap shot," Bednarik said. "It was a good, solid hit. Gifford knew it. He said so. What the hell, they aren't paying us to play two-hand touch out there. I knew the players on other teams were a little afraid of me. I'd hear 'em say, 'Watch out for that S.O.B.' I liked that. It gave me an edge. If you can intimidate your opponent, you've got him licked. Taylor does it now."

"When I think of intimidation, I think of one guy and that's Butkus," Paul Hornung said. "He went after you [the ball-carrier] like he hated you from the old neighborhood. I always got the feeling he was disappointed when he got up after a tackle and you were still breathing. It was like he hadn't done his job.

"Butkus was the only guy Vince [Lombardi] was ever wrong about. When we played him the first time, Vince said, 'This Butkus is big and sloppy. I can't believe everyone is so high on him. He lines up two yards deeper than most middle backers so you blockers should have a real good shot at him.'

"Well, we played the game and Butkus damn near killed us all. I got 32 yards on 15 carries, Jim Taylor had 60 yards on 28 carries, something like that. Butkus finished with 22 tackles and an interception. He beat our offensive linemen to death. He was like a one-man army.

"We came in for the meeting the next day and Vince said, 'Well, Butkus was right where we said he'd be and you blockers got to him but you couldn't handle him. All I can say is this guy must be one heckuva player.' He made All-Pro playing on one leg in '69.

"I've often said if we were choosing sides for an all-time football team and I had the No. 1 pick, I'd go for Butkus. I'd take him over any quarterback or halfback. I'd pick Taylor, too, but later. Butkus is the man I'd build around."

Huff disagrees. He would take Taylor ahead of Butkus, assuming Taylor has overcome the demons that almost ruined his life two years ago. If LT stays clean off the field, there's nothing he cannot accomplish on the field.

"I think part of the reason Taylor had such a great [1986] season is because he wanted to show people he could come back from his personal problems," Huff said.

"A lot of people said he'd never be what he was before. Taylor is such a competitor, he used that as a motivating factor. He wasn't satisfied to get back to where he was, he wanted to be better. And he was.

"The only person who can keep Lawrence Taylor out of the Hall of Fame is Lawrence Taylor. He understands that now."

INSIDE THE AFC

By PETER FINNEY JR.

PREDICTED ORDER OF FINISH

EAST	CENTRAL	WEST
New England	Cleveland	Denver
Miami	Cincinnati	Seattle
N.Y. Jets	Pittsburgh	L.A. Raiders
Buffalo	Houston	Kansas City
Indianapolis		San Diego

AFC Champion: Cleveland

The AFC Central used to make it so easy to get off a good laugh. You want a chuckle? In 1985, the Cleveland Browns, showing no shame, won the division with an 8-8 record. The quality of football was so bad nobody would have blamed the citizens of Cleveland, Pittsburgh, Cincinnati and Houston for petitioning the league for an NFL team.

But those days are over. The pendulum has swung back with a vengeance. How far? Well, here's a quiz for anyone handicapping the 1987 season. Would you take the Miami Dolphins over the Browns? Or the Los Angeles Raiders over the Bengals? If you're honest, you can't. The Browns came within a 98-yard touchdown drive by Denver quarterback John Elway of going to the Super Bowl last year. The Bengals, the NFL's answer to hot-and-cold running water, were arguably the hottest team in the conference at the end of the season.

Even the Central also-rans, the Steelers and the Oilers, rallied late in the year to show surprising strength. In the last half of 1986, the Central compiled a 20-12 record (62.5 percent). The

---

Peter Finney Jr. of the New York Post *has covered the New York Jets since coach Joe Walton's rookie year in 1983.*

Browns' Kevin Mack aims for 1,000-yard truckload.

closest rival was the NFC East at 20-18-2 (52.6). The Browns finished 7-1, the Bengals 5-3 and the Steelers and Oilers 4-4. Clearly, the division is on the move.

The Browns have to be rated as the favorites in the Central because they have what Cincinnati lacks—a solid defense. It will be interesting to see what effect the defection of secondary coach Tom Olivadotti to Miami has on Marty Schottenheimer's defensive scheme, but the Browns have the talent to carry on. Cornerbacks Hanford Dixon and Frank Minnifield could be the best

Miami's John Offerdahl: AFC's Defensive Rookie of Year.

tandem in the NFL, and the linebacking corps, even with the loss of Chip Banks, is one of the best.

On offense, Bernie Kosar has come of age in Lindy Infante's ball-control passing offense, and things should be even better with 1,000-yard rushers Kevin Mack and Earnest Byner healthy for a full season. The Bengals, behind Boomer Esiason's arm and improvisational ability and James Brooks' dazzling feet, had the most prolific offense in the NFL last year. They'll need it to compensate for a young defense that is learning the ropes.

The Steelers have defense and a running game, but Mark Malone isn't in Kosar's or Esiason's class. The Oilers haven't had a winning season since Bum Phillips left, but the talent is there after years of high draft picks.

In the West, the Denver Broncos again are the team to beat, but they'll be pressed by the Seattle Seahawks, who closed out 1986 with a 41-16 rout of the Broncos but missed the playoffs despite a 10-6 record. Elway is the most physically gifted quarterback in football, and his clutch drive into the teeth of the Cleveland Stadium wind was testament to his ability to win games on his own.

The Broncos' Achilles heel, however, may be the lack of a power running game. It may have cost them the Super Bowl when they failed to punch it in for a touchdown after a first-and-goal from the Giants' two-yard line. Joe Collier's defense bent more than he'd like last year, but it's solid.

If Chuck Knox can get a year's worth of Decembers like the one David Krieg had in 1986, the Seahawks might romp. The Seahawks have the running game to control the football and their special teams make things happen.

This is gut-check year for the Raiders, who are still in search of a quarterback and an offensive line. The Kansas City Chiefs made the playoffs in 1986 with defense and special teams, but they'll have to show more firepower to get back in. In San Diego, the questions are Dan Fouts' declining arm strength and a defense that may be shattered if pass-rusher Leslie O'Neal hasn't healed.

In the East, the New England Patriots are winning with Raymond Berry and with talent. When Berry saw how poorly the offensive line performed in 1986, he went out and stole guard Sean Farrell from Tampa Bay to give the running game an immediate shot in the arm. Tony Eason carried the Patriots with his arm last year. Now he won't have to. The defense is one of the top three in the conference.

While the Patriots are awesomely balanced, the New York Jets and the Miami Dolphins will be shootout kings once again. If Ken O'Brien can overcome the mystifying five-game losing streak at the end of last year, the Jet offense will be tough to contain. But it may have to score 35 points a game to win.

Don Shula demoted defensive coordinator Chuck Studley after two years of horrible results, but he needs a healthy Hugh Green to get back into the chase. That may be asking a lot, but Shula always does.

Buffalo played a lot of teams close in 1986 but won only four games. Now maybe new defensive coordinator Walt Corey can mold a Kansas City-style defense with some fresh talent. Indianapolis has too much ground to make up.

So who will be in San Diego in January? The Browns will beat the Patriots to get there. Stay tuned.

BUFFALO BILLS

TEAM DIRECTORY: Pres.: Ralph Wilson; GM/VP-Administration: Bill Polian; Dir. Player Personnel: Norm Pollom; Dir. Media Rel.; Dir. Pub. and Community Rel.: Denny Lynch; Head Coach: Hank Bullough. Home field: Rich Stadium (80,290). Colors: Scarlet red, royal blue and white.

SCOUTING REPORT

OFFENSE: Marv Levy has some convincing to do. He inherits one of the strongest guns in the Northeast—Jim Kelly—but his history as a head coach at Kansas City was to think run first . . . and run second. The highest any of Levy's five Chiefs' teams ranked in the NFL in passing was 21st, but Levy says he's changing with the times and his personnel. He's brought in former Colt head coach Ted Marchibroda to tutor Kelly, and the Bills have capable wideouts in Chris Burkett, Andre Reed and Jerry Butler, who had a metal plate removed from his fractured right fibula and should be at full speed in 1987. But Kelly would love some pint-sized track stars to throw to.

Kelly did dramatically improve the Bills' passing offense, but he still threw too many critical fourth-quarter interceptions. He'll also have to learn to be less rash in his critical judgments of teammates, because that's a quick road to alienation.

Running back Robb Riddick was a big surprise last year, but the Bills need a full season from Greg Bell, who spent most of 1986 in the tub. No. 1 pick Ronnie Harmon was a disappointment. The Bills are building a solid line to protect Kelly. Joe Devlin is a superior tackle and Will Wolford is entrenched at right guard.

DEFENSE: Levy's key staff move was to hire defensive coordinator Walt Corey, the mastermind behind the Chiefs' "Sic Em" defense. Corey believes in simplicity and having his players reacting instead of thinking, but he doesn't have anything close to the All-Pro secondary he had with the Chiefs. Opponents completed nearly 61 percent of their passes against the Bills last year and were intercepted only 10 times. Mostly at fault were the linebackers and safeties, who failed to cover receivers in the intermediate zones.

Corey has a stud pass rusher in Bruce Smith, who is everything he was cracked up to be, but he still needs someone to complement him on the other side. Nose tackle Fred Smerlas, who had played listlessly through several losing seasons, came to

Jim Kelly's receivers can help pay off his loan.

life after Hank Bullough was fired and has to sustain that level of play.

Insiders say linebacker Jim Haslett has recovered beautifully from a multiple fracture of the right leg, but missing a full season is always an iffy proposition. The Bills have to find a way to get more pressure on the passer, and they really don't have the outside linebackers to do it. Linebacker Shane Conlon of Penn State, the Bills' top pick, should be a factor. If Corey blitzes a lot, he'll expose cornerbacks Derrick Burroughs and Charles Romes to third-degree burns.

BILLS VETERAN ROSTER

HEAD COACH—Marv Levy. Assistant Coaches—Walt Corey, Ted Cottrell, Bruce DeHaven, Chuck Dickerson, Rusty Jones, Chuck Lester, Ted Marchibroda, Jim Ringo, Dick Roach, Ted Tollner.

No.	Name	Pos.	Ht.	Wt.	NFL Exp.	College
43	Bayless, Martin	S	6-2	200	4	Bowling Green
28	Bell, Greg	RB	5-10	210	4	Notre Dame
36	Bellinger, Rodney	CB	5-8	189	4	Miami
50	Bentley, Ray	LB	6-2	250	2	Central Michigan
81	Brookins, Mitchell	WR	5-11	196	3	Illinois
—	Broughton, Walter	WR	5-10	180	2	Jacksonville St.
85	Burkett, Chris	WR	6-4	198	3	Jackson St.
29	Burroughs, Derrick	CB	6-1	180	3	Memphis St.
61	Burton, Leonard	C	6-3	265	2	South Carolina
80	Butler, Jerry	WR	6-0	178	8	Clemson
35	Byrum, Carl	FB	6-0	232	2	Miss. Valley St.
—	Caron, Roger	OT	6-5	292	3	Harvard
69	Christy, Greg	G	6-4	285	2	Pittsburgh
41	Clark, Steve	S	6-3	186	1	Liberty Univ.
63	Cross, Justin	T	6-6	265	6	Western State (Colo.)
70	Devlin, Joe	T	6-5	280	11	Iowa
45	Drane, Dwight	S	6-1	200	2	Oklahoma
53	Furjanic, Tony	LB	6-1	228	2	Notre Dame
99	Garner, Hal	LB	6-4	225	3	Utah State
8	Gelbaugh, Stan	QB	6-3	207	2	Maryland
75	Hamby, Mike	DE	6-4	270	2	Utah State
33	Harmon, Ronnie	RB	5-11	192	2	Iowa
55	Haslett, Jim	LB	6-3	236	8	Indiana (Pa.)
71	Hellestrae, Dale	T	6-5	275	3	Southern Methodist
67	Hull, Kent	C	6-4	262	2	Mississippi St.
48	Johnson, Lawrence	S	5-11	202	7	Wisconsin
72	Jones, Ken	T	6-5	285	12	Arkansas St.
12	Kelly, Jim	QB	6-3	215	2	Miami
38	Kelso, Mark	S	5-11	177	2	William & Mary
84	Kern, Don	TE	6-4	235	3	Arizona St.
4	Kidd, John	P	6-3	208	4	Northwestern
49	King, Bruce	FB	6-1	219	3	Purdue
54	Marve, Eugene	LB	6-2	240	6	Saginaw Valley
13	McClure, Brian	QB	6-6	222	1	Bowling Green
95	McNanie, Sean	DE	6-5	270	4	San Diego St.
60	Melka, Jim	LB	6-1	228	1	Wisconsin
88	Metzelaars, Pete	TE	6-7	243	6	Wabash
11	Norwood, Scott	K	6-0	207	3	James Madison
64	Pike, Mark	LB	6-4	257	1	Georgia Tech
27	Pitts, Ron	CB-S	5-10	175	2	UCLA
68	Ploeger, Kurt	DE	6-5	260	2	Gustavus Adolphus
79	Prater, Dean	DE	6-4	256	6	Oklahoma St.
83	Reed, Andre	WR	6-0	186	3	Kutztown (Pa.)
14	Reich, Frank	QB	6-3	208	2	Maryland
84	Richardson, Eric	WR	6-1	185	3	San Jose St.
40	Riddick, Robb	RB	6-0	195	5	Millersville (Pa.)
51	Ritcher, Jim	G	6-3	265	8	North Carolina St.
87	Rolle, Butch	TE	6-3	242	2	Michigan St.
26	Romes, Charles	CB	6-1	190	11	North Carolina Cent.
57	Sanford, Lucius	LB	6-2	220	10	Georgia Tech
52	Seawright, James	LB	6-2	219	1	South Carolina
76	Smerlas, Fred	NT	6-3	280	9	Boston College
78	Smith, Bruce	DE	6-3	273	3	Virginia Tech
74	Smith, Don	NT	6-5	262	9	Miami
56	Talley, Darryl	LB	6-4	227	5	West Virginia
89	Tasker, Steve	WR-KR	5-9	185	3	Northwestern
86	Teal, Jimmy	WR	5-10	170	3	Texas A&M
65	Traynowicz, Mark	G	6-5	275	3	Nebraska
82	Vogler, Tim	G-T-C	6-3	285	9	Ohio State
34	Wilkins, Gary	FB	6-1	235	2	Georgia Tech
—	Williams, Bob	TE	6-3	238	1	Penn State
23	Williams, Kevin	CB	5-9	170	2	Iowa State
94	Witt, Billy	DE	6-5	265	1	North Alabama
73	Wolford, Will	G	6-5	276	2	Vanderbilt

FIVE TOP DRAFT CHOICES

Rd.	Name	Sel. No.	Pos.	Ht.	Wt.	College
1	Conlan Shane	8	LB	6-3	228	Penn State
2	Odomes, Nate	29	CB	5-10	186	Wisconsin
2	Mitchell, Roland	33	DB	5-11	180	Texas Tech
3	Brandon, David	60	LB	6-4	211	Memphis State
3	Mueller, Jamie	78	RB	6-2	229	Benedictine

KICKING GAME: Levy said it best when he took over: "The kicking game is shoddy right now." Kicker Scott Norwood, a USFL survivor, may not be the answer. He made only 17-of-27 field goals and missed five of his last six attempts. Punter John Kidd finished eighth in the AFC with a 40.4-yard average and was less accurate in placing punts inside the 20. Levy made an immediate impact. In his first three games, the Bills blocked a field goal and a punt and partially blocked another punt.

THE ROOKIES: Corey got the defensive clay he needs to mold a stronger defense. Linebacker Conlan, eighth overall in the draft, doesn't have Cornelius Bennett's big-play ability, but he's consistent, reliable and well-coached. The Bills got two cornerbacks in the second round—4.4 speedster Nate Odomes of Winconsin and Roland Mitchell of Texas Tech—to upgrade their woeful secondary.

OUTLOOK: The Bills are at least two good drafts away from being competitive. This year's schedule, which includes non-division games against the Giants, Redskins, Cowboys, Broncos and Raiders, doesn't make it any easier. The defense still needs plenty of help, but Indianapolis should keep the Bills out of the AFC East cellar. Five wins, maybe.

BILL PROFILES

JIM KELLY 27 6-3 215   Quarterback

The Franchise probably could afford to buy the Bills . . . Earned $3.15 million and received a $1 million loan last year as NFL's highest-paid player . . . He produced, too, completing 285 of 480 passes (59.4 percent) for 3,593 yards and 22 TDs with 17 interceptions, although Bills only won four games . . . Vocal leader ruffled feathers by criticizing his defensive teammates in close losses, but money has its privileges . . . Doubled season-ticket sales to 28,000 inside a month . . . Born Feb. 14, 1960, in East Brady, Pa. . . . May be the best in a great line of QBs from the University of Miami . . . Will do even more if Bills can get the small, fast receivers he likes . . . Threw for

9,842 yards and 83 TDs in two seasons with the USFL Houston Gamblers . . . He's color blind, but so is Jack Nicklaus.

ROBB RIDDICK 30 6-0 195   Running Back

Shed his injuries and burst from obscurity to lead the Bills in rushing with 632 yards and 4.2-yard average . . . Has been with the Bills since 1981 but spent 2½ seasons on injured reserve . . . Wasn't given much of a chance to make the roster in 1986 with Greg Bell, Joe Cribbs and Ronnie Harmon ahead of him in training camp . . . He not only made it but was the Bills' leading receiver for most of the season and averaged 25 yards on kickoff returns before becoming a starter . . . Born April 26, 1957, in Quakertown, Pa., and played at Millersville State . . . Marv Levy now knows he has a capable backup if Bell has another injury-filled season.

WILL WOLFORD 23 6-5 276   Guard

The Tractor moved a lot of piles in an impressive rookie season . . . The No. 1 pick from Vanderbilt started every game at right guard despite reporting three weeks late to camp due to a contract dispute . . . Education started in the opener when Jets' nose tackle Joe Klecko spooked him into tripping Jim Kelly as the QB went back to pass . . . Hall of Famer Jim Ringo, the Bills' line coach, says Wolford "made tremendous progress." . . . Father, Maurice, played in 1951 for the Los Angeles Rams for $7,000 . . . Will signed a four-year, $1.4-million contract . . . Born May 18, 1964, in Louisville, Ky.

BRUCE SMITH 24 6-3 273   Defensive End

Fifteen-sack season showed why the Bills made him the No. 1 pick in the entire 1985 draft . . . The Virginia Tech All-American has a prodigious appetite for quarterbacks and for food, which was his problem in his rookie season . . . Hovered close to 300 pounds in 1985, when he had 6½ sacks, but last year he was monstrously quick after slimming down to 273 and finished tied for second in sacks (15) in the AFC behind the Raiders' Sean Jones . . . Sack total was particularly impressive because he was constantly double-teamed on the right side... Voted only as a Pro Bowl alternate, but that's because of Bills' record... Born June 18, 1963, in Norfolk, Va.... Runs the 40 in 4.71 seconds... Can polish off 100 chicken wings at a sitting.

FRED SMERLAS 30 6-3 280   Nose Tackle

After several so-so seasons, Smerlas responded late in the year... Maybe it was the way the Bills overshifted him on the center, just like the Jets do with Joe Klecko... At $550,000 a year, the hard-nosed Boston College grad is a distant second to Jim Kelly on the Bills' payroll: "I guess I'm a street sweeper now," Smerlas joked... He stood up for defense when Kelly criticized it late in the season, cautioning the QB to "check his laundry."... Happy to see Hank Bullough leave because he can now do more reacting than reading... Born April 8, 1957, in Waltham, Mass.... Was a Pro Bowler between 1980-83 and wants to return.

JOE DEVLIN 33 6-5 280   Tackle

Outstanding 1986 was tarnished only by a Pro Bowl snub... In a year when Jim Kelly was dumped 43 times, almost none were his responsibility... Teammate Fred Smerlas says of Devlin: "He's the best tackle in football." ... That sentiment is shared across the AFC East... Jets' sack machine Mark Gastineau puts Devlin at the top of his Pro Bowl ballot every year... Born Feb. 23, 1954, in Phoenixville, Pa.... Voted to the Bills' silver anniversary all-time team in 1984... Devlin did a lot of boxing in high school and at Iowa.

EUGENE MARVE 27 6-2 240   Linebacker

The Bills showed a marked improvement against the run last year, and Marve was a key reason... Moved from weak to strong inside linebacker when Jim Haslett broke his leg in preseason, and he handled defensive signals flawlessly... Assumed greater leadership role with Haslett and Lucius Sanford sidelined... Was an obscure third-round pick out of Saginaw Valley State in 1982 but has improved each year... Had 13 solo tackles and three assists in a 14-13 loss to the Jets . . . Born Aug. 14, 1960, in Flint, Mich. . . . Went to college after working briefly on the auto assembly line.

GREG BELL 25 5-10 210   Running Back

He's an all-purpose back, but Bell was all-whirlpool last year, playing in only seven games . . . When healthy, as he showed in 1985 when he gained 883 yards rushing and caught 58 passes for 576 yards, he's a tough dual threat . . . Suffered a bad tear in the groin last year, and it was slow to heal . . . Coincidentally, it was a history of injuries that cut into his production at Notre Dame . . . Born Aug. 1, 1962, in Columbus, Ohio . . . Probably won't team in the same backfield with Robb Riddick because neither is an outstanding blocker . . . Set the Notre Dame indoor long-jump record at 24-6.

ANDRE REED 23 6-0 186   Wide Receiver

In two seasons he's turned into a consistent threat . . . Was Jim Kelly's main target last year, catching 53 passes for 739 yards and seven touchdowns . . . The fourth-round pick from Kutztown (Pa.) State in 1985 also led the Bills' receivers in his rookie year with 48 receptions for 637 yards and four scores . . . Teams up well with burner Chris Burkett, who led the Bills in '86 with a 22.9-yard average . . . Reed is no slow poke, either, with a 40-yard time of 4.35 seconds . . . Born Jan. 29, 1964, in Allentown, Pa. . . . May become even bigger part of passing game as Bills give Kelly freer rein to create his magic.

DERRICK BURROUGHS 25 6-1 180   Cornerback

The wait is still on for Burroughs to deliver . . . Hasn't been able to shake off nagging injuries and take a firm hold on the left side . . . Had a bad ankle in 1985 that limited him to eight starts and two interceptions . . . Last year he was benched for several games and was slowed by a bad knee . . . Bills haven't given up on him because of his great athletic ability, which he displayed often at Memphis State, but he'll have to become less fragile...Born May 18, 1962, in Mobile, Ala.

COACH MARV LEVY: Took over the hottest seat in pro football on Nov. 3, 1986, when owner Ralph Wilson fired Hank Bullough following a 2-7 start...The former Chiefs' head coach (1978-82) became the third Bills' coach in 14 months and the 10th in 27 years...He finished up 2-5...Overhauled staff, bringing in highly regarded defensive coordinator Walt Corey from Kansas City and Ted Marchibroda to tutor Jim Kelly...Known for his fine special teams and running attack at Kansas City, but he plans to open up the passing attack with Kelly...Given a two-year contract with the club's option for a third...After leaving the Chiefs, Levy worked as a television football analyst, coached the Chicago Blitz of the USFL for one year and served as director of football operations for the Montreal Alouettes of the CFL for three months...Born Aug. 3, 1928, in Chicago...Holds a master's degree in English history from Harvard, and organization is his strong suit...That didn't keep him from taking a wrong turn on his first day of work when he turned a 15-minute drive to Rich Stadium into an hour-and-45-minute ordeal...Main concern is the kicking game.

GREATEST KICKER

It might be easy to forget about Paul Maguire's punting ability when you see him clowning for the television camera these days, but the free spirit was a crackerjack punter in the old AFL. After leading the AFL in punting with San Diego in 1963, Maguire came to the Bills on waivers, a move that caused an open revolt in LaJolla. He went on to become the Bills' career punting leader over the next seven seasons.

Maguire, who led the nation with 10 touchdown catches in 1959 at The Citadel, still holds the club record for most punts in a career (552), in a season (100 in 1968) and in a game (11, twice). Obviously, the Bills had trouble moving the ball in 1967 and 1968.

Maguire also has the best lifetime average among all Bills' punters—42.1 yards. The best game of his career came against the Oilers on Sept. 21, 1969, when he averaged 55.1 yards on seven punts. His 78-yard punt in that game ties Marv Bateman for the longest punt in Buffalo history.

Maguire might be better known for his antics off the field. During training camp, Lou Saban would leave his players in a local motel while he went home to sleep. Maguire frequently drew the ire of hotel management by whacking real golf balls down the hallway. He also was a master at pool, which he described as "a hobby, not the result of a misspent youth." He still lives in Buffalo, where he owns a restaurant.

INDIVIDUAL BILL RECORDS

Rushing

Most Yards Game:	273	O. J. Simpson, vs Detroit, 1976
Season:	2,003	O. J. Simpson, 1973
Career:	10,183	O. J. Simpson, 1969-77

Passing

Most TD Passes Game:	5	Joe Ferguson, vs N.Y. Jets, 1979
Season:	26	Joe Ferguson, 1983
Career:	181	Joe Ferguson, 1973-84

Receiving

Most TD Passes Game:	4	Jerry Butler, vs N.Y. Jets, 1979
Season:	10	Elbert Dubenion, 1964
Career:	35	Elbert Dubenion, 1960-67

Scoring

Most Points Game:	30	Cookie Gilchrist, vs N.Y. Jets, 1963
Season:	138	O. J. Simpson, 1975
Career:	420	O. J. Simpson, 1969-77
Most TDs Game:	5	Cookie Gilchrist, vs N.Y. Jets, 1963
Season:	23	O. J. Simpson, 1975
Career:	70	O. J. Simpson, 1969-1977

CINCINNATI BENGALS

TEAM DIRECTORY: Chairman: Austin E. Knowlton; Pres.: John Sawyer; VP/GM: Paul Brown; Asst. GM: Michael Brown; Dir. Player Personnel: Pete Brown; Dir. Pub. Rel.: Allan Heim; Bus. Mgr.: Bill Connelly; Head Coach: Sam Wyche. Home field: Riverfront Stadium (59, 754). Colors: Orange, black and white.

SCOUTING REPORT

OFFENSE: We're talking high-octane. The Bengals led the NFL in total offense last season by averaging more than 405 yards a game. They did it with great balance. It starts, but doesn't end, with Boomer Esiason. The Bengals showcased a power running game highlighted by James Brooks, who rushed for 1,087 yards, and fullback Stanley Wilson, who rebounded from a drug suspension and a knee injury. But the Bengals reported that Wilson has been declared ineligible for an unspecified time.

Esiason caught fire in the last seven weeks, and there's no

Boomer Esiason led NFL in yards per attempt (8.44).

reason he can't carry over those good vibes to 1987. He gained the respect of this teammates by taking charge, and he has an Elway-like knack of improvising a big play. Cris Collinsworth will catch his 60 passes again this year, Eddie Brown is another year wiser and Brooks is the best there is out of the backfield.

Sam Wyche's embarrassment of riches doesn't stop there. The line is stocked with perennial Pro Bowler Anthony Munoz, who somehow keeps getting better, and bookend tackle Joe Walter, a 300-pounder who can pass-block.

The one thing the Bengals have to show is more resiliency. They were 10-0 last year when leading at halftime, 0-5 when they trailed and 0-1 when tied. They are a feast-and-famine team, but this offense is vicious enough to gobble up the AFC Central.

DEFENSE: You've heard the good news. Now for the bad. The Bengals gave up more points than any other team except the Colts last season, which has to change if they're going to be a solid playoff contender. The first order of business is to restore a pass rush without resorting to all-out blitzing. Defensive ends Ross Browner and Eddie Edwards couldn't do it, which is why nose tackle Tim Krumrie's superb play was even more surprising. The Bengals hope top draft choice Jason Buck, a tackle from BYU, can step right in.

There is a good nucleus of rising stars, however. Outside linebacker Emanuel King can be an overpowering blitzer, but he sometimes falls asleep. He's a long strider who needs work on his upper body strength. Linebacker Joe Kelly, who is on the smallish side to play inside but extremely fast, got his first start at midseason and made several impact plays. Inside linebacker Reggie Williams is 32 but still very productive.

The Bengals also have high hopes for strong safety David Fulcher, a massive hitter who made the all-rookie team, and cornerback Lewis Billups, another 1986 draft gem. Veteran Louis Breeden had seven interceptions last year and can still play the corner.

KICKING GAME: Look for changes. Punter Jeff Hayes was awful, finishing last in the AFC with a 35.1-yard gross average. Jim Breech finished fourth in the AFC in scoring with 101 points, but that was misleading because he made 50 extra points. Breech, who suffered with a bad back, missed almost 50 percent of his field goals, connecting on only 17-of-32.

THE ROOKIES: The Bengals went strong for defense in the first three rounds. They need a pass rush, and Buck, the 6-5,

BENGALS VETERAN ROSTER

HEAD COACH—Sam Wyche. Assistant Coaches—Jim Anderson, Bruce Coslet, Bill Johnson, Dick LeBeau, Jim McNally, Dick Selcer, Bill Urbanik, Kim Wood.

No.	Name	Pos.	Ht.	Wt.	NFL Exp.	College
14	Anderson, Ken	QB	6-3	212	17	Augustana (Ill.)
53	Barker, Leo	LB	6-2	227	4	New Mexico St.
24	Billups, Lewis	CB	5-11	190	4	North Alabama
74	Blados, Brian	G	6-5	295	4	North Carolina
55	Brady, Ed	LB	6-2	235	4	Illinois
3	Breech, Jim	K	5-6	161	9	California
34	Breeden, Louis	CB	5-11	185	10	N.C. Central
21	Brooks, James	RB	5-10	182	7	Auburn
81	Brown, Eddie	WR	6-0	185	3	Miami
79	Browner, Ross	DE	6-3	265	10	Notre Dame
27	Bussey, Barney	S	6-0	195	2	South Carolina St.
80	Collinsworth, Cris	WR	6-5	192	6	Florida
93	Deayala, Kiki	LB	6-1	225	2	Texas
67	Douglas, David	T	6-4	280	2	Tennessee
73	Edwards, Eddie	DE	6-5	256	11	Miami
7	Esiason, Boomer	QB	6-4	220	4	Maryland
33	Fulcher, David	S	6-3	228	2	Arizona St.
11	Gaynor, Doug	QB	6-2	205	2	Cal-Long Beach
71	Hammerstein, Mike	DE	6-4	270	2	Michigan
95	Herrmann, James	DE	6-6	255	1	Brigham Young
43	Hilary, Ira	WR	5-11	190	1	South Carolina
82	Holman, Rodney	TE	6-3	238	6	Tulane
20	Horton, Ray	CB	5-11	190	5	Washington
37	Jackson, Robert	S	5-10	186	7	Central Michigan
36	Jennings, Stanford	RB	6-1	205	4	Furman
30	Johnson, Bill	RB	6-2	230	3	Arkansas St.
84	Kattus, Eric	TE	6-5	235	2	Michigan
58	Kelly, Joe	LB	6-2	227	2	Washington
90	King, Emanuel	LB	6-4	251	3	Alabama
28	Kinnebrew, Larry	RB	6-1	258	5	Tennessee St.
64	Kozerski, Bruce	C	6-4	275	4	Holy Cross
86	Kreider, Steve	WR	6-3	192	9	Lehigh
69	Krumrie, Tim	NT	6-2	262	5	Wisconsin-Madison
88	Martin, Mike	WR	5-10	186	5	Illinois
85	McGee, Tim	WR	5-10	175	2	Tennessee
65	Montoya, Max	G	6-5	275	9	UCLA
78	Munoz, Anthony	T	6-6	278	8	USC
75	Reimers, Bruce	T	6-7	280	4	Iowa St.
50	Rimington, Dave	C	6-3	288	5	Nebraska
96	Shaw, Jeff	NT	6-1	280	1	Salem College
56	Simpkins, Ron	LB	6-1	235	7	Michigan
70	Skow, Jim	DE	6-3	250	2	Nebraska
63	Walter, Joe	T	6-6	290	3	Texas Tech
51	White, Leon	LB	6-2	236	2	Brigham Young
57	Williams, Reggie	LB	6-0	228	12	Dartmouth
32	Wilson, Stanley	RB	5-10	210	4	Oklahoma
91	Zander, Carl	LB	6-2	235	3	Tennessee

TOP FIVE DRAFT CHOICES

Rd.	Name	Sel. No.	Pos.	Ht.	Wt.	College
1	Buck, Jason	17	DE	6-5	256	Brigham Young
2	Thomas, Eric	49	DB	5-11	175	Tulane
3	Bell, Leonard	76	DB	5-11	210	Indiana
3	McClendon, Skip	77	DE	6-6	257	Arizona State
4	Riggs, Tim	!03	TE	6-5	245	Clemson

256-pound Outland Trophy winner, should be able to supply some heat, although his stock fell late in his senior season when his weight dropped to 245 pounds. Cornerback Eric Thomas from Tulane has 4.4 speed. Defensive end Skip McClendon of Arizona State was picked in the third round.

OUTLOOK: Offensively, the Bengals are awesome. If the youngsters on defense continue to improve and the Bengals find a pass rush, you'll hear from them in January. Wyche needs to show more self-control on and off the sidelines, which might help his team follow suit. This team is right on the verge of exploding, and the Browns know it.

BENGAL PROFILES

BOOMER ESIASON 26 6-4 220   Quarterback

Boomer packs a wallop... Went on a tear after being benched in the first half of a Nov. 9 loss to Houston... In the final 6½ games, the blond bomber completed 64.8 percent of his passes for 1,909 yards and 13 TDs with seven interceptions... Largely responsible for the Bengals' late surge... Tremendous improviser under pressure... Also loves going head-to-head with head coach Sam Wyche... Slammed helmet into the Astroturf on the sidelines when Wyche yanked him from the Houston game and then almost engineered an incredible second-half comeback... Born April 17, 1961, in East Islip, N.Y.... His mom felt him kick a lot during pregnancy. Hence the name "Boomer."... The Maryland flash finished third among AFC QBs last year and made the Pro Bowl when Dan Marino and Ken O'Brien bowed out with injuries.

CRIS COLLINSWORTH 28 6-5 192   Wide Receiver

Like Pete Rose banging out 200 hits a season in his prime, Collinsworth virtually guarantees 60 catches and 1,000 yards... Cris had a typical season in '86, grabbing 62 for 1,024 yards (16.4-yard average) and 10 TDs... His average was the third-highest of his career, so his legs haven't slowed up much... Master of precise routes... Has caught more than 60 passes five times in six seasons... Born Jan. 27, 1959, in

Dayton, Ohio... Was a freshman QB at Florida but made the best move of his life as a sophomore... Attends law school at the University of Cincinnati three mornings a week... Was a dean's list student in accounting with a 3.15 average at Florida.

EDDIE BROWN 24 6-0 185   Wide Receiver

Funny to talk about a 58-catch season as an off year, but that's how talented this University of Miami burner is... Hampered early last season by a tendon injury to his hand, which contributed to uncharacteristic drops... But he rallied at the end when the Bengals made a concerted effort to get him more involved in the offense... Fell 36 yards short of 1,000 yards, but that won't happen very often... Born Dec. 18, 1962, in Miami... Four touchdown catches were half as many as he posted as a rookie in 1985... He's still a game-breaker... Like Collinsworth, he started out in college playing another position —defensive back—before coming to his senses.

DAVID FULCHER 22 6-3 228   Strong Safety

Other than Miami's John Offerdahl, Fulcher may have had the best season of any defensive player in the AFC... He's as big as a linebacker and has the agility to cover wide receivers... Started every game and tied for second on the Bengals with 105 tackles... They love his fierce hitting and run support, the main reason Cincinnati's run defense improved dramatically... He was the Bengals' third pick in the third round out of Arizona State, but he showed well enough in camp that they moved veteran Bobby Kemp to free safety... Still green in coverage, but picked off four passes... Born Sept. 28, 1964, in Los Angeles.

JAMES BROOKS 28 5-10 182   Running Back

Continues his crusade to disprove the validity of computer specs... Next to Joe Morris, he is the best short running back in the NFL, and Morris can't touch him as a receiver... Brooks finished second in the AFC to Curt Warner in total yards (1,773) with 1,087 yards rushing and 686 yards receiving on 54 receptions... His club-record rushing total also was second to Warner's, but his 5.3-yard average was by far the best in the NFL . . . His success is the perfect marriage of an offense and player's talents . . . Set a Bengal record with 163 yards rushing against New England . . . Doesn't have breakaway speed, but is tough inside runner who's fast enough . . . Born Dec. 28, 1958, in Warner Robins, Ga., and played in Joe Cribbs' shadow at Auburn . . . Came to the Bengals from San Diego in a 1984 trade for Pete Johnson, which now looks like robbery.

ANTHONY MUNOZ 29 6-6 278   Tackle

Only wonder is why Munoz, the best tackle in the NFL, didn't make the Pro Bowl at wide receiver . . . The monster lineman snuck into the end zone twice to catch scoring passes from Boomer Esiason . . . In his career, the Merry Mex has caught three passes—all for TDs . . . Munoz dominated his position once again and was selected as a Pro Bowl starter for the sixth straight season . . . Ended Dwight Stephenson's three-year reign as Seagram's Offensive Lineman of the Year, an award voted on by 12 offensive and defensive coordinators . . . Line coach Jim McNally says Munoz got better because "he got a little bit nasty." . . . Born Aug. 19, 1958, in Ontario, Cal. . . . Rebounded from a series of knee operations at USC.

TIM KRUMRIE 27 6-2 262   Nose Tackle

The rarest of breeds: a nose tackle who led his team in tackles. Krumrie had 113 despite constant double-teaming and no production from his defensive ends . . . Serious injustice in being snubbed for the Pro Bowl . . . Was a highly honored defensive lineman at Wisconsin but wasn't drafted until the 10th round in 1982 . . . Pronounced CRUMB-rye, not CRUMMY . . . Born May 20, 1960, in Mondovi, Wis. . . . Has a full-sized poster of Clint Eastwood in his home and he calls Dirty Harry his hero . . . His Ohio license plate reads: "NTKLE." . . . Not many centers can handle him without help, and he puts his collegiate wrestling experience to good use . . . Says Cris Collinsworth: "He's like a shark out there who smells blood."

REGGIE WILLIAMS 32 6-0 228   Linebacker

A solid, steady year, maybe as good as his Super Bowl season in 1981 . . . Tied for second in tackles with 105 . . . Didn't do much blitzing—he only had 4½ sacks—but Bengals used him on stunts to open the lanes for other blitzers . . . Early reputation as a free-lancer has been replaced by his attention to assignments . . . Coming off an arthroscope on his left knee that was more than routine. Had loose cartilage removed and the bone shaved, but he should be ready . . . Born Sept. 19, 1954, in Flint, Mich. . . . Dartmouth grad, a tireless charity worker, was voted NFL Man of the Year.

JOE WALTER 24 6-6 290   Tackle

Bengals are raving about this massive Hope diamond they found in the seventh round of the 1985 draft . . . The Texas Tech mountain was good enough to send Brian Blados to the bench after five games, and now Blados will have to switch to guard to get any playing time . . . He's the prototype tackle of the '80s: huge and athletic with long arms and quick feet . . . Line coach Jim McNally, who loves the idea of bookend tackles, says Walter can pass-block all day . . . Born June 18, 1963, in Dallas.

LEWIS BILLUPS 22 5-11 190   Cornerback

It's not often a team finds two secondary starters in the same draft, but the Bengals struck gold in 1986. Billups was almost as impressive as David Fulcher, starting every game except for a four-week stretch he missed with a broken hand . . . Was so solid quarterbacks actually tested veteran CB Louis Breeden more than him . . . Held out for three weeks in a contract dispute but played well in the second preseason game at nickel back and was a starting corner the next week . . . Burned by Chicago's Willie Gault for a 53-yard score, but that was the exception . . . Born Oct. 10, 1964, in Niceville, Fla. and attended North Alabama.

COACH SAM WYCHE:  One of the brightest offensive minds in the NFL, but his emotional outbursts seem to mirror the hot-and-cold performances of his team...Blew his cool at a radio reporter after a tough loss at Denver and ripped away his microphone...Later apologized...He and Boomer Esiason sometimes get under each other's skin, but they feed off the excitement ...Has constructed as fearsome an offense as there is in the NFL, and his use of six first- or second-year starters on defense last year should begin paying dividends... Cincinnati and Seattle were the only 10-game winners not to make the playoffs...Bengal offense led the NFL with an average of 406 yards a game...Born Jan. 5, 1945, in Atlanta...A walk-on quarterback at Furman who played three seasons with the Bengals...Also had NFL stops with the Redskins, Lions, Cardinals and Bills...Was Bill Walsh's offensive assistant at San Francisco for four years and learned plenty about the passing game...Now if he could only make sure the same team shows up every week.

GREATEST KICKER

As John Houseman might say of a fellow Ivy Leaguer's success, "he earned it." Pat McInally was drafted by the Bengals out of Harvard in the fourth round of the 1975 draft and went on to become one of the most productive punters in the NFL during his 10-year career that ended in retirement before the 1986 season.

McInally led the NFL in punting in 1978 (43.1 yards) and in the Super Bowl season of 1981 (45.4). His career average was an outstanding 42.0. He went out on top, too, averaging 42.3 yards in 1985.

The 6-6, 212-pounder was an excellent all-around athlete. He played backup wide receiver between 1977 and 1981 and caught 57 passes for a 14.1-yard average and five touchdowns. He also completed three of the four passes he attempted out of punt formation.

He was a go-getter off the field as well. His syndicated column aimed at young athletes appeared in 90 newspapers.

McInally's NFL career got off on the wrong foot when he broke his leg in the 1975 College All-Star Game—remember that anachronism?—and he missed the entire season. But his leg came back stronger than ever.

INDIVIDUAL BENGAL RECORDS

Rushing

Most Yards Game:	163	James Brooks, vs New England, 1986
Season:	1,087	James Brooks, 1986
Career:	5,419	Pete Johnson, 1977-83

Passing

Most TD Passes Game:	5	Boomer Esiason, vs N.Y. Jets, 1986
Season:	29	Ken Anderson, 1981
Career:	196	Ken Anderson, 1971-85

Receiving

Most TD Passes Game:	3	Bob Trumpy, vs Houston, 1969
	3	Isaac Curtis, vs Cleveland, 1973
	3	Isaac Curtis, vs Baltimore, 1979
Season:	10	Isaac Curtis, 1974
Career:	53	Isaac Curtis, 1973-83

Scoring

Most Points Game:	24	Larry Kinnebrew, vs Houston, 1984
Season:	115	Jim Breech, 1981
Career:	616	Jim Breech, 1981-86
Most TDs Game:	4	Larry Kinnebrew, vs Houston, 1984
Season:	16	Pete Johnson, 1981
Career:	70	Pete Johnson, 1977-83

CLEVELAND BROWNS

TEAM DIRECTORY: Pres.: Art Modell; Exec. VP-Legal Administration: James Bailey; VP-Football Operations: Ernie Accorsi; Dir. Player Relations: Ricky Feacher; Dir. Player Personnel: Chip Falivene; VP-Pub. Rel.: Kevin Byrne; Head Coach: Marty Schottenheimer. Home field: Cleveland Stadium (80,098). Colors: Seal brown, orange and white.

SCOUTING REPORT

OFFENSE: Consider how far the Browns went last year with Kevin Mack and Earnest Byner suffering through nagging inju-

The Jets will long remember Bernie Kosar in the clutch.

ries, and you'll get an idea of how potent they can become in 1987 if both big backs remain healthy. Marty Schottenheimer doesn't think any injuries can be considered blessings in disguise, but Bernie Kosar blossomed when offensive coordinator Lindy Infante was allowed to open up the offense—by necessity—with a ball-control passing game.

Kosar is one of those quarterbacks who doesn't wow you with looks, but he is incredibly sharp at reading defenses and avoiding interceptions. Anyone who saw his dissection of the Jet secondary in the great playoff comeback knows that.

Kosar's receivers have nice balance. Brian Brennan is the possession man. Webster Slaughter and Reggie Langhorne have the speed to get deep. Gerald McNeil, the Ice Cube, was used mainly in the four-receiver set and can create havoc with his quickness. Herman Fontenot is the jack-of-all-trades, a back who also can be split wide. He's not fast, but he has great hands and moves.

Ozzie Newsome was hurt in so many places last season he briefly considered retirement. But he's back for his 10th season, and Kosar will find him. You know the line can block (Mack and Byner both surpassed 1,000 yards in 1985) and last year it did well protecting Kosar, who threw more passes (531) than any other AFC quarterback except Dan Marino.

DEFENSE: One AFC defensive coach said it best of Hanford Dixon and Frank Minnifield: "I'd die for those two corners." The Dawg Defense starts here. Dixon and Minnifield, who started barking at receivers once again, can play bump-and-run as well as any corner tandem in the NFL and they did a wonderful job disguising coverages. Free safety Chris Rockins, who broke up 13 passes, makes it tough to throw deep.

One thing the Browns could use is a more consistent pass rush. Carl Hairston led with nine sacks last year, but he's 34. Reggie Camp had 7½ sacks and played well in the playoffs, but the Browns could use an end who can apply some heat to take the pressure off nose tackle Bob Golic.

Schottenheimer's linebackers are excellent, even with the trade of Chip Banks to San Diego. Top draft pick Mike Junkin of Duke is expected to take his place. Inside linebacker Eddie Johnson, who doesn't get much ink, is coming off an excellent season. He's only 225 pounds, but he plays in the middle because he loves to hit. Clay Matthews is solid on the other outside spot, but he's not a blitzer, which is one thing the Browns need.

KICKING GAME: Matt Bahr was 20-of-26 on field-goal attempts until he tore knee ligaments with four weeks left in the

BROWNS VETERAN ROSTER

HEAD COACH—Marty Schottenheimer. Assistant Coaches—Dave Adolph, Bill Cowher, Lindy Infante, Richard Mann, Howard Mudd, Joe Pendry, Tom Pratt, Dave Redding, Kurt Schottenheimer, Darvin Wallis.

No.	Name	Pos.	Ht.	Wt.	NFL Exp.	College
4	Anderson, Greg	WR	5-10	170	1	Alabama State
66	Andrews, Tom	OG	6-4	267	3	Louisville
61	Baab, Mike	C	6-4	270	6	Texas
9	Bahr, Matt	K	5-10	175	9	Penn State
43	Baker, Tony	RB	5-10	175	2	East Carolina
99	Baldwin, Keith	DE	6-4	270	5	Texas A&M
77	Bolden, Rickey	T	6-6	280	4	So. Methodist
93	Bolzan, Scott	T	6-3	270	1	Northern Illinois
54	Bowser, Charles	LB	6-3	235	5	Duke
86	Brennan, Brian	WR	5-9	178	4	Boston College
44	Byner, Earnest	RB	5-10	215	4	East Carolina
96	Camp, Reggie	DE	6-4	280	5	California
91	Clancy, Sam	DE	6-7	260	4	Pittsburgh
18	Danielson, Gary	QB	6-2	196	10	Purdue
38	Davis, Johnny	RB	6-1	235	10	Alabama
33	Dickey, Curtis	RB	6-1	220	8	Texas A&M
29	Dixon, Hanford	CB	5-11	186	7	Southern Miss.
26	Duncan, Clyde	WR	6-2	211	3	Tennessee
24	Ellis, Ray	S	6-1	196	7	Ohio State
39	Everett, Major	RB	5-10	218	5	Miss. College
74	Farren, Paul	T-G	6-5	280	5	Boston University
69	Fike, Dan	G	6-7	280	3	Florida
28	Fontenot, Herman	RB-KR	6-0	206	3	Louisiana State
79	Golic, Bob	NT	6-2	270	8	Notre Dame
7	Gossett, Jeff	P	6-2	200	6	Eastern Illinois
80	Greer, Terry	WR	6-2	197	2	Alabama State
53	Griggs, Anthony	LB	6-3	230	6	Ohio State
27	Gross, Al	S	6-3	195	5	Arizona
78	Hairston, Carl	DE	6-4	260	12	Maryland (E. Shore)
23	Harper, Mark	CB	5-9	174	2	Alcorn State
48	Hoggard, D.D.	CB	6-0	188	2	No. Carolina St.
81	Holt, Harry	TE	6-4	240	5	Arizona
35	Jackson, Enis	CB	5-9	180	1	Memphis State
51	Johnson, Eddie	LB	6-1	225	7	Louisville
59	Johnson, Mike	LB	6-1	228	2	Virginia Tech
92	Kab, Vyto	TE	6-5	240	5	Penn State
19	Kosar, Bernie	QB	6-5	210	3	Miami
88	Langhorne, Reggie	WR	6-2	195	3	Elizabeth City St.
62	Lilja, George	G-C	6-4	270	6	Michigan
34	Mack, Kevin	FB	6-0	212	3	Clemson
90	Malone, Ralph	DE	6-5	225	2	Georgia Tech
57	Matthews, Clay	LB	6-2	235	10	So. California
89	McNeil, Gerald	WR-PR	5-7	143	1	Baylor
71	Meyer, Jim	T	6-5	295	1	Illinois State
52	Miller, Nick	LB	6-2	238	1	Arkansas
31	Minnifield, Frank	CB	5-9	180	4	Louisville
82	Newsome, Ozzie	TE	6-2	232	10	Alabama
58	Nicolas, Scott	LB	6-3	226	6	Miami
12	Norseth, Mike	QB	6-2	200	1	Kansas
10	Pagel, Mike	QB	6-2	200	6	Arizona State
72	Puzzuoli, Dave	NT	6-3	260	5	Pittsburgh
63	Risien, Cody	T	6-7	280	8	Texas A&M
37	Rockins, Chris	S	6-0	195	4	Oklahoma State
40	Simmons, King	S	6-2	200	1	Texas Tech
84	Slaughter, Webster	WR	6-0	170	2	San Diego State
87	Tucker, Travis	TE	6-3	240	3	So. Conn. State
50	Van Pelt, Brad	LB	6-5	235	15	Michigan State
85	Weathers, Clarence	WR-PR	5-9	170	5	Delaware State
55	Weathers, Curtis	LB	6-5	230	8	Mississippi
95	White, James	DE	6-3	245	1	Louisiana State
70	Williams, Larry	G	6-5	290	2	Notre Dame
22	Wright, Felix	CB-S	6-2	190	3	Drake
83	Young, Glen	WR-KR	6-2	205	4	Mississippi State

TOP FIVE DRAFT CHOICES

Rd.	Name	Sel. No.	Pos.	Ht.	Wt.	College
1	Junkin, Mike	5	LB	6-3	235	Duke
2	Rakoczy, Greg	32	C	6-5	281	Miami
3	Manoa, Tim	80	RB	6-1	227	Penn State
3	Jaeger, Jeff	82	K	5-11	189	Washington
6	Braggs, Stephen	165	DB	5-9	173	Texas

regular season. He has his old job back, with no competition from the released Mark Moseley, the veteran who missed a 23-yard field goal in overtime against the Jets but came back with a 27-yarder in the sixth quarter. Punter Jeff Gossett was solid, finishing fifth in the AFC with a 41.2-yard average.

THE ROOKIES: Schottenheimer used the fifth overall pick to take Junkin, a 6-3, 235-pounder who's a better prospect than Tim Green, John Offerdahl and Pepper Johnson, the three top inside linebackers in the 1986 draft. Gregg Rakoczy of Miami was the nation's premier center in 1987 and should fit in well behind Mike Baab.

OUTLOOK: Excellent. The Browns would have been in the Super Bowl last year if they could have held off John Elway for one more series. Skill personnel on offense are still kids, with the exception of Newsome, and there are no gaping holes on defense. Forget the AFC Central jokes. The Browns, division winners for two straight years, are as good as any team in the conference.

BROWN PROFILES

BERNIE KOSAR 23 6-5 210   Quarterback

Had it not been for John Elway's 98-yard scoring drive in the AFC championship game, Kosar would have been the youngest quarterback in Super Bowl history... Doesn't have the athletic grace of an Elway—who does?—but he blossomed when the Browns diversified their run-oriented attack... Completed 310 of 531 passes (58.4 percent) for 3,854 yards and 17 TDs with 10 interceptions... Clutch performer carried Browns to one of the greatest comebacks in playoff history by rallying his team from 10 points down to the Jets with four minutes to go. His 489 yards passing were a playoff record... Browns will do anything on offense now, including five wide receivers... Born Nov. 25, 1963, in Boardman, Ohio, and led the University of Miami to the national championship in 1983 as a redshirt freshman.

GERALD McNEIL 25 5-7 143   Kick Returner

The Bears have the Fridge, but the Browns have the Ice Cube . . . The lightest player in the NFL also is the most slippery . . . Set a Browns' record with an 84-yard punt return for a touchdown in a 24-21 win over the Lions and returned a kickoff 100 yards for a TD in a 27-24 victory over the Steelers . . . Mistaken for a ballboy when he first stepped on the practice field at Baylor . . . Would have grown a few more inches but his curvature of the spine was not detected in childhood and went untreated . . . The Mouseketeer starred with the USFL Houston Gamblers and caught 58 passes from Jim Kelly for 1,017 yards in his last season . . . Born Mar. 27, 1962, in Killeen, Tex.

BRIAN BRENNAN 25 5-9 178   Wide Receiver

Browns' leading wide receiver in his first two years surpassed even Ozzie Newsome last year with 55 catches for 838 yards and six TDs . . . Always had to fight an uphill battle because of his size, but he's a great route-runner who can read on the run . . . Scoffed when Raider cornerback Lester Hayes claimed he was hurt and thus contributed to a five-catch afternoon. "Now I know I'm a good player," Brennan said, "rather than just thinking I am." . . . Born Feb. 15, 1962, in Bloomfield Mich., and attended Boston College, where he was a small target for a small QB named Doug Flutie . . . Loves to mix it up over the middle.

HANFORD DIXON 28 5-11 186   Cornerback

Dawg Defense relies on two cornerbacks who can play aggressive bump-and-run coverage, and Dixon and Frank Minnifield are two of the best . . . Dixon finally made the Pro Bowl with five interceptions, which is great for a corner who plays so much man-to-man and isn't tested often . . . Also led the Browns with 19 passes defensed . . . Has 20 interceptions in six seasons . . . His hands cost him a trip to the Pro Bowl in 1985 when he intercepted three but dropped several more . . . He's as good a corner as there is in the AFC . . . Born on Christmas Day, 1958, in Mobile, Ala., and was a first-round pick out of Southern Mississippi in 1981.

FRANK MINNIFIELD 27 5-9 180   Cornerback

Deserved Pro Bowl recognition, but it's hard to take two starters from the same team... Blinding 4.5 speed makes up for his lack of size, but he can be overpowered by receivers who have both size and speed... Doesn't lack for confidence: "I'm the best defensive back in the game."... Also a great special teams performer. Almost singlehandedly won game against Minnesota by blocking a punt for one TD and deflecting a 45-yard field goal that would have tied it on the last play... Came to the Browns in 1984 as a free agent after playing two seasons with the Arizona Wranglers of the USFL... Born Jan. 1, 1960, in Lexington, Ky.... Was nicknamed "Sky" at Louisville because of his 44-inch vertical leap.

KEVIN MACK 25 6-0 212   Running Back

The Browns' Mack Truck was in for frequent repair on his left shoulder, but he gutted out 665 yards on 174 carries and scored 10 touchdowns... Suffered a severe bruise on his shoulder in the season opener against Chicago and might have qualified for injured reserve. He returned in Week 4 against Detroit and re-injured it... Didn't hit full stride until the last five weeks of the season when he put together 100-yard games in wins over the Steelers and Oilers... In 1985, he teamed with Earnest Byner to form only the third NFL backfield to produce a pair of 1,000-yard rushers... Born Aug. 8, 1962, in Kings Mountain, N.C., and was a first-round pick in 1985 out of Clemson.

EARNEST BYNER 24 5-10 215   Running Back

Maybe it was fitting that Byner and Kevin Mack, so complementary on the field, both had injury problems last year... Byner severely sprained his ankle in Week 7 against Green Bay and returned only for a cameo appearance in the playoffs... Rushing totals dropped from 1,002 yards in 1985 to 277 last year, but he'll be back full speed in '87... He's a great receiver and lead blocker... Born Sept. 15, 1962, in Milledgeville, Ga., and was an obscure 10th-round pick out of East Carolina in 1984... Doesn't have breakaway speed, but he ran 55 yards with a fumble for a touchdown in his rookie year, so he's not slow.

OZZIE NEWSOME 31 6-2 232   Tight End

The years finally may be catching up with the Wizard of Oz, who limped through the season like the Tin Man but still showed a lot of heart . . . He sprained an ankle in the opener and then sprained a shoulder two weeks later, which accounts for only 39 catches for 417 yards . . . That was the lowest total since his rookie year of 1978 . . . The NFL's all-time pass-receiving tight end said he doesn't want to retire until he gets a Super Bowl ring . . . Born March 16, 1956, in Muscle Shoals, Ala., and was a two-time All American at Alabama . . . Proved he could still play when he ripped apart Jet secondary in playoffs . . . The three-time Pro Bowler has 50 or more catches in six of his last eight years.

BOB GOLIC 29 6-2 270   Nose Tackle

"Mad Dog" is the ultimate overachiever . . . He was an All-American linebacker at Notre Dame and the Patriots' second-round pick in 1979, but they never knew he could be converted to a down lineman's position . . . He's flourished in the middle since arriving in Cleveland on waivers in 1982, using the leverage and athletic ability he needed as an outstanding wrestler in high school and college . . . Born Oct. 26, 1957, in Cleveland . . . Asked what would happen if the NFL enforced a ban on steroids: "There would be a lot of offensive linemen playing indoor soccer next year. They'd look like raisins."

COACH MARTY SCHOTTENHEIMER: All he does is win

. . . In his first two seasons as a head coach, the Browns have won the AFC Central Division. Last year they went 12-4 and secured the home-field advantage throughout the AFC playoffs . . . They were just a defensive series away from going to the Super Bowl, but John Elway was other-worldly in a 23-20 victory in the AFC championship game . . . Richly deserved Coach-of-the-Year honors because he still won despite injuries to Kevin Mack, Earnest Byner and Ozzie Newsome and the cocaine-induced death of Don Rogers... Opened up the offense to give Bernie Kosar a chance to use his arm and intelligence. That's called adjusting... Future is bright because most of the Browns' money players are young and there are no gaping holes on defense... Came to the Browns as defensive coordinator in 1980 and replaced Sam Rutigliano midway through the 1984 season... Born Sept. 23, 1943, in Canonsburg, Pa.... He was an All-American linebacker at Pitt but survived for six seasons as a special teams player for the Bills and the Patriots... Maybe that's why the Browns' special teams are so good.

GREATEST KICKER

The Browns have had many distinguished kickers and punters in their history, including Don Cockroft, the ultimate two-way performer who led the Browns in scoring from 1968-80 and in punting from 1968-76.

But Paul Brown wouldn't have any trouble identifying the best Browns' kicker of all time. You go by the number of championships won, and there's no doubt that puts Hall of Famer Lou Groza at the top of the list.

Groza played tackle and handled the kicking for the Browns between 1946-59 and 1961-67. In that span, the Browns won four All-America Conference titles and four NFL championships and played in five other NFL title games. Groza holds the Cleveland records for most career points (1,349), most consecutive games scoring (107), most points after touchdown (641), most consecutive PATs made (138), most field goals (234) and highest field-goal percentage in a season (88.5 in 1953).

He kicked five field goals of 50 yards or longer, but oddly enough, both of his career-best 52-yarders came in losing efforts. He also kicked three field goals against Detroit in the 1953 NFL championship game, but the Browns lost, 17-16. His best season was 1953, when he led the NFL by making 23-of-26 field goals and finished with 108 points. He scored a career-high 115 points in 1964 on the strength of 49 PATs in 50 attempts. Groza runs his own insurance company in Cleveland.

INDIVIDUAL BROWN RECORDS

Rushing

Most Yards Game:	237	Jim Brown, vs Los Angeles, 1957	
	237	Jim Brown, vs Philadelphia, 1961	
Season:	1,863	Jim Brown, 1963	
Career:	12,312	Jim Brown, 1957-65	

Passing

Most TD Passes Game:	5	Frank Ryan, vs N.Y. Giants, 1964
	5	Bill Nelsen, vs Dallas, 1969
	5	Brian Sipe, vs Pittsburgh, 1979
Season:	30	Brian Sipe, 1980
Career:	154	Brian Sipe, 1974-83

Receiving

Most TD Passes Game:	3	Mac Speedie, vs Chicago, 1951
	3	Darrell Brewster, vs N.Y. Giants, 1953
	3	Ray Renfro, vs Pittsburgh, 1959
	3	Gary Collins, vs Philadelphia, 1963
	3	Reggie Rucker, vs N.Y. Jets, 1976
	3	Larry Poole, vs Pittsburgh, 1977
	3	Calvin Hill, vs Baltimore, 1978
Season:	13	Gary Collins, 1963
Career:	70	Gary Collins, 1962-71

Scoring

Most Points Game:	36	Dub Jones, vs Chicago Bears, 1951
Season:	126	Jim Brown, 1965
Career:	1,349	Lou Groza, 1950-59, 1961-67
Most TDs Game:	6	Dub Jones, vs Chicago Bears, 1951
Season:	21	Jim Brown, 1965
Career:	126	Jim Brown, 1957-65

DENVER BRONCOS

TEAM DIRECTORY: Owner: Patrick D. Bowlen; GM: John Beake; Dir. Media Rel.: Jim Saccomano; Head Coach: Dan Reeves. Home field: Mile High Stadium (76,274). Colors: Orange, blue, and white.

SCOUTING REPORT

OFFENSE: Loads of talent, starting with the most physically gifted quarterback in the NFL. John Elway's coming-out party in last year's playoffs wowed America, but his teammates already knew what he could do. Don't let anyone kid you. The Broncos would have had the Giants in serious trouble in Super Bowl XXI if they had a quality running back who could have punched it in

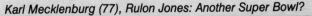

Karl Mecklenburg (77), Rulon Jones: Another Super Bowl?

from the two-yard line in the first half. Instead, Dan Reeves had to resort to a run-pass option by Elway and the drive fizzled.

Getting that big back is the Broncos' top priority. Sammy Winder averaged only 3.3 yards a carry, and Gerald Willhite is more of a threat as a receiver than a runner.

Elway doesn't lack for targets—both big and small. The biggest is 6-foot-5, 265-pound tight end Orson Mobley, who has suction cups for hands and made several outstanding catches when he filled in during Clarence Kay's absence for drug rehab. Steve Watson is the crafty possession receiver, while Vance Johnson and rookie find Mark Jackson are small, fast guys who can get deep. Rookie Ricky Nattiel, the No. 1 pick from Florida, will compete for playing time.

Elway's line is a big question mark. It's on the small side, which definitely hurts the run blocking. You can count on left guard Keith Bishop and right tackle Ken Lanier, but rookie Jim Juriga, coming off knee surgery, is being projected as an immediate starter.

DEFENSE: Despite a trip to the Super Bowl, Dan Reeves was concerned by the performance of his defense in the final four weeks of the season. Cincinnati scored 28 points, Kansas City 37, Washington 30 and Seattle 41. And, of course, the Giants scored 39 in the Super Bowl.

Defensive coordinator Joe Collier, who has been in Denver for 19 years, preaches bend-but-don't break tactics, but they broke down several times. Rulon Jones was switched to left defensive end before the season, but that created a problem at right end when Andre Townsend failed to make an impact. Nose tackle Greg Kragen is smart, but he had trouble plugging the middle against the run.

Karl Mecklenburg's sack production fell off in 1986, but the Broncos think his lack of dominance was more a case of offenses loading up against him. Ricky Hunley, the other inside linebacker, improved with each game, but outside linebacker Jim Ryan is undersized at 218 pounds.

Cornerback Mike Harden made the Broncos forget about Mark Haynes. In fact, owner Patrick Bowlen's biggest mistake was in awarding Haynes a four-year, $2.5-million contract. That price tag made him difficult to trade when the Broncos had no more use for him. Veteran left corner Louie Wright talked about retirement, but he'll be back. Strong safety Dennis Smith made his second straight Pro Bowl despite injuring his knee.

KICKING GAME: Rich Karlis felt as though he let the Broncos down with his misses from point-blank range in the

BRONCOS VETERAN ROSTER

HEAD COACH—Dan Reeves. Assistant Coaches—Marvin Bass, Ruben Carter, Joe Collier, Kay Dalton, Chan Gailey, Alex Gibbs, Stan Jones, Al Miller, Myrel Moore, Nick Nicolau, Mike Shanahan, Charlie West.

No.	Name	Pos.	Ht.	Wt.	NFL Exp.	College
2	Horan, Mike	P	6-0	180	6	Long Beach State
3	Karlis, Rich	K	6-0	180	6	Cincinnati
7	Elway, John	QB	6-3	210	5	Stanford
8	Kubiak, Gary	QB	6-0	192	5	Texas A&M
20	Wright, Louis	CB	6-3	200	13	San Jose State
22	Lilly, Tony	S	6-0	199	4	Florida
23	Winder, Sammy	RB	5-11	203	6	Southern Mississippi
30	Sewell, Steve	RB-WR	6-3	210	3	Oklahoma
31	Harden, Mike	CB	6-1	192	8	Michigan
33	Lang, Gene	RB	5-10	196	4	Louisiana State
35	Bell, Ken	RB	5-10	190	2	Boston College
36	Haynes, Mark	CB	5-11	195	8	Colorado
43	Foley, Steve	S	6-3	190	12	Tulane
45	Wilson, Steve	CB	5-10	195	9	Howard
47	Willhite, Gerald	RB	5-10	200	5	San Jose State
48	Robbins, Randy	S	6-2	189	4	Arizona
49	Smith, Dennis	S	6-3	200	7	Southern California
50	Ryan, Jim	LB	6-1	218	8	William & Mary
52	Woodard, Ken	LB	6-1	218	6	Tuskegee Institute
54	Bishop, Keith	C-G	6-3	265	7	Baylor
55	Dennison, Rick	LB	6-3	220	6	Colorado State
59	Comeaux, Darren	LB	6-1	227	6	Arizona State
61	Townsend, Andre	DE-NT	6-3	265	4	Mississippi
62	Freeman, Mike	G-C	6-3	256	3	Arizona
63	Cooper, Mark	G	6-5	267	5	Miami
64	Bryan, Bill	C	6-2	255	11	Duke
69	Colorito, Tony	NT	6-5	260	2	Southern California
70	Studdard, Dave	T	6-4	260	9	Texas
71	Kragen, Greg	NT	6-3	245	3	Utah State
73	Fletcher, Simon	DE	6-5	240	3	Houston
74	Remsberg, Dan	T	6-6	275	2	Abilene Christian
75	Jones, Rulon	DE	6-6	260	8	Utah State
76	Lanier, Ken	T	6-3	269	7	Florida State
77	Meckienburg, Karl	DE-LB	6-3	250	5	Minnesota
80	Jackson, Mark	WR	5-9	174	2	Purdue
81	Watson, Steve	WR	6-4	195	9	Temple
82	Johnson, Vance	WR	5-11	174	3	Arizona
84	Sampson, Clint	WR	5-11	183	5	San Diego State
85	Hackett, Joey	TE	6-5	267	2	Elon
87	Micho, Bobby	TE	6-3	240	3	Texas
88	Kay, Clarence	TE	6-2	237	4	Georgia
89	Mobley, Orson	TE	6-5	256	2	Salem College
90	Gilbert, Freddie	DE	6-4	275	2	Georgia
98	Hunley, Ricky	LB	6-2	238	4	Arizona

TOP FIVE DRAFT CHOICES

Rd.	Name	Sel. No.	Pos.	Ht.	Wt.	College
1	Nattiel, Ricky	27	WR	5-9	180	Florida
3	Brooks, Michael	83	LB	6-1	235	Louisiana State
4	Munford, Marc	111	LB	6-2	231	Nebraska
6	Marshall, Warren	167	RB	6-0	216	James Madison
7	Strozier, Wilbur	194	OL	6-4	264	Georgia

Super Bowl, but he probably only hastened the inevitable. Karlis had a big-kick season, including the overtime field goal against Cleveland that won the AFC championship game. Mike Horan was signed after Week 12 and solidified the Broncos' woeful punting. He averaged 43.9 yards in the playoffs.

THE ROOKIES: The draft was a major disappointment in that the Broncos couldn't land the big back they wanted. But they did get Nattiel, a 5-9 wide receiver—a Smurf with blazing speed and strength to bench-press 340 pounds—to swell their bulging receiver corps. A third-round trade with Dallas fell through at the last second, but the Broncos recovered by taking LSU linebacker Michael Brooks, who is coming off knee surgery but is a demon when healthy.

OUTLOOK: Elway learned patience last year to go with his flash, and that makes the Broncos a threat to repeat. But Denver needs more depth on the offensive line and a big-time running back. Reeves has won 44 games and two division titles in the last four years, so the Broncos are once again the team to beat in the West.

BRONCO PROFILES

JOHN ELWAY 27 6-3 210   **Quarterback**

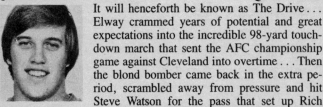

It will henceforth be known as The Drive... Elway crammed years of potential and great expectations into the incredible 98-yard touchdown march that sent the AFC championship game against Cleveland into overtime... Then the blond bomber came back in the extra period, scrambled away from pressure and hit Steve Watson for the pass that set up Rich Karlis' winning field goal... "I may have finally lived up to my potential," Elway smiled... The crazy QB ratings ranked him only ninth in the AFC, but they don't account for his superior athletic talent... Completed 280 of 504 passes (55.6 percent) for 3,485 yards and 19 TDs, with 13 interceptions... He had the Giants on the run in Super Bowl XXI, but lack of running game crushed Broncos' hopes... Born June 28, 1960, in Port Angeles, Wash., and ended his college career at Stanford with five major NCAA passing records... Look out world.

VANCE JOHNSON 24 5-11 174   Wide Receiver

His favorite river is the stream of consciousness... Off-the-wall fun-lover wowed Super Bowl media with his wild antics... Claimed there were really two Vances: one shy and one aggressive. The shy Vance starts a game, runs a few patterns, and then the aggressive Vance takes over... Forget the dramatics, this guy can play... Missed four games with a sprained knee, but he caught 31 passes for 363 yards and two TDs... He was Denver's leading receiver in the playoffs with 12 catches for 235 yards (19.6-yard average) and two scores... Born Mar. 13, 1963, in Trenton, N.J., and was the Broncos' second-round pick out of Arizona in 1985... Was walking through a shopping mall when he decided to get his ears pierced. But when Dan Reeves looked at him funny, he took the earrings out.

STEVE WATSON 30 6-4 195   Wide Receiver

Biggest catch in 1986 set up Rich Karlis' game-winning field goal in the AFC championship game and showcased his craftiness. Watson saw John Elway scrambling to the left and he took off down the field into an open area... Has led Bronco receivers in receptions for the last six seasons. Caught 45 passes for 699 yards (15.5-yard average) and three TDs last year... Watson is a true rags-to-riches story. He was signed as a free agent out of Temple in 1979 and played primarily on special teams his first two years. Then in 1981 he became a starter in Week 2 and went on to catch 60 passes for 1244 yards and a career-high 13 TDs... Born May 28, 1957, in Baltimore ... Fearless over the middle and he can block.

MARK JACKSON 24 5-9 174   Wide Receiver

The Broncos committed grand theft when they plucked Jackson, Purdue's second-leading receiver, in the sixth round... The rookie was expected to fit in as fourth receiver, but he kept making the big play... Finished with 38 receptions for 738 yards and a 19.4-yard average, highest on the team... Really shined on The Drive, making a huge catch on third-

and-20 to keep the march alive and then catching the tying TD pass from John Elway as dog biscuits rained down from the Cleveland bleachers . . . "He's so fast, plus he's tough," said Elway. "He's not afraid to get hit and he'll go after it in a crowd." . . . Born July 23, 1963, in Chicago . . . He's a late-bloomer. Was a walk-on in 1983 at Purdue, and he made 47 of his 51 career receptions in his senior year.

ORSON MOBLEY 24 6-5 256   **Tight End**

Like Jackson, the "Big O" was another Bronco scouting find in the sixth round . . . Mobley was thought to be too big to play tight end, but Bronco scouts loved what they saw at the scouting combine. "He caught everything in sight and he's got huge hands," Dan Reeves said . . . Starred when Clarence Kay was sent into drug rehab . . . Caught 22 passes for 332 yards (15.1-yard average) in the regular season, and he had a 49-yard catch against the Patriots in the playoffs . . . Only problem is his weight. He played at more than 265 pounds last year . . . Played defensive end and tight end for two years for Bobby Bowden at Florida State before transferring to tiny Salem (W.V.) College and playing for Bowden's son, Terry . . . Born Mar. 4, 1963, in Brooksville, Fla. . . . Drafted by baseball's Expos out of high school.

RULON JONES 29 6-6 260   **Defensive End**

Signed a $3.5 million four-year contract at the beginning of the 1986 season, and then he went out and earned his money . . . Finished fourth in the AFC with club-record 13½ sacks, but significantly, he does it more with consistency than with overwhelming single-game performances . . . His best game came against Seattle in Week 8 when he had 2½ sacks . . . Trapped New England quarterback Tony Eason for a safety in the playoffs . . . Broncos played more four-man line last year, which freed up Jones to make more plays . . . His easy-going nature off the field changes radically when he steps between the lines. Says line coach Stan Jones: "He may portray the model of good citizenship, but inside, I think he'd really rather be a bad guy." . . . Born March 25, 1958, in Salt Lake City, and was a second-round pick out of Utah State in 1980.

KEITH BISHOP 30 6-3 265 Guard

Played 1986 under considerable duress after the death of both of his parents within a month of each other... But Bishop had his finest season, earning Pro Bowl honors for the first time in six seasons... Suffered a rare "broken" larynx when he jumped on Jet defensive end Barry Bennett, who had slammed John Elway to the turf in Week 7. Didn't hurt much because Bishop doesn't talk much, anyway... Born Mar. 10, 1957, in Midland, Tex.... Began his college career at Nebraska before transferring to Baylor after two years... His strengths are pulling and trapping because he doesn't have the size to overpower people... One of the best long snappers in the league.

KARL MECKLENBURG 27 6-3 250 Linebacker

His sack production was slightly down from 13 to nine, but wary opponents were loading up their blocking schemes to take care of this hybrid pass-rusher... Defensive coordinator Joe Collier used Mecklenburg and Rulon Jones frequently on the same side in 1985, but he split them up more often last year... One of the NFL's biggest success stories in 1985 when he made the Pro Bowl despite not starting until the 10th week of the season... He was a 12th-round pick out of Minnesota in 1983, and he probably wouldn't have made it had the roster not been expanded to 49 that year... Tried first at nose guard but was a washout. But he's a great linebacker... Born Sept. 1, 1960, in Edina, Minn.

MIKE HARDEN 29 6-1 192 Cornerback

It was a serious injustice keeping Harden out of the Pro Bowl... Set a club record for touchdowns by a defensive player with three. Returned two of his six interceptions for scores and also returned a punt 41 yards for another... His six interceptions tied him for fifth in the AFC... He played so well that Mark Haynes, who was acquired from the Giants for two No. 2s and a No. 6, never saw the light of day ... The Pro Bowl snub hurt. "One of the complaints I have with pro football is that too often people go by reputation when judging players instead of performance," Harden said... Born Feb. 16, 1958, in Memphis, Tenn., and attended Michigan.

RICKY HUNLEY 25 6-2 238   Linebacker

Bitter preseason battle with Steve Busick for a starting inside linebacker position ended when the Broncos traded Busick to the Rams for two low-round draft picks before the opener. Hunley made the trade look good . . . Led the Broncos with 164 tackles, 99 solos . . . Called defensive signals most of the season until he handed over that responsibility to Jim Ryan . . . The Bengals drafted the Arizona All-American with the seventh pick in the 1984 draft, but Hunley refused to sign. The Broncos gave up a No. 1, No. 3 and No. 5 for him . . . Has the speed to go sideline to sideline . . . Born Nov. 11, 1961, in Petersburgh, Va. . . . One of 11 children . . . His mother, Scarlette, has reared more than 40 foster children . . . Hunley donated money based on his tackles to two Denver adoption agencies.

COACH DAN REEVES: As his television commercial suggested, he never let anyone see him sweat . . .

Got Broncos into the Super Bowl for the first time since 1977, but it wasn't all a Rocky Mountain high . . . Regrouped well after Denver went 4-4 in last eight regular-season games, and then picked up momentum in the playoffs . . . Has collected a lethal receiving corps to use his biggest weapon—John Elway —more effectively. Now all he needs is a running game . . . The former Cowboy halfback and assistant coach under Tom Landry is the most successful coach in Broncos' history. He's gone 56-33 (.629) in six seasons, which ranks as fifth best in the NFL since 1981 . . . The Broncos have made the playoffs three times, won the AFC West twice and won at least 10 games four times . . . Born Jan. 19, 1944, in Americus, Ga. . . . Played quarterback at South Carolina, but he was a tough-nosed halfback in eight seasons with the Cowboys . . . His toughest assignment as an assistant was dealing with Duane Thomas, whose private rebellion was one reason he decided to try the real estate business for a year. When construction schedules lagged, Reeves said: "I found out pretty quickly that I was dealing with 100 Duane Thomases." . . . Spent most of his early childhood in and out of hospitals because of rheumatic fever. His mother remembers carrying him to church. He's always been a battler.

GREATEST KICKER

It was a straight-up deal in 1971—the Broncos sent Bobby Howfield to the Jets in exchange for Jim Turner. There's no question the Broncos got the best of that transaction. Turner led the Broncos in scoring for eight of the next nine seasons, while Howfield was cut by the Jets in 1974.

Turner, a Utah State graduate who now hosts a radio show in Denver, scored 697 points in seven seasons with the Jets and added 742 in nine years with the Broncos.

Denver didn't have much of an offense when it advanced to the Super Bowl in 1977, but Turner made the most of his few opportunities. In a 34-21 divisional playoff victory over Pittsburgh, Turner put the Broncos ahead for good with a 44-yard field goal in the fourth quarter. He also broke the ice for Denver in Super Bowl XII with a 47-yard field goal in the third quarter, but the Broncos lost to Dallas, 27-10.

Turner's shining moment may have come earlier in the 1977 season when he caught a touchdown pass in a 30-7 win over the Raiders.

As a Bronco, Turner made 151-of-233 field goals for a .648 percentage. The conventional kicker had his best season in 1975, when he converted 21-of-29 attempts (.724).

INDIVIDUAL BRONCO RECORDS

Rushing

Most Yards Game:	183	Otis Armstrong, vs Houston, 1974	
Season:	1,407	Otis Armstrong, 1974	
Career:	6,323	Floyd Little, 1967-75	

Passing

Most TD Passes Game:	5	Frank Tripucka, vs Buffalo, 1962	
	5	John Elway, vs Minnesota, 1984	
Season:	24	Frank Tripucka, 1960	
Career:	74	Craig Morton, 1977-82	

Receiving

Most TD Passes Game:	3	Lionel Taylor, vs Buffalo, 1960
	3	Bob Scarpitto, vs Buffalo, 1966
	3	Haven Moses, vs Houston, 1973
	3	Steve Watson, vs Baltimore, 1981
Season:	13	Steve Watson, 1981
Career:	44	Lionel Taylor, 1960-66
	44	Haven Moses, 1972-81

Scoring

Most Points Game:	21	Gene Mingo, vs Los Angeles, 1960
Season:	137	Gene Mingo, 1962
Career:	736	Jim Turner, 1971-79
Most TDs Game:	3	Lionel Taylor, vs Buffalo, 1960
	3	Don Stone, vs San Diego, 1962
	3	Bob Scarpitto, vs Buffalo, 1966
	3	Floyd Little, vs Minnesota, 1972
	3	Floyd Little, vs Cincinnati, 1973
	3	Haven Moses, vs Houston, 1973
	3	Otis Armstrong, vs Houston, 1974
	3	Jon Keyworth, vs Kansas City, 1974
	3	Steve Watson, vs Baltimore, 1981
	3	Gerald Willhite, vs Dallas, 1986
	3	Gerald Willhite, vs Kansas City, 1986
Season:	13	Floyd Little, 1972
	13	Floyd Little, 1973
	13	Steve Watson, 1981
Career:	54	Floyd Little, 1967-75

HOUSTON OILERS

TEAM DIRECTORY: Pres./Owner K.S. (Bud) Adams Jr.; Exec. VP/GM: Ladd Herzeg; VP/Player Personnel: Mike Holovak; Dir. Adm.: Rick Nichols; Dir. Media Rel.: Chip Namias; Head Coach: Jerry Glanville. Home field: Astrodome (50,452). Colors: Scarlet, Columbia blue and white.

SCOUTING REPORT

OFFENSE: It's tough to produce a quality assembly-line product when the nuts and bolts keep getting in the way. The Oilers simply committed too many turnovers in 1986. Warren Moon threw for more yards (3,489) than all but five AFC quarterbacks,

Ernest Givins had a grand reception as a rookie.

but he also threw 27 interceptions, most in the NFL. The Oilers' 44 turnovers were more than all but five teams.

When given some protection, Moon can play, although he is living through the same problem Archie Manning had during his career in New Orleans. June Jones will be his fourth quarterback coach in four years, and that lack of stability reflects on the Oilers' larger organizational problems.

The Oilers finished 4-4 in the second half of 1986 because they went with their strength—Moon pitching and Ernest Givins and Drew Hill catching. The running game is iffy, but Miami running back Alonzo Highsmith, the Oilers' top pick, could change that. Mike Rozier averaged only 3.3 yards a crack before he went down with a knee injury with four games left. Ray Wallace, who played defensive back at Purdue before switching to running back as a senior, has shown flashes of ability. Alan Pinkett is only 5-9 and he goes down too easily. Butch Woolfolk is not an every-down back.

The key to the line will be how well guard Mike Munchak and Jim Romano return from knee injuries. Ex-Ram Kent Hill, who came over in the Jim Everett trade, will be fighting for a job.

DEFENSE: The Oilers were the second-most improved defensive team in the NFL last year, in part because they blitzed from every spot on the field. Only four opposing quarterbacks completed at least 50 percent of their passes, but that daring strategy only produced 16 interceptions and 32 sacks.

Defensive end Ray Childress has been excellent against the run, but the Oilers are counting on William Fuller, acquired in the Everett trade, to become their designated pass-rusher.

The secondary is solid. Patrick Allen was placed frequently in man coverage and held up well, breaking up a team-leading 18 passes. Depending on the coverage, strong safety Jeff Donaldson, who moved into the starting lineup when Bo Eason injured his ankle, can play cornerback, safety or inside linebacker.

The Oilers were devastated by injuries last season, and the most serious was a spine injury that forced outside linebacker Frank Bush into retirement. Bush had been considered the Oilers' best overall linebacker. John Grimsley picked up some of the slack by leading the team in tackles from his left inside position.

KICKING GAME: Outstanding. The Oilers robbed the Redskins when they acquired Tony Zendejas in 1985 for a fifth-round pick. He's working on a streak of seven straight field goals entering 1987. In addition to finishing sixth in the AFC in punting with a 41.2-yard average, Lee Johnson kicks off extremely deep.

OILERS VETERAN ROSTER

HEAD COACH—Jerry Glanville. Assistant Coaches—Tom Bettis, Kim Helton, Dick Jamieson, Milt Jackson, June Jones, Miller McCalmon, Floyd Reese, Doug Shively.

No.	Name	Pos.	Ht.	Wt.	NFL Exp.	College
56	Abraham, Robert	LB	6-1	236	6	North Carolina St.
86	Akiu, Mike	WR	5-9	182	3	Hawaii
29	Allen, Patrick	CB	5-10	179	4	Utah State
75	Baker, Jesse	DE	6-5	271	9	Jacksonville State
36	Banks, Chuck	FB	6-2	225	4	West Virginia Tech
25	Bostic, Keith	S	6-1	223	5	Michigan
92	Briehl, Tom	LB	6-3	246	2	Stanford
24	Brown, Steve	CB	5-11	187	5	Oregon
94	Bush, Frank	LB	6-1	228	3	North Carolina St.
71	Byrd, Richard	DE	6-3	264	3	S. Mississippi
79	Childress, Ray	DE	6-6	276	3	Texas A&M
50	Dodge, Kirk	LB	6-1	231	3	Nevada-Las Vegas
31	Donaldson, Jeff	S	6-0	194	4	Colorado
88	Dressel, Chris	TE	6-4	239	5	Stanford
82	Drewrey, Willie	WR-KR	5-7	164	3	West Virginia
21	Eason, Bo	S	6-2	204	4	Cal-Davis
51	Fairs, Eric	LB	6-3	235	2	Memphis State
95	Fuller, William	DE	6-3	255	2	North Carolina
81	Givins, Ernest	WR	5-9	175	2	Louisville
68	Golic, Mike	DT	6-5	272	2	Notre Dame
59	Grimsley, John	LB	6-2	236	4	Kentucky
85	Hill, Drew	WR	5-9	168	8	Georgia Tech
72	Hill, Kent	G	6-5	260	9	Georgia Tech
22	Johnson, Kenny	S	5-11	172	7	Mississippi State
11	Johnson, Lee	P	6-1	199	3	Brigham Young
23	Johnson, Richard	CB	6-1	190	3	Wisconsin
38	Jordan, Donald	RB	6-0	215	2	Houston
58	Kelley, Mike	C-G	6-5	281	2	Notre Dame
37	Kush, Rod	S	6-1	198	7	Nebraska-Omaha
10	Luck, Oliver	QB	6-2	196	6	West Virginia
28	Lyday, Allen	S	5-10	197	4	Nebraska
93	Lyles, Robert	LB	6-1	225	4	TCU
98	Madsen, Lynn	DE	6-4	260	2	Washington
78	Maggs, Don	T-G	6-5	279	2	Tulane
74	Matthews, Bruce	T	6-4	283	5	USC
26	McMillian, Audrey	CB	6-0	190	3	Houston
91	Meads, Johnny	LB	6-2	235	4	Nicholls State
1	Moon, Warren	QB	6-3	210	4	Washington
76	Moran, Eric	T-G	6-5	294	4	Washington
67	Morgan, Karl	OT	6-1	255	4	UCLA
63	Munchak, Mike	G	6-3	278	5	Penn State
39	Oliver, Hubert	FB	5-10	230	6	Arizona
89	Parks, Jeff	TE	6-4	236	2	Auburn
52	Pennison, Jay	C	6-1	265	2	Nicholls State
20	Pinkett, Allen	RB	5-9	185	2	Notre Dame
53	Riley, Avon	LB	6-3	240	7	UCLA
55	Romano, Jim	C	6-3	264	6	Penn State
33	Rozier, Mike	RB	5-10	211	3	Nebraska
99	Smith, Doug	DT	6-4	287	3	Auburn
70	Steinkuhler, Dean	T-G	6-3	275	4	Nebraska
35	Wallace, Ray	FB	6-0	221	2	Purdue
69	Williams, Doug	T-G	6-5	285	2	Texas A&M
87	Williams, Jamie	TE	6-4	245	5	Nebraska
80	Williams, Oliver	WR	6-2	195	2	Illinois
12	Witkowski, John	QB	6-1	205	3	Columbia
40	Woolfolk, Butch	RB	6-1	215	6	Michigan
7	Zendejas, Tony	PK	5-8	165	3	Nevada-Reno

TOP FIVE DRAFT CHOICES

Rd.	Name	Sel. No.	Pos.	Ht.	Wt.	College
1	Highsmith, Alonzo	3	RB	6-1	235	Miami
1	Jeffires, Haywood	20	WR	6-2	198	North Carolina St.
2	Johnson, Walter	46	LB	6-0	218	Louisiana Tech
3	Carlson, Cody	64	QB	6-3	203	Baylor
4	Dusbabek, Mark	105	LB	6-5	232	Minnesota

THE ROOKIES: The Oilers traded up with Buffalo to get Highsmith, the consummate big back combining power with the speed to bounce outside. Highsmith played in Miami's pass-oriented offense and has excellent hands. Haywood Jeffires of North Carolina State was rated by some to be the best wide receiver in the draft after a spectacular senior season, and he can run a 4.37. Third-round linebacker Walter Johnson of Louisiana Tech is a 6-foot, 235-pound sleeper.

OUTLOOK: The Oilers made improvements on offense and defense in 1986, but turnovers and penalties negated a big chunk of that. Jerry Glanville is glib, but he has to instill a winning attitude. GM Ladd Herzeg has hired three coaches and has only 23 wins over the last six seasons to show for it. The Oilers have too much talent to be this bad.

OILER PROFILES

WARREN MOON 30 6-3 210   Quarterback

The shame is he's never been used properly since arriving from the CFL in 1984, but that could be changing . . . Oilers would run on first and second down, leaving Moon to run for his life on third down or throw into stacked coverages . . . But indications are Jerry Glanville wants to open up the offense because of the strength of his wide receivers . . . Moon beat out only Indianapolis' Jack Trudeau in the AFC quarterback ratings . . . He completed 256 of 488 passes (52.5 percent) for 3,489 yards and 13 touchdowns with 26 interceptions . . . Had arthroscopic surgery on a kneecap tendon in the offseason, but he should be OK . . . Born Nov. 18, 1956, in Los Angeles, and attended Washington . . . Won five straight Grey Cups at Edmonton.

ERNEST GIVINS 23 5-9 175   Wide Receiver

Oilers struck gold with this second-round speed-burner from Louisville, the same school that produced Mark Clayton . . . Made the All-Rookie team with 61 catches for 1,062 yards, which gave him a team-leading 17.4-yard average. He was only the ninth rookie in NFL history to surpass 1,000 yards . . . He's acrobatic, extremely quick and can make the great catch in traffic . . . Oilers also love his toughness over the middle and willingness to block downfield . . . Also averaged 16.4 yards on nine reverses and can return punts . . . Born Sept. 3, 1964, in St. Petersburg, Fla. . . . His father played minor-league baseball.

DREW HILL 30 5-9 168   Wide Receiver

The Oilers haven't exactly cornered the market on good trades, but this is one GM Ladd Herzeg can be proud of . . . Gave up fourth- and seventh-round picks to the Rams before the 1985 season, and Hill has responded with 129 receptions and 2,281 yards over the last two seasons . . . He caught a career-high 65 balls for 1,112 yards last year . . . Not quite as fast as Givins, who runs a 4.4, but he makes great adjustments to the ball . . . Only the second time in Oiler history that a pair of receivers surpassed 1,000 yards in a season. Charlie Hennigan (1,746) and Bill Groman (1,175) did it in 1961 . . . In five active seasons with the Rams, Hill caught only 60 passes, but he had an eye-popping 22.6-yard average . . . He was a great kick-returner at Georgia Tech . . . Born Oct. 5, 1956, in Newnan, Ga.

JOHN GRIMSLEY 25 6-2 236   Linebacker

In his first full season, Grimsley led the Oilers with 199 tackles—112 solos and 87 assists—and drew favorable comparisons with former Houston linebacker Greg Bingham for his toughness and intelligence . . . Grimsley did all that despite not starting until Week 7 against Cincinnati . . . He averaged nearly 14 tackles in his last 12 games . . . Part of the Oilers' 1984 draft class that was considered weak because so many signed with the USFL. But the sixth-rounder from Kentucky has improved every year . . . Born Feb. 25, 1962, in Canton, Ohio . . . In the NFL, that's not a bad place to call home.

PATRICK ALLEN 26 5-10 179   Cornerback

Instead of jewelry or fancy clothes, Allen wears wide receivers . . . Since the Oilers send everyone after the quarterback, their corners are placed in almost constant man-to-man jeopardy. Allen thrives on the pressure. He didn't give up a touchdown in single coverage all season . . . He says: "It's a game of confidence. If you're scared, you're not going to win the battle. I'm not scared to get beat." . . . Oilers allowed a completion rate of just 46.5 percent, the NFL's best mark, and

Allen led the Oilers with three interceptions... The fourth-round pick out of Utah State in 1984 credits his success to endless hours of film study and visualization... Born Aug. 26, 1961, in Seattle.

KENT HILL 30 6-5 260   Guard

Part of the blockbuster trade that sent holdout quarterback Jim Everett to the Rams... The five-time Pro Bowler had trouble moving from left to right guard and may have to hold off second-year guard Don Maggs or Mike Kelley for a starting job... The change in positions made Hill adjust his footwork on pass sets and leading sweeps, which he did exceptionally well with the Rams... Hill was expendable because the Rams drafted Tom Newberry in the second round last year, but he still was shocked by the trade... Born Mar. 7, 1957, in Americus, Ga., and played at Georgia Tech... His main rap is consistency. He destroyed Cowboy defensive tackle Randy White in a 1985 playoff game but has had trouble against players with lesser reputations.

RAY CHILDRESS 24 6-6 276   Defensive End

Even though he led the Oilers with five sacks, Childress isn't a man-eating pass rusher, which is probably why the Oilers drafted him No. 1 with the third pick in 1985... He does have great size and strength, though, and that makes him a bear against the run... Finished second to John Grimsley in tackles with 172 ... One reason the Oilers blitz so much is that they need some kind of gimmick to produce heat on the passer ... Runnerup in 1985 to the Colts' Duane Bickett for AFC Defensive Rookie of the Year... Born Oct. 20, 1962, in Memphis, Tenn., and was an All-American at Texas A&M.

MIKE ROZIER 26 5-10 211   Running Back

The 1983 Heisman Trophy winner from Nebraska was running well until he suffered a knee injury while picking up a blitz against Cleveland in Week 13. Underwent arthroscopic surgery to repair ligament and cartilage damage... Finished 10th in the AFC with 662 yards on 199 carries (3.3-yard average) ... Oilers would like to feature him, but they've fallen behind so quickly they've had to abandon the run ... Rozier had 20 carries in only one game last year ... It hasn't helped that the Oilers' run-blocking has been terrible ... Born Mar. 1, 1961, in Camden, N.J. ... In three years at Nebraska, the Jersey Flash ran for 4,780 yards and had a 7.2-yard rushing average ... Rozier was playing for Pittsburgh in the USFL when the Oilers obtained his rights in the 1984 supplemental draft.

JIM ROMANO 27 6-3 264   Center

Oilers found out how valuable Romano was when he was out for five weeks with ligament damage in his right knee ... During an unbeaten preseason and a 31-3 rout of Green Bay in the opener, Romano helped the Oilers control the ball on the ground ... He suffered the knee injury in Week 2 against Cleveland, and the Oilers lost all five games without him ... He was reactivated in Week 8 against his former team, the Raiders, and struggled through most of the season until his knee gave out in the final two weeks ... Born Sept. 7, 1959, in Glen Cove, N.Y., and played with Oiler guard Mike Munchak at Penn State ... He can also swing a golf club. He won an automobile at the 1985 Super Bowl golf tournament with a hole-in-one.

TONY ZENDEJAS 27 5-8 165   Kicker

One of the few mistakes the Redskin braintrust has made ... The Skins gave away the talented Zendejas for a fifth-round pick before the 1985 season and later regretted it when Mark Moseley started clanging the uprights ... In his first two seasons with the Oilers, Zendejas has converted 43-of-54 field-goal attempts (79.6 percent) ... He was 21-of-27 last year, including five field goals of 45 yards or longer ... Oilers don't use Zendejas to kick off because punter Lee Johnson can boom those ... Born May 15, 1960, in Curimeo, Michucan, Mexico, and set a Division 1-AA record with 70 field goals in four years at Nevada-Reno ... Also played two years with the Los Angeles Express of the USFL and was 24-of-27 on field goals inside 50 yards.

COACH JERRY GLANVILLE: Oilers have a lot of talent.  Now it's up to Glanville to build on last year's promising 4-4 finish . . . Glanville is probably best known for his one-liners. Asked why he didn't bench players who kept making mistakes, Glanville replied: "What do you want me to do, throw a hand grenade in the dressing room and play who's left?" . . . Spent 12 years as an NFL assistant at Detroit, Atlanta, Buffalo and Houston before taking over for Hugh Campbell in '86 . . . The 5-11 Oilers had great stats but killed themselves with penalties and turnovers . . . Glanville's easy to spot on the sidelines—he's the Man in Black. He owns two cars, both black . . . After one flag-filled game, he wore a black-and-white striped shirt to his Monday press conference . . . Hired a former NFL ref to officiate practice in an attempt to cut out the penalties. When that didn't work, he suggested hypnosis. "Anybody got a voodoo doll?" he asked . . . Instituted "Operation Headstart" the last two seasons, which is not a welfare program but an offseason training session . . . Warren Moon criticized his run-oriented offensive philosophy, and the Oilers opened it up late in the season . . . Born Oct. 14, 1941, in Detroit . . . Played linebacker at Northern Michigan . . . Coached for six seasons at Georgie Tech.

GREATEST KICKER

Toni Fritsch's five seasons with the Oilers (1977-81) coincided with their greatest success. The soccer-style kicker didn't have the strongest leg in the world, but he was deadly accurate. He converted 81-of-105 field-goal attempts for an excellent .771 percentage. Stack that up against George Blanda's .481 percentage (on 91-of-189 attempts), and you'll really see how good it was.

Fritsch was the NFL's best kicker in 1979, when the Oilers went 11-5. He made 21-of-25 attempts (.840) and was one of six Oilers named to the Pro Bowl. But his most memorable game may have come the next year in a Monday Night Game against the nemesis Steelers. Before a sellout Astrodome crowd, Fritsch kicked two field goals to provide all the points the Oilers would need in a 6-0 shutout.

Blanda made the Hall of Fame mainly on the strength of his passing abilities, but he does hold NFL records for most points (2,002) and most points after touchdown (943) and he is second all-time in field goals (335). In an age of specialization, Fritsch was the far superior kicker.

INDIVIDUAL OILER RECORDS

Rushing

Most Yards Game:	216	Billy Cannon, vs N.Y. Jets, 1961
Season:	1,934	Earl Campbell, 1980
Career:	8,574	Earl Campbell, 1978-84

Passing

Most TD Passes Game:	7	George Blanda, vs N.Y. Jets, 1961
Season:	36	George Blanda, 1961
Career:	165	George Blanda, 1960-66

Receiving

Most TD Passes Game:	3	Bill Groman, vs N.Y. Jets, 1960
	3	Bill Groman, vs N.Y. Jets, 1961
	3	Billy Cannon, vs N.Y. Jets, 1961
	3	Charlie Hennigan, vs San Diego, 1961
	3	Charlie Hennigan, vs Buffalo, 1963
	3	Charles Frazier, vs Denver, 1966 (twice)
	3	Dave Casper, vs Pittsburgh, 1981
Season:	17	Bill Groman, 1961
Career:	51	Charlie Hennigan, 1960-66

Scoring

Most Points Game:	30	Billy Cannon, vs N.Y. Jets, 1961
Season:	115	George Blanda, 1960
Career:	596	George Blanda, 1960-66
Most TDs Game:	5	Billy Cannon, vs N.Y. Jets, 1961
Season:	19	Earl Campbell, 1979
Career:	73	Earl Campbell, 1978-84

INDIANAPOLIS COLTS

TEAM DIRECTORY: Pres./Treas.: Robert Irsay; VP/GM: Jim Irsay; VP/Gen. Counsel: Michael Chernoff; Dir. Player Personnel: Jack Bushofsky; Dir. Pub. Rel.: Craig Kelley; Head Coach: Ron Meyer. Home field: Hoosier Dome (60,127). Colors: Royal blue, white and silver.

SCOUTING REPORT

OFFENSE: Maybe Robert Irsay should write the Cardinals a thank-you note. Only St. Louis' feeble offense, which scored 218 points last year, accounted for fewer points than the Colts (229), who have no game-breaking running backs or wide receivers. Rookie receiver Bill Brooks had a marvelous year by catching everything thrown to him. But the one ingredient Brooks lacks is something you can't teach—speed. That shortcoming is particularly noticeable because on the other side, Matt Bouza is another possession receiver.

The Colts should benefit by having Gary Hogeboom healthy for an entire season. The ex-Cowboy knocked himself out for most of the season by trying to stiff-arm Dolphin Lyle Blackwood near the sidelines rather than just running out of bounds, and he paid the price with a separated shoulder. When Ron Meyer took over the 0-13 Colts from Rod Dowhower, he inserted Hogeboom for Jack Trudeau and the Colts won their last three, losing the rights to Vinny Testaverde.

The big mystery is what happened to the Colts' running game. In 1985, they averaged a league-leading 5.0-yards a carry; a year later, the team average was down to 3.8. It doesn't figure to improve following the loss of Randy McMillan, who broke his leg in a car accident in April. A lot will be up to Albert Bentley, who had only 73 carries but a team-leading average of 4.8 yards.

He also may shift left tackle Chris Hinton to left guard, lining him up next to underrated center Ray Donaldson and right guard Ron Solt. It's the old baseball theory of strength up the middle.

DEFENSE: Linebacker Barry Krauss is coming off his fourth surgery in two years, and this is the most serious yet—total reconstructive knee surgery. But defensive end and cornerback are bigger concerns. Jon Hand, the No. 1 pick in 1986, was a mild disappointment because he lacked the upper-body strength to shed tacklers at the line of scrimmage.

Duane Bickett, the No. 1 pick from 1985, has performed solidly against the run at right outside linebacker, and although he

Jon Hand was the Colts' leading sack man.

doesn't have blazing speed, he has improved his pass drops and is extremely intelligent. Inside linebacker Cliff Odom gets little recognition, but he's led the Colts in tackles for two straight years. No. 1 pick Cornelius Bennett, the Alabama linebacker, should have an immediate impact.

The Colts had only 16 interceptions, and they are looking to improve their secondary. Leonard Coleman, a No. 1 in 1984, had three interceptions against New Orleans but only one more the rest of the season. This is a make-or-break season for safeties Dwight Hicks and Dextor Clinkscale.

KICKING GAME: Not only is Rohn Stark the best punter in the NFL, he is the best punter, statistically, in NFL history with a

COLTS VETERAN ROSTER

HEAD COACH—Ron Meyer. Assistant Coaches—John Becker, Greg Briner, Leon Burtnett, George Catavolos, George Hill, Tom Lovat, John Marshall, Chip Myers, Keith Rowen, Rick Venturi, Tom Zupancic.

No.	Name	Pos.	Ht.	Wt.	NFL Exp.	College
57	Ahrens Dave	LB	6-3	245	7	Wisconsin
79	Armstrong, Harvey	NT	6-3	261	5	Southern Methodist
72	Baldischwiler, Karl	OT	6-5	276	9	Oklahoma
81	Beach, Pat	TE	6-4	244	5	Washington State
20	Bentley, Albert	RB	5-11	215	3	Miami
4	Biasucci, Dean	K	6-0	198	3	Western Carolina
50	Bickett, Duane	LB	6-5	241	3	Southern Cal
85	Bouza, Matt	WR	6-3	208	6	California
84	Boyer, Mark	TE	6-4	232	3	Southern Cal
80	Brooks, Bill	WR	5-11	187	2	Boston University
74	Brotzki, Bob	OT	6-5	269	2	Syracuse
68	Broughton, Willie	NT	6-5	282	3	Miami
71	Call, Kevin	OT	6-7	288	4	Colorado State
47	Clinkscale, Dextor	S	5-11	195	7	S. Carolina State
31	Coleman, Leonard	S	6-2	211	3	Vanderbilt
98	Cooks, Johnie	LB	6-4	243	6	Mississippi State
38	Daniel, Eugene	CB	5-11	184	4	Louisiana State
23	Daniel, Kenny	CB	5-10	180	4	San Jose State
53	Donaldson, Ray	C	6-4	282	8	Georgia
44	Gill, Owen	FB	6-1	230	3	Iowa
25	Glasgow, Nesby	FS	5-10	191	9	Washington
90	Haines, John	DL	6-7	266	3	Texas
78	Hand, Jon	DE	6-6	280	2	Alabama
87	Harbour, James	WR	6-0	192	2	Mississippi
29	Hicks, Dwight	S	6-1	192	9	Michigan
75	Hinton, Chris	OT-G	6-4	285	5	Northwestern
7	Hogeboom, Gary	QB	6-4	207	8	Central Michigan
21	Holt, John	CB	5-11	180	7	West Texas State
56	Hunley, LaMonte	LB	6-2	238	3	Arizona
94	Kellar, Scott	NT	6-3	278	2	Northern Illinois
5	Kiel, Blair	QB	6-0	200	3	Notre Dame
63	Kirchner, Mark	OT	6-3	265	4	Baylor
55	Krauss, Barry	LB	6-3	253	9	Alabama
92	Leiding, Jeff	LB	6-3	232	2	Texas
59	Lowry, Orlando	LB	6-4	238	3	Ohio State
88	Martin, Robbie	WR	5-8	187	7	Cal Poly-SLO
32	McMillan, Randy	FB	6-0	220	7	Pittsburgh
86	Murray, Walter	WR	6-4	200	2	Hawaii
93	Odom, Cliff	LB	6-2	241	7	Texas-Arlington
35	Randle, Tate	DB	6-0	204	6	Texas Tech
58	Redd, Glen	LB	6-1	232	6	Brigham Young
83	Sherwin, Tim	TE	6-6	246	7	Boston College
66	Sott, Ron	OG	6-3	283	4	Maryland
—	Springs, Kirk	S-KR	6-0	197	7	Miami (Ohio)
3	Stark, Rohn	P	6-3	202	6	Florida State
99	Thompson, Donnell	DE	6-5	269	7	North Carolina
10	Trudeau, Jack	QB	6-3	207	2	Illinois
64	Utt, Ben	OG	6-5	281	6	Georgia Tech
34	Wonsley, George	RB	6-0	221	4	Mississippi State

TOP FIVE DRAFT CHOICES

Rd.	Name	Sel. No.	Pos.	Ht.	Wt.	College
1	Bennett, Cornelius	2	LB	6-2	236	Alabama
3	Gambol, Chris	58	OT	6-7	285	Iowa
4	Dixon, Randy	86	OT	6-4	286	Pittsburgh
5	Banks, Roy	114	WR	5-11	190	Eastern Illinois
6	Robinson, Freddie	142	DB	6-0	185	Alabama

career average of 45.16 yards per punt. Stark improved even his high standards last year by downing 22 kicks inside the 20, against only five touchbacks. Kicker Dean Biasucci had a shaky season—he was 13-of-25 on field-goal attempts—and he was certain to be challenged in training camp.

THE ROOKIES: The Colts decided to keep their first pick— the second overall—and used it wisely on Bennett. He's not as big or strong as Lawrence Taylor, but he's faster. The Colts needed to shore up their offensive line after a terrible rushing season and added Iowa tackle Chris Gambol in the third round and Pitt tackle Randy Dixon in the fourth. They still don't have a star back.

OUTLOOK: This is a franchise that has gone 38-90-1 over the last nine seasons and hasn't been close to breaking even since 1983. Meyer will crack the whip, but it's hard to see much improvement without an influx of talent. Even when Meyer was loaded with players at New England, he struggled. Raymond Berry took that same team to the Super Bowl. Suffice it to say the Colts will be looking up at the rest of the AFC East once again.

COLT PROFILES

GARY HOGEBOOM 29 6-4 207   Quarterback

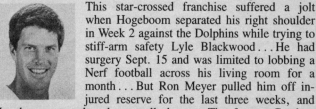

This star-crossed franchise suffered a jolt when Hogeboom separated his right shoulder in Week 2 against the Dolphins while trying to stiff-arm safety Lyle Blackwood...He had surgery Sept. 15 and was limited to lobbing a Nerf football across his living room for a month...But Ron Meyer pulled him off injured reserve for the last three weeks, and Hogeboom started and won all three...The former Cowboy completed 85 of 144 passes (59.0 percent) for 1,154 yards and six touchdowns, with six interceptions...The late winning streak kept the Colts out of the Vinny Testaverde Derby, so it might have been counter-productive...Born Aug. 21, 1958, in Grand Rapids, Mich., and attended Central Michigan... Selected in the fifth-round by Dallas in 1980, but he never could put Danny White on the bench...He's got a strong arm but he tries to force the ball.

BILL BROOKS 23 5-11 187   Wide Receiver

Playing at Boston University—not Boston College—Brooks didn't have a long pedigree. But the Colt scouts loved what they saw at the Senior Bowl and stole him in the fourth round ... Brooks exploded with 65 catches for 1,131 yards and eight touchdowns ... The yardage was the third-highest in NFL history for a rookie ... He led all rookie receivers in yards and receptions ... Brooks went low in the draft because he was timed at 4.58 seconds in the 40. The Colts worked on his start and got him slightly under that ... He was the 86th player drafted and received only $77,000 in base salary and $85,000 in signing and reporting bonuses ... Smooth, gliding stride ... Had two drops among 79 catches his senior year ... Born April 6, 1964, in Milton, Mass.

MATT BOUZA 29 6-3 208   Wide Receiver

Ideally, the Colts would love to have at least one speed receiver, but Bouza mirrors Bill Brooks in that he gets by with excellent routes and great hands ... He's the prototypical possession receiver ... Finished sixth in the AFC with 71 catches for 830 yards (11.7-yard average) and five touchdowns in the best season of his five-year career ... Like many players, he's extremely superstitious. Before every home game, he spits his gum into the same drain pipe on the field. On the road, he wears the same shoes and never unpacks his suitcase ... He caught seven passes in games against the Bills (twice), Saints and Jets and has a 25-game receiving streak going into 1987 ... Born April 8, 1958, in San Jose, Cal. ... He was a freshman walk-on at California, so he knows how to battle for a job.

CHRIS HINTON 26 6-4 280   Guard

Ron Meyer made controversial decision to move the three-time Pro Bowler from left tackle to left guard for the final two games of the 1986 season. Meyer's theory is to build strength up the middle, which is why he wants Hinton, center Ray Donaldson and right guard Ron Solt lined up as a trio ... Remains to be seen if Hinton will stay there or return to his more comfortable spot . . . Pro-Bowl selection may have been based more on reputation than production . . . Part of Swap Shop deal that sent John Elway to Denver in 1983. Colts also got quarterback Mark Herrmann, who was cut, and Solt. The Broncos win by a landslide . . . Born July 31, 1961, in Chicago . . . Unfortunately, he knows all about losing. He played at Northwestern.

ROHN STARK 28 6-3 202   Punter

Became a better punter, if that's possible, by working on his finesse punts without sacrificing any distance . . . Led NFL with a 45.2-yard average on 76 punts, and his 37.2-yard net average was second in the NFL to Miami's Reggie Roby (37.4) . . . What sent Stark apart was his decision not to overpower the ball near the end zone. He had only five touchbacks and placed 22 punts inside the 20-yard line, both personal records . . . He usually can boom away because he has the whole field in front of him due to the Colts' poor offense . . . From midfield, he worked on dropping punts at the five between the numbers and the sideline, aiming for a 4.5-second hang time . . . His 45.16-yard career average is slightly better than Sammy Baugh's mark of 45.10 . . . Born June 4, 1959, in Minneapolis, and attended Florida State.

JON HAND 23 6-6 280   Defensive End

Steady, not spectacular . . . You'd expect more out of the fourth overall pick in the 1986 draft, and the Colts are holding their breath . . . Hand led all Colt linemen with five sacks, but he needs to build up his upper-body strength to become more physical. In fact, he will receive $26,700 in each of the next three seasons for following an offseason weight-lifting program . . . He started out slowly and was spelled by Harvey Armstrong at right end. But he came on at the end of the season, which is a good sign . . . Could he be the next Bubba Smith? Well, he wears a No. 78 jersey and he also "stood in" for Smith during the filming of *Stroker Ace* . . . But it's Monday's films that are important now . . . Born Nov. 13, 1963, in Sylacauga, Ala., and was part of the last class recruited at Alabama by Bear Bryant.

DUANE BICKETT 24 6-5 241   Linebacker

The Colts passed up Al Toon, Jerry Rice and Eddie Brown on Draft Day '85 to go for this rangy, big-play linebacker from USC, and he hasn't disappointed... Led the Colts with 104 unassisted tackles and six sacks while becoming more comfortable with the system... Had his best game in his native state when he chased down 49er quarterback Jeff Kemp for a 15-yard loss, made nine tackles and recovered a fumble... His pass coverage also improved from 1985, when he was named NFL Defensive Rookie of the Year by the AP despite sitting out three weeks of training camp in a contract dispute... Born Dec. 1, 1962, in Los Angeles... Graduated from USC with a 3.62 average in business accounting.

CLIFF ODOM 29 6-2 241   Linebacker

Quietly led the Colts in total tackles for the second straight year, but he got little notice because of the club's terrible record... Life isn't fair, but Odom knows all about adversity. When he was cut by the Browns in 1981, he was forced to make the transition from loading up on running backs to unloading 18-wheel trucks... He was cut by the Raiders in 1982, but he's prospered since the Colts picked him up... Took on a bigger load after Barry Krauss went down with a serious knee injury in Week 4... Didn't report until Aug. 17 because of a salary dispute... His nickname is "The Dude."... Born Aug. 15, 1958, in Beaumont, Tex., and attended Texas-Arlington.

RAY DONALDSON 29 6-4 282   Center

Colts' Iron Man started every game to extend his streak of consecutive starts to 89, and he was rewarded with his first trip to the Pro Bowl... Tough to earn recognition playing center in the same conference as Miami's Dwight Stephenson, but Donaldson is one of the best in the business... He's got the speed to chase after linebackers and is also a highly rated pass-blocker... He makes all the blocking calls on the line and also snaps for field goals and punts... Says Donaldson: "

think it would be hard to find a label for my talent, but I have the respect of the men I've fought."...Born May 18, 1958, in Rome, Ga....He did as most Romans do and attended Georgia, where he was an All-American under Vince Dooley.

ALBERT BENTLEY 27 5-11 215   Running Back

With the offseason injury to Randy McMillan, the Colts' No. 1 rusher in the last two seasons, Bentley becomes more important in Ron Meyer's plans, especially if he emphasizes the one-back philosophy...Finished second to McMillan in 1986 with 351 yards on only 73 carries, but his 4.8-yard average was the best on the team...Also caught 25 passes for 230 yards...He played two seasons in the USFL with Michigan and Oakland before coming to the Colts in 1985...Born Aug. 15, 1960, in Immokalee, Fla., and was a walk-on his first two years at Miami...Has shown flashes of ability...Rushed for 162 yards in the season finale against the Raiders, the sixth-highest rushing total in Colt history.

COACH RON MEYER: The Irsays know how to keep the

merry-go-round spinning. Rather than waiting until the end of the season when more candidates might be available, they canned Rod Dowhower after an 0-13 start and called in Meyer...The former Patriot head coach is a legendary wheeler-dealer. He had verbally accepted the Purdue head coaching job before he was contacted by GM Jimmy Irsay. He even had a photostat of a Purdue contract in his pocket...Meyer strengthened his case by winning the last three games, but at what cost? The Colts lost a shot at Vinny Testaverde...Meyer was the first coach in NFL history to be fired in the midst of a winning season. The Patriots released Meyer after he went 5-3 in 1984, and a lot of veterans who didn't like his disciplinary code rejoiced...Like him or not, Meyer went 18-16 in 2½ seasons with the Patriots, although it could be argued they should have done even better with their superior talent...The first three years of Meyer's contract are guaranteed, and the last two are guaranteed only if the Colts go 8-8 in any of his first three seasons...He'll also get a $100,000 bonus if the Colts win the Super

Bowl... Born Feb. 17, 1941, in Westerville, Ohio... Was a walk-on defensive back at Purdue and served as an assistant there from 1965-70... Went 34-31-1 as head coach at SMU from 1976-81.

GREATEST KICKER

There's a lot of kick in the Colts. Everyone remembers rookie Jim O'Brien's 32-yard field goal with five seconds left to beat Dallas, 16-13, in Super Bowl V. And for 18 years, Bert Rechichar held the NFL record for longest field goal—56 yards—until Tom Dempsey came along with a 63-yarder to break it.

But the kicker of record for the Colts these days is Rohn Stark, who breaks the curve every time he drops back to punt. After five seasons, Stark is the leading punter in NFL history with a 45.16-yard average on 389 boots. That's better than Sammy Baugh's career mark of 45.10 on 338 punts between 1937-52.

Stark, a decathlete champ at Florida State and mid-70s golfer, has been remarkably consistent since the Colts made him their second pick in 1982. He averaged 44.4 yards in 1982, 45.3 in 1983, 44.7 in 1984, 45.9 in 1985 and 45.2 last year.

Last year's average was tops in the NFL, beating out the Giants' Sean Landeta (44.8). Stark also improved his finesse, with a career low of five touchbacks on 76 punts. He had an advantage punting inside the Hoosier Dome, but he simply is better than everyone else.

INDIVIDUAL COLT RECORDS
Rushing

Most Yards Game:	198	Norm Bulaich, vs N.Y. Jets, 1971
Season:	1,200	Lydell Mitchell, 1976
Career:	5,487	Lydell Mitchell, 1972-77

Passing

Most TD Passes Game:	5	Gary Cuozzo, vs Minnesota, 1965
Season:	32	John Unitas, 1959
Career:	287	John Unitas, 1956-72

Receiving

Most TD Passes Game:	3	Jim Mutscheller, vs Green Bay, 1957
	3	Raymond Berry, vs Dallas, 1960
	3	Raymond Berry, vs Green Bay, 1960
	3	Jimmy Orr, vs Washington, 1962
	3	Jimmy Orr, vs Los Angeles, 1964
	3	Roger Carr, vs Cincinnati, 1976
Season:	14	Raymond Berry, 1959
Career:	68	Raymond Berry, 1955-67

Scoring

Most Points Game:	24	Lenny Moore, vs Chicago, 1958
	24	Lenny Moore, vs Los Angeles, 1960
	24	Lenny Moore, vs Minnesota, 1961
	24	Lydell Mitchell, vs Buffalo, 1975
Season:	120	Lenny Moore, 1964
Career:	678	Lenny Moore, 1956-67
Most TDs Game:	4	Lenny Moore, vs Chicago, 1958
	4	Lenny Moore, vs Los Angeles, 1960
	4	Lenny Moore, vs Minnesota, 1961
	4	Lydell Mitchell, vs Buffalo, 1975
Season:	20	Lenny Moore, 1964
Career:	113	Lenny Moore, 1956-67

KANSAS CITY CHIEFS

TEAM DIRECTORY: Owner: Lamar Hunt; Pres.: Jack Steadman; VP/GM: Jim Schaaf; VP-Administration: Don Steadman; Pro Personnel Dir.: Whitey Dovell; College Personnel Dir.: Les Miller; Dir. Pub. Rel.: Bob Sprenger; Head coach: Frank Gansz. Home field: Arrowhead Stadium (78,094). Colors: Red and gold.

SCOUTING REPORT

OFFENSE: Rookie head coach Frank Gansz was a jet pilot in the Air Force, so it's no surprise he uses military analogies to describe the ineffectiveness of the Chiefs' offense, which ranked last in total yards (27th rushing, 21st passing) in 1986. "We have to get away from wasted plays," Gansz said. "It's like an F-16 out there. It's a great-looking bird, but it doesn't come alive until

Awesome Dino Hackett led Chiefs in tackles as a rookie.

you put someone in the seat who's well prepared."

The dilemma starts in the cockpit. Gansz says Bill Kenney, Todd Blackledge and Frank Seurer are on equal footing going into 1987, but indications are that Blackledge could be in trouble if he doesn't show improvement in training camp. Kenney has produced when he's been healthy and Seurer has some promise.

The running game is in even worse shape. Only the Patriots rushed for fewer yards last year. Leading rusher Mike Pruitt gained only 448 yards, and he's 33. Maybe Paul Palmer, the rookie halfback from Temple, can change things. Gansz is banking on building "the finest offensive line in the NFL." He already has one of the biggest. Rick Donnalley has solidified the center spot, and guards Mark Adickes and Brian Jozwiak are converted tackles. Left tackle Irv Eatman needs to shake off bad habits, but right tackle David Lutz is excellent.

DEFENSE: The only change is the loss of coordinator Walt Corey to the Bills. Line coach John Paul Young was elevated to that job, and he may emphasize the 4-3 defense because of his strength up front. End Art Still is coming off a fantastic year in which he had 95 tackles and a team-high 10½ sacks, and Mike Bell is back from a year in prison on a drug charge. Peter Koch filled in well for Bell, and nose tackle Bill Maas is one of the best in the business.

The linebacking corps is equally talent. Rookie Dino Hackett became a folk hero for his hard hitting, and free agent Tim Cofield unleashed his aggressiveness in Corey's attacking system.

Topping it all off is the best secondary—bar none—in football. Free safety Deron Cherry and strong safety Lloyd Burruss made the Pro Bowl by combining for 14 interceptions, but cornerback Albert Lewis was voted MVP by his teammates for his suffocating coverage. That should tell you how good he is. Lewis and right corner Kevin Ross each grabbed four interceptions.

KICKING GAME: How good was it? In a season-ending 24-19 win over Pittsburgh, the kicking teams scored all 24 points on a blocked field goal, a blocked punt, a kickoff return and a field goal. The Chiefs won despite being outgained 515 yards to 171. Nick Lowery, who entered the season as the NFL's best percentage kicker, had a year below his standards. He made 19-of-26 field goals and missed an attempt inside 30 yards for the first time in his career. Rookie punter Lewis Colbert finished seventh in the AFC with a 40.7-yard average. Gansz' special teams blocked or deflected 10 kicks and scored five touchdowns during the season, and added a blocked punt and touchdown in the playoffs.

CHIEFS VETERAN ROSTER

HEAD COACH—Frank Gansz. Assistant Coaches—Ed Beckman, Dave Brazil, Mark Hatley, J.D. Helm, C.T. Hewgley, Don Lawrence, Billie Matthews, Carl Mauck, Homer Smith, Dick Wood, John Paul Young.

No.	Name	Pos.	Ht.	Wt.	NFL Exp.	College
61	Adickes, Mark	G	6-4	274	2	Baylor
76	Alt, John	T	6-7	282	4	Iowa
87	Arnold, Walt	TE	6-3	224	8	New Mexico
91	Baldinger, Gary	DE	6-3	265	2	Wake Forest
77	Baldinger, Rich	G-T	6-4	285	5	Wake Forest
58	Baugh, Tom	C	6-3	274	2	Southern Illinois
99	Bell, Mike	DE	6-4	259	7	Colorado State
81	Bergmann, Paul	TE	6-2	235	1	UCLA
14	Blackledge, Todd	QB	6-3	223	5	Penn State
71	Budde, Brad	G	6-4	271	8	Southern California
34	Burruss, Lloyd	SS	6-0	209	7	Maryland
88	Carson, Carlos	WR	5-11	184	8	Louisiana State
20	Cherry, Deron	FS	5-11	196	7	Rutgers
22	Cocroft, Sherman	S-CB	6-1	195	3	San Jose State
84	Coffman, Paul	TE	6-3	225	10	Kansas State
54	Cofield, Tim	OLB	6-2	245	2	Elizabeth City State
5	Colbert, Lewis	P	5-11	180	2	Auburn
55	Cooper, Louis	OLB	6-2	235	3	Western Carolina
51	Donnalley, Rick	C	6-2	270	7	North Carolina
75	Eatman, Irv	T	6-7	293	2	UCLA
80	Fox, Chas	WR	5-11	180	2	Furman
48	Garron, Andre	RB	5-11	193	1	New Hampshire
40	Green, Boyce	RB	5-11	215	5	Carson Newman
98	Griffin, Leonard	DE	6-4	252	2	Grambling
56	Hackett, Dino	ILB	6-3	225	2	Appalachian State
82	Hancock, Anthony	WR-KR	6-0	204	6	Tennessee
92	Harris, Bob	LB	6-2	223	4	Auburn
86	Harry, Emile	WR	5-11	175	2	Stanford
85	Hayes, Jonathan	TE	6-5	236	3	Iowa
44	Heard, Herman	RB	5-10	190	4	Southern Coloardo
23	Hill, Greg	CB	6-1	199	5	Oklahoma State
93	Holle, Eric	DE-NT	6-5	265	4	Texas
73	Jozwiak, Brian	T	6-5	308	2	West Virginia
9	Kenney, Bill	QB	6-4	211	9	Northern Coloardo
74	Koch, Pete	DE	6-6	275	4	Maryland
70	Lathrop, Kit	DE	6-5	261	4	Arizona State
29	Lewis, Albert	CB	6-2	192	5	Grambling
8	Lowery, Nick	PK	6-4	189	8	Dartmouth
72	Lutz, David	T	6-6	295	5	Georgia Tech
63	Maas, Bill	NT	6-5	268	4	Pittsburgh
89	Marshall, Henry	WR	6-2	216	12	Missouri
94	McAlister, Ken	OLB	6-5	230	5	San Francisco
32	Moriarty, Larry	RB	6-1	237	5	Notre Dame
83	Paige, Stephone	WR	6-2	183	5	Fresno State
57	Paul, Whitney	OLB	6-4	219	12	Colorado
96	Pearson, Aaron	ILB	6-0	236	2	Mississippi State
24	Pearson, J.C.	CB	5-11	183	2	Washington
43	Pruitt, Mike	RB	6-0	235	12	Purdue
97	Radecic, Scott	ILB	6-3	242	4	Penn State
30	Robinson, Mark	S	5-11	206	4	Penn State
31	Ross, Kevin	CB	5-9	182	4	Temple
10	Seurer, Frank	QB	6-1	195	2	Kansas
47	Smith, Chris	RB	6-0	222	1	Notre Dame
42	Smith, Jeff	RB-KR	5-9	201	3	Nebraska
59	Spani, Gary	ILB	6-2	229	10	Kansas State
67	Still, Art	DE	6-7	255	10	Kentucky

TOP FIVE DRAFT CHOICES

Rd.	Name	Sel. No.	Pos.	Ht.	Wt.	College
1	Palmer, Paul	19	RB	5-10	185	Temple
2	Okoye, Christian	35	RB	6-2	255	Azusa Pacific
3	Howard, Todd	73	LB	6-2	235	Texas A&M
5	Taylor, Kittrick	128	WR	5-11	181	Washington State
7	Hudson, Doug	186	QB	6-3	205	Nicholls State

THE ROOKIES: The Chiefs don't want to finish last in rushing again. They took Palmer in the first round and 255-pound fullback Christian Okoye of Azusa Pacific in the second. Despite his 5-10, 185-pound frame, Palmer is a great all-purpose back. But can he take the pounding? Okoye has only three years of football experience and will be 26 when the season starts, but he's a physical specimen who can run a 4.49.

OUTLOOK: If the Chiefs can find a pilot and a lead gunner—er, a quarterback and a big running back—they'll be tough to handle. They can't continue to rely solely on their defense and special teams to carry them. Gansz also is a rookie head coach. You can't minimize the problems of on-the-job training. But the Chiefs should be fighting for a division title.

CHIEF PROFILES

BILL KENNEY 32 6-4 211   Quarterback

Kenney's main competition for the starting job may be second-year Frank Seurer rather than Todd Blackledge, who's been a major disappointment ... Kenney finished 11th among AFC quarterbacks last year, completing 161 of 308 passes (52.3 percent) for 1,922 yards and 13 touchdowns with 11 interceptions ... Blackledge started the season, but Kenney came off the bench in a 42-41 win over San Diego and was named the starter in Week 8 ... Sprained his right thumb and was available only for mop-up duty in playoff loss to the Jets ... Born Jan. 20, 1955, in San Francisco, and attended Northern Colorado ... Was the second-to-last player taken in the 1978 draft by the Dolphins.

DINO HACKETT 23 6-3 225   Linebacker

Miami's John Offerdahl got most of the ink, but this second-round pick from Division 1-AA Appalachian State was the kamikaze, big-play force in the Chiefs' excellent defense ... Led the team with 140 tackles, 32 more than second-place Deron Cherry. That's no surprise. In his senior season he made 200 tackles in 11 games ... He didn't blitz much from the inside because the Chiefs loved to put him into coverage . . . Wasn't invited to any postseason bowl games but impressed scouts with excellent 40 time . . . Born June 18, 1964, in Greensboro, N.C. . . . Became public folk hero in second exhibition game when he nailed Ottis Anderson with a vicious tackle and got up screaming, "Aaaah! Not here buddy!"

TIM COFIELD 24 6-2 245   Linebacker

When a linebacker knocks out four quarterbacks in one season, you've got yourself a hit man . . . The unheralded free agent out of Elizabeth City State turned heads at the beginning of training camp and proved to be the Chiefs' most intense outside linebacker since Bobby Bell . . . Prospered under simple defensive system of Walt Corey—he could attack one man —but leveled off late in the year . . . "He's a 250-pounder who can run as fast as a wide-out," Corey said . . . Outstanding 4.5 speed makes him a good blitzer, and he had five sacks . . . Quiet guy who lets his hitting do the talking . . . Born May 18, 1963, in Murfreesboro, N.C.

DERON CHERRY 27 5-11 196   Free Safety

Continues to build on his legend . . . Earned fourth straight Pro Bowl berth by leading the AFC with nine interceptions . . . He has 30 interceptions in last four years, more than any player in the NFL . . . For the first time in four years, Cherry didn't lead the Chiefs in tackles, but he had 108 to finish second . . . Every team in the league had a chance to sign him in 1981 when he was inked by the Chiefs as a free-agent punter. He was cut when he couldn't beat out Bob Grupp, but was switched to the secondary and caught on . . . Born Sept. 12, 1959, in Palmyra, N.J., and attended Rutgers.

ALBERT LEWIS 26 6-2 192   Cornerback

How good is Lewis? On a team that sent three defensive players to the Pro Bowl—defensive backs Deron Cherry and Lloyd Burruss, and nose tackle Bill Maas—Lewis was voted MVP by his teammates . . . They know what the Pro Bowl voters don't. Chiefs' scheme places man-to-man pressure on cornerbacks, and Lewis, who picked off four passes, regularly

ate up his receiver . . . Batted away five passes against Buffalo in
Week 13 . . . Also a terror on special teams. He blocked three
kicks and deflected one other . . . Blocked Dave Jennings' punt
and recovered in the end zone in the playoff game against the
Jets . . . Born Oct. 6, 1960, in Mansfield, La., and was a third-
round pick out of Grambling . . . Tied for AFC lead in interceptions with eight in '85.

LLOYD BURRUSS 29 6-0 209   Strong Safety

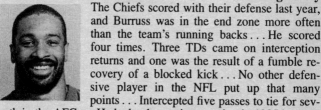

The Chiefs scored with their defense last year,
and Burruss was in the end zone more often
than the team's running backs . . . He scored
four times. Three TDs came on interception
returns and one was the result of a fumble recovery of a blocked kick . . . No other defensive player in the NFL put up that many
points . . . Intercepted five passes to tie for seventh in the AFC . . . He had only one interception in 1985 but was
voted team MVP . . . Born Oct. 31, 1957, in Charlottesville, Va.,
and was a third-round pick out of Maryland in 1981 . . . Finally
made Pro Bowl in '86 after years of consistency.

BILL MAAS 25 6-5 268   Nose Tackle

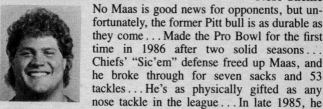

No Maas is good news for opponents, but unfortunately, the former Pitt bull is as durable as
they come . . . Made the Pro Bowl for the first
time in 1986 after two solid seasons . . .
Chiefs' "Sic'em" defense freed up Maas, and
he broke through for seven sacks and 53
tackles . . . He's as physically gifted as any
nose tackle in the league . . . In late 1985, he
switched to end and played equally as well . . . The No. 1 pick in
1984 is exceptionally strong against the run and uses his awesome strength to rush the passer . . . Born Mar. 2, 1962, in
Philadelphia . . . Married to Dan Marino's sister, Cindy.

NICK LOWERY 31 6-4 189   Kicker

For most kickers, making 19-of-26 field goals
(73.1 percent) is considered an excellent season. Lowery is so good it was considered an
off year . . . For the first time in his career, he
missed a field goal of less than 30 yards. It
was blocked . . . He also surrendered his No. 1
spot in career percentage when the Steelers'
Gary Anderson qualified with enough kicks to

lead 77.2 to 76.3 . . . Lowery's average miss, however, is much longer . . . Has career totals of 155 field goals in 203 attempts and has scored at least 100 points in the last four seasons . . . Says Lowery: "The No. 1 priority is never having a bad year. Even your worst year must be good." . . . Failed tryouts with eight other teams before coming to Kansas City in 1980 . . . Born May 27, 1956, in Munich, Germany, and attended Dartmouth.

IRV EATMAN 26 6-7 293   Tackle

Had a rocky first season in the NFL after destroying defensive linemen in three USFL seasons with the Philadelphia Stars . . . Part of the problem was moving from the right side to the left, and Eatman said: "Anybody who thinks that's easy has never tried." . . . Eatman didn't have to work very hard to dominate in the USFL, and now he does. Chiefs want him to work on his technique because he fell into bad habits . . . They still think the former UCLA great will adjust and be a fixture on an improving line . . . Born Jan. 1, 1961, in Dayton, Ohio . . . Chiefs selected Eatman in the eight round of the 1983 draft while he was playing his first USFL season.

STEPHONE PAIGE 25 6-2 183   Wide Receiver

Quietly has become the NFL's leader in touchdown receptions over the last two years. He has 21, which is one more than Philadelphia's Mike Quick . . . Hasn't had a 1,000-yard season yet, but he's one of the few big-play offensive performers for the Chiefs . . . Caught 11 touchdown passes last year, which ranked him just behind the Jets' Wesley Walker for most in the AFC . . . His most dazzling game came at the end of the 1985 season, when he shattered a 40-year-old record with a 309-yard performance against San Diego. Caught eight passes that day for 84, 56, 51, 39, 30, 20, 17 and 12 yards . . . Born Oct. 15, 1961, in Slidell, La., and played in the shadow of Henry Ellard at Fresno State.

COACH FRANK GANSZ: Maybe it could only happen in Kansas City . . . Gansz, the Chiefs' charismatic special teams coach, resigned after the club's first playoff season since 1971 and then was named head coach three days later . . . Former head man John Mackovic was the fall guy. The day after Gansz quit, a group of 15 players met with owner Lamar Hunt at kicker Nick Lowery's house to protest his departure. Three hours later, Mackovic was fired even though he had been offered a two-year contract extension the week before . . . Hunt offered Gansz the top job an hour later . . . Obvious dilemma is what Gansz will do if he has to make a coaching decision on the players responsible for getting him his job. Sticky, sticky . . . The former Air Force jet pilot is known as a great motivator . . . He coached the Chiefs' special teams in 1981 and 1982 before going to the Eagles for three years . . . He returned to Kansas City in 1986 as assistant head coach . . . Born Nov. 22, 1938, in Altoona, Pa. . . . Didn't get into full-time coaching until he was nearly 30 and has never been a head coach at any level in 23 years of coaching . . . His nickname is "Crash" because of some of the daredevil stories he tells to pump up the team . . . In one speech, he mentioned Neil Armstrong, John Wooden, Chuck Yeager, Michael Jordan, Jack Nicklaus and Genghis Khan. Says cornerback Albert Lewis: "When Frank tells you that you can do something, he has a way of making you believe it's possible." . . . Gansz was a guard, center and linebacker at the U.S. Naval Academy.

GREATEST KICKER

There may never be another kicker like Jan Stenerud. The Chief's all-time leading scorer (1,231 points) was at the forefront of the soccer-style kicking explosion in the 1960s, and no specialist was better in terms of success and longevity.

The Chiefs made the Montana State kicker a pick in the 1966 future draft, and he arrived in 1967 and kicked through 1979. In his Kansas City career, Stenerud made 279 field goals, had five consecutive seasons (1967-71) of scoring at least 100 points and was named to four Pro Bowls. Although his distance was limited late in his career, he made eight field goals of 52 yards or longer.

Stenerud kicked two field goals in a 13-6 playoff win over the Jets in 1969 and added another field goal a week later when the Chiefs advanced to Super Bowl IV with a 17-7 win over the Raiders. Then, in the biggest game of his career, he put Minnesota in a 9-0 hole with field goals of 48, 32 and 25 yards, and the Chiefs buried the Vikings, 23-7.

One of his few failures came in the 1971 Christmas Day playoff game against Miami. He missed two field goals that would have won the game, and Miami wound up winning, 24-21, in the second overtime period.

INDIVIDUAL CHIEF RECORDS

Rushing

Most Yards Game:	193	Joe Delaney, vs Houston, 1981
Season:	1,121	Joe Delaney, 1981
Career:	4,451	Ed Podolak, 1969-77

Passing

Most TD Passes Game:	6	Len Dawson, vs Denver, 1964
Season:	30	Len Dawson, 1964
Career:	237	Len Dawson, 1962-75

Receiving

Most TD Passes Game:	4	Frank Jackson, vs San Diego, 1964
Season:	12	Chris Burford, 1962
Career:	57	Otis Taylor, 1965-75

Scoring

Most Points Game:	30	Abner Haynes, vs Oakland, 1961
Season:	129	Jan Stenerud, 1968
Career:	1,231	Jan Stenerud, 1967-79
Most TDs Game:	5	Abner Haynes, vs Oakland, 1961
Season:	19	Abner Haynes, 1962
Career:	60	Otis Taylor, 1965-75

LOS ANGELES RAIDERS

TEAM DIRECTORY: Managing Gen. Partner: Al Davis; Exec. Asst.: Al LoCasale; Senior Administrators: Irv Kaze, John Herrera; Bus. Mgr.: Ken LaRue; Dir. Marketing/Promotions: Mike Ornstein; Head Coach: Tom Flores. Home field: Los Angeles Memorial Coliseum (92,516). Colors: Silver and black.

SCOUTING REPORT

OFFENSE: The Raiders are trying anything to pump life back into their long-ball passing attack. First, they went into Canada to

Ankle healed, Marcus Allen seeks return to '85 form.

sign wide receiver Mervyn Fernandez to a $1.85 million, four-year contract, which included $500,000 in guarantees. Then they traded a third-round 1987 pick and a conditional 1988 pick to Green Bay for talented but troubled James Lofton, whose availability might be affected by the result of his trial on sexual assault charges.

The quarterback picture is as cloudy as ever. Al Davis indicated seldom-used Rusty Hilger was at the top of his depth chart going into training camp, but anything could happen. Jim Plunkett will be 40 in December, and he is coming off delayed shoulder surgery that cut into his rehab time.

The Raiders shot themselves in the foot last season with a league-high 49 turnovers. Marc Wilson threw 15 interceptions before being benched after nine games, and Marcus Allen, who couldn't push off a bad ankle, was haunted by several key fumbles.

The biggest concern, however, is a graybeard line that allowed the most sacks in the NFL—63. Right tackle Henry Lawrence, 36, may be at the end of his career after being benched late in the season and replaced by Shelby Jordan, 35. Left tackle Bruce Davis and right guard Mickey Marvin are 31. John Clay, a tackle from Missouri who was the Raiders' top draft choice, should be playing before too long.

The Raiders still have some dangerous weapons in tight end Todd Christensen and receiver Dokie Williams, but whoever the quarterback is—he'll need time to throw.

DEFENSE: The Raiders always have prided themselves in brass-knuckles defense, but last year only eight teams gave up more points than they did (21.6 per game). Howie Long made the Pro Bowl for the fourth consecutive year, but he was limited by a blood clot in his knee. He's one of the best when he's running on two good legs. On the other side, Sean Jones became a pass-rushing force and led the NFL with 15½ sacks. Nose tackle Bill Pickel is returning from another fine season and arthroscopic knee ... and have ... year. The Raiders may have blown their No. 1 pick ... season ... and ... year. The Raiders ... bad Bob Buczkowski missed the entire ... had trouble running ... operations in five months. ... broke his foot two ... ausposing secondary. Mike Haynes can still play. Haynes ... a calf injury and Lester Hayes converted receiver, ... the end of the season, but both corner. ... Hayes is 32. Sammy Seale, a

The Raiders fired ... ing adeptness at playing the

... coach Bob Zeman and brought

RAIDERS VETERAN ROSTER

HEAD COACH—Tom Flores. Assistant Coaches—Sam Boghosian, Willie Brown, Chet Franklin, Larry Kennan, Earl Leggett, Bob Mischak, Terry Robiskie, Joe Scannella, Art Shell, Charlie Sumner, Tom Walsh, Ray Willsey.

No.	Name	Pos.	Ht.	Wt.	NFL Exp.	College
44	Adams, Stefon	S	5-10	185	2	East Carolina
32	Allen, Marcus	RB	6-2	205	6	Southern California
10	Bahr, Chris	K	5-10	170	12	Penn State
88	Barksdale, Rod	WR	6-1	180	2	Arizona
56	Barnes, Jeff	LB	6-2	230	11	California
82	Branton, Gene	TE	6-5	245	1	Texas Southern
46	Christensen, Todd	TE	6-3	230	9	Brigham Young
38	Cochran, Brad	CB	6-3	200	1	Michigan
79	Davis, Bruce	T	6-6	280	8	UCLA
45	Davis, James	CB	6-0	190	6	Southern
36	Davis, Mike	S	6-3	200	9	Colorado
80	Fernandez, Mervyn	WR	6-3	205	1	San Jose State
94	Franks, Elvis	DE	6-4	265	8	Morgan State
8	Guy, Ray	P	6-3	200	15	Southern Mississippi
73	Hannah, Charley	G	6-5	265	11	Alabama
27	Hawkins, Frank	RB	5-9	210	7	Nevada-Reno
37	Hayes, Lester	CB	6-0	200	11	Texas A&M
22	Haynes, Mike	CB	6-2	190	12	Arizona State
84	Hester, Jessie	WR	5-11	170	3	Florida State
12	Hilger, Rusty	QB	6-4	200	3	Oklahoma State
99	Jones, Sean	DE	6-7	265	4	Northeastern
74	Jordan, Shelby	T	6-7	280	11	Washington (Mo.)
87	Junkin, Trey	TE	6-2	225	5	Louisiana Tech
59	Kimmel, Jamie	LB	6-3	235	2	Syracuse
33	King, Kenny	RB	5-11	205	8	Oklahoma
52	King, Linden	LB	6-4	245	10	Colorado State
70	Lawrence, Henry	T	6-4	270	14	Florida A&M
51	Lewis, Bill	C	6-7	275	2	Nebraska
80	Lofton, James	WR	6-3	195	10	Stanford
75	Long, Howie	DE	6-5	270	7	Villanova
11	Luther, Ed	QB	6-2	205	8	San Jose State
60	Marsh, Curt	G	6-5	270	5	Washington
53	Martin, Rod	LB	6-2	225	11	Southern California
65	Marvin, Mickey	G	6-4	265	11	Tennessee
7	Mathison, Bruce	QB	6-3	210	4	Nebraska
34	McCallum, Napoleon	RB	6-2	215	2	Naval Academy
26	McElroy, Vann	S	6-0	195	6	Baylor
54	McKenzie, Reggie	LB	6-1	240	3	Tennessee
55	Millen, Matt	LB	6-2	250	8	Penn State
64	Miraldi, Dean	T	6-5	285	4	Utah
83	Moffett, Tim	WR	6-2	180	3	Mississippi
72	Mosebar, Don	C	6-6	275	5	Southern California
42	Mueller, Vance	RB	6-0	210	2	Occidental
81	Parker, Andy	TE	6-5	240	4	Utah
89	Pattison, Mark	WR	6-2	190	2	Washington
71	Pickel, Bill	DT	6-5	260	5	Rutgers
16	Plunkett, Jim	QB	6-2	220	17	Stanford
77	Riehm, Chris	G	6-6	275	2	Ohio State
57	Robinson, Jerry	LB	6-2	225	9	UCLA
69	Russell, Rusty	T	6-5	275	2	South Carolina
43	Seale, Sam	CB	5-9	180	4	Western State (Colo.)
39	Strachan, Steve	RB	6-1	215	3	Boston College
5	Talley, Stan	P	6-5	225	1	Texas Christian
30	Toran, Stacey	S	6-2	200	4	Notre Dame
93	Townsend, Greg	DE	6-3	250	5	Texas Christian
41	Walker, Fulton	S	5-11	195	7	West Virginia
48	Washington, Lionel	CB	6-0	180	5	Tulane
85	Williams, Dokie	WR	5-11	180	5	UCLA
98	Willis, Mitch	DT	6-8	275	3	Southern Methodist
6	Wilson, Marc	QB	6-6	205	8	Brigham Young
90	Wise, Mike	DE	6-6	260	2	Cal-Davis

TOP FIVE DRAFT CHOICES

Rd.	Name	Sel. No.	Pos.	Ht.	Wt.	College
1	Clay, John	15	OT	6-5	315	Missouri
2	Wilkerson, Bruce	52	OT	6-5	272	Tennessee
3	Smith, Steve	81	RB	6-1	232	Penn State
4	Beuerlein, Steve	110	QB	6-3	201	Notre Dame
7	Jackson, Bo	183	RB	6-1	222	Auburn

back long-time defensive assistant Charlie Sumner. They need some fresh young talent more than a new coach.

KICKING GAME: This might be Ray Guy's final season. He's in the final year of his contract and he'll be 38 in December. He barely averaged 40 yards in his 14th season and he dropped two center snaps that cost the Raiders touchdowns. But he's a pro and he wants to go out on top. Chris Bahr missed his fourth consecutive 100-point year by a point, but he connected on 75 percent of his field goals (21-of-28).

THE ROOKIES: How bad was the offensive line last year? It was so bad the Raiders used their first two picks to select two tackles—Clay and Tennessee's Bruce Wilkerson. Clay is 6-5 and 315, but has questionable upper-body strength. But he's a great drive-blocker. Wilkerson is 6-5 and 272 with room to grow. Penn State fullback Steve Smith, taken in the third round, could be a sleeper.

OUTLOOK: The Raiders played about as well last year as their 8-8 record would indicate. Their offensive line, linebackers and secondary are growing old, and the quarterback controversy that has raged since 1984 figures only to intensify. Lofton could be a key acquisition if he plays and if he can play to his All-Pro level. A lot of ifs, but somehow you know the Raiders will be in the thick of the division race.

RAIDER PROFILES

RUSTY HILGER 25 6-4 200   **Quarterback**

Maybe Al Davis was just kidding, but the Raiders' managing general partner said Hilger, who has thrown only 51 passes in two seasons, was his No. 1 going into '87 . . . Hilger has some raw ability, but no one knows whether he can lead an NFL team into the playoffs . . . In very brief appearances last year, the sixth-rounder out of Oklahoma State completed 19 of 38 passes for 266 yards and one touchdown, with one interception . . . Unless there's a trade, it looks like another three-way battle between Hilger, Jim Plunkett and Marc Wilson . . . Born May 5, 1962, in Oklahoma City, Okla. . . . Embarrassing

moment in his rookie season came when he replaced the injured Wilson and couldn't snap on his chin strap. He's progressed since then.

JIM PLUNKETT 39 6-2 220　　　　　　Quarterback

And in the beginning, there was Jim. Plunkett will turn 40 on Dec. 5, and that makes him the oldest player in the NFL . . . While he can't really be considered a full-time starter at his advanced age, the Raiders still think he can be the cool, experienced backup who can perform in a pinch . . . Coming off late surgery for a rotator cuff tear in his right shoulder that wasn't diagnosed immediately after the season. It cost him about two months of rehab time . . . Plunkett finished ahead of Marc Wilson in the AFC quarterback ratings last year, completing 133 of 252 passes (52.8 percent) for 1,986 yards and 14 touchdowns, with nine interceptions . . . Hard to believe that the 1970 Heisman Trophy winner from Stanford is still around . . . Was the MVP of Super Bowl XV win over Eagles and also played well in Super Bowl XVIII victory over Redskins.

MARCUS ALLEN 27 6-2 205　　　　　　Running Back

It was a season of frustration for the franchise back . . . Bad ankle limited his production to 759 yards on 208 carries—exactly 1,000 yards less than when he led the NFL in rushing in 1985 . . . It was the first time he'd failed to break the 1,000-yard mark in a 16-game season. His average per carry also was a career-low 3.6 yards . . . Allen's toughest day came in Week 13 when he fumbled at the Eagle 15 in overtime and the ball was returned 81 yards by cornerback Andre Waters for the winning TD . . . Allen also was set back by poor run-blocking . . . One good thing did happen. He broke Walter Payton's record for consecutive 100-yard games with 10 in an opening loss to Denver . . . Born Mar. 26, 1960, in San Diego, and was the 1980 Heisman Trophy winner at USC . . . His weekly manicure reflects poorly on the Raider image.

JAMES LOFTON 31 6-3 195   Wide Receiver

Nine-year veteran was suspended by Packers before final game last year following charges of sexual assault... In April, Green Bay traded him to Raiders for Raiders' 1987 third-round draft choice and undisclosed conditional choice in '88... Ironically, Lofton, a Stanford grad, was once a finalist in prestigious NFL Man-of-the-Year competition and was heavily involved in many charities. He was the leader... Had never missed a game until suspension. Started 136 in a row. Had 64 catches for 840 yards, but averaged only 13.1 yards per catch, well below his 18.9 average for eight previous seasons... Only fifth receiver in NFL to gain 1,000 yards in five or more seasons ... String of six straight Pro Bowl appearances was snapped... Became 15th player with more than 500 catches. Now has 530... Born July 5, 1956, in Los Angeles.

TODD CHRISTENSEN 31 6-3 230   Tight End

The one constant in the Raider offense... He became the first player in NFL history to catch at least 80 passes in four consecutive seasons ...Last year was his best ever, when he caught 95 for 1,153 yards and eight touchdowns. San Francisco's Jerry Rice was No. 2 in catches with 86... His figures over the last four seasons are outrageous: 349 catches for 4,394 yards and 33 TDs... Helps that he's in the Raiders' long-ball offense, which stretches a defense and allows him to shake free underneath... Born Aug. 3, 1956, in Bellefonte, Pa., and attended BYU... Both the Cowboys and the Giants let him slip through their fingers.

HOWIE LONG 27 6-5 270   Defensive End

It wasn't easy being Howie Long last year. The Raiders' first four-time Pro Bowl defensive lineman was plagued by a right knee injury most of the season and was limited to seven sacks... Underwent surgery in Week 11 to remove a blood clot from an area above the knee. Said Dr. Robert Rosenfeld: "We tried to drain the fluid out with a needle, but no matter how often you drained it, it filled up right away." The knee joint wasn't involved ... Long got into TV, hosting a weekly diary of his painful season on HBO's "Inside the NFL." One week he begged off, saying: "Folks, I've got nothing to say." ... Born Jan. 6, 1960, in Sommerville, Mass., and played at Villanova before they deemphasized football ... At $650,000 in base salary this year, he's fourth-highest paid lineman behind the Jets' Joe Klecko and Mark Gastineau and Chicago's Dan Hampton.

SEAN JONES 24 6-7 265   Defensive End

In his first year as a starter, Jones became a pass-rushing force despite a subpar season on the other side by Howie Long ... The Kingston, Jamaica, native took over at right end for the retired Lyle Alzado and led the AFC with 15½ sacks ... Jones first showed great promise in 1985 when he recorded 8½ sacks without even playing full time ... The Raiders love to find physical specimens in out-of-the-way places, and Northeastern certainly doesn't qualify as a major football power. Still, they made Jones their No. 2 pick in 1984 ... He's about as big a rusher as there is in the league, but he's also got great leverage and quickness ... Born Dec. 19, 1962 ... He also played lacrosse at Northeastern. How would you like to be the goalie?

BILL PICKEL 27 6-5 260   Nose Tackle

The Raiders love to find defensive linemen in the East, maybe because no one else looks there ... They found Pickel at Rutgers, which hasn't been exactly a spawning ground for future pros ... But Pickel is as hard-nosed as they come. He led all AFC nose tackles with 11½ sacks in 1986 ... Over the last 48 games, the Pro Bowler has 36½ sacks, outstanding production for a nose man. He's benefited by the Raiders' philosophy of moving him around on the line, and he's also rangier than most nose men ... Born Nov. 5, 1959, in Queens, N.Y. ... Played only six games in his junior and senior seasons, but that didn't scare off the Raiders ... Had arthroscopic knee surgery on Dec. 16 to remove bone chips.

MIKE HAYNES 34 6-2 190   Cornerback

Got to the Pro Bowl for the ninth time—one short of the record held by Houston safety Ken Houston—but even he would admit his performance didn't back it up...Suffered a bruised calf against Seattle in Week 6 and was hobbling so badly he was replaced by Sammy Seale for three games...Only had two interceptions, his lowest total since he joined the Raiders in a midseason trade with the Patriots in 1983...He's still a terror on bump-and-run coverage when he's healthy...Born July 1, 1953, in Denison, Tex., and was a two-time All-American at Arizona State...Was drafted No. 1 by the Patriots in 1976 and had 28 interceptions in seven seasons.

MATT MILLEN 29 6-2 250   Linebacker

So-so season for the run-stuffer from Penn State...He was off the field more than ever when the Raiders went to their nickel-and-dime coverages, but he's still a force against the run...The Raiders finished fourth in the AFC in run defense, allowing 108 yards a game...Millen's claim to fame are his stories of growing up as a pain-loving schoolboy in Hokendauqua, Pa. Calcium deposits on his elbow had locked his arm at a 90-angle, so he put the arm in a vice and had someone drop a weight on it. Instant range of motion...Born March 12, 1958...Played defensive tackle at Penn State, lining up next to Bruce Clark...Fiery, emotional leader...Helped Howie Long give Patriot GM Patrick Sullivan a knuckle sandwich after 1985 playoff loss.

COACH TOM FLORES:

Quiet demeanor isn't in keeping with Raider image, but he's one of the best coaches in the NFL...Has to be feeling some heat because the Raiders haven't won a playoff game since their Super Bowl season in 1983, but he remains calm. "I can't create something that isn't there," he says. "My stoic presence doesn't put our team to sleep. We've won two Super Bowls since I've been here."

...Which is the bottom line...Flores, an ex-Raider quarterback, has been up to his ears in quarterback problems over the last three seasons, and that figures to be the key to 1987, as well...He's 78-43 in eight seasons, a winning percentage of .645, and he's won as many Super Bowls as Don Shula...Born March 21, 1937, in Fresno, Cal....He comes from humble beginnings. Worked as a farm laborer alongside his family...He's the first NFL head coach of Mexican heritage...Played quarterback at the College of the Pacific and signed a pro contract in 1958 with the CFL's Calgary Stampeders. A shoulder injury short-circuited him and he returned to teaching, only to be signed by the pre-Al Davis Raiders in 1960...A lung ailment sidelined him in 1962, but he returned in 1963 under Davis and threw six TD passes against the Oilers, still a club record...He was traded in 1967 to the Bills and then in 1969 to the Chiefs, where he won the first of his four Super Bowl rings...Came back as a Raider assistant in 1972 and took over from John Madden in 1979.

GREATEST KICKER

Drafting kickers or punters in the first round is a lot like investing in oil wells—you either go boom or bust. Ray Guy has been the gusher by which all other specialists will be measured. Everyone agreed Guy was the best punter in the nation after an All-American career at Southern Mississippi, where he averaged 44.7 yards over three seasons. But never before had any team been willing to invest that high a pick in a punter. Those that have done it since then have been burned (see: New Orleans, Russell Erxleben).

Guy has averaged 42.42 yards on 1,050 punts since 1973, and he has led the NFL in punting average in 1974, 1975 and 1977, and finished second three times. The stories about his leg strength are legendary. He was the first punter to hit the ceiling television screen in the Louisiana Superdome. The Oilers once stole one of his footballs and sent it to Rice University to see if there was helium inside.

There is concern that Guy, at 37, has lost the pop in his leg. The Raiders brought in punters last year for weekly tryouts, and he is in the final year of his contract. Before he goes, though, Guy would like to break Jerrel Wilson's NFL record of 46,139 punting yards. He has 44,541 going in. One more season should do it.

INDIVIDUAL RAIDER RECORDS

Rushing

Most Yards Game:	200	Clem Daniels, vs N.Y. Jets, 1963
Season:	1,759	Marcus Allen, 1985
Career:	5,907	Mark van Eeghen, 1974-81

Passing

Most TD Passes Game:	6	Tom Flores, vs Houston, 1963
	6	Daryle Lamonica, vs Buffalo, 1969
Season:	34	Daryle Lamonica, 1969
Career:	150	Ken Stabler, 1970-79

Receiving

Most TD Passes Game:	4	Art Powell, vs Houston, 1963
Season:	16	Art Powell, 1963
Career:	76	Fred Biletnikoff, 1965-78

Scoring

Most Points Game:	24	Art Powell, vs Houston, 1963
	24	Marcus Allen, vs San Diego, 1984
Season:	117	George Blanda, 1968
Career:	863	George Blanda, 1967-75
Most TDs Game:	4	Art Powell, vs Houston, 1963
	4	Marcus Allen, vs San Diego, 1984
Season:	18	Marcus Allen, 1984
Career:	77	Fred Biletnikoff, 1965-78

MIAMI DOLPHINS

TEAM DIRECTORY: Pres.: Joseph Robbie; VP/Head Coach: Don Shula; Dir. Pro Scouting: Charley Winner; Dir. Player Personnel: Chuck Connor: Dir. Publicity: Eddie White. Home field: Dolphin Stadium (75,000). Colors: Aqua and orange.

SCOUTING REPORT

OFFENSE: With apologies to Rogers and Hammerstein, defensive coordinators across the league are singing the blues: "How do you solve a problem like Marino?" In four seasons, Dan Mar-

Dan Marino continues to rewrite the NFL record book.

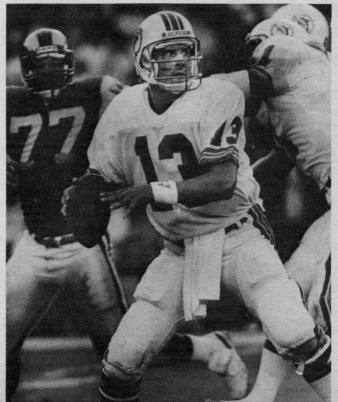

ino has posted numbers that numb the senses. He's thrown for 16,177 yards and 142 touchdowns and is the only NFL quarterback ever to throw more than 40 touchdown passes in two seasons. "He's done things that nobody has ever done before in the league," says Don Shula.

Mark Duper and Mark Clayton simply reap the benefits. Duper is faster, Clayton is more acrobatic, but the two are as inseparable as any wide-receiver tandem in the league. In fact, they feed off each other, Shula says, because "they both want to be known as the best." Duper had 70 catches for 11 TDs last year; Clayton had 60 and 10. They're that close.

The league's most powerful offense averaged 26.9 points a game last year, and it was improved because Lorenzo Hampton backed up his No. 1 selection in 1985 and became both the breakaway back and excellent receiver the Dolphins thought he could be. Tight end Bruce Hardy, with 54 catches, had his best year as a pro.

Even with a decimated line, Marino was sacked only 17 times. Center Dwight Stephenson is the best in football and Roy Foster made the Pro Bowl at left guard. The other spots are up for grabs. Left tackle John Giesler played only seven games because of injuries.

DEFENSE: Two stats tell the tale of how desperate the Dolphins are for defense. Outside linebacker Hugh Green, who started three games, was second on the team with four sacks, and the Dolphins' leading interceptor had two (four players were tied). The Dolphins had allowed more points (405) than Indianapolis and Buffalo.

Green was working out full speed before training camp, and Shula said his comeback was the key to any defensive improvement. But the Dolphins, who had only 33 sacks, still need a dominating pass-rusher, whether it's a defensive end or a blitzing linebacker. Nose tackle Bob Baumhower got over a hurdle last year by completing the season after he spent 1985 rehabbing a knee, but he was hardly a force. John Boza, a defensive end from Boston College, may be counted on heavily.

Inside linebacker John Offerdahl, the AFC Rookie of the Year, was the bright spot in a dark year. The only concern is whether he can continue to throw his body around with the same abandon and still be standing at the end of the season. A.J. Duhe got beat up doing that. Veteran Bob Brudzinski is coming off a disappointing year, and Jackie Shipp was too inconsistent.

Shula hired Tom Olivadotti from the Browns as his new defensive coordinator and shifted Chuck Studley to linebacker

DOLPHINS VETERAN ROSTER

HEAD COACH—Don Shula. Assistant Coaches—Tom Olivadotti, Mel Phillips, John Sandusky, Dan Sekanovich, David Shula, Chuck Studley, Carl Taseff, Junior Wade, Mike Westhoff.

No.	Name	Pos.	Ht.	Wt.	NFL Exp.	College
73	Baumhower, Bob	NT	6-5	265	10	Alabama
34	Bennett, Woody	FB	6-2	225	9	Miami
75	Betters, Doug	DE	6-7	265	10	Nevada-Reno
47	Blackwood, Glenn	S	6-0	190	9	Texas
43	Brown, Bud	S	6-0	194	4	Southern Mississippi
32	Brown, Donald	CB	5-11	189	2	Maryland
51	Brown, Mark	LB	6-2	230	5	Purdue
59	Brudzinski, Bob	LB	6-4	223	11	Ohio State
71	Charles, Mike	NT	6-4	287	5	Syracuse
—	Clark, Steve	G	6-4	260	5	Utah
83	Clayton, Mark	WR	5-9	175	5	Louisville
30	Davenport, Ron	FB	6-2	230	3	Louisville
65	Dellenbach, Jeff	T	6-6	280	3	Wisconsin
85	Duper, Mark	WR	5-9	187	6	Northwestern St. (La.)
33	Ellis, Craig	RB	5-11	180	2	San Diego State
61	Foster, Roy	G	6-4	275	6	Southern California
53	Frye, David	LB	6-2	227	5	Purdue
79	Giesler, Jon	T	6-5	265	9	Michigan
55	Green, Hugh	LB	6-2	225	7	Pittsburgh
27	Hampton, Lorenzo	RB	6-0	212	3	Florida
84	Hardy, Bruce	TE	6-5	232	10	Arizona State
90	Hendel, Andy	LB	6-1	230	2	North Carolina State
11	Jensen, Jim	WR-QB	6-4	215	7	Boston University
87	Johnson, Dan	TE	6-3	240	5	Iowa State
49	Judson, William	CB	6-2	190	6	South Carolina State
64	Katolin, Mike	C	6-3	270	1	San Jose State
68	Koch, Greg	T	6-4	276	11	Arkansas
94	Kolic, Larry	LB	6-1	242	2	Ohio State
40	Kozlowski, Mike	S	6-1	198	8	Colorado
44	Lankford, Paul	CB	6-2	184	6	Penn State
66	Lee, Larry	C-G	6-2	263	7	UCLA
72	Lee, Ronnie	G	6-4	265	9	Baylor
99	Little, George	DE	6-4	278	3	Iowa
13	Marino, Dan	QB	6-4	214	5	Pittsburgh
28	McNeal, Don	CB	5-11	192	7	Alabama
89	Moore, Nat	WR	5-9	188	14	Florida
22	Nathan, Tony	RB	6-0	206	9	Alabama
56	Offerdahl, John	LB	6-2	232	2	Western Michigan
82	Pruitt, James	WR	6-2	199	2	Cal State-Fullerton
7	Reveiz, Fuad	K	5-11	222	3	Tennessee
91	Robinson, Fred	LB	6-5	238	4	Miami
4	Roby, Reggie	P	6-2	243	5	Iowa
26	Rose, Donovan	S	6-1	190	3	Hampton Institute
80	Rose, Joe	TE	6-3	230	7	California
52	Sendlein, Robin	LB	6-3	225	6	Texas
50	Shipp, Jackie	LB	6-2	236	4	Oklahoma
25	Smith, Mike	CB	6-0	171	3	Texas-El Paso
70	Sochia, Brian	NT-DE	6-3	274	5	N.W. Oklahoma State
57	Stephenson, Dwight	C	6-2	255	8	Alabama
10	Strock, Don	QB	6-5	225	14	Virginia Tech
24	Thompson, Reyna	CB	5-11	194	2	Baylor
76	Toth, Tom	T	6-5	275	2	Western Michigan
95	Turner, T.J.	DE	6-4	265	2	Houston

TOP FIVE DRAFT CHOICES

Rd.	Name	Sel. No.	Pos.	Ht.	Wt.	College
1	Bosa, John	16	DE	6-4	257	Boston College
2	Graf, Rick	43	LB	6-5	235	Wisconsin
2	Schwedes, Scott	56	WR	5-11	171	Syracuse
4	Stradford, Troy	99	WR	5-8	189	Boston College
5	Conlin, Chris	132	OT	6-4	280	Penn State

coach. Olivadotti also is in charge of a secondary that gave up too many big plays last year, but Reyna Thompson has great athletic ability to be a fine corner.

KICKING GAME: Shula says punter Reggie Roby has the strongest leg in the league. Roby finished second in the AFC to Rohn Stark in punting average (44.2). Fuad Reveiz kicked more PATs—52—than anyone else in the league, but he was erratic on the field goals (14-of-22) after an outstanding rookie year.

THE ROOKIES: Shula said he needed "defense, defense, defense," and he backed those words up by taking Bosa in the first round and Wisconsin linebacker Rick Graf in the second. Bosa is a fine athlete who showed versatility in lining up at linebacker in certain situations. Shula couldn't resist offense, however, moving up in the third round to grab Syracuse wide receiver Scott Schwedes, described as a faster Steve Largent.

OUTLOOK: Shula has moved to improve the defense, but there are so many holes to fill that it's unlikely he can do it with one draft. Most of the improvement hinges on what kind of impact Green can make, and that's highly speculative. The answers could come early because the Dolphins play four playoff teams in first six weeks, plus Seattle, which won 10 games. It looks tough, but never count out Shula.

DOLPHIN PROFILES

DAN MARINO 25 6-4 214   Quarterback

The $9-million man is worth every cent... Qualified last year for the all-time NFL quarterback ratings, and he zoomed to the top with a 95.21 mark, just ahead of Joe Montana ...In four incredible seasons, he has completed 1,249 of 2,050 passes (60.9 percent) for 16,177 yards and 142 touchdowns with 67 interceptions... Set NFL records last year for attempts (623) and completions (378)... Threw for more than 400 yards in three games, giving him a career total of seven 400-yard games, another record... Marino was the only passer to throw a TD pass in every game, and he has a 23-game streak going into 1987... Threw for 4,746 yards, the third-highest total in league history, and for 44 TDs, the second-highest total... Marino, of course, holds both records from his 1984 season

(5,084 yards and 48 TDs)... Threw for a career-high six scores in a 51-45 loss to the Jets... Whew... Born Sept. 15, 1961, in Pittsburgh, and was an All-American at Pitt... Now he's truly All-World.

MARK DUPER 28 5-9 187   Wide Receiver

Super Duper set a Dolphin record with eight 100-yard games in his super 1986 season... Finished with 67 receptions and his 1,313 yards and 11 TDs were both single-season highs... Came to the Dolphins in 1982 as a sleeper, second-round pick out of Northwest (La.) State and initially had trouble running precise patterns, but now he has experience and patience to go with his 4.3 speed... Had arthroscopic knee surgery after the season and was replaced in the Pro Bowl by teammate Mark Clayton... Born Jan. 25, 1959, in Pineville, La.... Ran on the NCAA championship 400-meter relay team with the late Joe Delaney.

LORENZO HAMPTON 25 6-0 212   Running Back

Dolphins were only 25th in rushing offense, but Hampton was the reason they weren't last... First-round pick out of Florida in 1985 gave the Dolphins much-needed ground punch in the second half of the season... Broke a Miami string of 36 regular-season games (41 overall) without a 100-yard rusher when he gained 148 against the Jets... Also ran for 109 yards in finale against Patriots... Finished with 830 yards on 189 carries and nine TDs and also was the team's second-leading receiver with 61 catches for 446 yards... Can return kickoffs, too... Born March 12, 1962, in Lake Wales, Fla.

MARK CLAYTON 26 5-9 175   Wide Receiver

Amazing what a trip to the eye doctor will do... Clayton was making some uncharacteristic drops in the middle of the 1985 season and finally discovered he's far-sighted. He wore prescription goggles all last season and caught 60 passes for 1,150 yards and 10 TDs... Has averaged at least 19 yards a catch in three out of four seasons... Runs more refined patterns than Mark Duper but isn't as fast...Loves catching the ball underneath a zone and then motoring...Asked what Clayton needs to improve on, Don Shula says: "We just have to keep throwing the ball to him."...Born April 8, 1961, in Indianapolis...He was an eighth-round pick out of Louisville in 1983.

BRUCE HARDY 31 6-5 232   Tight End

A vintage season...The nine-year veteran exploded for 54 catches for 430 yards and five TDs and became Dan Marino's possession receiver against double zones...Hardy played so well the Dolphins kept Joe Rose, who has better speed, on injured reserve...Was on the cover of *Sports Illustrated* in 1974 as an 18-year-old high-school superstar. He had been named MVP of the state of Utah in football and basketball in two straight years...Good blocker and awareness at finding open areas...Born June 1, 1956, in Murray, Utah, and attended Arizona State, where he was a teammate of John Jefferson.

DWIGHT STEPHENSON 29 6-2 255   Center

Tuesday is Dwight's Day. That's the day he and his Dolphin teammates watch the videotapes of Sunday's game and see him knocking a linebacker through the end zone. Stephenson gets so embarrassed he turns away from the screen...For the fourth straight season, Stephenson started in the Pro Bowl. He's that good...Utilizes strength and lightning quickness to occupy nose tackles one-on-one...Even though he's relatively light, he's durable, starting every game in the last five seasons...Born Nov. 20, 1957, in Murfreesboro, N.C....At Alabama, Bear Bryant called him "the greatest center I have ever coached."...Voted NFL Man of the Year in 1985.

JOHN OFFERDAHL 23 6-2 232   Linebacker

Fifty-one players were picked ahead of this head-hunter from Western Michigan, but none made his impact...Voted Defensive Rookie of the Year in the AFC and started in the Pro Bowl after leading the Dolphins with 135 tackles, 50 more than second-place Jackie Shipp...Also had two sacks, an interception, forced three fumbles and broke up eight passes...He did all of this while calling the defensive signals, an unbelievable feat for a rookie . . . Saved a 17-13 victory over the Colts with an open-field tackle with 33 seconds left . . . Born Aug. 17, 1964, in Wisconsin Rapids, Wis. . . . After being picked by the Dolphins, he moved to Miami in the summer to learn the defensive system, living in an apartment with no furniture.

HUGH GREEN 28 6-2 225   Linebacker

On the comeback trail after serious knee injury in Week 3 against the Jets. The patella tendon in his right knee ruptured and the kneecap rolled out of place . . . Injury was similar to the one suffered by the Dodgers' Pedro Guerrero . . . Doctors say his rehab is going fine and he may be back for the start of the season . . . Green's absence was a crushing blow to beleaguered Dolphin D. He had four sacks in less than three games, and that total led the team until Week 15 . . . He is such an impact player that Don Shula gave up a first- and a second-round pick in 1986 to Tampa Bay . . . Born July 27, 1959, in Natchez, Miss., and was the 1980 Heisman Trophy runnerup at Pitt.

REYNA THOMPSON 24 5-11 194   Cornerback

Another find, but that didn't keep Don Shula from almost getting rid of him . . . In the roster cut to 60 players, Shula waived the ninth-round speedster from Baylor but then couldn't sleep. The next morning, Shula got to his office at 7:30 and told pro scouting director Charley Winner to get him back . . . Reyna (pronounced rah-NAY) has 4.45 speed and was the Southwest Conference high-hurdles champion . . . He played well at nickel back and then started the last four games at left corner when Paul Lankford was injured . . . Born Aug. 28, 1963, in Dallas . . . He was burned a few times, but you can't teach speed.

REGGIE ROBY 26 6-2 243   Punter

A thunder leg who gives hang time a new meaning . . . Finished second to Indianapolis' Rohn Stark with a gross average of 44.2 yards on 56 punts, but he was first in net average at 37.4 . . . His 56 punts tied him with Cincinnati's Jeff Hayes for the fewest punts by a regular in the NFL last season, a sign of potent offense . . . Had the longest punts in the NFL,

booming 73-yarders against San Francisco and New England...
Born July 30, 1961, in Waterloo, Iowa, and led the nation in
punting at Iowa in his junior and senior seasons...He also can
kick off...He's a two-step punter who has the strength to con-
tact the ball higher and produce a 4.5-second hang time...Only
negative last year were two dropped snaps.

COACH DON SHULA: Even the greatest coach in the game

must get a taste of humility...The break-even
season was the first time since 1980 that the
Dolphins fell short of a winning record. Shula
still has only one losing season at Miami in
17 years...Injuries crippled the defense, but
Shula never uses that as an excuse...Decided
to go with a fresh approach by hiring Cleveland defensive back coach Tom Olivadotti as
defensive coordinator to replace Chuck Studley. But the defense
needs a healthy Hugh Green and better players, especially with
tough schedule coming up against the NFC East...Winningest
active coach in the NFL. In 24 seasons, Shula is 263-107-6 for
.707 winning percentage. He's 63 wins short of George Halas'
all-time record of 326 victories...Born Jan. 4, 1930, in Grand
River, Ohio...He has taken six teams to the Super Bowl and
won twice. One of his Super Bowl teams had David Woodley at
quarterback. The man can coach...Some teams would have died
after opening 1-5. Dolphins won six of their last nine...Major
force on the league's competition committee. He pushed for rein-
statement of the instant-replay system even though it cost him a
game against the Jets...Played running back at John Carroll
University and played seven years in the NFL as a defensive back
for the Browns, Colts and Redskins.

GREATEST KICKER

Whenever the Super Bowl's greatest bloopers are discussed
Garo Yepremian's name won't be far from the top. The 197?
Dolphins were in the midst of their perfect season and were looking to extend a 14-0 lead over the Redskins in the fourth quarte
of Super Bowl VII. But Yepremian's field-goal attempt wa
blocked and the ball bounced back into his hands. Instead o

eating it, Yepremian tried a "pass" that slipped out of his hands and was returned 49 yards by Mike Bass for Washington's only score.

Yepremian can accept the notoriety because he was a pro at his craft. The Dolphins have lit up the scoreboard recently, but Yepremian still holds the season scoring record with 117 points in 1971. And that was in a 14-game season.

Yepremian was a money kicker. He won the 1971 Christmas Day marathon against Kansas City with a 37-yard field goal 7:40 into the sixth quarter. In nine seasons with Miami, Yepremian scored 830 points on 165 field goals (in 242 attempts) and 335 extra points (in 351 tries). His best percentage season came in 1978 when he converted 19-of-23 field-goal attempts (.826).

INDIVIDUAL DOLPHIN RECORDS

Rushing

Most Yards Game:		197	Mercury Morris, vs New England, 1973
	Season:	1,258	Delvin Williams, 1978
	Career:	6,737	Larry Csonka, 1968-74, 1979

Passing

Most TD Passes Game:		6	Bob Griese, vs St. Louis, 1977
		6	Dan Marino, vs N.Y. Jets, 1986
	Season:	48	Dan Marino, 1984
	Career:	192	Bob Griese, 1967-80

Receiving

Most TD Passes Game:		4	Paul Warfield, vs Detroit, 1973
	Season:	18	Mark Clayton, 1984
	Career:	74	Nat Moore, 1974-86

Scoring

Most Points Game:		24	Paul Warfield, vs Detroit, 1973
	Season:	117	Garo Yepremian, 1971
	Career:	830	Garo Yepremian, 1970-78
Most TDs Game:		4	Paul Warfield, vs Detroit, 1973
	Season:	18	Mark Clayton, 1984
	Career:	75	Nat Moore, 1974-86

NEW ENGLAND PATRIOTS

TEAM DIRECTORY: Pres.: William Sullivan Jr.; VP: Bucko Kilroy; GM: Patrick J. Sullivan; Dir. Pub. Rel.: Dave Wintergrass; Dir. Publicity: Jim Greenidge; Head Coach: Raymond Berry. Home field: Sullivan Stadium (61,000). Colors: Red, white and blue.

SCOUTING REPORT

OFFENSE: Raymond Berry says his dad, a former high-school coach in Paris, Tex., used to preach to him that the most important ingredient an offensive team can have is balance. Well, Berry didn't follow his dad's advice last year and still won the AFC East.

With the retirement of John Hannah and the injury to blocking tight end Lin Dawson, the Patriots had absolutely zero punch on the ground. They averaged a pitiful 2.9 yards per rush, last in the NFL, after getting to the Super Bowl in 1985 with a crunching ground attack that was second best in the AFC.

Part of the problem were nagging knee and shoulder injuries to Craig James, who rushed for only 428 yards and a 2.8-yard average. But the run-blocking was lacking, too, which is why Berry aggressively pursued Tampa Bay guard Sean Farrell, who will give New England a great push up front. The Patriots surrendered second-, seventh- and ninth-round picks for Farrell, and it was well worth the price. Louisville tackle Bruce Armstrong, the Pats' No. 1 pick, should help, too.

The Patriots are set in most other offensive areas. Tony Eason rebounded from a rough Super Bowl to establish his leadership. He completed 61.6 percent of his passes and threw only 10 interceptions. Stanley Morgan, who lost weight and had finger surgery before the 1986 season, seemed reborn with 84 catches for 10 touchdowns. Berry will continue to live with Irving Fryar's lapses because of his big-play ability.

In two playoff seasons, Berry has instilled a winning attitude in a franchise that at one time seemed rudderless. It took an offbeat thinker like Berry to concoct the idea of having Steve Grogan call Eason's plays from the sidelines, and, of course, it worked.

DEFENSE: The biggest uncertainty seems to be the same every year. Will defensive end Ken Sims, the No. 1 overall pick in 1982, be able to shake his back problems and become an every-down player? Maybe the Patriots should move on. Garin Veris,

Tony Eason's passing made up for Pats' poor rushing.

the other end, has had 21 sacks in two seasons.

Linebacker looks particularly solid. Steve Nelson, who had surgery to repair ligaments in his left knee, is expected back for a 14th season, and Andre Tippett and Don Blackmon might be reaching their peaks. Tippett never was put on injured reserve with his right knee injury, but he missed five games and never was quite the same when he returned. But he spent the offseason lifting more weights than he normally does and should be back in top shape.

Ray Clayborn may be as good as any cornerback in the league and Ronnie Lippett, who finished second in the AFC with eight interceptions, isn't far from that class. Clayborn said the major difference in the Patriots' pass defense, which held quarterbacks to a league low of 186.1 yards a game, was Lippett's play. But safeties Roland James and Fred Marion will have to play better.

PATRIOTS VETERAN ROSTER

HEAD COACH—Raymond Berry. Assistant Coaches—Dean Brittenham, Jim Carr, Bobby Grier, Ray Hamilton, Rod Humenuik, Harold Jackson, Eddie Khayat, John Polonchek, Rod Rust, Dante Scarnecchia, Don Shinnick, Les Steckel.

No.	Name	Pos.	Ht.	Wt.	NFL Exp.	College
62	Bain, Bill	T	6-4	260	13	USC
48	Baty, Greg	TE	6-5	241	2	Stanford
94	Black, Mel	LB	6-2	228	2	Eastern Illinois
55	Blackmon, Don	LB	6-3	235	7	Tulsa
28	Bowman, Jim	S	6-2	210	3	Central Michigan
58	Brock, Pete	C	6-5	275	12	Colorado
3	Camarillo, Rich	P	5-11	185	7	Washington
46	Chapman, David	TE	6-4	245	2	W. Va. Inst. Tech.
26	Clayborn, Raymond	CB	6-0	186	11	Texas
33	Collins, Tony	HB	5-11	212	7	East Carolina
87	Dawson, Lin	TE	6-3	240	7	NC State
59	Doig, Steve	LB	6-2	240	5	New Hampshire
21	Dupard, Reggie	HB	5-11	205	2	SMU
11	Eason, Tony	QB	6-4	212	5	Illinois
66	Fairchild, Paul	G	6-4	270	4	Kansas
62	Farrell, Sean	G-T	6-3	260	6	Penn State
1	Franklin, Tony	K	5-8	182	9	Texas A&M
80	Fryar, Irving	WR-KR	6-0	200	4	Nebraska
43	Gibson, Ernest	CB	5-10	185	4	Furman
14	Grogan, Steve	QB	6-4	210	13	Kansas State
68	Haley, Darryl	T-G	6-4	265	5	Utah
27	Hawthorne, Greg	TE	6-2	235	9	Baylor
97	Hodge, Milford	DE	6-3	278	2	Washington State
76	Holloway, Brian	T	6-7	288	7	Stanford
51	Ingram, Brian	LB	6-4	235	6	Tennessee
32	James, Craig	RB	6-0	215	4	SMU
38	James, Roland	S	6-2	191	8	Tennessee
83	Jones, Cedric	WR	6-1	184	6	Duke
36	Jordan, Eric	RB-KR	6-0	190	2	Purdue
45	Keel, Mark	TE	6-3	242	2	Arizona
42	Lippett, Ronnie	CB	5-11	180	5	Miami
31	Marion, Fred	S	6-2	191	6	Miami
64	Matich, Trevor	C	6-4	270	3	Brigham Young
50	McGrew, Lawrence	LB	6-5	233	7	USC
23	McSwain, Rod	CB	6-1	198	4	Clemson
67	Moore, Steve	G-T	6-5	305	5	Tenn. A&I State
86	Morgan, Stanley	WR	5-11	181	11	Tennessee
75	Morriss, Guy	C-G	6-4	275	15	Texas Christian
57	Nelson, Steve	LB	6-2	230	14	North Dakota State
98	Owens, Dennis	NT	6-1	258	6	NC State
70	Plunkett, Art	T	6-8	282	7	Nevada-Las Vegas
22	Profit, Eugene	DB	5-10	165	2	Yale
12	Ramsey, Tom	QB	6-1	189	3	UCLA
52	Rembert, Johnny	LB	6-3	234	5	Clemson
95	Reynolds, Ed	LB	6-5	242	5	Virginia
65	Ruth, Mike	DT	6-1	266	2	Boston College
88	Scott, Willie	TE	6-4	245	7	South Carolina
77	Sims, Kenneth	DE	6-5	271	6	Texas
81	Starring, Stephen	WR-KR	5-10	172	5	McNeese
30	Tatupu, Mosi	RB	6-0	227	10	USC
56	Tippett, Andre	LB	6-3	241	6	Iowa
60	Veris, Garin	DE	6-4	255	3	Stanford
24	Weathers, Robert	RB	6-2	225	6	Arizona State
53	Weishuhn, Clayton	LB	6-1	218	4	Angelo State
96	Williams, Brent	DT	6-3	278	2	Toledo
82	Williams, Derwin	WR	6-1	185	3	New Mexico
54	Williams, Ed	LB	6-4	244	4	Texas
90	Williams, Toby	DL	6-4	270	5	Nebraska
61	Wooten, Ron	G	6-4	273	6	North Carolina

TOP FIVE DRAFT CHOICES

Rd.	Name	Sel. No.	Pos.	Ht.	Wt.	College
1	Armstrong, Bruce	23	G	6-4	260	Louisville
3	Perryman, Bob	79	RB	6-1	232	Michigan
4	Gannon, Richard	98	QB-RB	6-3	200	Delaware
4	Beasley, Derrick	102	DB	6-2	195	Winston-Salem
4	Jordan, Tim	107	LB	6-3	221	Wisconsin

KICKING GAME: There may not be a better combo in the AFC. Kicker Tony Franklin had his finest season with 140 points on 32-of-41 field-goal attempts, and he made the Pro Bowl for the first time. Offseason surgery to clean out both knees may even add to his distance. Punter Rich Camarillo finished third in punting with a 42.1 average and was adept at dropping the ball inside the 20.

THE ROOKIES: When you evaluate this draft, you have to count four-year NFL vet Farrell in a sense as a great second-round pick. He'll start at guard immediately. Ray Berry also beefed up his line with Armstrong, 23rd overall. Fourth-rounder Rich Gannon of Delaware was a highly athletic quarterback who may be tried at running back.

OUTLOOK: The Patriots overcame an unbelievable rash of injuries to win the AFC East, and it's hard to see anybody touching them this season. Farrell will help the running game immensely, and James, Tippett and Nelson are back at full strength. The Patriots not only have the best talent in the division—they've got a coach who knows what buttons to push.

PATRIOT PROFILES

TONY EASON 27 6-4 212   **Quarterback**

The Patriots were the worst rushing team in the NFL and still finished No. 2 in scoring, so Eason must have done a lot of things right... Finished third in the AFC quarterback ratings behind Dan Marino and Dave Krieg, completing 276 of 448 passes (61.6 percent) for 3,328 yards and 19 touchdowns, with 10 interceptions... He answered the big question from the 1985 Super Bowl: would he be able to recover mentally after being yanked following an 0-for-6 horror show against the Bears? A resounding yes... Missed two starts with bruised ribs and was knocked out in the finale against Miami with a pinched nerve in his right shoulder... Born Oct. 8, 1959, in Blythe, Cal., and had a decorated career at Illinois.

STEVE GROGAN 34 6-4 210   Quarterback

He has replaced Don Strock as the premier relief pitcher in football... With the AFC East title and a playoff spot on the line, he came in for Tony Eason early in the second quarter in the finale against Miami and directed an inspiring 34-27 win, throwing for two TDs and running seven yards for another... Overall, Grogan completed 62 of 102 passes (60.8 percent) for 976 yards and nine TDs, with two interceptions... He was 2-1 in the games in which he saw extensive action... Of course, he pulled off an even more incredible feat in 1985 when he stepped in and won six straight games after not having played in 18 months... Born July 24, 1953, in San Antonio, Tex., and attended Kansas State... Set an unusual precedent when he became the first backup quarterback to call the offensive plays from the sidelines... Had elbow surgery in the offseason.

IRVING FRYAR 24 6-0 200   Wide Receiver

Just when you thought it was safe to watch Fryar, he made it dangerous... Trailing the Jets by seven points, Fryar made a fair catch of a Dave Jennings punt as time expired. Against the Broncos in the playoffs, he fielded a punt inside his five with a minute left, leading to a safety on the next play... A tremendous but flighty talent... Caught 43 passes for 737 yards and six TDs... Finished third in the AFC with a 10.5-yard average on punt returns... After separating his shoulder against the Bills, he left Sullivan Stadium early and drove his Mercedes into a tree. He suffered a concussion and was fined $20 by police. Fryar said he lost control while talking on his car phone... Born Sept. 28, 1962, in Mount Holly, N.J., and was an All-American wingback at Nebraska.

STANLEY MORGAN 32 5-11 181   Wide Receiver

He was leaner and much meaner. It only took Morgan 10 seasons to have his greatest year as a pro... Shed 10 pounds from his 1985 playing weight of 185, and the results were amazing. Morgan caught 84 passes for 1,491 yards, both career highs, and scored 10 touchdowns. Only Jerry Rice of the 49ers, who accounted for 1,570 yards, had better production, and

Rice is running around on 24-year-old legs . . . Morgan said he dropped the weight to avoid nagging hamstring pulls and to improve his quickness. He also did track work in the offseason and had surgery on the little finger of his left hand. The middle joint was removed, curved slightly to imitate the circumference of a football and then fused into place. Said Morgan: "It looked as if there had been a little rat in there, eating away at the bone." . . . Born Feb. 17, 1955, at Easley, S.C. . . . Product of Tennessee.

CRAIG JAMES 26 6-0 215   Running Back

The James Gang was mowed down at High Noon and in the rest of the afternoon last season . . . In the absence of guard John Hannah and tight end Lin Dawson, the line failed to open enough holes for James, who rushed for 1,227 yards in 1985 but only 427 yards (and a 2.8-yard average) last year . . . James was slowed by a knee injury at midseason, but he balked at wearing a protective brace. Finally agreed to wear it . . . The Patriots dropped from the No. 2 rushing team in the NFL to dead last . . . Said James: "Momentum is a lethal thing if you let it work against you." Unfortunately, that's what happened . . . Born Feb. 2, 1961, in Jacksonville, Fla., he was Eric Dickerson's running mate in the Pony Express backfield at SMU.

SEAN FARRELL 27 6-3 260   Guard

The Patriots moved aggressively to shore up their offensive line by acquiring this unhappy but talented Buc in exchange for a No. 2, No. 7 and No. 9 . . . The former Penn Stater had asked to be traded after the season because he was disgruntled over the club's lack of progress in five years. "I know what I want for Christmas; I want to get out of Tampa Bay," he said . . . Now he's with a winner and he's got a reason to whip himself back into marvelous shape . . . Farrell will be given a chance to fill John Hannah's left guard spot, which was handled by Paul Fairchild in 1986 . . . Had offseason arthroscopic surgery on his knee . . . He can also play tackle . . . Born May 25, 1960, in Westhampton Beach, N.Y.

ANDRE TIPPETT 27 6-3 241   Linebacker

Before the 1986 season, Tippett declared: "When it comes to linebackers, I'm the man." ...Talk about backfiring. Tippett suffered a sprained right knee in Week 9 against Atlanta and underwent arthroscopic surgery to remove loose cartilage...He never was placed on injured reserve, but he missed five games and never was 100 percent when he came back...
He went from AFC Defensive Player of the Year in 1985 with 16½ sacks to 9½ sacks last season...He's a black belt in karate, and no linebacker is stronger or quicker when he's healthy...Born Dec. 27, 1959, in Birmingham, Ala....Grew up in Newark, N.J., and the young man went west to Iowa, where he was All-American and led the Hawkeyes to the 1981 Rose Bowl.

GARIN VERIS 24 6-4 255   Defensive End

With Ken Sims out once again with a bad back and Julius Adams retired, Veris picked up the sack slack with a second consecutive season of superb play...Led the Patriots with 11 sacks, which gives him 21 in two years...Came on early in his rookie year to become a starter, confounding those who said the second-round pick out of Stanford was too small and too slow to be effective...Born Feb. 27, 1963, in Chillicothe, Ohio ...Decided on Stanford rather than Ohio State because he wanted to throw the shot as well as play football...His most impressive play as a rookie was recovering a fumble by the Jets about 50 yards away from where he had begun pursuing the play.

RONNIE LIPPETT 26 5-11 180   Cornerback

The joke around Foxboro used to be Lippett's terrible hands. In 1985, he dropped at least a half-dozen sure interceptions, so Raymond Berry ordered all the defensive backs to participate in the wide-receiver drills during training camp...It must have worked. Lippett (pronounced Lip-PET) hung on to eight interceptions last year to finish second in the AFC to Kansas City's Deron Cherry...He also broke up 10 passes...Has started at left cornerback since 1984 when Mike Haynes was traded to the Raiders...Born Dec. 10, 1960, in Melbourne, Fla., and attended the University of Miami...Intercepted two passes in games against Miami, Buffalo and Indianapolis.

RAYMOND CLAYBORN 32 6-0 186   Cornerback

Quarterbacks tested the veteran a little more because of Lippett's emergence, but he was more than up to the task . . . Intercepted three passes and led the Patriots by breaking up 16 . . . Has a streak of 151 consecutive games going into 1987, which is one short of the club record. Already owns the Patriot mark for 138 consecutive starts . . . Usually draws the opposing team's best receiver and seldom gives up a deep ball . . . Born Jan. 2, 1955, in Fort Worth, Tex. . . . Played running back at Texas until he saw Earl Campbell in the flesh. Switched to defense and became an All-American and the Patriots' No. 1 pick in 1977 . . . Likes to taunt receivers because he knows he usually has the upper hand.

COACH RAYMOND BERRY: Since Berry arrived midway

through the 1984 season, the Patriots don't just promise the big play—they make it . . . Had to beat Miami in the Orange Bowl in the final Monday night game to win the AFC East and secure a playoff spot, and they did it . . . Berry went 10-6 with a club that could have been crushed by injuries to Andre Tippett, Steve Nelson, Tony Eason, Craig James, Ken Sims and Lin Dawson and by the retirement of John Hannah and Julius Adams . . . Always looking for novel ideas, and his best was handing over the sideline play-calling responsibilities to backup quarterback Steve Grogan . . . Defused furor over revelations that several of his players had tested positive for illegal drugs . . . Patriots had never gotten to the Super Bowl before he took them as a wild-card team in 1985 . . . Born Feb. 27, 1933, in Corpus Christi, Tex. . . . Wants his players stronger and in better condition in 1987 . . . The Hall of Fame receiver with the Colts caught 631 yards in his 13 seasons in the NFL . . . He's taught all his receivers the art of tucking away the football once they catch it . . . Patriots also practice the proper way of falling on fumbles . . . Credits his dad, a high-school coach in Paris, Tex., with teaching him about the importance of a balanced offensive and defensive team.

GREATEST KICKER

It looks like one of the best trades in Patriot history. New England acquired Tony Franklin in 1984 from Philadelphia in exchange for a sixth-round pick in the 1985 draft, and Franklin has given the Patriots incredible consistency at a vital position. Last year he led the NFL in scoring (140) and in field goals (32). In fact, 1986 was the third straight season in which the former Texas A&M kicker surpassed 100 points, and his three-season accuracy is a phenomenal 78.7 percent.

Franklin does not have incredible leg strength, but he separates himself from the field with his consistency inside the 40. Last year he made 23-of-25 field goals of 39 yards or less and he was rewarded with his first Pro Bowl appearance. In his New England career, he has missed only 4-of-63 field goals inside the 40, a .937 success rate.

Franklin could be even tougher this year. He had offseason arthroscopic surgery to remove calcium deposits behind both knees. The Patriots feel that will enable him to put more weight on his plant leg and thus increase his distance on kickoffs.

Franklin originally was drafted by the Eagles in the third round of the 1979 draft. He kicked 80 field goals in five years with Philadelphia and has kicked 78 in three years with New England.

INDIVIDUAL PATRIOT RECORDS
Rushing

Most Yards Game:	212	Tony Collins, N.Y. Jets, 1983
Season:	1,458	Jim Nance, 1966
Career:	5,453	Sam Cunningham, 1973-79, 1981-82

Passing

Most TD Passes Game:	5	Babe Parilli, vs Buffalo, 1964
	5	Babe Parilli, vs Miami, 1967
	5	Steve Grogan, vs N.Y. Jets, 1979
Season:	31	Babe Parilli, 1964
Career:	155	Steve Grogan, 1975-86

Receiving

Most TD Passes Game:	3	Billy Lott, vs Buffalo, 1961
	3	Gino Cappelletti, vs Buffalo, 1964
	3	Jim Whalen, vs Miami, 1967
	3	Harold Jackson, vs N.Y. Jets, 1979
	3	Derrick Ramsey, vs Indianapolis, 1984
	3	Stanley Morgan, vs Seattle, 1986
Season:	12	Stanley Morgan, 1979
Career:	57	Stanley Morgan, 1977-86

Scoring

Most Points Game:	28	Gino Cappelletti, vs Houston, 1965
Season:	155	Gino Cappelletti, 1964
Career:	1,130	Gino Cappelletti, 1960-70
Most TDs Game:	3	Billy Lott, vs Buffalo, 1961
	3	Billy Lott, vs Oakland, 1961
	3	Larry Garron, vs Oakland, 1964
	3	Gino Cappelletti, vs Buffalo, 1964
	3	Larry Garron, vs San Diego, 1966
	3	Jim Whalen, vs Miami, 1967
	3	Sam Cunningham, vs Buffalo, 1974
	3	Mack Herron, vs Buffalo, 1974
	3	Sam Cunningham, vs Buffalo, 1975
	3	Harold Jackson, vs N.Y. Jets, 1979
	3	Tony Collins, vs N.Y. Jets, 1983
	3	Mosi Tatupu, vs L.A. Rams, 1983
	3	Derrick Ramsey, vs Indianapolis, 1984
	3	Stanley Morgan, vs Seattle, 1986
Season:	13	Steve Grogan, 1976
	13	Stanley Morgan, 1979
Career:	58	Stanley Morgan, 1977-86

NEW YORK JETS

TEAM DIRECTORY: Chairman: Leon Hess; Pres.: Jim Kensil; Dir. Player Personnel: Mike Hickey; Dir. Pro Personnel: Jim Royer; Dir. Pub. Rel.: Frank Ramos; Head Coach: Joe Walton. Home field: Giants Stadium (76,891). Colors: Kelly green and white.

SCOUTING REPORT

OFFENSE: If the Jet offense looked like two completely different operations last year, that's because it was. While most of the devastating injuries occurred on defense, it was the offense that collapsed in the final five weeks after a 10-1 start.

There are a lot of theories as to what happened. The most

Al Toon topped AFC wide receivers with 85 catches.

current, as held by Joe Walton, is that the line simply was overpowered late in the season because several key players were too injured to lift weights. Left tackle Jim Sweeney and left guard Ted Banker both had offseason shoulder surgery, and each couldn't lift a pound in the final two months.

Ironically, the line play suffered when center Joe Fields returned from seven weeks on injured reserve with a sprained knee. The Jets were 7-0 with backup center Guy Bingham, but Fields finished up 0-5 and admitted he picked up some bad habits.

The lack of protection turned Ken O'Brien into a different quarterback as well. He had thrown 23 touchdown passes and only eight interceptions in the first 11 weeks; that ratio went to two touchdowns and 12 interceptions in the last five. O'Brien, who also suffered a broken pinky finger on his right hand, was the best quarterback in football during the winning streak. Now the test is for him to bounce back.

Freeman McNeil got off to a slow start—dislocating his right elbow in the second week—but he closed with a rush. Johnny Hector is too good to keep out of the lineup, so the Jets may use him at fullback this year. Top draft pick Roger Vick of Texas A&M should get some time at fullback, too.

Al Toon and Wesley Walker combined to give the Jets as lethal a receiving combo as there is in football. Toon is tall, rangy, acrobatic and tough. Walker can still burn. Mickey Shuler is an excellent tight end. All O'Brien needs is time to find them.

DEFENSE: Get out the scalpels. Nose tackle Joe Klecko and linebacker Lance Mehl are trying to return from major reconstructive knee surgery, and neither will be back before October. Marty Lyons had surgery on both shoulders but should be ready for the season. Mark Gastineau, who had a career-low two sacks, has a torn anterior cruciate ligament in his knee but did not have knee surgery. Will it hold up? Good question.

The Jets are in dire need of a pass rush, which is one reason they will try to convert Tim Crawford, a linebacker who spent the season on injured reserve, to a light defensive end. Outside linebacker Bob Crable has made good recovery from his knee troubles, but Rusty Guilbeau was manhandled on the outside.

Cornerback Russell Carter is the Jets' best cover man, but he's been nagged by injuries. Coverted wide receiver Bobby Humphery might challenge for a starting job. Defensive coordinator Bud Carson would always like another corner.

KICKING GAME: The Jets have two of the oldest legs in the NFL in Pat Leahy, 36, and Dave Jennings, 35, but they'll proba-

JETS VETERAN ROSTER

HEAD COACH—Joe Walton. Assistant Coaches—Zeke Bratkowski, Ray Callahan, Bud Carson, Mike Faulkiner, Bobby Hammond, Rich Kotite, Larry Pasquale, Dan Radakovich, Jim Vechiarella.

No.	Name	Pos.	Ht.	Wt.	NFL Exp.	College
60	Alexander, Dan	G	6-4	268	10	Louisiana State
43	Amoia, Vince	RB	5-11	222	1	Arizona State
95	Baldwin, Tom	DT	6-4	270	3	Tulsa
63	Banker, Ted	G-T-C	6-2	265	3	SE Missouri
31	Barber, Marion	FB	6-3	228	5	Minnesota
78	Bennett, Barry	DE-DT	6-4	260	9	Concordia (Minn.)
54	Benson, Troy	LB	6-2	235	1	Pittsburgh
64	Bingham, Guy	C-T-G	6-3	260	7	Montana
22	Bruckner, Nick	WR	5-11	185	5	Syracuse
27	Carter, Russell	CB-S	6-2	195	3	SMU
59	Clifton, Kyle	LB	6-4	230	3	TCU
50	Crable, Bob	LB	6-3	230	5	Notre Dame
52	Crawford, Tim	LB	6-4	230	1	Texas Tech
30	Faaola, Nuu	RB	5-11	215	1	Hawaii
65	Fields, Joe	C	6-2	253	12	Widener
98	Foster, Jerome	DE	6-2	275	3	Ohio State
99	Gastineau, Mark	DE	6-5	270	8	E. Central Oklahoma
35	Glenn, Kerry	CB	5-9	175	3	Minnesota
81	Griggs, Billy	TE	6-3	230	2	Virginia
94	Guilbeau, Rusty	LB	6-4	235	5	McNeese State
79	Haight, Mike	G-T	6-4	270	1	Iowa
39	Hamilton, Harry	S	6-0	195	3	Penn State
84	Harper, Michael	WR	5-10	180	1	Southern California
34	Hector, Johnny	RB	5-11	200	4	Texas A&M
47	Holmes, Jerry	CB	6-2	175	5	West Virginia
28	Howard, Carl	CB-S	6-2	190	3	Rutgers
48	Humphery, Bobby	CB-KR	5-10	180	3	New Mexico State
13	Jennings, Dave	P	6-4	200	13	St. Lawrence
80	Jones, Johnny "Lam"	WR	5-11	180	7	Texas
72	King, Gordon	T-G	6-6	270	8	Stanford
73	Klecko, Joe	DT-DE	6-3	265	11	Temple
89	Klever, Rocky	TE	6-3	228	4	Montana
5	Leahy, Pat	K	6-0	200	13	St. Louis
26	Lyles, Lester	S-LB	6-3	218	2	Virginia
93	Lyons, Marty	DE-DT	6-5	269	8	Alabama
57	McArthur, Kevin	LB	6-2	230	1	Lamar
68	McElroy, Reggie	T	6-6	270	5	West Texas State
24	McNeil, Freeman	RB	5-11	214	6	UCLA
56	Mehl, Lance	LB	6-3	233	8	Penn State
36	Miano, Rich	S	6-0	200	2	Hawaii
74	Moore, Derland	NT	6-4	273	14	Oklahoma
58	Monger, Matt	LB	6-1	238	2	Oklahoma State
7	O'Brien, Ken	QB	6-4	208	4	Cal-Davis
49	Paige, Tony	FB	5-10	225	3	Virginia Tech
10	Ryan, Pat	QB	6-3	210	9	Tennessee
82	Shuler, Mickey	TE	6-3	231	9	Penn State
87	Sohn, Kurt	WR-KR	5-11	180	5	Fordham
21	Springs, Kirk	S-KR	6-0	197	7	Miami (Ohio)
53	Sweeney, Jim	T-G	6-4	260	3	Pittsburgh
88	Toon, Al	WR	6-4	205	2	Wisconsin
83	Townsell, JoJo	WR	5-9	180	2	UCLA
70	Waldemore, Stan	G-C-T	6-4	269	9	Nebraska
85	Walker, Wesley	WR	6-0	182	10	California

TOP FIVE DRAFT CHOICES

Rd.	Name	Sel. No.	Pos.	Ht.	Wt.	College
1	Vick, Roger	21	RB	6-3	220	Texas A&M
2	Gordon, Alex	42	LB	6-4	243	Cincinnati
3	Elam, Onzy	75	LB	6-2	215	Tennessee State
5	Jackson, Kirby	129	DB	6-1	180	Mississippi State
6	Martin, Tracy	161	WR	6-2	190	North Dakota

bly be together at least one more season. Jennings didn't average 40 yards a punt last season, but the Jets could get by with that because he frequently was punting from near midfield, where accuracy was more important. Leahy's consecutive field-goal streak was snapped at 22. His major goal is to get back some of the length he lost on kickoffs last year.

THE ROOKIES: The Jets had crying needs on defense, but they couldn't pass up Vick, a 220-pounder who has 4.6 speed and excellent hands. He'll make the running attack that much more versatile since defenses no longer can load up on McNeil and Hector. The Jets addressed their speed problems at outside linebacker by trading up in the second round to take 6-4, 243-pound Alex Gordon of Cincinnati and then tabbing Onzy Elam, a 215-pound speedball from Tennessee State, in the third.

OUTLOOK: If this were a weather report, the Jets would have to be considered cloudy to partly cloudy. No one knows how well the defense can hang in without Klecko and Mehl. It finished 28th in pass defense last season, but a non-existent pass rush was a big reason for that. O'Brien can bounce back, but Jets don't have a defense to go far in the playoffs.

JET PROFILES

KEN O'BRIEN 26 6-4 208   Quarterback

If ever there was a tale of two seasons, O'Brien experienced it...Led all NFL quarterbacks through 11 weeks, completing 66.6 percent of his passes for 23 touchdowns with only eight interceptions...But in the five-game losing streak, O'Brien completed only 54.4 percent for two touchdowns with 12 interceptions...He's still the starter, but the big question is whether his confidence was permanently shaken ...Pulled from the starting lineup for backup Pat Ryan in the Jets' 35-15 wild-card playoff victory over Kansas City...Came back the next week when Ryan suffered a pulled groin...Born Nov. 27, 1960, in Brooklyn, but his family moved to California when he was three...Surprise first-round pick in 1983 out of Cal-Davis.

PAT RYAN 31 6-3 210 Quarterback

Joe Walton has a winner if Ken O'Brien falters... "Mr. Guts" started and won two critical early-season games against New England and Denver when O'Brien was out with a knee sprain... Came off the bench after two-month layoff and engineered wild-card win over the Chiefs and also had Jets ahead of Cleveland when he left with a groin injury... The 10-year veteran out of Tennessee knows he's in a relief role, but he says: "I know I can win."... His QB rating in the playoffs was a dazzling 126.6... Born Sept. 16, 1955, in Oklahoma City ... Played on the same high school football team with Seattle's Steve Largent... Pat Leahy credits Ryan's perfect holds for much of his kicking success.

FREEMAN McNEIL 28 5-11 214 Running Back

Again proved he's one of the most dangerous, multi-purpose backs in football when he's healthy... Started slowly and then missed four games with a dislocated right elbow in Week 2, so he was way behind... Rallied in the last 10 weeks to finish fifth in the AFC in rushing with 856 yards and five TDs... Also shined as a receiver with 49 catches for 410 yards... McNeil has yet to complete a 16-game season since coming to the Jets as their No. 1 pick out of UCLA in 1981... Born April 22, 1959, in Jackson, Miss.... Early injuries may have saved his legs for the playoffs, when he rushed for 206 yards in two games... He's a car nut and has a 1938 Chevy Coupe as a prized possession.

WESLEY WALKER 32 6-0 182 Wide Receiver

Other half of Jets' lethal receiving combo... Still has sprinter's speed to bend defenses... Six of his career-high 12 scoring catches were for 83, 71, 65, 50, 46 and 43 yards... Had his finest day as a pro in 51-45 overtime win over Miami, catching four TD passes, including game-winner... Season totals of 49 catches for 1,016 yards... His 20.7-yard average marked second straight year in which he topped 20 yards a catch, which proves value of Toon in keeping defenses occupied... Born May 26, 1955, in San Bernadino, Calif., and was Jets' second-round pick out of California in 1977... Legally blind in left eye... Has greatly improved his toughness over the middle.

AL TOON 24 6-4 205   Wide Receiver

Became one of the most feared wide outs in the NFL last year... His calling card is grace, leaping ability and incredible toughness... His 85 catches (for 1,176 yards and eight TDs) led all AFC wide receivers and shattered the club record for receptions... Lasting image was his 62-yard romp through the Saint secondary in which he broke four tackles... The rarest of commodities: a possession receiver with the speed to get deep... Caught one TD pass against Seattle by cradling ball between his knees... Born April 30, 1963, in Newport News, Va.... Set Wisconsin triple-jump record at 54-7½ and has a 43-inch vertical leap... A student of modern dance, and it shows.

MICKEY SHULER 31 6-3 231   Tight End

Finally achieved professional dream by making the Pro Bowl in his ninth season... Took on more of a blocking role but still managed to catch 69 passes for 675 yards and four TDs... Finished second in receptions to the Raiders' Todd Christensen among AFC tight ends... Has a 53-game streak in which he has caught at least one pass... Most important catch came in the final minute of a 14-13 win over Buffalo when he sliced through the Bill secondary for a 32-yard score... Played virtually the entire playoff game against Cleveland in a daze after getting kicked in the head. He may be lucky he doesn't remember that game... Born Aug. 21, 1956, in Harrisburg, Pa., and attended Penn State.

LANCE MEHL 29 6-3 233   Linebacker

Another major question mark... The 1985 Pro Bowler tore his left knee in Week 8 against New Orleans after catching his foot in the artificial turf... Needed major reconstructive surgery and may not be able to compete until October... His loss, coupled with the absence of Joe Klecko, turned the Jets' No. 2-rated run defense into a sieve... Even though he missed nearly nine games, he finished fifth in tackles with 60... Defensive coordinator Bud Carson said he missed Mehl's signal-calling abilities the most... Born Feb. 14, 1958, in Bellaire, Ohio, and carried on the tradition of great Penn State linebackers... Worked three summers in the coal mines, which convinced him football was easier.

JOE KLECKO 33 6-3 265   Nose Tackle

The guts of the Jet defense has come back from serious knee surgery before, so never count him out... But this latest injury to his left knee required major reconstructive surgery and he may not be ready until mid-season... First hurt the knee in Week 8 against New Orleans and didn't play the following week. Returned in Week 10 against Atlanta and re-injured it, forcing him out of the next four weeks... Came back again in Week 15 against Pittsburgh and tore the knee for good ... Until Klecko went out, Jets were ranked No. 2 in the NFL against the run, but the floodgates opened without him... When healthy, he's the best in the business because of his incredible first step and bull strength... Born Oct. 15, 1953, in Chester, Pa.... Played at Temple after playing semi-pro football after high school... Gave up boxing after sparring with Joe Frazier.

MARK GASTINEAU 30 6-5 270   Defensive End

Most frustrating year of his career... Two-time NFL sack leader recorded only two sacks in 1986 by sharing in two sacks and chasing Denver's John Elway out of bounds for the other... Problems started when he reported to training camp at 290 pounds, but extra weight may have contributed to groin and abdomen pulls that limited his quickness... Then he tore the anterior cruciate ligament in his right knee in Week 11 against Indianapolis and didn't return until the playoffs... His roughing penalty on Bernie Kosar fueled the Browns' incredible comeback... Probably will play with a knee brace this season, but the Jets need him to become a force... Born Nov. 20, 1956, in Ardmore, Okla.... First player drafted from East Central (Okla.) State.

BOB CRABLE 27 6-3 230   Linebacker

Crable's successful rehab of a major knee injury offers Joe Klecko and Lance Mehl reason to hope... Crable underwent major reconstructive surgery in November 1984, and it took him about a year to fully recover... The former middle linebacker looked quick and active last year, finishing third in tackles (87) and leading all linebackers with 3½ sacks...

Finished the season at left outside linebacker but played every position because of injuries...Hates artificial turf, which he thinks contributed to his and Mehl's injuries: "I think the turf threatens your career."...The former Notre Dame All-America was born Sept. 22, 1959, in Cincinnati, Ohio.

COACH JOE WALTON: Tiger Joe has gotten the Jets out of box quickly in the last three seasons, but his teams have had trouble finishing...Since 1984, the Jets are 19-5 in the first eight weeks of the season and 9-15 in the last eight weeks ...Last year's team was the first in NFL history to lose its last five games and still make the playoffs...Despite the collapse, Walton was given a new three-year contract that runs through the 1989 season...Overall, he did a great job getting the Jets into the playoffs with an avalanche of injuries, but the slide from 10-1 to 10-6 left a bitter taste...Born Dec. 15, 1935, in Beaver Falls, Pa., the same town that produced Joe Namath... In fact, one of Walton's summer jobs when he attended the University of Pittsburgh was to mow the Little League diamond where Namath played...Played seven years in the NFL with the Redskins and Giants after an All-America career at tight end and linebacker...Kept coaching staff intact after 1986 for the first time in four years...Relationship with Ken O'Brien seemed to cool late in the season and bears watching.

GREATEST KICKER

No NFL kicker has been with his team longer than Pat Leahy has been with the Jets, and there's a good reason. Leahy, who replaced Bobby Howfield in the middle of the 1974 season, has been among the NFL's most consistent performers, especially since the Jets have moved away from the wind tunnel and poor field conditions at Shea Stadium.

In three seasons at Giants Stadium, Leahy has converted 59-of-77 field-goal attempts for a sparkling .776 percentage. He was never better than last year, when he made his first 10 field goals to give him a streak of 22 in a row dating back to 1985. Leahy had a chance to tie Mark Moseley's all-time NFL record of

23 consecutive field goals, but he missed a 46-yard attempt in a heavy rain against New Orleans. His response? "No big deal," he said. "I'll just have to start another streak."

Leahy finished the season making 16-of-19 field goals. In his 13-year career, he has become the Jets' leading scorer with 993 points on 200-of-292 field goals (.684) and 393-of-418 extra points.

Leahy, 36, has no retirement plans on the horizon. One area he wants to improve on in 1987 is his kickoff distance, which slipped a bit from 1986.

INDIVIDUAL JET RECORDS
Rushing

Most Yards Game:	192	Freeman McNeil, vs Buffalo, 1985
Season:	1,331	Freeman McNeil, 1985
Career:	5,320	Freeman McNeil, 1981-86

Passing

Most TD Passes Game:	6	Joe Namath, vs Baltimore, 1972
Season:	26	Al Dorow, 1960
	26	Joe Namath, 1967
Career:	170	Joe Namath, 1965-76

Receiving

Most TD Passes Game:	4	Wesley Walker, vs Miami, 1986
Season:	14	Art Powell, 1960
	14	Don Maynard, 1965
Career:	88	Don Maynard, 1960-72

Scoring

Most Points Game:	19	Jim Turner, vs Buffalo, 1968
	19	Pat Leahy, vs Cincinnati, 1984
Season:	145	Jim Turner, 1968
Career:	993	Pat Leahy, 1974-86
Most TDs Game:	4	Wesley Walker, vs Miami, 1986
Season:	14	Art Powell, 1960
	14	Don Maynard, 1965
	14	Emerson Boozer, 1972
Career:	88	Don Maynard, 1960-72

PITTSBURGH STEELERS

TEAM DIRECTORY: Chairman: Art Rooney; Pres.: Daniel Rooney; VP: John McGinley; VP: Art Rooney Jr.; Dir. Player Personnel: Dick Haley; Bus. Mgr.: Joe Gordon; Dir. Publicity: Dan Edwards; Head Coach: Chuck Noll. Home field: Three Rivers Stadium (59,000). Colors: Black and gold.

SCOUTING REPORT

OFFENSE: High-tech the Steelers ain't, but they proved late in the 1986 season they could grind out some ball-control marches. Once center Mike Webster returned from an elbow injury and guard Craig Wolfley rebounded from a bad knee, the running game, led by Eagle castoff Earnest Jackson and Walter Abercrombie, really took off.

Earnest Jackson just missed 1,000 yards in 13 games.

Jackson wasn't signed until the fourth week, but he finished as the AFC's third-leading rusher with 910 yards and a 4.2 average. Abercrombie gradually regained his strength after a bout with asceptic meningitis to finish fourth with 877 yards and a 4.1 average.

The success of the running game took pressure off Mark Malone, who pressed in the first four games and completed only 40 percent of his passes and threw nine interceptions. But after taking two weeks off with a thumb injury, Malone decided to rely on the running game and low-risk passes and turned around his season. His dump-off passing, however, resulted in the AFC's second-lowest average gain per pass (5.75).

After all the injury problems, the line is now considered one of the team's strength. Tackle Tunch Ilkin, who should get Pro Bowl recognition with another good season, allowed only one sack last year. The entire unit allowed only 20 sacks, second only to Miami.

John Stallworth, 35, and Louis Lipps played in only nine games together because of injuries and combined for only 72 catches and four touchdowns. They'll have to do better or else defenses will simply load up against the run.

DEFENSE: Joe Greene has four Super Bowl rings as a charter member of the Steel Curtain, and he'll use that experience this year in his first season as line coach. Actually, the line was the most improved aspect of the Steeler defense last year, accounting for 30½ of the team's 43 sacks. End Keith Willis led the way with 12 sacks, and 10-year nose tackle Gary Dunn shut down the run after having two knee operations before the season.

This could be the season outside linebacker Bryan Hinkle emerges from Mike Merriweather's shadow. Merriweather made the Pro Bowl for the third straight year, but Hinkle was voted team MVP and was considered the more solid player from the beginning of the season. Defensive coordinator Tony Dungy, who most expect to be the first black head coach in the NFL, unleashed his linebackers in an unusual 3-5 defense and got good results.

The secondary may be improved if cornerback Dwayne Woodruff, who missed the entire season with a knee injury, is able to play up to his previous standards. The Steelers need more big plays from their secondary, and Woodruff is their best cover man. Purdue cornerback Rod Woodson, the Steelers' No. 1 pick, will fight for a job. Lupe Sanchez is looking to break into a starting safety spot. Strong safety Donnie Shell is back for his 13th season.

STEELERS VETERAN ROSTER

HEAD COACH—Chuck Noll. Assistant Coaches—Ron Blackledge, Tony Dungy, Dennis Fitzgerald, Joe Greene, Dick Hoak, Jed Hughes, H?' Hunter, Jon Kolb, Tom Moore.

No.	Name	Pos.	Ht.	Wt.	NFL Exp.	College
34	Abercrombie, Walter	RB	6-0	210	6	Baylor
1	Anderson, Gary	PK	5-11	179	6	Syracuse
15	Baker, Andrew	WR	6-1	195	1	Rutgers
66	Behning, Mark	OT	6-6	285	2	Nebraska
6	Brister, Bubby	QB	6-2	192	2	Northeast Louisiana
88	Britt, Jessie	WR	6-4	200	2	North Carolina A&T
35	Brown, Gordon	RB	5-10½	225	1	Tulsa
91	Carr, Gregg	LB	6-1½	220	3	Auburn
44	Carter, Rodney	RB	5-11½	213	1	Purdue
33	Clayton, Harvey	CB	5-9	186	5	Florida State
56	Cole, Robin	LB	6-2	225	11	New Mexico
67	Dunn, Gary	NT	6-3	275	11	Miami
42	Edwards, Dave	SS	6-0	198	3	Illinois
24	Erenberg, Rich	RB	5-10	205	4	Colgate
92	Gary, Keith	DE	6-3	269	5	Oklahoma
86	Gothard, Preston	TE	6-4	242	3	Alabama
96	Henton, Anthony	LB	6-1	218	2	Troy State
38	Herron, Donald	LB	6-2	225	1	North Carolina State
53	Hinkle, Bryan	LB	6-2	220	6	Oregon
36	Hughes, David	RB	6-0	220	7	Boise State
62	Ilkin, Tunch	OT	6-3	265	8	Indiana State
43	Jackson, Earnest	RB	5-9	202	5	Texas A&M
—	Jones, Bruce	SS	6-1	195	1	North Alabama
—	Kimmel, Jerry	LB	6-2	250	1	Syracuse
83	Lipps, Louis	WR-PR	5-10	185	4	Southern Mississippi
50	Little, David	LB	6-1	242	7	Florida
74	Long, Terry	G	5-11	270	4	East Carolina
16	Malone, Mark	QB	6-4	220	8	Arizona State
84	McCombs, Glenn	TE	6-4	225	1	Central Florida
57	Merriweather, Mike	LB	6-2	215	6	Pacific
64	Nelson, Edmund	DE-DT	6-3	271	4	Auburn
18	Newsome, Harry	P	6-0	186	3	Wake Forest
65	Pinney, Ray	OT	6-4	247	9	Washington
30	Pollard, Frank	RB	5-10	230	8	Baylor
76	Quick, Jerry	OT	6-5	270	1	Wichita State
60	Rasmussen, Randy	C-G	6-1½	254	2	Minnesota
40	Reeder, Dan	RB	5-11	235	2	Delaware
79	Rienstra, John	G	6-4½	275	2	Temple
63	Rostosky, Pete	OT	6-4	265	4	Connecticut
28	Sanchez, Lupe	CB-KR	5-10	192	2	UCLA
45	Sanders, Chuck	RB	6-1	233	2	Slippery Rock
80	Seitz, Warren	TE	6-4	223	2	Missouri
41	Sheffield, Chris	CB	6-1	188	2	Albany State
31	Shell, Donnie	SS	5-11	198	14	South Carolina State
99	Sims, Darryl	DE-DT	6-3	284	3	Wisconsin
82	Stallworth, John	WR	6-2	202	14	Alabama A&M
90	Station, Larry	LB	5-11	232	2	Iowa
26	Swain, John	CB	6-1	200	7	Miami
85	Sweeney, Calvin	WR	6-2	192	8	Southern California
87	Thompson, Weegie	WR	6-6	210	4	Florida State
20	Tucker, Erroll	CB-KR	5-7½	170	1	Utah
52	Webster, Mike	C	6-1½	260	14	Wisconsin
21	Williams, Eric	FS	6-1	190	5	North Carolina State
98	Williams, Gerald	NT	6-3	280	2	Auburn
93	Willis, Keith	DE	6-1	255	6	Northeastern
55	Winston, Dennis	LB	6-0	224	11	Arkansas
73	Wolfley, Craig	G	6-1	268	8	Syracuse
49	Woodruff, Dwayne	CB	6-0	198	8	Louisville
22	Wood, Rick	S-CB	6-1	195	6	Boise State

TOP FIVE DRAFT CHOICES

Rd.	Name	Sel. No.	Pos.	Ht.	Wt.	College
1	Woodson, Rod	10	CB	6-0	195	Purdue
2	Hall, Delton	38	CB	6-1	195	Clemson
3	Lockett, Charles	66	WR	6-0	175	Cal-Long Beach
4	Everett, Tom	94	DB	5-9	177	Baylor
5	Nickerson, Hardy	122	LB	6-2	230	California

KICKING GAME: Kicking field goals is a three-man operation. Gary Anderson, who became the NFL's career percentage leader, suffered through a subpar season as he adjusted to a new holder (punter Harry Newsome) and snapper (Dan Turk in Mike Webster's absence). Several kicks were affected. Newsome had his best punting performance early in the season before tailing off. He finished 10th in the AFC with a 40.1 average. Kick coverage must improve, which is one reason Chuck Noll hired two new special-teams assistants.

THE ROOKIES: The Steelers were shocked when Woodson slipped down to the 10th overall pick. He was the best pure athlete in the draft, running a 4.29 at the scouting combine. He played safety, cornerback, wide receiver, running back and returned kicks. He can also block kicks. The Steelers also drafted two other defensive backs in the first four rounds—Delton Hall of Clemson and Thomas Everett of Baylor.

OUTLOOK: The Steelers closed with five wins in their last nine games, but there still is a gap between them and the Browns and the Bengals, the AFC Central's big boys. Front-office reorganization gave Noll more power. But can he win with Mark Malone and a shaky secondary?

STEELER PROFILES

MARK MALONE 28 6-4 220   Quarterback

Maybe his thumb injury in Week 5 was a blessing in disguise . . . In the first four weeks, a healthy Malone completed 40 percent of his passes for two touchdowns, nine interceptions and a 31.6 rating . . . But in his first three games after returning from the injury, Malone forgot about the home-run ball and went to high-percentage passes. He completed 63.5 percent for seven TDs, one interception and a 105.7 rating . . . "I had to withdraw myself from the situation and say, 'OK, play some smart football,'" Malone said. "Get it to the open guy, regardless of whether it's four yards or 40 yards." . . . Overall, he completed 50.8 percent for 15 TDs and 18 interceptions . . . Born Nov. 22, 1958, in El Cajon, Calif. . . . He was an option quarterback at Arizona State.

EARNEST JACKSON 27 5-9 202   Running Back

You explain it. In 1984, Jackson rushed for 1,179 yards, a Chargers' record, and was dumped for fourth- and eighth-round draft choices . . . In 1985, he became only the third player in Eagles' history to run for 1,000 yards (1,028), but then he was criticized and cut during 1986 training camp by Buddy Ryan . . . Jackson signed with the Steelers as a free agent after the third game and proceeded to pump life into a woeful running attack that was averaging 65 yards a game . . . He finished with 910 yards and a 4.2-yard average and would have had a third consecutive 1,000-yard season had he played in more than 13 games . . . After Jackson arrived, the Steelers averaged about 156 yards rushing a game . . . Born Dec. 18, 1959, in Needville, Tex., and attended Texas A&M . . . Doesn't have breakaway speed, but he's perfect in a quick-trapping offense.

WALTER ABERCROMBIE 27 6-0 210   Running Back

Earnest Jackson wasn't the only one responsible for turning around the Steeler running game . . . Abercrombie was weakened by meningitis before training camp and then sustained a painful hip-pointer in the opener . . . But he recovered gradually, and with Malone more underneath-conscious, he became the team's leading receiver with 47 catches for 395 yards . . . Until Jackson overtook him in the final week, Abercrombie also was the club's leading rusher. He finished fourth in the AFC with 877 yards on 214 carries (4.1-yard average) . . . The Steelers expected a lot when they drafted him No. 1 out of Baylor in 1982, and he may be getting close . . . Born Sept. 26, 1959, in Waco, Tex.

LOUIS LIPPS 25 5-10 185   Wide Receiver

Much of his game-breaking talent was wasted because the Steelers couldn't get him the deep ball . . . Slowed most of the season by a hamstring pull, and he never really came on to hang up the numbers . . . Caught 38 passes for 590 yards and three touchdowns . . . Roughest moment came Nov. 30 against the Bears when he ran in motion and took a vicious forearm to the head from linebacker Otis Wilson. Lipps suffered a concussion, but the officials didn't call a penalty because they didn't see the hit. Wilson sent a letter of apology to Lipps. "I think he showed a lot of class," Lipps said . . . Missed the Pro Bowl for the first time in his three-year career . . . Born Aug. 9, 1962, in New Orleans, and attended Southern Mississippi . . . Scored 26 touchdowns in his first 30 NFL games.

LUPE SANCHEZ 25 5-10 192   Cornerback

One of the season's big surprises . . . Came to the Steelers on waivers from Kansas City and was supposed to be a stop-gap safety because Donnie Shell was hurt. But he went on to lead the AFC in kickoff returns with an average runback of 23.6 yards . . . He also started the last three games at right cornerback for Harvey Clayton and wound up with an interception in each game. He also tipped a fourth theft to Shell . . . He'll be given a chance to win a starting job from the outset in 1987 . . . Born Oct. 28, 1961, in Tulare, Cal., and attended UCLA.

BRYAN HINKLE 28 6-2 220   Linebacker

Mike Merriweather continued to get the recognition—and the Pro Bowl berth—but insiders say Hinkle played better and deserved to go . . . Led the Steelers in tackles, but he didn't do a lot of blitzing, so he doesn't get the sacks . . . When the Steelers used their exotic, 3-5-3 "Press" defense, Hinkle would take the place of the strong safety and cover the tight end man-to-man all over the field . . . Very intelligent and very solid . . . Born June 4, 1959, in Long Beach, Cal. . . . He was a freshman quarterback at Oregon before he switched to linebacker . . . Former Steeler linebacker Jack Ham called Hinkle the club's best defensive player.

MIKE WEBSTER 35 6-1½ 260   Center

Iron Mike finally showed he was human, but not by much . . . His Ironman streak ended at 177 consecutive games, five short of the Steeler record held by Ray Mansfield, when he was on injured reserve for the opener with a dislocated elbow . . . Actually, Mansfield used some craftiness in 1981 to keep his streak alive. He was injured, but he ran onto the field for a kickoff return . . . When Webster returned, however, he was the same dominant player who had earned eight consecutive Pro Bowls through 1985 . . . He graded out at about 90 percent in the last nine weeks. Said strength coach Walt Evans: "He came back after the injury and just dominated people again, just like he did last year." . . . Born March 18, 1952, in Tomahawk, Wis., and attended Wisconsin.

MIKE MERRIWEATHER 26 6-2 215   Linebacker

Merriweather may not have had the season that Hinkle did, but he made the Pro Bowl for the third consecutive season. It was the 17th straight year in which the Steelers had a linebacker in the Pro Bowl, which must be a record . . . May be hard to live up to the year he had in 1984 when he finished third in the AFC with 15 sacks . . . But the Steelers use their outside linebackers in coverage more than most teams . . . The 4.55 speedster has acrobatic flair. Says Hinkle: "Mike's a great player and deserves everything he's gotten. He can fly around the field. He looks great on film." . . . Born Nov. 26, 1960, in St. Albans, N.Y. . . . Steelers got him in the third round of the 1982 draft from the University of Pacific.

WEEGIE THOMPSON 26 6-6 210   Wide Receiver

He can play. The only question is, where? Chuck Noll loves the lanky wide receiver but he was toying with the idea of trying him at tight end in training camp . . . With John Stallworth on injured reserve with a bad knee and Louis Lipps sidelined with a strained back, Thompson started at wide receiver against the Packers in Week 9 and caught three touchdown passes . . . He was used mostly as a third receiver on third downs. Five of his 17 catches went for TDs . . . Tough thing is getting playing time behind Lipps, which is why the move to tight end might make sense. But he'd have to gain a lot of weight . . . Born March 21, 1961, in Pensacola, Fla. . . . He played quarterback in his first two years at Florida State before switching to receiver . . . His real first name is Willis, but his little brother couldn't pronounce it and called him Weegie.

KEITH WILLIS 28 6-1 255   Defensive End

On a team where high-round defensive line-men have been a bust—see Darryl Sims, No. 1 in 1985—Willis has arrived from free-agent obscurity to become its feature pass-rusher . . . Led the Steelers with 12 sacks, the third time in four years he has done that. His sack total also placed him in a tie for fifth in the AFC . . . He comes from the same college, Northeastern, that produced AFC sack leader Sean Jones of the Raiders . . . Has 36½ sacks in his last 58 games . . . Born July 29, 1959, in Newark, N.J. . . . Earned his roster spot in 1982 when Steel Curtain mainstay L.C. Greenwood was waived.

COACH CHUCK NOLL: Another frustrating year for the only

coach to win four Super Bowls . . . The Steelers were decimated by injuries during a 1-6 start, but they actually were playing decent football when they closed out the season 5-4 . . . Took the Bears and the Browns into over-time before losing and manhandled the Jets in the final weeks . . . Consolidated his power when the Steelers made their first front-office shakeup since the late 1960s by ousting long-time player personnel chief Art Rooney Jr., who had been candidly critical of Noll . . . Noll's promotion to director of football operations may indicate he will become the Steelers' general manager when his coaching career is over . . . And who knows when that will be? The Steelers enter 1987 off 7-9 and 6-10 seasons . . . Noll took heat for being the only head coach not to have a special teams assistant on his staff . . . Weak drafts have gotten the Steelers into this predicament, and Noll has the final say on the selections. But Rooney and his scouts were responsible for assembling the information . . . Noll is one of the few head coaches who was a very good player . . . The Dayton grad had a seven-year NFL career, beginning in 1953 in Cleveland, as a linebacker and guard . . . Born Jan. 5, 1932, in Cleveland . . . Has the longest tenure (19 seasons) of any coach in the AFC . . . Among coaches with 100 wins, Noll's postseason record of 15-7 is topped only by Vince Lombardi (9-1) and Weeb Ewbank (4-1).

GREATEST KICKER

Gary Anderson became the NFL's all-time leader in career field-goal accuracy last season—a .771 success rate—but that was the only bright spot in an otherwise frustrating season. Anderson made 21-of-32 field-goal attempts in 1986, but his .656 accuracy rate was far below his .803 mark in four previous seasons with the Steelers.

The two-time Pro Bowl kicker had led the AFC in scoring for three previous seasons, but he slipped to seventh last year with 95 points. That was partly related to the Steelers' impotent offense, which didn't give him many chances early in the season. He also went through several changes in his holder and snapper, and at least five kicks were affected.

Anderson enters 1987 ranked third in career scoring for the Steelers, trailing Roy Gerela (731) and Franco Harris (600). He needs 79 points to move past Harris into second place. He also needs 32 field goals to set a Steeler record in career field goals. He has 115 to Gerela's 146, and that record is within reach because he made 33 field goals in 1985.

Anderson also takes into the season a streak of 153 straight extra points made. His last miss was on Sept. 11, 1983, against Green Bay. Anderson, a native of South Africa, is the son of a former professional soccer player in England.

INDIVIDUAL STEELER RECORDS

Rushing

Most Yards Game:	218	John Fuqua, vs Philadelphia, 1970
Season:	1,246	Franco Harris, 1975
Career:	11,950	Franco Harris, 1972-83

Passing

Most TD Passes Game:	5	Terry Bradshaw, vs Atlanta, 1981
	5	Mark Malone, vs Indianapolis, 1985
Season:	28	Terry Bradshaw, 1978
Career:	210	Terry Bradshaw, 1970-82

Receiving

Most TD Passes Game:	4	Roy Jefferson, vs Atlanta, 1968
Season:	12	Buddy Dial, 1961
	12	Louis Lipps, 1985
Career:	61	John Stallworth, 1974-86

Scoring

Most Points Game:	24	Ray Mathews, vs Cleveland, 1954
	24	Roy Jefferson, vs Atlanta, 1968
Season:	139	Gary Anderson, 1985
Career:	731	Roy Gerela, 1971-78
Most TDs Game:	4	Ray Mathews, vs Cleveland, 1954
	4	Roy Jefferson, vs Atlanta, 1968
Season:	14	Franco Harris, 1976
Career:	100	Franco Harris, 1972-83

SAN DIEGO CHARGERS

TEAM DIRECTORY: Owner/Chairman of Board: Alex G. Spanos; Dir. of Administration: Jack Teele; Dir. Football Operations: Steve Ortmayer; Asst. Dir. Football Operations: John Sanders; Dir. Pub. Rel.: Rick Smith; Head Coach: Al Saunders. Home field: San Diego Jack Murphy Stadium (60,100). Colors: Blue, white and gold.

Billy Ray Smith has soared with his sacks—11 in '86.

SCOUTING REPORT

OFFENSE: The remnants of Air Coryell are still in the hangar, but new Charger coach Al Saunders wants to add some ground artillery to his arsenal. Saunders, who took over for Don Coryell after a 1-7 start, says he'll stay with Coryell's pass-oriented philosophy, but he wants to see better balance in an offense that finished 24th in rushing and seventh in passing.

"Our philosophy in the last several years has been, if we didn't score 35 points our chances of winning were not very good," Saunders says. "We felt we had to get the ball into the end zone every possession. But I'd hope we wouldn't be that daring offensively."

Gary Anderson led the Chargers with 442 yards rushing, but he was used more as a receiver and he's too light at 182 pounds to be considered an every-down back. Lionel James, Buford McGee, Curtis Adams and Tim Spencer are solid but are coming off an injury-filled season.

Saunders won't stray too far from Dan Fouts, 36, who no longer can gun the ball deep but adjusted well to the new ball-control passing offense. The future Hall of Famer is entering his 14th season, and he took his lumps last year with two concussions and a broken nose. But wide receiver Wes Chandler and tight end Kellen Winslow are still outstanding targets and the line is solid. Top draft choice Rod Bernstine of Texas A&M adds depth at tight end.

DEFENSE: New defensive coordinator Ron Lynn's goal was to institute a penetrating, pressure-oriented defense, and he succeeded to some extent. Rookie defensive end Leslie O'Neal recorded 12½ sacks until he tore up his knee late in the season. Adding pop to the pass rush was end Lee Williams, who tied for second in the AFC with 15 sacks, and Billy Ray Smith, who had 11. The Chargers finished with 62 sacks, second only to the Raiders in the NFL, but O'Neal's injury means they may have to look again for another lineman.

The Chargers gave up more points (396) than anyone in the AFC except the Dolphins and the Colts, but they were respectable in stopping the run. They ranked 24th in the NFL against the pass and gave up far too many big plays. There are crying needs at linebacker and in the secondary, although safety Vencie Glenn and cornerback Daniel Hunter were pleasant surprises. Chip Banks, obtained from Cleveland on draft day, should lend immediate help at one linebacker spot.

If Saunders wants 35 points on offense to hold up, he'll have to keep making improvements.

CHARGERS VETERAN ROSTER

HEAD COACH—Al Saunders. Assistant Coaches—Gunther Cunningham, Mike Haluchak, Bobby Jackson, Charlie Joiner, Dave Levy, Ron Lynn, Wayne Sevier, Roger Theder, Ed White.

No.	Name	Pos.	Ht.	Wt.	NFL Exp.	College
42	Adams, Curtis	RB	6-1	194	2	Central Michigan
56	Allert, Ty	LB	6-2	233	2	Texas
40	Anderson, Gary	RB	6-0	182	3	Arkansas
—	Banks, Chip	LB	6-4	233	6	Southern California
6	Benirschke, Rolf	K	6-1	183	10	Cal-Davis
57	Benson, Thomas	LB	6-2	235	4	Oklahoma
22	Byrd, Gill	S	5-11	194	5	San Jose State
89	Chandler, Wes	WR	6-0	182	10	Florida
77	Claphan, Sam	T	6-6	288	7	Oklahoma
37	Dale, Jeff	S	6-3	213	3	Louisiana State
61	Dallafior, Ken	G	6-4	277	3	Minnesota
20	Davis, Wayne	CB	5-11	175	3	Indiana State
75	DiGiacomo, Curt	G	6-4	275	2	Arizona
78	Ehin, Chuck	NT	6-4	257	5	Brigham Young
52	Fellows, Mark	RB	6-1	233	1	Montana State
70	FitzPatrick, James	T	6-7½	295	2	Southern California
12	Flick, Tom	QB	6-3	191	4	Washington
14	Fouts, Dan	QB	6-3	208	15	Oregon
25	Glenn, Vencie	S	6-0	183	2	Indiana State
92	Hardison, Dee	DE	6-4	274	10	North Carolina
59	Hawkins, Andy	LB	6-2	230	6	Texas A&I
29	Hendy, John	CB	5-11	199	2	Long Beach State
9	Herrmann, Mark	QB	6-4	199	7	Purdue
88	Holohan, Pete	TE	6-4	232	7	Notre Dame
27	Hunter, Daniel	CB	5-11	180	3	Henderson State (Ark.)
26	James, Lionel	RB-KR	5-6	170	4	Auburn
83	Johnson, Trumaine	WR	6-1	191	3	Grambling
68	Kowalski, Gary	G-T	6-6	280	4	Boston College
74	Lachey, Jim	T	6-6½	287	3	Ohio State
63	Leonard, Jim	C-G	6-3	270	7	Santa Clara
51	Lowe, Woodrow	LB	6-1	229	12	Alabama
62	Macek, Don	C	6-2	270	12	Boston College
21	McGee, Buford	RB	6-0	206	4	Mississippi
60	McKnight, Dennis	C-G	6-3½	270	6	Drake
2	Mojsiejenko, Rolf	P-K	6-2½	210	3	Michigan State
90	Moore, Mack	DE	6-4	258	3	Texas A&M
87	Moore, Malcolm	TE	6-3½	236	1	Southern California
55	Nelson, Derrie	ILB	6-2	239	5	Nebraska
91	O'Neal, Leslie	DE	6-4	251	2	Oklahoma State
50	Plummer, Gary	ILB	6-2	230	2	California
—	Powell, Jeff	WR	5-10	185	1	Tennessee
—	Rome, Tag	WR	5-9	175	1	Northeast Louisiana
—	Shepherd, Larry	WR	6-3	204	1	Houston
85	Sievers, Eric	TE	6-4	235	7	Maryland
97	Simmons, Tony	DE	6-4½	268	2	Tennessee
54	Smith, Billy Ray	OLB	6-3	233	5	Arkansas
—	Smith, Tim	WR	6-2	206	8	Nebraska
52	Snipes, Angelo	OLB	6-0	215	2	West Georgia
43	Spencer, Tim	FB	6-1½	227	3	Ohio State
33	Sullivan, John L	CB-S	6-1	190	2	California
24	Taylor, Ken	CB	6-1	186	3	Oregon State
98	Unrein, Terry	NT	6-5	283	2	Colorado State
72	Walker, Jeff	G	6-4½	295	2	Memphis State
23	Walters, Danny	CB	6-1½	190	4	Arkansas
81	Ware, Timmie	WR	5-10	171	2	Southern California
99	Williams, Lee	DE	6-5½	263	4	Bethune-Cookman
93	Wilson, Earl	DE	6-4	280	3	Kentucky
80	Winslow, Kellen	TE	6-5½	242	9	Missouri
96	Winter, Blaise	DE	6-3	274	3	Syracuse
30	Wyatt, Kevin	CB	5-10	190	2	Arkansas

TOP FIVE DRAFT CHOICES

Rd.	Name	Sel. No.	Pos.	Ht.	Wt.	College
1	Bernstine, Rod	24	TE	6-3	247	Texas A&M
2	Brock, Louis	53	CB	5-11	165	USC
3	Wilson, Karl	59	DE	6-4	251	Louisiana State
4	Vlasic, Mark	89	QB	6-3	206	Iowa
5	Jones, Nelson	115	DB	6-0	190	NC State

KICKING GAME: Rolf Benirschke suffered through a tough year, and the toughest moment probably came in 42-41 loss to the Chiefs that hastened Coryell's departure. Benirschke's 35-yard field-goal try sailed wide in the final seconds. Punter Ralf Mojsiejenko, a left-footer, averaged 42 yards a kick and also served as the Chargers' kickoff man.

THE ROOKIES: With the 24th overall pick, the Chargers took Bernstine, a sure-handed clutch receiver who has added weight and strength every year. They may have stolen USC cornerback Lou Brock Jr. in the second round and they added LSU defensive end Karl Wilson in the third as pass-rushing insurance in case O'Neal can't return.

OUTLOOK: Owner Alex Spanos is in no mood to wait for the Chargers to become a playoff contender. "The eight weeks after the Miami game to open the season (all losses) were the most miserable in my life," Spanos said. "You can't believe what a big fan I am, or what those weeks did to me." Unfortunately, the wait for a winner could be long. If O'Neal doesn't return in good shape, the defense loses a dominant pass rusher. The Chargers can't afford that. The defense is suspect.

CHARGER PROFILES

DAN FOUTS 36 6-3 208   Quarterback

At this stage in his career, Fouts is adjusting to his slowing fastball. He no longer can throw the home-run but he's the master of rhythm passing... In the first half of 1986 he threw 19 interceptions and nine TD passes, but he rallied in the second half when Al Saunders stripped down the offense and went to a high-percentage, ball-control attack... Overall, Fouts completed 252 of 430 passes (58.6 percent) for 3,031 yards and 16 TDs, with 22 interceptions... Moved past Johnny Unitas into second place in career passing yardage with 40,523 yards. Fran Tarkenton (47,003) is No. 1... Biggest concern is his health. Suffered concussions against the Raiders and the Chiefs, which is the kind of thing that convinced Roger Staubach to hang it up... Born June 10, 1951, in San Francisco, and attended Oregon.

WES CHANDLER 31 6-0 182   Wide Receiver

By the standards he set in 1985, last year was a lukewarm season... Caught 56 passes for 874 yards (15.6-yard average) and four touchdowns, but he seemed to sulk when he wasn't getting the ball enough... He's still the class of the Charger wide receivers, although he was bothered by a foot injury in 1986... Had his best season a year earlier when he caught 67 passes for 1,199 yards and 10 TDs and earned his fourth Pro Bowl berth... Showed his versatility by punting twice (for a 36.5 average) for the first time in his career against the Cowboys ... Born Aug. 22, 1956, in New Smyrna Beach, Fla., and attended Florida... Drafted No. 1 by the Saints in 1978, but Bum Phillips didn't care for his aloofness and traded him in 1981.

GARY ANDERSON 26 6-0 182   Running Back

In the Chargers' offense, Anderson is a hybrid running back/wide receiver, and he's a rare species indeed... Finished fourth in the AFC with 80 catches—most of them on swing passes—for 871 yards and eight TDs... Also ran 127 times for 442 yards and one score... His 1,313 yards in total offense placed him fourth in the AFC behind Seattle's Curt Warner (1,823), Cincinnati's James Brooks (1,773) and New England's Stanley Morgan (1,491)... He's not an every-down player, but he can stretch a defense... Split out more as a receiver in second half of season... Born April 18, 1961, in Columbia, Mo., and attended Arkansas... Rushed for 2,731 yards and caught 167 passes in three seasons with Tampa Bay in the USFL.

LEE WILLIAMS 24 6-5½ 263   Defensive End

Continued his meteoric rise as one of the NFL's best young pass-rushers... Recorded 15 sacks, tying him with Buffalo's Bruce Smith for second place in the AFC behind the Raiders' Sean Jones with 15½... The addition of rookie Leslie O'Neal at right end helped him tremendously, because teams couldn't stack their blocking schemes to stop him... He was signed out of Bethune-Cookman in 1984 by the Los Angeles Express and then joined the Chargers later in the year. By the end of those 16 months, his body could have been donated to medical science... Born Oct. 15, 1962, in Ft. Lauderdale, Fla.... Proved in 1985 what a year of rest could do. Deflected a pass and ran 66 yards for a TD against the Bears... Runs a 4.7.

CHIP BANKS 27 6-4 233 — Linebacker

Will Chip Banks finally find happiness as a Charger?... He's back in southern California (USC is his alma mater) after five years with the Browns... In '85 he bucked a trade to Buffalo and he sat out the summer of '86 before signing a two-year deal that was to pay him $700,000 this season... He was a force, as usual, finishing second on the team in tackles (119) and recording 4½ sacks... The third player selected in 1982... Came to San Diego on draft day when Browns traded him and first- and second-round choices for Chargers' first- and second-round picks... Born Sept. 18, 1959, in Ft. Lawton, Okla.

BILLY RAY SMITH 26 6-3 233 — Linebacker

Thrived when aggressive defensive coordinator Ron Lynn moved him from inside to outside linebacker—his college position... The former No. 1 pick from Arkansas showed great blitzing ability on the left side, and he finished with 11 sacks. That's more than Smith had in his first three seasons combined, but he was left off the Pro Bowl team... Says linebacker coach Mike Haluchak: "On the outside you're looking for a player who can rush and cover. Billy's got the abilities." ... Now he's found a home. "It's kind of like riding a bicycle," Smith says... Born Aug. 10, 1961, in Fayetteville, Ark.... His father, Billy Ray, Sr., was a 14-year NFL player and All-Pro with the Colts.

LESLIE O'NEAL 23 6-4 251 — Defensive End

One of the tragedies of the 1986 season occurred when O'Neal tore up his knee in a Week 13 win over the Colts... The No. 1 pick out of Oklahoma State was leading the AFC with 12½ sacks at the time of the non-contact injury, but now even a return for the 1987 season is in jeopardy... O'Neal tore the anterior cruciate and medial collateral ligaments, an injury similar to one that kept Kellen Winslow out for a year . . . Most frustrating thing is O'Neal wasn't wearing a knee brace for the first time. "You can't force anybody to wear a piece of protective material," said Al Saunders, "but they are encouraged to wear it." . . . Several teams had passed on O'Neal in the draft because they felt his knees were questionable . . . Born May 7, 1964, in Pulaski County, Ark.

KELLEN WINSLOW 29 6-5½ 242   Tight End

He may not be the Winslow of old, but he showed in the second half of last year that he can still be a force . . . After openly complaining about not getting the ball enough, he became a major target of Dan Fouts once again. He finished the season with 64 catches, the most since he sustained a severe knee injury midway through 1984 . . . The Chargers feel Winslow can become a dominant player again, although he's not as fearless in the open field . . . He's been struggling to regain the form that allowed him to catch 374 passes in 64 games (an average of six a game) from 1980-84. He is a playwright, and he entitled his first work *Struggle*. It is not autobiographical . . . Born Nov. 5, 1957, in St. Louis, Mo., and was an All-American at Missouri.

VENCIE GLENN 22 6-0 183   Free Safety

The Chargers were in a bind when free safety Danny Walters ruptured his Achilles tendon in the second week. They helped themselves immensely by trading a fifth-round pick to New England for Glenn, the Indiana State rookie the Pats had drafted in the second round . . . Glenn helped solidify the secondary and showed good leadership . . . He had 17 career interceptions in college and breaks well on the ball . . . His dentist worked overtime after a game against the Cowboys in Week 12. His face was mashed against his facemask as he lay on the turf. The blow broke Glenn's jaw, knocked loose five teeth and required eight stitches to close cuts on the lips . . . Born Oct. 26, 1964, in Terre Haute, Ind.

JIM LACHEY 24 6-6½ 287   Tackle

May be one of the Chargers' top three players ... The massive left tackle stepped in as a starter in his rookie season and then continued to improve last year ... The only question about the No. 1 pick out of Ohio State was deciding if he was a guard or a tackle, and the Chargers apparently made the right decision ... He's a rock. All he needs to become a consistent Pro Bowler is more experience in pass-blocking. He was a polished run-blocker from the start ... Born June 4, 1963, in St. Henry, Ohio ... Pronounced Lah-SHAY ... He was the fifth lineman taken in the 1985 draft, but only Atlanta's Bill Fralic is his equal.

JAMES FITZPATRICK 23 6-7½ 295   Tackle

The Chargers like their tackles big, but not *this* big ... FitzPatrick, the No. 1 pick from USC in 1986, was grossly overweight and finished the season on injured reserve ... The Chargers had him on an intensive weight training and conditioning program, and by the end of the season he had lost 25 pounds from his early-season weight of 312 pounds ... He would be a great bookend to complement Lachey if he can come through. Says FitzPatrick: "I know the coaches can't trust me because I came in here out of shape, but I am going to be in the best shape possible [in 1987]" ... Born Feb. 1, 1964, in Heidelberg, Germany.

COACH AL SAUNDERS:

Got his first head-coaching shot when Don Coryell "resigned" following a 1-7 start ... But cards were on the table much earlier. Charger owner Alex Spanos rarely spoke to Coryell, preferring to do his communicating through Saunders, whom he had named assistant head coach after the 1985 season ... Saunders, who doubled as the receivers coach, went 3-5 in the second half of the season as he re-tooled the offense to cut down on turnovers . . . Saunders has a five-year contract and left little doubt about who was in control: "I am the spokesman for this team. Me. I don't want 15 guys going in 15 different directions." . . . Served as a Charger assistant for four years after arriving in 1983 from Tennessee, where he was offensive coordinator and quarterback coach . . . Was an academic All-American defensive back at San Jose State and began his coaching career as a graduate assistant at USC in 1970 . . . Tried to restore discipline to the Chargers. When he speaks to the team, his players must kneel on one knee . . . Born Feb. 1, 1947, in London, England . . . His priorities with the Chargers are to improve the defense, special teams and running game. Sounds like a tall order.

GREATEST KICKER

There are few stories more uplifting than that of a person overcoming physical adversity, and Rolf Benirschke is a glowing tribute to the human spirit. During the 1978 season, he began experiencing stomach discomfort which doctors diagnosed as Crohn's Disease.

The pain returned in 1979, causing him to lose weight and strength, yet he still made all four field goals he attempted in a 33-16 opening-game victory over Seattle. His condition deteriorated until he was placed in a hospital less than a month later and almost died of complications after surgery to remove part of his colon.

His weight dropped from 174 pounds to 123, but he returned to visit his teammates late in the season and walked to midfield for the coin toss before a game against the Steelers. His comeback in 1980 was nothing short of amazing. He made 24-of-36 field-goal attempts, including a 53-yarder, and scored a career-high 118 points. The NFL Players Association named him "Hero of the Year" and the Philadelphia Sports Writers' Association named him "Most Courageous Athlete" in 1980.

In 1982, doctors at Mt. Sinai Hospital in New York determined that Benirschke has been suffering from ulcerative colitis and not Crohn's Disease, which means his medical prognosis is good.

The Chargers picked up Benirschke on waivers from the Raiders in 1977, and the Cal-Davis graduate took over for Toni Fritsch.

INDIVIDUAL CHARGER RECORDS

Rushing

Most Yards Game:	206	Keith Lincoln, vs Boston, 1964
Season:	1,179	Earnest Jackson, 1984
Career:	4,963	Paul Lowe, 1960-67

Passing

Most TD Passes Game:	6	Dan Fouts, vs Oakland, 1981
Season:	33	Dan Fouts, 1981
Career:	244	Dan Fouts, 1973-86

Receiving

Most TD Passes Game:	5	Kellen Winslow, vs Oakland, 1981
Season:	14	Lance Alworth, 1965
Career:	81	Lance Alworth, 1962-70

Scoring

Most Points Game:	30	Kellen Winslow, vs Oakland, 1981
Season:	118	Rolf Benirschke, 1980
Career:	766	Rolf Benirschke, 1977-86
Most TDs Game:	5	Kellen Winslow, vs Oakland, 1981
Season:	19	Chuck Muncie, 1981
Career:	83	Lance Alworth, 1962-70

SEATTLE SEAHAWKS

TEAM DIRECTORY: Pres./GM: Mike McCormack; Asst. GM: Chuck Allen; Dir. Player Personnel: Mike Allman; Dir. Pub. Rel.: Gary Wright; Head Coach: Chuck Knox. Home field: Kingdome (64,757). Colors: Blue, green and silver.

SCOUTING REPORT

OFFENSE: Funny thing about Dave Krieg. Everybody wants to keep burying him, but the former free agent from Milton College keeps digging himself out of the deepest holes. Maybe this time he can enjoy the fruits of success. Krieg bounced back from a

Curt Warner's 1,481 yards topped AFC rushers.

midseason benching and persistent rumors he would be replaced by sparking a late five-game winning streak that fell just short of the playoffs.

Krieg gambled on a one-year contract before the 1986 season, hoping a good year would create a heavy demand for his services. His plan almost backfired. He sat while Gale Gilbert quarterbacked Seattle to two losses and then looked awful in a relief appearance against Kansas City. But Chuck Knox said he had a gut feeling and gave the starting job back to Krieg the following week. Krieg threw for 11 touchdowns and only one interception in the streak, and only Dan Marino was a hotter quarterback in December.

If Krieg stays on track, the Seahawks will be tough to beat in the AFC West. That's because Ground Chuck is alive and kicking with Curt Warner, the AFC leader in rushing and total yardage, and blockbuster fullback John L. Williams.

Steve Largent is moving closer to NFL career records with each catch, and hasn't skipped a beat. Wide receiver Daryl Turner was plagued by dropped passes.

Knox had expressed some interest in Vinny Testaverde before the draft, but Krieg's late-season surge may have convinced him Krieg can take the Seahawks to the playoffs.

DEFENSE: End Jacob Green had a Pro Bowl season with 12 sacks, but the Seahawks were hurt by ineffective play at nose tackle. Joe Nash was affected by a preseason ankle injury, and he was benched later in the season. Jeff Bryant, the other end, suffered through ankle and shoulder injuries. The Seahawks don't like to blitz, and they were frequently burned by quarterbacks who ran away from the pressure and completed scoring passes.

Strong safety Ken Easley manifested a high threshold for pain. He was bothered by knee and ankle injuries all season, but he didn't go on injured reserve until he collapsed in the bathroom after a game. Easley underwent surgery to remove two large bone spurs from his ankle, and he should be completely healthy. Ironically, the Seahawks were 6-0 in the games Easley missed and was replaced by Paul Moyer.

Inside linebacker Fredd Young made his third straight Pro Bowl, but this was the first time he merited attention for something other than his outstanding special teams play. Knox is looking for more depth at linebacker—thus the selection of Pitt's Tony Woods as the team's No. 1 pick.

In the secondary, rookie corner Patrick Hunter showed enough that he will push veteran Dave Brown for a starting job. Brown had five interceptions last year but had a tough year. The Sea-

SEAHAWKS VETERAN ROSTER

HEAD COACH—Chuck Knox. Assistant Coaches—Tom Catlin, George Dyer, Chick Harris, Ralph Hawkins, Ken Meyer, Steve Moore, Russ Purnell, Kent Stephenson, Rusty Tillman, Joe Vitt.

No.	Name	Pos.	Ht.	Wt.	NFL Exp.	College
2	Gamache, Vince	P	5-11	176	2	Cal-Fullerton
7	Gilbert, Gale	QB	6-3	206	3	California
8	Salisbury, Sean	QB	6-5	215	1	Southern California
9	Johnson, Norm	K	6-2	198	6	UCLA
17	Krieg, Dave	QB	6-1	196	8	Milton
20	Taylor, Terry	CB	5-10	191	4	Southern Illinois
21	Moyer, Paul	S	6-1	203	5	Arizona State
22	Brown, Dave	CB	6-1	197	13	Michigan
23	Hunter, Patrick	CB	5-11	185	2	Nevada-Reno
26	Justin, Kerry	CB	5-11	175	7	Oregon State
27	Johnson, Greggory	S	6-1	195	5	Oklahoma State
28	Warner, Curt	RB	5-11	204	4	Penn State
30	Edmonds, Bobby Joe	RB	5-11	186	2	Arkansas
32	Williams, John L.	FB	5-11	226	2	Florida
37	Lane, Eric	FB	6-0	201	7	Brigham Young
41	Robinson, Eugene	S	6-0	186	3	Colgate
43	Morris, Randall	RB	6-0	200	4	Tennessee
45	Easley, Kenny	S	6-3	206	7	UCLA
47	Anderson, Eddie	S	6-1	199	2	Fort Valley State
50	Young, Fredd	LB	6-1	233	4	New Mexico State
51	Merriman, Sam	LB	6-3	232	5	Idaho
52	Grant, Will	C	6-3	268	10	Kentucky
53	Butler, Keith	LB	6-4	239	10	Memphis State
54	Kaiser, John	LB	6-3	233	4	Arizona
56	Gaines, Greg	LB	6-3	222	6	Tennessee
58	Scholtz, Bruce	LB	6-6	244	6	Texas
59	Bush, Blair	C	6-3	272	10	Washington
60	Hyde, Glenn	C	6-3	255	10	Pittsburgh
61	Mitz, Alonzo	DE	6-3	275	2	Florida
62	Kauahi, Kani	C	6-2	261	6	Hawaii
63	Kinlaw, Reggie	NT	6-2	249	8	Oklahoma
64	Essink, Ron	T	6-6	282	6	Grand Valley St.
65	Bailey, Edwin	G	6-4	276	7	South Carolina State
66	Eisenhooth, Stan	C	6-5	278	1	Towson State
68	Edwards, Randy	DE	6-4	267	4	Alabama
70	Mattes, Ron	T	6-6	306	2	Virginia
71	Millard, Bryan	G	6-5	284	4	Texas
72	Nash, Joe	NT	6-2	257	6	Boston College
73	Powell, Alvin	G	6-5	296	1	Winston-Salem
74	Singer, Curt	T	6-5	279	2	Tennessee
75	Wilson, Mike	T	6-5	280	10	Georgia
76	Borchardt, Jon	G	6-5	272	9	Montana State
77	Bryant, Jeff	DE	6-5	272	6	Clemson
79	Green, Jacob	DE	6-3	252	8	Texas A&M
80	Largent, Steve	WR	5-11	191	12	Tulsa
81	Turner, Daryl	WR	6-3	194	4	Michigan State
82	Skansi, Paul	WR	5-11	183	5	Washington
83	Butler, Ray	WR	6-3	206	8	Southern California
84	Greene, Danny	WR	5-11	190	2	Washington
85	Hudson, Gordon	TE	6-4	241	2	Brigham Young
86	Tice, Mike	TE	6-7	247	7	Maryland
87	Davis, Tony	TE	6-5	239	1	Missouri
88	Franklin, Byron	WR	6-1	183	4	Auburn
89	Walker, Byron	WR	6-4	188	6	Citadel
94	Graves, Rory	T	6-6	290	1	Ohio State
—	Kemp, Jeff	QB	6-0	201	6	Dartmouth

TOP FIVE DRAFT CHOICES

Rd.	Name	Sel. No.	Pos.	Ht.	Wt.	College
1	Woods, Tony	18	DE	6-4	244	Pittsburgh
2	Wyman, David	45	LB	6-2	229	Stanford
4	Moore, Mark	104	DB	6-0	194	Oklahoma State
5	Agee, Tommie	119	RB	5-11	211	Auburn
5	Rodriguez, Ruben	131	P	6-2	220	Arizona

hawks also may consider shifting Easley from strong to free safety, leaving Moyer and Eugene Robinson to fight it out for the strong safety job.

KICKING GAME: Rusty Tillman's special teams always are something special. Rookie Bobby Joe Edmonds became one of the top kick-returners in the NFL. Kicker Norm Johnson, who finished second to New England's Tony Franklin with 108 points, had an unusually streaky season, but he's solid. Punter Vince Gamache will be given a lot of competition after finishing 12th in the AFC with a paltry average of 38.6. That's terrible inside a dome.

THE ROOKIES: Chuck Knox honed in on defense, taking two linebackers—Stanford's Dave Wyman in addition to Woods—and safety Mark Moore of Oklahoma State in the first three rounds. Wyman played well after returning from a serious knee injury, but the injury dropped him from a first-rounder to the 45th pick. Moore is a heavy hitter but not especially quick. The Seahawks also picked up blocking fullback Tommie Agee of Auburn in the fifth round.

OUTLOOK: The 10-6 Seahawks were playing perhaps the best football in the AFC at the end of the season, but their four-game losing streak in the middle of the season cost them a wild-card playoff spot. The key always seems to be Krieg, who may not be talented enough to carry a team through a slump but can operate when things are going well. Maybe this year the good vibes will carry over.

SEAHAWK PROFILES

STEVE LARGENT 32 5-11 191   **Wide Receiver**

 We're talking Hall-of-Fame numbers here... The classiest receiver in football extended his NFL-record streak of catching at least one pass to 139 consecutive games...Those numbers are only the beginning. He enters 1987 No. 2 all-time in career receptions (694) and needs 57 to pass Charlie Joiner (750) for No. 1. He ranks No. 3 all-time in career yardage (11,129) and needs 1,018 to pass Joiner (12,146) for No. 1. Those goals are reachable this season...The amazing thing

about Largent is that he has done all this without a franchise quarterback. Jim Zorn and Dave Krieg were both free agents . . . Largent established another NFL record last year with his seventh 1,000-yard season, breaking a tie with Lance Alworth. He caught 70 passes for 1070 yards and nine TDs . . . Born Sept. 28, 1954, in Tulsa, Okla, and attended Tulsa . . . Bum Phillips cut him from the Oilers, maybe the worst personnel decision in NFL history.

CURT WARNER 26 5-11 205   Running Back

There were two new weapons in Warner's incredible offensive arsenal last year: blocking fullback John L. Williams and a full season of health . . . The Seahawks' all-time leading rusher buried his competition for the AFC rushing crown with 1,481 yards, nearly 400 more than Cincinnati's James Brooks (1,087) . . . His 1,823 total yards also topped the AFC and put him second in the NFL to the Rams' Eric Dickerson (2,026) . . . He finished the season galloping for 192 yards in a 41-16 rout of the Broncos. It was his seventh 100-yard game of the season, another Seattle record . . . Warner also scored 13 rushing TDs to finish just behind Denver's Sammy Winder (14) in scoring . . . The former Penn State All-American has made a remarkable recovery from a severe 1984 knee injury . . . Born Mar. 18, 1961, in Wyoming, W.Va.

DAVE KRIEG 28 6-1 196   Quarterback

These things usually are explained only by biorhythms or the position of the stars. Krieg's return from oblivion surpassed even his streaky nature . . . Chuck Knox benched him for two weeks, but he returned to become the hottest quarterback in the NFL as the Seahawks closed out with five consecutive wins . . . Threw for 11 TDs and only one interception in the winning streak while compiling 132.0 rating . . . Eight weeks after he was benched, he was the NFL's third-rated passer behind Dan Marino and Tommy Kramer . . . For the season, he completed 225 of 375 passes (60.0 percent) for 2,921 yards and 21 TDs, with 11 interceptions . . . Offensive coordinator Steve Moore said of Krieg: "Something just clicked." He thinks it will last . . . Born Oct. 20, 1958, in Iola, Wis., and is the only NFL quarterback whose alma mater, Milton College, went out of business.

JOHN L. WILLIAMS 22 5-11 225   Fullback

John L. is quite a heavyweight...Any team that runs successfully from the I needs a great lead blocker, and the No. 1 pick out of Florida did that and more for Curt Warner...Rushed for 538 yards on 129 carries, an excellent 4.2-yard average...But his wipe-out blocks were the real story, opening huge holes for Warner..."He did everything we asked him to do," said Chuck Knox...Two vintage blocks came late in the season. He slammed into Raider linebacker Matt Millen and knocked him woozy. Against Dallas, he hit safety Bill Bates so hard that Bates' mouthpiece flew out—just like it does at a prize-fight. John L. is a good name after all...Born Nov. 23, 1964, in Palatka, Fla.

BOBBY JOE EDMONDS 22 5-11 183   Kick Returner

On a team that emphasizes special teams play, the rookie from Arkansas made the Pro Bowl as the AFC's best return specialist...Led the entire NFL in returning punts, motoring 12.3 yards every time he touched the ball... He also finished sixth in the AFC on kickoff returns, averaging 22.5 yards on 34 tries... The Seahawks also tried to use his big-play ability when they went to a four-wide receiver set...Special teams coach Rusty Tillman, who worked out Edmonds before the draft, said he was "flabbergasted" by his quickness and running ability...The fifth-round pick has 4.45 speed and great acceleration and he also has sure hands...Born Sept. 26, 1964, in St. Louis.

JACOB GREEN 30 6-3 257   Defensive End

Finally made the Pro Bowl after years of coming close...Finished sixth in the AFC with 12 sacks, which was 1½ fewer than he had in 1985...He has been one of the most consistent pass-rushers in the NFL, as his four consecutive seasons with at least 10 sacks will attest...His best game came in Week 12 against Philadelphia when he had three sacks ...He's always been a big-play man. In 1985 he returned a fumble 79 yards for a TD against the Jets and an interception 19 yards for a score against the Saints...Born Jan. 21, 1957, in

Pasadena, Tex., and attended Texas A&M . . . Has 58 sacks in his last 73 games.

KEN EASLEY 28 6-3 206   Strong Safety

It was a year of suffering for the perennial Pro Bowler . . . Underwent arthroscopic surgery to remove loose cartilage in his right knee and almost played six days later . . . He hurt the knee in the opener against Pittsburgh when he was leg-whipped on a blitz, and it finally gave out the day after he played the Raiders in Week 6 . . . Easley also had recurring pain in his left ankle. But that problem should be cleared up because he had bone chips removed from the ankle . . . Strange but true: the Seahawks won all six games he missed . . . The four-time Pro Bowler led the NFL in interceptions in 1984 with 10 . . . Born Jan. 15, 1959, in Chesapeake, Va., and was a three-time All-American at UCLA . . . He's a low-handicap golfer who usually gets up at dawn during training camp to play nine holes before two-a-day practices begin.

PATRICK HUNTER 23 5-11 185   Cornerback

Veteran Dave Brown had five interceptions at right cornerback last year, but Hunter showed signs that he will push him for a starting job . . . The second-round pick from Nevada-Reno had extensive man-to-man coverage responsibilities in the pass-oriented Big Sky Conference, which is why the Seahawk scouts liked him . . . He can also return kickoffs in a pinch, but Bobby Joe Edmonds fills that bill for the Seahawks . . . Born Oct. 24, 1963, in San Francisco . . . Chuck Knox is counting on him to be part of a revamped secondary . . . Was a first-team Division 1-AA All American as a senior.

PAUL MOYER 26 6-1 201   Strong Safety

When Ken Easley went down with injuries, the former free agent from Arizona State stepped in and more than held his own . . . Easley may move to free safety to free him from man-to-man coverage responsibilities, and that would put Moyer in competition with free safety Eugene Robinson and Eddie Anderson for the starting strong safety spot . . .

Moyer also is no stranger to pain. He played half of the Denver game in Week 8 with a ruptured testicle...Made an important sack of Giant quarterback Phil Simms in Week 7, which was the last time New York lost in 1986...Born July 26, 1961, in Villa Park, Cal.

FREDD YOUNG 25 6-1 233   Linebacker

OK, quick. How many Pro Bowls has Young been to? If you said three, you deserve Seahawk season tickets because not many outside of Seattle know of Young's ability...Young made the Pro Bowl in 1984 and 1985 as one of the premier special teams performers in the league. Last year he made it on front-line merit as a starting inside linebacker...Led the Seahawks with 121 tackles, 22 more than free safety Eugene Robinson...Also led the club in tackles in 1985...The third-rounder out of New Mexico State opened his NFL career in 1984 by blocking a punt, forcing a fumble and making four tackles inside the 20 on kickoff coverage against Cleveland...Born Nov. 14, 1961, in Dallas.

COACH CHUCK KNOX: Seahawks could have disintegrated

after mysterious four-game losing streak in the middle of the season, but Knox steadied the course and finished with five straight wins to barely miss the playoffs...They probably were the hottest team in the AFC at the end of the year, crushing Super Bowl finalist Denver, 41-16, in the final week...Toughness of character is no surprise in a Knox team. He's the only coach in NFL history to take three different teams to the playoffs (the Rams and the Bills were the others)...Maybe his best coaching job ever came in 1984 when he lost Curt Warner for 15 games and still went 12-4, the best record in club history ...Tied with Weeb Ewbank for 10th place on the all-time victory list...His lifetime mark is 130-76-1, which places him second in winning percentage (.631) among active coaches with at least 100 wins. Don Shula (.724) is No. 1 and Tom Landry slipped to No. 3 (.628) last season...Born Apr. 27, 1932, in Sewickley,

Pa., and attended Juniata College in Pennsylvania, where he lettered four years as a tackle . . . In 14 years as a head coach, Knox has made the playoffs nine times and won six division titles . . . He's had glittering success without a top-flight quarterback at any of his stops . . . He's not called "Ground Chuck" for nothing.

GREATEST KICKER

Norm Johnson bounced back from a so-so 1985 by attacking the NFL record book last year. The former free-agent kicker from UCLA tied two NFL records by making five field goals of at least 50 yards and by making two of them in one game against the Raiders.

Everyone knew Johnson had the leg, but in his first four seasons with the Seahawks he only made 3-of-10 from beyond the 50. Johnson also set Seattle records for most field goals (22) and most field-goal attempts (35) and tied records for most field goals in a game (four against the Chargers) and longest field goal (54, vs. the Chargers).

It was the third time in four seasons that Johnson, 27, has surpassed 100 points. He had 103 in 1983, 110 in his Pro Bowl season of 1984 and 108 last year to finish second in scoring to Tony Franklin in the AFC.

Johnson led UCLA in scoring during his senior season, but no NFL team drafted him. In his five-year career he has made 84-of-123 field goals (.683). With 446 points, he trails only Steve Largent (529) as the Seahawks' all-time leading scorer.

INDIVIDUAL SEAHAWK RECORDS

Rushing

Most Yards Game:	207	Curt Warner, vs Kansas City, 1983
Season:	1,481	Curt Warner, 1986
Career:	4,064	Curt Warner, 1983-86

Passing

Most TD Passes Game:	5	Dave Krieg, vs Detroit, 1984
	5	Dave Krieg, vs San Diego, 1985
Season:	32	Dave Krieg, 1984
Career:	107	Jim Zorn, 1976-84
	107	Dave Krieg, 1980-86

The Seahawks hope Dave Krieg can keep the heat on.

Receiving

Most TD Passes Game:	4	Daryl Turner, vs San Diego, 1985
Season:	13	Daryl Turner, 1985
Career:	87	Steve Largent, 1976-86

Scoring

Most Points Game:	24	Daryl Turner, vs San Diego, 1985
Season:	110	Norm Johnson, 1984
Career:	529	Steve Largent, 1976-86
Most TDs Game:	4	Daryl Turner, vs San Diego, 1985
Season:	15	David Sims, 1978
	15	Sherman Smith, 1979
Career:	88	Steve Largent, 1976-86

INSIDE THE NFC

By BILL VERIGAN

PREDICTED ORDER OF FINISH

EAST	CENTRAL	WEST
N.Y. Giants	Chicago	L.A. Rams
Washington	Minnesota	San Francisco
Dallas	Green Bay	New Orleans
Philadelphia	Detroit	Atlanta
St. Louis	Tampa Bay	

NFC Champion: N.Y. Giants

Hey, how's this for a twist? Instead of playing for the NFC championship at the end of the season, let's get it over in the first week, prime time, Monday night. That's when the New York Giants and the Chicago Bears, the world champs of the last two seasons, will lay it all on the line. Call it Super Bowl XXI½. The winner will be instantly proclaimed the best team in the conference; the loser will be trying to catch up with the rest of the season.

And right now it looks like the Giants have an edge. It is Phil Simms. The Bears have all those quarterbacks. They even added one more by selecting Michigan's Jim Harbaugh with their first pick in the draft. But none of them are as good as Simms. Not even Jim McMahon, who still hadn't picked up a football in the middle of May because of his injured shoulder.

While the Bears appear to be a team in decline, the Giants are definitely still on the rise. New York has the depth that Chicago lacks. New York also has the dedication that Chicago lacks.

Remember the bickering in Chicago after the Bears won Super Bowl XX? The coach and quarterback were taking shots at each

---

Bill Verigan of the New York Daily News *has been covering pro football—in particular the New York Giants—for a decade.*

other in print. Nothing like that happened in New York. Indeed, the Giants had more players in their offseason conditioning program than ever before.

The Giants will have no challenger in the East. The Redskins will make a run, then fade just the way they did last year. They simply don't have linebackers the Giants possess. Monte Coleman, Rich Milot and Neal Olkewicz all came into the league at the same time, and they are growing old together. The secondary is suspect, too.

The Eagles might have made matters more interesting with a couple of upsets in the East. They will have a tough one-two defensive punch with Jerome Brown joining Reggie White on the defensive line, but Keith Byars' fractured foot has brought pain all around.

And Dallas is rebuilding, and St. Louis is still nowhere close to becoming a challenger. The Cardinals will be testing a new quarterback, and that's always a tedious procedure.

In the Central, the Vikings will put some heat on the Bears. The Vikings are not as good as Chicago, but they are young and aggressive. If Tommy Kramer can hold together for another year and D.J. Dozier contributes, Minnesota will be a wild card.

The rest of the competition is so weak it will fatten any record in the Central Division. Green Bay, Detroit and Tampa Bay will fight it out for last place. The Packers are a sad lot who lost their only star, fallen James Lofton; the Lions used mirrors to put together a half-decent defense last year but the cracks are showing; and Ray Perkins will tear apart the Bucs before he puts them back together.

But there will be a change in the order in the West. Jim Everett will become a passing threat in a new offense, and that's all the Rams were lacking a year ago. They finished last in the NFL in passing, and they still made the playoffs. Then they fumbled it all away.

This season, the wild card will be the 49ers. Bill Walsh did a wonderful job in the offseason, trading for Steve Young, the heir to Joe Montana, and adding help in the draft. And they could make it interesting.

Bobby Hebert, a slow learner who still throws right into the heart of a defense, is hanging like an albatross around the neck of Jim Mora at New Orleans. Mora is a terrific coach, and Jim Finks has a knack for finding players. Those two men deserve a better fate.

Then there are the Falcons, who are forever rebuilding. Marion Campbell's defense will hold ground, but the offense must wait for Chris Miller, a rookie quarterback.

ATLANTA FALCONS

TEAM DIRECTORY: Chairman: Rankin Smith Sr.; Pres.; Rankin Smith Jr.; VP: Taylor Smith; Dir. Pub. Rel.: Charlie Taylor; Head Coach: Marion Campbell. Home field: Atlanta Stadium (59,643). Colors: Red, black, silver and white.

SCOUTING REPORT

OFFENSE: With the departure of Dan Henning, Rod Dowhower and Jim Hanifan have designed a two-back game plan—Gerald Riggs and guess who? It could be anybody on the roster now, or it could be a surprise. One thing's certain. Riggs won't be blocking. Maybe William Andrews can come back from injuries to lead the way, but a speed back would be nice.

Then the Falcons must decide on a quarterback. Dave Archer missed five late games with a separated shoulder, and the old coaching staff showed little confidence in Turk Schonert after his acquisition from Cincinnati. First-round pick Chris Miller of Oregon will push Archer for the starting job in the not-too-distant future.

If the line can stay healthy, the Falcons will be a lot better than last year. They had strangers playing next to each other. Poor Bill Fralic was doing everybody's job and playing next to a rookie. John Scully, Brett Miller and Jeff Kiewel all suffered serious injuries. If Scully fully recovers from his broken leg, he'll possibly get a chance to compete with Wayne Radloff at center now that Jeff Van Note has retired.

There is a shortage of depth at receiver, but the Falcons have a good pair in Charlie Brown and Floyd Dixon, a sixth-round draft choice. To improve the passing game, which ranked 11th in the NFC and gave up 56 sacks, the Falcons will use a shotgun extensively.

DEFENSE: Marion Campbell's baby has a lot of growing up to do. Only the defensive line is solid with Mike Gann, Tony Casillas (last year's No. 1) and Rick Bryan as starters and adequate backups.

The linebackers are in need of an overhaul. Buddy Curry was being phased out before coming back for a big year. Tim Green, a disappointing first-round draft choice who was a projected move from the line, was moved outside after the season, and maybe he can challenge for a job there.

A bunch of no-names are in the secondary. Strong safety Robert Moore was a free agent, and free safety Bret Clark came from the USFL. The corners were equally unheralded James Britt and Scott Case, but Bobby Butler, who missed time with a broken leg, might come back to challenge. In the meantime, the Falcons are getting by with a combination zone defense instead of over-powering folks.

Despite their shortcomings, they showed a lot of improvement last season. After giving up 452 points in 1985, they allowed only 280. That's dramatic. Perhaps Clark, who led the team in interceptions and special-teams hits, and Casillas were the major reasons.

KICKING GAME: Mick Luckhurst injured his groin after 10 games, and the Falcons were forced to search for a replacement kicker. They signed Ali Haji-Sheikh, who was a rookie phenom with the Giants, then got hurt and drifted into oblivion. Ali made seven of nine field goals and could make it interesting for Luckhurst in camp.

Return specialist Billy Johnson didn't get into the fray until the final game, and it was obvious the Falcons missed him. They

Gerald Riggs was the fourth-leading rusher in NFC.

FALCONS VETERAN ROSTER

HEAD COACH—Marion Campbell. Assistant Coaches—Tom Brasher, Fred Bruney, Scott Campbell, Chuck Clawsen, Steve Crosby, Rod Dowhower, Al Groh, Jim Hanifan, Claude Humphrey, Tim Jorgensen, Jimmy Raye.

No.	Name	Pos.	Ht.	Wt.	NFL Exp.	College
85	Allen, Anthony	WR	5-11	182	3	Washington
16	Archer, Dave	QB	6-2	203	4	Iowa State
31	Andrews, William	RB	6-0	220	7	Auburn
39	Austin, Cliff	RB	6-1	213	5	Clemson
82	Bailey, Stacey	WR	6-0	157	6	San Jose State
—	Belk, Veno	TE	6-3	229	1	Michigan State
26	Britt, James	CB	6-0	185	5	LSU
52	Brown, Aaron	LB	6-2	238	5	Ohio State
89	Brown, Charlie	WR	5-10	179	6	South Carolina State
77	Bryan, Rick	DE	6-4	265	4	Oklahoma
91	Burnette, Dave	T	6-6	285	1	Central Arkansas
23	Butler, Bobby	CB	5-11	182	7	Florida State
10	Campbell, Scott	QB	6-0	195	4	Purdue
—	Caravello, Joe	NT	6-3	270	1	Tulane
25	Case, Scott	CB	6-0	178	4	Oklahoma
75	Casillas, Tony	NT	6-3	280	2	Oklahoma
20	Cason, Wendell	CB	5-11	197	3	Oregon
28	Clark, Bret	S	6-2	195	2	Nebraska
56	Costello, Joe	LB	6-3	250	2	Central Conn. State
88	Cox, Arthur	TE	6-2	262	5	Texas Southern
30	Croudip, David	CB	5-8	185	4	San Diego State
50	Curry, Buddy	LB	6-4	222	8	North Carolina
86	Dixon, Floyd	WR	5-9	170	2	Stephen F. Austin
3	Donnelly, Rick	P	6-0	190	3	Wyoming
73	Dukes, Jamie	G	6-1	270	2	Florida State
79	Fralic, Bill	T-G	6-5	280	3	Pittsburgh
76	Gann, Mike	DE	6-5	265	3	Notre Dame
99	Green, Tim	LB	6-2	249	2	Syracuse
6	Haji-Sheikh, Ali	PK	6-0	172	5	Michigan
68	Harrison, Dennis	DE	6-8	280	10	Vanderbilt
66	Hinson, Billy	G	6-1	278	2	Florida
71	Howe, Glen	T	6-7	298	3	So. Mississippi
—	Hudgens, Kevin	DE	6-4	270	2	Idaho State
81	Johnson, Billy	WR	5-9	170	13	Widener
43	Jones, Daryll	DB	6-1	195	4	Georgia
84	Jones, Joey	WR	5-8	165	2	Alabama
78	Kenn, Mike	T	6-7	277	10	Michigan
63	Kiewel, Jeff	G	6-3	277	2	Arizona
80	Landrum, Mike	TE	6-2	231	2	So. Mississippi
18	Luckhurst, Mick	K	6-1	178	7	California
83	Matthews, Aubrey	WR	5-7	165	2	Delta State
87	Middleton, Ron	TE	6-2	252	2	Auburn
62	Miller, Brett	T	6-7	290	5	Iowa
34	Moore, Robert	S	5-11	190	2	Northwestern St.
—	Morris, Dwaine	DT	6-2	260	1	SE Louisiana
64	Pellegrini, Joe	G-C	6-4	265	6	Harvard
53	Phillips, Ray	LB	6-3	245	1	North Carolina St.
74	Pitts, Mike	DE	6-5	277	4	Alabama
72	Provence, Andrew	DE	6-3	267	5	South Carolina
59	Rade, John	LB	6-1	240	5	Boise State
55	Radloff, Wayne	G-C	6-5	277	3	Georgia
42	Riggs, Gerald	RB	6-1	232	6	Arizona State
14	Schonert, Turk	QB	6-1	196	8	Stanford
61	Scully, John	G	6-6	270	7	Notre Dame
48	Sharp, Dan	TE	6-2	235	1	Texas Christian
29	Stamps, Sylvester	RB	5-7	175	4	Jackson State
21	Turner, Jimmy	CB	6-0	187	5	UCLA
65	Upchurch, Andy	C	6-2	260	1	Arkansas
45	Whisenhunt, Ken	TE	6-2	233	3	Georgia Tech
51	Wilkes, Reggie	LB	6-4	242	10	Georgia Tech
54	Williams, Joel	LB	6-1	227	9	Wisconsin-La Crosse
35	Williams, Keith	WR/RB	5-10	173	2	SW Missouri
22	Woodberry, Dennis	CB	5-10	183	2	Southern Arkansas

TOP FIVE DRAFT CHOICES

Rd.	Name	Sel. No.	Pos.	Ht.	Wt.	College
1	Miller, Chris	13	QB	6-2	195	Oregon
2	Flowers, Kenny	31	RB	6-0	207	Clemson
4	Van Dyke, Ralph	97	OT	6-6	260	Southern Illinois
5	Mraz, Mark	125	DE	6-4	255	Utah State
6	Kiser, Paul	153	G	6-3	272	Wake Forest

had one of the lowest punt-return averages in the league.

But there was no problem with the punting. Rick Donnelly had the second-best gross average in the conference (43.9 yards).

THE ROOKIES: Miller, the new quarterback hope, completed 216 of 356 passes for 2,053 yards and 12 TDs in his senior year at Oregon, and his stock rose in the postseason. The addition of running back Kenny Flowers of Clemson and offensive linemen Ralph Van Dyke of Southern Illinois and Paul Kiser of Wake Forest might provide immediate offensive help. Flowers (109 carries, 528 yards) can complement Riggs the way he did Terrence Flagler.

OUTLOOK: Despite the difficulty in finding a head coach, the Falcons have put together a remarkable staff. If the players stay healthy, they could surprise a lot of people. They seem certain to improve on last year's 7-8-1 record.

FALCON PROFILES

BUDDY CURRY 29 6-4 222   Linebacker

Led team in tackles (156) for seventh straight season . . . Has started 105 straight games . . . Had 15 tackles vs. Saints . . . Plays left inside linebacker and teams up nicely with right inside backer John Rade, who was second in tackles and had 103 in final 10 weeks of season . . . Breathing down their necks is Tim Green, a first rounder in '85. But Green didn't sign until Aug. 15 and went on injured reserve Sept. 5 for five weeks with a calf injury . . . Curry played with Lawrence Taylor at North Carolina . . . Born June 4, 1958, in Danville, Va.

DAVE ARCHER 25 6-2 203   Quarterback

Former free agent . . . Already has 23 starts at age of 25 . . . Completed 150 of 294 passes for 2,007 yards and 10 TDs and had 52 carries for 298 yards, then wound up on injured reserve for five games . . . Shoulder was separated vs. Bears on Nov. 16, but injury was repaired by minor surgery . . . Began throwing again in March . . . Turk Schonert, acquired in trade with Bengals, was expected to challenge for starting job. Schonert was 95-for-154 for 1,032 yards while Archer was hurt... But Archer is first on depth chart, and Schonert looks like permanent backup unless rookie Chris Miller comes fast... Born Feb. 15, 1962, in Fayetteville, N.C. Attended Iowa State.

MIKE GANN 23 6-5 265   **Defensive End**

Very quick off snap... Beat Mike Pitts for last spot on line and started all 16 games for second straight season... Had 5½ sacks and 43 QB pressures... Lanky player from Notre Dame was second-round draft choice in 1985 ... Recurring shoulder problems hindered productivity as rookie, but surgery solved them... With Rick Bryan, Falcons seem well fixed for ends... Born Oct. 19, 1963, in Stillwater, Okla.

CHARLIE BROWN 28 5-10 179   **Wide Receiver**

Had 63 catches for 918 yards in '86, best season since 1983... Key was staying healthy ... Spent rookie season ('81) on the injured reserve list with Redskins. In strike-shortened '82 had 32 catches for 690 yards and in 1983 had Pro Bowl-caliber stats with 78 catches for 1,225 yards. Tremendous in playoffs both of those years... Redskins traded him for R. C. Thielemann on Aug. 26, 1985. Injured in first season with Atlanta and caught only 24 passes for 412 yards... Finally came up with big year. Could have been bigger if two TD passes hadn't been called back because of penalties vs. Saints in December... Born Oct. 29, 1958, in Charleston, S.C.... Attended South Carolina State.

BILL FRALIC 24 6-5 280   **Tackle/Guard**

Entering third season of contract worth $2.3-million over four years... Played right guard as rookie, but he moved to right tackle when Brett Miller went on IR in seventh week with knee... Had to cover up a lot of mistakes by Jamie Dukes and Glen Howe, his inexperienced partners on that side of the line... Falcons finished third in NFL in rushing thanks to his strength... Born Oct. 31, 1962, in Penn Hills, Pa.

... Attended Pitt and was second player taken in '85 draft ...
One of four Pitt players to have jersey retired (others are Tony
Dorsett, Hugh Green and Dan Marino).

GERALD RIGGS 26 6-1 232   Running Back

Nasty training camp holdout ... But still went
to Pro Bowl ... Gained 1,327 yards and nine
TDs on 343 carries. Another 136 yards
receiving ... No. 5 rusher in NFC ...
Offensive line injuries and inexperience made
life tough. But Falcons still finished second in
NFC in rushing with 2,524 net yards. Last two
games were particularly punishing behind
makeshift line ... Drafted in first round in 1982 out of Arizona
State ... Spent two seasons as understudy to William Andrews
... Took over when Andrews was hurt in '84 ... Has club-record
45 career TDs ... Only Falcon to have three 1,000-yard rushing
seasons. Had 1,486 yards in '84 and 1,719 in '85 ... Second to
Andrews in rushing attempts and yards ... Born Nov. 6, 1960, in
Tilluha, La.

TONY CASILLAS 23 6-3 280   Nose Tackle

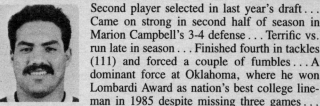

Second player selected in last year's draft ...
Came on strong in second half of season in
Marion Campbell's 3-4 defense ... Terrific vs.
run late in season ... Finished fourth in tackles
(111) and forced a couple of fumbles ... A
dominant force at Oklahoma, where he won
Lombardi Award as nation's best college lineman in 1985 despite missing three games ...
Described as best Oklahoma lineman since Lee Roy Selmon
... Born Oct. 26, 1963, in Tulsa, Okla., one of seven children
of Mexican-American descent.

BRET CLARK 26 6-2 195   Free Safety

Tough guy led team in interceptions and spe-
cial teams tackles ... Drafted by Raiders in
1985 in seventh round, but never played due to
contract conflict with Tampa Bay in USFL.
Atlanta acquired him on draft day from the
Raiders for a fourth-round draft choice ...
Became indispensible when starting DBs
Kenny Johnson and Bobby Butler were placed

on injured reserve at midseason... Wound up starting next to rookie Robert Moore, a free agent from Northwestern State... Born Feb. 24, 1961, in Nebraska City, Neb. Attended Nebraska.

WILLIAM ANDREWS 31 6-0 220   Running Back

Courage... A third-round draft choice out of Auburn, he was NFL's most productive running back from 1979-83, accumulating 8,382 yards... Suffered left knee injury in August 1984, tearing ligaments, damaging cartilage and stretching peroneal nerve... Missed 1984 and 1985 seasons and wasn't expected to return... But remarkable determination brought him back for spot duty last year, when he averaged 4.1 yards on 52 carries... Big finish in final game with 18 carries for 76 yards vs. Detroit... Underwent offseason surgery to remove bone chips from knee... Maybe it's over, but never count him out... Born Dec. 25, 1955, in Thomasville, Ga.

SCOTT CASE 25 6-0 178   Cornerback

Only white cornerback starting in NFL last year... When designated to play position by Marion Campbell, Case said, "I thought they were crazy."... Second-round draft choice out of Oklahoma in 1984... Played corner as junior for Sooners, then moved to safety... Strange as it sounds, Case was too aggressive at safety. He was flagged for only one interference call in '85, but coaches thought he was better suited to RCB and he beat out Tom Pridemore in camp... Intercepted four passes, defended 41... Born May 17, 1962, in Waynoka, Okla., and lives in Buford, Ga.

COACH MARION CAMPBELL: Falcons sought everywhere

for someone to accept job after firing Dan Henning... Finally looked around inside the organization and promoted Campbell for second time to head coach... A brilliant defensive history... Was all-conference at Georgia three times, entered Army, then played for 49ers in 1954 and 1955 and Eagles from 1956-61... Two-time Pro Bowl selection... Coached defensive lines with Patriots, Vikings (Purple People

Eaters), and Rams (Fearsome Foursome)... Hired as defensive coordinator of Falcons in 1974 and was promoted to head coach in 1974... Fired in 1977, moved to Eagles under Dick Vermeil ... Upon Vermeil's retirement, Campbell was named head coach at Philadelphia... Fired and returned to Atlanta under Dan Henning in 1985... A merry-go-round... Born May 25, 1929, in Chester, S.C.

GREATEST KICKER

The 1986 season was a bit of a trial for Mick Luckhurst. He entered the season with the third-best field-goal percentage in NFL history (.724), and after a back injury he exited as the fifth-best (.702). He made 14-of-24 field goals, below .700 for the first time in five years, and he will have to battle for his job against Ali Haji-Sheikh in camp.

But the former free agent is still the best the Falcons ever had. His 514 points are a club career record, nearly twice as many as the next Falcon, Nick Mike-Mayer (270). He also holds the record for most FGs attempted (151), FGs made (106), PATs attempted (199) and PATs made (196). He has hit his last 117 extra points.

Born in England, Luckhurst won MVP honors in a collegiate rugby tournament in '80. He caddies for his wife, Terri, on the LPGA tour. He attended St. Cloud, then transferred to California.

INDIVIDUAL FALCON RECORDS
Rushing

Most Yards Game:	202	Gerald Riggs, vs New Orleans, 1984	
Season:	1,719	Gerald Riggs, 1985	
Career:	5,986	William Andrews, 1979-86	

Passing

Most TD Passes Game:	4	Randy Johnson, vs Chicago, 1969	
	4	Steve Bartkowski, vs New Orleans, 1980	
	4	Steve Bartkowski, vs St. Louis, 1981	
Season:	31	Steve Bartkowski, 1980	
Career:	149	Steve Bartkowski, 1975-85	

Receiving

Most TD Passes Game:	3	Lynn Cain, vs Oakland, 1979
	3	Alfred Jenkins, vs New Orleans, 1981
	3	William Andrews, vs Denver, 1982
	3	William Andrews, vs Green Bay, 1983
	3	Lynn Cain, vs L.A. Rams, 1984
	3	Gerald Riggs, vs. L.A. Rams, 1985
Season:	13	Alfred Jenkins, 1981
Career:	40	Alfred Jenkins, 1975-83

Scoring

Most Points Game:	18	Lynn Cain, vs Oakland, 1979
	18	Alfred Jenkins, vs New Orleans, 1981
	18	William Andrews, vs Denver, 1982
	18	William Andrews, vs Green Bay, 1983
	18	Lynn Cain, vs L.A. Rams, 1984
	18	Gerald Riggs, vs L.A. Rams, 1985
Season:	114	Mick Luckhurst, 1981
Career:	514	Mick Luckhurst 1981-86
Most TDs Game:	3	Shared by Lynn Cain, Alfred Jenkins, William Andrews and Gerald Riggs
Season:	13	Alfred Jenkins, 1981
	13	Gerald Riggs, 1984
Career:	45	Gerald Riggs 1982-86

CHICAGO BEARS

TEAM DIRECTORY: Chairman: Edward B. McCaskey; Pres.: Michael B. McCaskey; VP Player Personnel: Bill Tobin; Dir. Administration: Bill McGrine; Dir. Finance: Ted Phillips; Pub. Rel. Dir.: Ken Valdiserri; Head Coach: Mike Ditka. Home field: Soldier Field (66,030). Colors: Orange, navy blue and white.

SCOUTING REPORT

OFFENSE: Mike Ditka keeps the pot (and tempers) boiling during the offseason. He keeps the laughs coming, too. You probably thought the absence of Jim McMahon was the major reason the Bears didn't get to the NFC title game for a crack at the

The Bears look forward to the return of Jim McMahon.

Giants last year. But Ditka said, "We've won 39 games over the past three years and Jim's only been on the field 54 percent of the time. The proof's in the pudding, we can win with the other guys. If he can't go, you play Flutie, you win with him, you go to the Super Bowl with him, then he becomes a national hero, he runs for President, makes me Secretary of Defense and we go on to conquer the whole world."

However, he admitted he wishes the 5-9 Flutie were "a little taller. We've had him on the stretching machine for three months and he's 6-foot-7 now." The Bears now have five QBs. McMahon is the only one they need. They've won 23 straight games when he started. His rehab from last year's shoulder injury remains a question and Ditka couldn't resist making a surprise first-round choice of Michigan quarterback Jim Harbaugh.

Without McMahon, the Bears ran. They averaged 168.8 yards per game, and they ranked first in the NFC. Walter Payton gained 1,333 yards and went to the Pro Bowl again, and he was the unquestioned leader of the offense. But Ditka, while acknowledging that contribution and adding that Payton is also one of the best blocking backs in the league, still plans to begin phasing out the legendary back. The coach said Neal Anderson, a first-round draft choice from Florida last year, will take some of the carries so Payton can rest.

Certainly having Anderson around will be reassuring, and so will the return of receiver Dennis McKinnon, who missed all of last season with a knee injury. And then there is Willie Gault, who had his best season as the Bears' leading receiver.

The Chicago defense gets most of the attention, but the offense is good and will get better.

DEFENSE: Maybe the Giants won the Super Bowl, but the Bears can still lay claim to having the best defense in the league. They were first in total defense (258.1 yards per game compared to the Giants' 297.3) and they were first in scoring defense (187 points vs. 236). The defense didn't die when Buddy Ryan left for Philadelphia.

Cornerback Leslie Frazier didn't come back after wrecking his knee in Super Bowl XX, and he probably won't be back this season. Such a loss might be disastrous for some teams, but Vestee Jackson, a second-round draft choice, quickly moved in as a starter.

Maybe it's near the time to replace free safety Gary Fencik, 33, and defensive end Dan Hampton. Defensive tackle Steve McMichael and linebacker Otis Wilson will reach 30 this year. But the defense is comparatively young.

BEARS VETERAN ROSTER

HEAD COACH—Mike Ditka. Assistant Coaches—Jim Dooley, Ed Hughes, Steve Kazor, Greg Landry, Jim LaRue, John Levra, Dave McGinnis, Johnny Roland, Dick Stanfel, Vince Tobin.

No.	Name	Pos.	Ht.	Wt.	NFL Exp.	College
35	Anderson, Neal	RB	5-11	210	2	Florida
81	Barnes, Lew	WR	5-8	163	2	Oregon
79	Becker, Kurt	G	6-5	267	6	Michigan
25	Bell, Todd	S	6-1	205	6	Ohio State
68	Blair, Paul	OT	6-4	295	2	Oklahoma State
62	Bortz, Mark	G	6-6	269	5	Iowa
8	Buford, Maury	P	6-1	191	6	Texas Tech
6	Butler, Kevin	K	6-1	195	3	Georgia
54	Cabral, Brian	LB	6-1	232	8	Colorado
74	Covert, Jim	T	6-4	271	5	Pittsburgh
95	Dent, Richard	DE	6-5	263	5	Tennessee State
36	Douglass, Maurice	DB	5-11	200	2	Kentucky
22	Duerson, Dave	S	6-1	203	5	Notre Dame
45	Fencik, Gary	S	6-1	196	12	Yale
2	Flutie, Doug	QB	5-9	176	2	Boston College
21	Frazier, Leslie	CB	6-0	187	6	Alcorn State
71	Frederick, Andy	T	6-6	265	10	New Mexico
4	Fuller, Steve	QB	6-4	195	9	Clemson
83	Gault, Willie	WR	6-1	183	5	Tennessee
23	Gayle, Shaun	CB	5-11	193	3	Ohio State
29	Gentry, Dennis	RB	5-8	181	6	Baylor
99	Hampton, Dan	DT	6-5	267	9	Arkansas
90	Harris, Al	LB	6-5	253	8	Arizona State
73	Hartenstine, Mike	DE	6-3	254	13	Penn State
63	Hilgenberg, Jay	C	6-3	258	7	Iowa
75	Humphries, Stefan	G	6-3	268	4	Michigan
24	Jackson, Vestee	DB	6-0	186	2	Washington
88	Kozlowski, Glen	WR	6-1	193	1	BYU
58	Marshall, Wilber	LB	6-1	225	4	Florida
85	McKinnon, Dennis	WR	6-1	190	4	Florida State
9	McMahon, Jim	QB	6-1	190	6	BYU
76	McMichael, Steve	DT	6-2	260	8	Texas
87	Moorehead, Emery	TE	6-2	220	11	Colorado
51	Morrissey, Jim	LB	6-3	215	3	Michigan State
89	Ortego, Keith	WR	6-0	180	3	McNeese State
34	Payton, Walter	RB	5-10	202	13	Jackson St.
72	Perry, William	DT	6-2	325	3	Clemson
48	Phillips, Reggie	DB	5-10	170	3	Southern Methodist
53	Rains, Dan	LB	6-1	222	4	Cincinnati
27	Richardson, Mike	CB	6-0	188	5	Arizona State
59	Rivera, Ron	LB	6-3	239	4	California
52	Rubens, Larry	C	6-2	262	4	Montana State
20	Sanders, Thomas	RB	5-11	203	3	Texas A&M
50	Singletary, Mike	LB	6-0	228	7	Baylor
26	Suhey, Matt	FB	5-11	216	8	Penn State
57	Thayer, Tom	G-C	6-4	261	3	Notre Dame
33	Thomas, Calvin	FB	5-11	245	6	Illinois
18	Tomczak, Mike	QB	6-1	195	3	Ohio State
78	Van Horne, Keith	T	6-6	280	7	USC
70	Waechter, Henry	DT	6-5	275	6	Nebraska
49	Walton, Riley	TE	6-3	230	1	Tennessee State
55	Wilson, Otis	LB	6-2	232	8	Louisville
80	Wrightman, Tim	TE	6-3	237	5	UCLA

TOP FIVE DRAFT CHOICES

Rd.	Name	Sel. No.	Pos.	Ht.	Wt.	College
1	Harbaugh, Jim	26	QB	6-3	207	Michigan
2	Morris, Ron	54	WR	6-1	192	Southern Methodist
4	Smith, Sean	101	DE	6-4	275	Grambling
5	Bryan, Steve	120	DE	6-3	260	Oklahoma
5	Johnson, Will	138	DE	6-5	240	NE Louisiana

The Bears had five defensive players chosen for the Pro Bowl, and Vince Tobin's style has done nothing to diminish the effectiveness of the unit.

KICKING GAME: Maury Buford is not so hot, but his teammates overcome any problems. He grossed only 41.3 yards per punt, but his net average was 36.9 yards, second-best in the NFC. And he got 19 punts inside the 20.

Kevin Butler made 28-of-41 field-goal attempts, and he could have been better. Dennis Gentry led the NFC with 28.8 yards per kickoff return, and Lew Barnes averaged a so-so 8.5 yards on punt returns. But individuals don't make this unit effective. It is the aggressiveness of backups like Thomas Sanders, Jim Morrissey, Dan Rains, Ron Rivera and Shaun Gayle.

THE ROOKIES: McMahon was still unable to toss a tennis ball across the room by the day of the draft, forcing the Bears to add Harbaugh to their extensive quarterback collection. The Michigan grad ranked second in the NCAA in passing, hitting 65.75 percent of his passes for 2,557 yards with only eight interceptions. The likely return of McKinnon removed some of the pressure to get a wide receiver, but second-round wide receiver Ron Morris of SMU could be the steal of the draft if his knee heals. He's big, brave and productive.

OUTLOOK: The Bears will be back if McMahon is healthy. Watch for them to meet the Giants on Monday night in Week One and in the NFC championship game at the end of the year.

BEAR PROFILES

JIM McMAHON 27 6-1 190   Quarterback

Center of turmoil in a season of injuries, controversy and big-bucks commercials... Absence might have kept the Bears from reaching the Super Bowl again. Steve Fuller, Mike Tomczak and Doug Flutie could not provide the answers...McMahon and coach Mike Ditka traded barbs in their books and also during the season. Barbs flew faster after Flutie signed and started final regular-season game and in playoff loss to Washington... There is supposed to be a QB competition in camp, but it seems inconceivable considering McMahon's record of success. Chicago won 23 consecutive games that McMahon started. Last victory was against Green Bay when Charles Martin mauled him in the 12th game . . . He had these stats: six starts, 77 completions, 150 attempts, 995 yards, five TDs, eight interceptions . . . Time off allowed ex-BYU star to pursue more endorsements. He made $1.5-million or so off the field after Super Bowl XX, and he passed up another $1-million or so in offers . . . How he comes back from arthroscopic shoulder surgery performed Dec. 12 and how he is able to coexist with Ditka will determine the fate of the Bears in '87 . . . Born Aug. 21, 1959, in Jersey City, N.J.

WILBER MARSHALL 25 6-1 225   Linebacker

Led Bears in forced fumbles (four), second in fumble recoveries (three), third in interceptions (five), fourth in tackles (105) and sacks (5.5) . . . Stats reveal what a big-play specialist the outside linebacker has become after being the 11th player picked in the 1984 draft . . . Returned a fumble and interception for touchdowns on opportunistic defense . . . Was Lombardi Award finalist as junior and senior at Florida . . . Giants took close look at him and chose Carl Banks instead, possibly because of his agent's threats to go to USFL . . . One of 13 children . . . Father was from Bahamas . . . Elected to Pro Bowl for first time . . . Born April 18, 1962, in Titusville, Fla.

WALTER PAYTON 33 5-10 202   Running Back

A legend that keeps growing . . . Ran 321 times for 1,333 yards and eight TDs. Caught 37 passes for 382 yards . . . Only Eric Dickerson and Joe Morris had more yards from scrimmage in the NFC than his 1,715 . . . His NFL rushing record has now reached 16,193 yards . . . Has led Bears in rushing every season since entering league in 1975 from Jackson State . . . Nine Pro Bowls in 12 seasons . . . Playful in the locker room . . . Loves to grab a microphone and interview teammates for TV, and his questions are better than most . . . Plans to play two more seasons and surpass 18,000 yards, but there seem to be no limits . . . Never hurt seriously . . . Missed one game in 12 years . . . Tied Jim Brown's NFL career record with 106 rushing TDs. His 120 total TDs trail Brown's NFL-record 126 . . . Born July 25, 1954, in Columbia, Miss.

MIKE SINGLETARY 28 6-0 228   Linebacker

Key to Bears' defense, he made transition from Buddy Ryan's "46" with no problem... Scholarly demeanor off the field, signal-caller and captain on the field... Made Pro Bowl for fourth consecutive year... Despite comparatively short stature, he is a mean hitter. Noted for being relentless against the run. But he also defenses passes effectively... Tied for team lead with 129 tackles... Was Southwest Conference Player of the Year in 1979 and 1980 at Baylor... Positive attitude is revealed by title of his favorite book: Dr. Norman Vincent Peale's *The Power of Positive Thinking*... Missed two games with groin injury in '86... Born Oct. 9, 1958, in Houston.

WILLIE GAULT 26 6-1 183   Wide Receiver

With 42 catches for 818 yards and five TDs, he's first receiver to lead the Bears in receptions since James Scott with 50 in 1977... Appeared to come of age, but his wife damaged that image with an interview in a national magazine. She complained that Jim McMahon wouldn't throw to her husband and linked the quarterback's absence to Gault's success... Second-best hurdler in world in 1982, his transition to pro football was not easy... He was heavily used to return kicks until last season... Dennis Gentry and Thomas Sanders allowed Gault to concentrate on using his 4.4 speed as a receiver... Loss of Dennis McKinnon for season added to his role... Born Sept. 5, 1960, in Griffin, Ga.... Attended Tennessee... Competed on track circuit last winter.

RICHARD DENT 26 6-5 263   Defensive End

Resolved bitter contract dispute with four-year, $2.5-million deal, but sacks fell off in '86... He had 17½ in '84 and 17 in '85 in the "46" defense, when he came from everywhere, looping and stunting to take advantage of an opponent's weakness... His 11½ sacks last season paced the Bears anyway... He's no longer vulnerable to runs directed at him ... An all-around athlete... Likes to play racquetball, tennis, swim and horseback-ride—no contact sports... Failed to make Pro Bowl after being Honolulu starter for two consecutive years, but remains a respected member of an awesome defense with his 4.6 speed...Bargain pick in eighth round of 1983 draft out of Tennessee State...Born Dec. 13, 1960, in Atlanta.

JIM COVERT 27 6-4 271   Tackle

Named youngest captain in the NFL in 1984 ...Since joining Bears as sixth player selected in 1983 draft, he has started all but one game ...Bears have led the NFL in rushing every year since his arrival...Elected to Pro Bowl for second time despite hyperextending elbow in sixth game...Also scored with fans to win Miller Lite Lineman-of-the-Year award... Walter Payton calls him "best tackle in NFL."...Best man at wedding of Dan Marino, a Pitt teammate...Champion wrestler in high school...Underwent arthroscopic knee and elbow surgery in offseason...Born March 22, 1960, in Conway, Pa.

DAVE DUERSON 26 6-1 203   Safety

Selected to Pro Bowl in both seasons he has started...Gets around and is always near the ball. Fifth in sacks, second in interceptions, passes defensed and fumble recoveries... Also a special teams leader...When another Pro Bowler, Todd Bell, held out, Duerson got his opportunity in 1985 and was instrumental in Super Bowl title...Can cover most tight ends and hits like a linebacker...His six interceptions and seven sacks were career highs in '86...A third-round selection in 1983 draft out of Notre Dame...Speaks out against drugs and alcohol ...Born Nov. 28, 1960, in Muncie, Ind.

STEVE McMICHAEL 29 6-2 260   Defensive Tackle

The guy hunts rattlesnakes for a hobby. You just know he's a defensive lineman...Coming off his finest season with eight sacks...Was told by Patriot coach Ron Erhardt in 1981 to forget about a football career. Chicago got him as a free agent...Started every game over the last three seasons...Selected to Pro Bowl, an honor that eluded him in 1985...One of the strongest players on the field since his college days at Texas... Was third-round draft choice in 1980...Bad knees have not prevented him from being one of the leading defensive linemen in the league... Born Oct. 17, 1957, in Houston.

MIKE RICHARDSON 26 6-0 188   Cornerback

A strong finish gave him seven interceptions. He's only fourth Bear since 1963 to get that many... Also led the team in passes defensed ... Safeties get most of the attention in the Bears' secondary, but Richardson had impressive stats. With Leslie Frazier injured, Chicago used rookie Vestee Jackson on right side... Richardson is effective against the run, too... Perhaps the Bears' secondary is underrated because of the pressure applied by the front seven... Lists "Mexican food" as a hobby... Born May 23, 1961, in Compton, Cal.... A second-round draft selection out of Arizona State in 1983... Has six sisters.

COACH MIKE DITKA: Loved, hated... A winner... With

14-2 record in '86 without a quarterback, Ditka moved ahead of George Halas as most successful coach in Bears' history. Halas was 320-148-31 (.672), Ditka is 54-25 (.685) in five seasons... His '86 Bears lost to Redskins in NFL playoffs... Expressed anger when GM Jerry Vainisi was fired at end of last season... Poked at former defensive coordinator Buddy Ryan and even QB Jim McMahon... All-American (tight end, linebacker) at Pitt... A 25-year NFL veteran. Twelve years as tight end with Bears (1961-66), Eagles (1967-68) and Cowboys (1970-72)... Cowboys' offensive coach from 1973-81 before becoming Bears' 10th head coach... Coach of Year in 1985 when Bears won Super Bowl XX... Born Oct. 13, 1939, in Carnegie, Pa.

GREATEST KICKER

George Blanda is a legend whose career spanned 26 years and led to the Hall of Fame in 1981. But it began in Chicago in 1949.

He was briefly with the Colts in 1950, but came back to spend 10 seasons in Chicago. During that decade he made 247 of 250 PATs and 88 of 201 field-goal attempts.

His career appeared to be over in 1959, but he came out of retirement to spend seven seasons with Houston and nine with Oakland in the AFL. He got to throw the ball with those teams, a job that was denied him for the most part with the Bears. At the age of 48, in 1975, he finally retired with 26,920 yards passing for 236 TDs. His kicking stats are 638 FGs attempted (NFL record) 335 made, 959 PATs attempted (NFL record), 2,002 points (NFL record).

He led the league in extra points for eight seasons and had 54 consecutive PATs in 1968, only two shy of the all-time record for a single season. But it all began in Chicago.

INDIVIDUAL BEAR RECORDS

Rushing

Most Yards Game:	275	Walter Payton, vs Minnesota, 1977
Season:	1,852	Walter Payton, 1977
Career:	16,193	Walter Payton, 1975-86

Passing

Most TD Passes Game:	7	Sid Luckman, vs N.Y. Giants, 1943
Season:	28	Sid Luckman, 1943
Career:	137	Sid Luckman, 1939-50

Receiving

Most TD Passes Game:	4	Harlon Hill, vs San Francisco, 1954
	4	Mike Ditka, vs Los Angeles, 1963
Season:	13	Dick Gordon, 1970
	13	Ken Kavanaugh, 1947
Career:	50	Ken Kavanaugh, 1940-41, 1945-50

Scoring

Most Points Game:	36	Gale Sayers, vs San Francisco, 1965
Season:	144	Kevin Butler, 1985
Career:	720	Walter Payton, 1975-86
Most TDs Game:	6	Gale Sayers, vs San Francisco, 1965
Season:	22	Gale Sayers, 1965
Career:	120	Walter Payton, 1975-86

DALLAS COWBOYS

TEAM DIRECTORY: General Partner: H.R. Bright; Pres./GM: Tex Schramm; VP-Player Development: Gil Brandt; VP-Administration: Joe Bailey; VP-Treasurer: Don Wilson; VP-Pro Personnel: Bob Ackles; Pub. Rel. Dir.: Doug Todd; Head Coach: Tom Landry. Home field: Texas Stadium (63,855). Colors: Royal blue, metallic blue and white.

SCOUTING REPORT

OFFENSE: There are big problems in Big D. Danny White's wrist was healing so slowly that the team didn't know if he'd be ready for the season. But the quarterback was postponing any operation. Of course, it's rather ironic that White, who has been blamed so often for the Cowboys' offensive woes, is now such a cause for concern. "My biggest concern," said Tom Landry.

But that's not the only worry. The offensive line has been a wasteland, and Jim Erkenbeck has been brought in from New Orleans as offensive line coach to see what can be salvaged. "It just never solidified," said Landry, who went into the draft looking for help on the line. Gil Brandt will have to find better players than he has in other recent drafts.

The retirement of Jim Cooper is a blow to a unit that badly needs leadership. Center Tom Rafferty and guard Crawford Ker tried to pick up slack last year when guard Kurt Petersen was injured. But there was too much ineptitude on the line.

The problems temper the excitement over the addition of former 49er offensive specialist Paul Hackett, receiver Mike Sherrard and running back Herschel Walker. And a healthy Tony Dorsett will add to the flow. But nothing works without a line and quarterback.

DEFENSE: "We definitely need to improve our defense," said Landry. "We discovered last year that the defense couldn't carry us if the offense had problems. When Walker and Dorsett were hurt and Danny White was on injured reserve we couldn't win. But the Bears could win without their quarterback, and the Giants could win when the offense didn't get many points."

The Cowboys will experiment more with different fronts, but the familiar flex will be the basic core. The Cowboys don't have dominating linebackers, and they ranked 11th in the NFC in both rushing defense (137.5 yards per game) and scoring defense (337 points allowed).

The defensive line has begun showing its age. For the first

time in 11 seasons, no defensive lineman reached the Pro Bowl. Indeed, it was the first time in the club's history that no Cowboy at all made the Pro Bowl. Jim Jeffcoat, a No. 1 in '83, is the only kid on the line, but maybe the No. 1 in '85, Kevin Brooks, will be ready to contribute. Top draft pick Danny Noonan of Nebraska should help immediately.

Behind the line are some smallish linebackers (Jeff Rohrer and Mike Hegman outside), and behind the linebackers are a couple of very marginal safeties and talented but mistake-prone cornerback Ron Fellows. Landry wants more aggressive players in both areas. The shortage of interceptions (17) was a major shortcoming.

Surgery and guts keep Randy White in the game.

COWBOYS VETERAN ROSTER

HEAD COACH—Tom Landry. Assistant Coaches—Neill Armstrong, Jim Erkenbeck, Paul Hackett, Al Lavan, Alan Lowry, Dick Nolan, Mike Solari, Ernie Stautner, Jerry Tubbs, Bob Ward.

No.	Name	Pos.	Ht.	Wt.	NFL Exp.	College
36	Albritton, Vince	S	6-2	210	4	Washington
62	Baldinger, Brian	G	6-4	261	5	Duke
87	Banks, Gordon	WR	5-10	173	5	Stanford
40	Bates, Bill	S	6-1	204	5	Tennessee
99	Brooks, Kevin	DL	6-6	273	3	Michigan
85	Chandler, Thornton	TE	6-5	245	2	Alabama
42	Clack, Darryl	RB	5-10	218	2	Arizona State
10	Collier, Reggie	QB	6-3	207	2	Southern Mississippi
84	Cosbie, Doug	TE	6-6	238	9	Santa Clara
55	DeOssie, Steve	LB	6-2	245	4	Boston College
33	Dorsett, Tony	RB	5-11	189	11	Pittsburgh
26	Downs, Michael	S	6-3	204	7	Rice
78	Dutton, John	DT	6-7	261	14	Nebraska
27	Fellows, Ron	CB	6-0	173	7	Missouri
46	Fowler, Todd	FB	6-3	221	3	Stephen F. Austin
28	Granger, Norm	RB	5-10	225	2	Iowa
58	Hegman, Mike	LB	6-1	227	12	Tennessee State
45	Hendrix, Manny	DB	5-10	178	2	Utah
80	Hill, Tony	WR	6-2	205	11	Stanford
23	Holloway, Johnny	CB	5-11	182	2	Kansas
53	Jax, Garth	LB	6-2	225	2	Florida State
77	Jeffcoat, Jim	DE	6-5	260	5	Arizona State
72	Jones, Ed	DE	6-9	273	13	Tennessee State
68	Ker, Crawford	G	6-3	285	3	Florida
29	Lavette, Robert	RB	5-11	190	3	Georgia Tech
56	Lockhart, Eugene	LB	6-2	235	4	Houston
14	McDonald, Paul	QB	6-2	185	8	Southern California
30	Newsome, Timmy	FB	6-1	237	8	Winston-Salem State
67	Newton, Nate	G	6-3	317	2	Florida A&M
16	Pelluer, Steve	QB	6-4	208	4	Washington
59	Penn, Jesse	LB	6-3	218	3	Virginia Tech
65	Petersen, Kurt	G	6-4	272	7	Missouri
81	Powe, Karl	WR	6-2	178	2	Alabama State
75	Pozderac, Phil	T	6-9	282	6	Notre Dame
64	Rafferty, Tom	C	6-3	262	12	Penn State
82	Renfro, Mike	WR	6-0	187	10	Texas Christian
70	Richards, Howard	T	6-6	269	7	Missouri
50	Rohrer, Jeff	LB	6-2	227	6	Yale
89	Salonen, Brian	LB	6-3	223	3	Montana
4	Saxon, Mike	P	6-3	188	3	San Diego State
22	Scott, Victor	DB	6-0	203	4	Colorado
86	Sherrard, Mike	WR	6-2	187	2	UCLA
60	Smerek, Don	DT	6-7	262	7	Nevada-Reno
63	Titensor, Glen	G	6-4	270	7	Brigham Young
71	Tuinei, Mark	T	6-5	283	5	Hawaii
34	Walker, Herschel	RB	6-1	223	2	Georgia
24	Walls, Everson	CB	6-1	193	7	Grambling
11	White, Danny	QB	6-3	197	12	Arizona State
54	White, Randy	DT	6-4	265	13	Maryland

TOP FIVE DRAFT CHOICES

Rd.	Name	Sel. No.	Pos.	Ht.	Wt.	College
1	Noonan, Danny	12	DT	6-4	280	Nebraska
2	Francis, Ron	39	CB	5-9	206	Baylor
3	Zimmerman, Jeff	68	G	6-4	322	Florida
4	Martin, Kelvin	95	WR	5-9	161	Boston College
5	Gay, Everett	124	WR	6-2	204	Texas

KICKING GAME: The greatest kicker in Cowboys' history, Rafael Septien, was waived after pleading guilty to molesting a 10-year-old girl. It's a severe blow to a special teams unit that doesn't look so special. Punter Mike Saxon had an unimpressive 40.7 gross and 34.4 net, and return specialists ranked near the bottom.

THE ROOKIES: Noonan is described as a hard worker who should help run the defense, and Baylor's Ron Francis should find somewhere to play now in a secondary that has some serious flaws. The offensive line, which has been trying every combination available, added a guard, Jeff Zimmerman of Florida, in the third round. And Sherrard, a successful choice a year ago, got two wide-receiver playmates in Kelvin Martin of Boston College and Everett Gay of Texas.

OUTLOOK: Landry calls this season a "challenge." That's a euphemism for a very rough job. The Cowboys had 12 new players on their team at the end of last season, and they'll have more this year. For the first time since 1960, the club is having to rebuild from the bottom.

COWBOY PROFILES

HERSCHEL WALKER 25 6-1 223   Running Back

Won "Superstars" TV competition during offseason . . . Established himself as truly great back in USFL and confirmed it in first NFL season. Ran for 737 yards and 12 TDs and caught 76 passes for 837 yards and two more TDs . . . Accomplished that while sharing position with Tony Dorsett . . . Played with sprained ankle and bursitis in right knee . . . Averaged 4.9 yards a carry . . . Came through in very first game, getting the critical yards and TD to beat Giants . . . An 84-yard run vs. Eagles was longest in NFL last season . . . Amassed 292 yards (6 for 122 rushing, 9 for 170 receiving) in Eagle game . . . Cowboys snatched former Heisman Trophy winner from Georgia in fifth round of '85 draft . . . Gained more than 7,000 yards rushing and receiving in three seasons with New Jersey Generals and scored 61 TDs. His 2,411 yards rushing in a season is pro record . . . Ranks third on NCAA rushing list with 5,259 yards in three seasons . . . Born March 3, 1962, in Wrightsville, Ga.

TONY DORSETT 33 5-11 189   Running Back

Wanted a trade when he heard about Walker's $1-million-a-year deal . . . Reconsidered next day . . . Gained 748 yards on 184 carries . . . Fourth-leading rusher in NFL history, and by end of '87 he should trail only Walter Payton . . . Played on sheer guts in some games. Injured left knee in third game and missed several games . . . Led team in rushing for 10th consecutive season . . . Has 11,580 yards . . . First-rounder in 1977 out of Pitt, where he won Heisman Trophy . . . Set NCAA record with 6,082 yards rushing and 58 TDs . . . Born April 7, 1954, in Aliquippa, Pa.

DANNY WHITE 35 6-3 197   Quarterback

Injured wrist is reason for concern . . . Was placed on injured reserve list Nov. 8 after big hit by Giant LB Carl Banks. Surgery was postponed in offseason and Cowboys won't know until camp whether it has healed . . . Didn't throw enough passes to be included among leaders . . . Completed 95 of 153 for 1,157 yards, 12 TDs, 5 interceptions. Those stats gave him 97.9 rating, which was better than NFL's official passing leader, Tommy Kramer . . . The 7.8-yards per pass was best average among NFC passers . . . Third-rounder out of Arizona State. NCAA's all-time passing leader at end of college career . . . Born Feb. 9, 1952, in Mesa, Ariz.

MIKE SHERRARD 24 6-2 187   Wide Receiver

Cowboys traded ahead of Giants in '86 draft so they wouldn't miss former UCLA walk-on . . . Missed most of preseason with knee injury, but was ready for opener . . . A rare combination, of speed (4.4 in the 40) and height . . . Hands appeared to be no problem . . . Caught 41 passes for 744 yards and five TDs . . . Five catches, 111 yards vs. Cardinals and four catches, 115 yards vs. Chargers . . . Moved ahead of Mike Renfro on depth chart . . . Averaged 18.1 yards per catch, team's best since Tony Hill's 20.7 average in 1981 . . . Born June 21, 1963, in Chico, Cal. . . . First wide receiver chosen in the draft by Dallas since Dennis Homan in 1968.

CRAWFORD KER 25 6-3 285   Guard

Potential All-Pro . . . Became starter in training camp when RG Kurt Petersen injured knee . . . Drafted in round three in 1985. Appeared likely to replace Petersen as rookie, but injured back when chair collapsed under him. "Killer chairs" were soon replaced, but it was too late . . . Reinjured back in game and missed rest of season . . . Former Florida Gator ran 4.8 in 40 and bench-pressed 500 pounds . . . Called "Crawdaddy" . . . Claims karate lessons and acupuncture helped heal back . . . Father was guard, too. But he was a Scot who guarded queen at Buckingham Palace . . . Never allowed her to be sacked . . . Born May 5, 1962, in Philadelphia.

JIM JEFFCOAT 26 6-5 260   Defensive End

Rising star on fading defensive line . . . Fourth in NFC with 14 sacks, behind only Giants' Lawrence Taylor, Redskins' Dexter Manley and Eagles' Reggie White . . . Had 65 tackles . . . Bothered part of season by ankle injury . . . Played some left tackle when Dom Smerek was hurt . . . First-rounder out of Arizona State in 1983 . . . Has 27½ sacks in last three years since replacing Harvey Martin . . . Trains with aerobic dancing . . . Born April 1, 1961, in Cliffwood, N.J. . . . Was a high-school wrestler . . . Made 16 tackles in Arizona State's 1983 Fiesta Bowl victory over Oklahoma.

STEVE PELLUER 25 6-4 208   Quarterback

Ever since Roger Staubach rode into the sunset, the quarterbacks on the bench have looked better than the quarterback on the field. At least to the fans. So the cry went up for Pelluer to replace Danny White as soon as the Cowboys reached training camp . . . White was able to fend off Gary Hogeboom. Might not be so lucky this time . . . Pelluer has mobility, which comes in handy with all those offensive line changes . . . Completed 215 of 378 passes last season for 2,727 yards, a respectable average gain of 7.21 yards . . . Also killed the Cowboys with 17 interceptions . . . A fifth-round draft choice in '84, he followed in footsteps of his grandfather and father as a player at Washington State . . . His brother, Scott, was a Cowboy draft choice and now plays linebacker for the Saints... Born July 29, 1962, in Yakima, Wash.

EUGENE LOCKHART 26 6-2 235   Linebacker

Hardest hitter on defense... Intelligent, but took time to pick up intricacies of flex defense. "I got tired of hearing about my mistakes. I let receivers come over the middle. It was a freeway back there. I'm putting up some stop signs now."... Only fourth regular middle linebacker in Cowboys' history, succeeding Jerry Tubbs, Lee Roy Jordan and Bob Breunig... Started eight games as rookie after being drafted out of Houston in sixth round in 1984... Had 121 tackles, leading team for second straight season. Added five sacks... Born April 2, 1961, in Crockett, Tex.... Has degree in marketing and owns one-hour photo shop in Dallas.

RANDY WHITE 34 6-4 265   Defensive Tackle

Gets spare parts and never wears out... Surgery on both knees at end of 1985 season... Shoulder and elbow surgery to remove bone spurs at end of 1986 season... Never complained... Concealed painful injury all year... Third in tackles (103) and second in sacks (6½)... Defensed three passes and recovered two fumbles... Had 17 tackles in Week 16 vs. Eagles. Defensive coordinator Ernie Stautner called it best game he ever saw White play... Seven trips to Pro Bowl, but hasn't gone last two years... Born Jan. 15, 1953, in Wilmington, Del.... Won Outland and Vince Lombardi awards as college football's No. 1 lineman at Maryland in 1974.

MICHAEL DOWNS 28 6-3 204   Safety

Led the Cowboys with six interceptions... Emerged as leader of the secondary when flamboyant Dennis Thurman was released and Dexter Clinkscale's holdout led to oblivion in St. Louis... Was elected captain for second straight year... Gained attention as rookie free agent in 1981 when he arrived in camp from Rice with a gold star set in his front tooth... Has been anonymous since then... Should have made Pro Bowl in 1984 when he had seven interceptions, one for a TD, two fumble recoveries and 136 tackles, including 96 solos, but he was overlooked . . . Secondary seemed to reflect his quiet personality. Instead of gambling for interceptions, defensive backs were more conservative . . . Dallas still played man-to-man 80 percent of the time, but it cut way down on opponents' passing yards . . . A good special teams player, particularly at blocking punts and field-goal attempts . . . Born June 9, 1959, in Dallas.

COACH TOM LANDRY: Coming off first losing record (7-9) since 1964 . . . Oldest head coach in NFL at 63, he is entering 28th season with Cowboys . . . After five consecutive losing seasons, Cowboys were 7-7 in 1965. Since then they have won 12 division championships, five NFC titles and two Super Bowls (VI and XII) . . . Devout born-again Christian . . . Said excitement of building a team is greater than winning Super Bowl. Has had a chance for a lot of thrills . . . Career at Texas as fullback was interrupted by World War II service. Flew 30 B-17 missions . . . Played for New York Yankees of All-American Conference in 1949 . . . Joined Giants following year and was All-Pro defensive back in 1954 . . . Retired as player in '55 and became a defensive coach for Giants through 1959 . . . Has no thought of retirement entering this season . . . Born Sept. 11, 1924, in Mission, Tex.

GREATEST KICKER

Rafael Septien's career appeared to be over when a back injury tormented him throughout 1985, and Max Zendejas was drafted in the fourth round last year to replace him. But when the season ended, Septien had made 15 of 21 field goals and all 43 of his extra-point attempts.

His life took a tragic turn, however, when he was arrested early this year and charged with molesting a 10-year-old girl. After pleading guilty, he was placed on 10 years' probation and was subsequently waived by the Cowboys.

But his performance on the field leaves no questions.

Deadly from inside 40 yards, the native of Mexico has hit

better than 70 percent of his field-goal tries in 10 NFL seasons. A 10th-round draft choice (Southwest Louisiana) by the Saints in 1977, he was cut in training camp and picked up by the Rams. Although he had an outstanding rookie year, he was cut again just before the 1978 season and signed by the Cowboys. He has made 388 of 398 PATs and 180 of 256 FGs for 874 points. At his best under pressure, he has made 18 of 21 FGs in playoff games.

Tony Dorsett gets incentive from Herschel Walker.

INDIVIDUAL COWBOY RECORDS

Rushing

Most Yards Game:	206	Tony Dorsett, vs Philadelphia, 1978
Season:	1,646	Tony Dorsett, 1981
Career:	11,580	Tony Dorsett, 1977-86

Passing

Most TD Passes Game:	5	Eddie LeBaron, vs Pittsburgh, 1962
	5	Don Meredith, vs N.Y. Giants, 1966
	5	Don Meredith, vs Philadelphia, 1966
	5	Don Meredith, vs Philadelphia, 1968
	5	Craig Morton, vs Philadelphia, 1969
	5	Craig Morton, vs Houston, 1970
	5	Danny White, vs N.Y. Giants, 1983
Season:	29	Danny White, 1983
Career:	153	Roger Staubach, 1969-79

Receiving

Most TD Passes Game:	4	Bob Hayes, vs Houston, 1970
Season:	14	Frank Clarke, 1962
Career:	71	Bob Hayes, 1965-74

Scoring

Most Points Game:	24	Dan Reeves, vs Atlanta, 1967
	24	Bob Hayes, vs Houston, 1970
	24	Calvin Hill, vs Buffalo, 1971
	24	Duane Thomas, vs St. Louis, 1971
Season:	123	Rafael Septien, 1983
Career:	874	Rafael Septien, 1978-86
Most TDs Game:	4	Dan Reeves, vs Atlanta, 1967
	4	Bob Hayes, vs Houston, 1970
	4	Calvin Hill, vs Buffalo, 1971
	4	Duane Thomas, vs St. Louis, 1971
Season:	16	Dan Reeves, 1966
Career:	85	Tony Dorsett, 1977-86

DETROIT LIONS

TEAM DIRECTORY: Pres.: William Clay Ford; Exec. VP/GM: Russ Thomas; Dir. Football Operations/Head Coach: Darryl Rogers; Dir. Pub. Rel.: George Heddleston. Home field: Pontiac Silverdome (80,638). Colors: Honolulu blue and silver.

SCOUTING REPORT

OFFENSE: The Lions gained more yards but scored less points in 1986. They ranked 11th in the NFC. And when the games were on the line they didn't score. But maybe the offense is not as bad as it looked.

James Jones paced Lions in rushing, receiving, TDs.

Lions' fans have bemoaned the lack of a quarterback for years. Well, this year they might get Chuck Long instead of Eric Hipple. Maybe the change will help, maybe it won't. Hipple has always been unfairly maligned, and Long isn't going to strong-arm anybody to death. Any quarterback the Lions get will have the same problem—no receivers.

Jeff Chadwick, a lanky receiver with a long stride, gained 18.8 yards per catch and five TDs. He would have had 1,000-plus yards, but he injured his Achilles in the 15th game. That's his problem. He's fragile. And the other receivers are bland, as in Carl Bland and Leonard Thompson, and one, Pete Mandley, is an outright busted second-round draft pick. Another busted pick is tight end David Lewis, who has produced nothing since he was chosen in the first round in 1984. He was replaced in midseason by Tampa Bay discard Jimmie Giles, but that one-time Pro Bowler is fading fast.

The Lions' strongest starters are to be found on the offensive line and at running back. There is little depth, but fullback James Jones had 1,245 all-purpose offensive yards, and Garry James, a second-rounder who had to make the transition from wingback at LSU, had 899 yards. The addition of Harvey Salem from Houston made the Lions solid across the line, and Lomas Brown at left tackle might have been a Pro Bowler for a winning team.

All in all, not great. But not as bad as it looks. And a new running backs coach (Vic Rapp from Tampa Bay) and receivers coach (Lew Carpenter from Green Bay) might add some fresh ideas.

DEFENSE: Defensive coordinator Wayne Fontes holds this unit together by sheer willpower. In the last two drafts the Lions took only nine defensive players, and only one of them is starting. The offense adopted its dink-passing style just to keep the defense off the field. Injuries to Bobby Watkins and Jimmy Williams added to the problems, and so did several players' lousy attitudes.

On the line, the Lions lack a good nose tackle and a pass rusher. Eric Williams spent several afternoons on his back. Keith Ferguson was the defensive MVP with 9½ sacks, but the Lions need another aggressive player. That's why they selected Washington defensive end Reggie Rogers in the first round.

Jimmy Williams and Mike Cofer are respectable outside linebackers, but the center is as soft as a jelly doughnut. Vernon Maxwell, who came into the league with such fanfare, was a castoff that the Lions snatched, and he seemed under better control when they moved him inside. But the Lions still gave up 146.8 yards rushing per game. Only the Bucs were worse.

LIONS VETERAN ROSTER

HEAD COACH—Darryl Rogers. Assistant Coaches—Bob Baker, Carl Battershell, Lew Carpenter, Don Doll, Wayne Fontes, Bill Muir, Mike Murphy, Rex Norris, Vic Rapp, Willie Shaw.

No.	Name	Pos.	Ht.	Wt.	NFL Exp.	College
6	Arnold, Jim	P	6-3	211	5	Vanderbilt
68	Baack, Steve	G	6-4	265	4	Oregon
61	Barrows, Scott	C-G	6-2	278	2	West Virginia
80	Bland, Carl	WR	5-11	182	4	Virginia Union
23	Brown, Arnold	CB	5-10	185	2	North Carolina St.
75	Brown, Lomas	T	6-4	282	3	Florida
42	Bostic, John	CB	5-10	178	3	Bethune-Cookman
96	Butcher, Paul	LB	6-0	223	2	Wayne State
89	Chadwick, Jeff	WR	6-3	190	5	Grand Valley St.
55	Cofer, Michael	LB	6-5	245	5	Tennessee
70	Dorney, Keith	G-T	6-5	285	9	Penn State
94	Drake, Joe	NT	6-3	285	2	Arizona
43	Elder, Donnie	CB	5-9	175	3	Memphis State
15	Erxleben, Russell	P	6-5	230	5	Texas
66	Evans, Leon	DE	6-5	282	3	Miami
12	Ferguson, Joe	QB	6-1	195	15	Arkansas
77	Ferguson, Keith	DE	6-5	260	7	Ohio State
40	Galloway, Duane	DB	5-8	181	2	Arizona State
79	Gay, William	DE	6-5	260	10	Southern California
81	Giles, Jimmie	TE	6-3	240	11	Alcorn State
53	Glover, Kevin	C-G	6-2	267	3	Maryland
33	Graham, William	S	5-11	191	6	Texas
62	Green, Curtis	NT-DE	6-3	265	7	Alabama State
34	Griffin, James	S	6-2	197	5	Middle Tennessee St.
58	Harrell, James	LB	6-1	245	8	Florida
47	Hill, Rod	CB	6-0	188	5	Kentucky State
17	Hipple, Eric	QB	6-2	198	8	Utah State
98	Hughes, Allen	DE	6-3	254	1	Western Michigan
36	Hunter, Herman	RB	6-1	193	3	Tennessee State
32	James, Garry	RB	5-10	214	2	Louisiana State
95	Jamison, George	LB	6-1	226	1	Cincinnati
21	Johnson, Demetrious	S	5-11	190	5	Missouri
54	Johnson, James	LB	6-2	236	2	San Diego State
30	Jones, James	RB	6-2	229	5	Florida
92	King, Angelo	LB	6-1	222	7	South Carolina St.
87	Lewis, David	TE	6-3	235	4	California
16	Long, Chuck	QB	6-4	211	2	Iowa
82	Mandley, Pete	WR	5-1	191	4	Northern Arizona
57	Maxwell, Vernon	LB	6-2	235	4	Arizona State
29	McNorton, Bruce	CB	5-11	175	6	Georgetown (Ky.)
74	Milinichik, Joe	G-T	6-5	300	1	North Carolina St.
31	Mitchell, Devon	S	6-1	195	2	Iowa
24	Moore, Alvin	RB	6-0	194	5	Arizona State
52	Mott, Steve	C	6-3	270	5	Alabama
3	Murray, Eddie	K	5-10	175	8	Tulane
86	Nichols, Mark	WR	6-2	208	6	San Jose State
51	Robinson, Shelton	LB	6-2	236	6	North Carolina
84	Rubick, Rob	TE	6-3	234	6	Grand Valley St.
73	Salem, Harvey	G-T	6-6	285	5	California
64	Sanders, Eric	G-T	6-7	280	7	Nevada-Reno
25	Smith, Oscar	RB	5-9	203	1	Nicholls State
26	Smith, Steve	S	6-0	200	1	Michigan
71	Strenger, Rich	T	6-7	285	4	Michigan
39	Thompson, Leonard	WR	5-11	192	13	Oklahoma State
27	Watkins, Bobby	CB	5-10	184	6	Southwest Texas State
76	Williams, Eric	NT	6-4	280	4	Washington State
59	Williams, Jimmy	LB	6-3	230	6	Nebraska
38	Williams, Scott	FB	6-2	234	2	Georgia

TOP FIVE DRAFT CHOICES

Rd.	Name	Sel. No.	Pos.	Ht.	Wt.	College
1	Rogers, Reggie	7	DE	6-7	255	Washington
3	Ball, Jerry	63	DT	6-0	281	Southern Methodist
4	Rivers, Garland	92	DB	6-1	190	Michigan
6	Lockett, Danny	148	LB	6-3	226	Arizona
7	Saleaumua, Dan	175	DT	6-0	285	Arizona State

The Lions were missing their best defensive back, cornerback Bobby Watkins, with an arch injury. His absence left rookie Duane Galloway and erratic Bruce McNorton hanging out on the corners. One of the few pleasant surprises last season was Devon Mitchell, a fourth-rounder who turned into a player. At strong safety, Demetrious Johnson took over from pouty William Graham and fooled a lot of people before they discovered he couldn't run. Watkins' return will help.

KICKING GAME: Eddie Murray is called Eddie Money in Detroit after making 18-of-25 last season. He ranks among the best during his career (152-of-204). But critics complain that he misses when games are on the line. Acquisition of Jim Arnold (42.6) helped the punting game. But the Lions would love another return specialist who can double as a receiver. Herman Hunter set records for kickoff returns and return yardage, but he's still not the flyer the Lions want.

THE ROOKIES: Some folks are mystified why the Lions chose Rogers when they could have had Miami's Jerome Brown. However, Rogers is a pressure lineman. And the Lions' next choice in the third round was a nose tackle, SMU's Jerry Ball, who grew to 281 pounds after playing fullback in high school. The first five picks were all defensive, which shows where the real weakness lies.

OUTLOOK: The Lions still look like the third-best team in the NFC Central, and that's not very good. But if they could come up with two or three defensive players they might spring a few surprises. And Long better take charge in his second year.

LION PROFILES

JAMES JONES 26 6-2 229   Fullback

Led team in rushing and receiving with career-high 911 yards rushing (3.6 per carry) and 54 catches (6.4-yard average)...Also led team with nine TDs...Biggest game was opener against Minnesota: 36 carries, 174 yards... Tied team record with 12 catches vs. Browns in Sept....Battering back had tough act to follow, Billy Sims...Shared team's offensive

MVP honors with Keith Dorney...J. J. has been a starter since first game of rookie season...Selected 1985 "Lion of the Year" by the Michigan March of Dimes...Lions' player rep in '86...Was 13th overall selection out of Florida in '83 draft...Born March 21, 1961, in Pompano Beach, Fla....Full name is James Roosevelt Jones.

CHUCK LONG 24 6-4 211   **Quarterback**

Pencil him in as the starter. Threw 40 passes in 1986 after being drafted in first round out of Iowa...At end of rookie year he was listed first on depth chart ahead of Joe Ferguson and Eric Hipple, an unsigned free agent who underwent elbow surgery during the offseason ...Ferguson is a very old pro, 10th-most completions (2,292) and 11th-most yards (28,925) in NFL history...Long's first pass came in 12th game, a 34-yard TD toss to Leonard Thompson...First start was against Bears in Week 15, and he had Lions ahead 13-3 in third quarter. Bears won, but Long was 12 for 24 for 167 yards, 1 TD, 1 interception...Born Feb. 18, 1963, in Norman, Okla.

VERNON MAXWELL 25 6-2 235   **Linebacker**

Found a home in Detroit...Great rookie season with Colts in 1983 when he was 29th player chosen in draft. Had 11 sacks and was named Rookie of the Year by AP and Pro Football Writers...But Colts traded him to Chargers during training camp in 1985, and he was cut before season opened...Signed with Lions on Oct. 25, 1985, his 24th birthday...Played outside for Colts and Chargers, but Lions moved him to left inside linebacker...Third on Lions in '86 with 106 tackles, 87 solos. Led team with four fumble recoveries and defended five passes...Free agent during offseason, but Detroit—in particular Darryl Rogers—had every reason to want him back: Rogers had been Maxwell's coach at Arizona State...Born Oct. 25, 1961. in Birmingham, Ala.

JIMMY WILLIAMS 26 6-3 230   Linebacker

A very unhappy fella in 1986 . . . Missed 40 practices during training-camp holdout in option year . . . Injured knee in 11th game and missed rest of year . . . Said he wanted trade to Washington . . . Those unhappy circumstances followed a brilliant 1985 season when he was switched from right to left outside linebacker . . . He was team's defensive MVP in 1985 . . . Dropped to 53 tackles (40 solos) and two sacks . . . But signed a new multiyear contract after season and announced how pleased he was to be a Lion . . . His return would give Detroit two very good OLBs . . . Mike Cofer, a former down lineman, is on the other side . . . Born Nov. 15, 1960, in Washington, D.C. . . . Made Nebraska roster with brother, Toby, as walk-ons.

DEVON MITCHELL 24 6-1 195   Safety

Drafted in fourth round in '86 . . . Broke into starting lineup before former Iowa teammate, Chuck Long, who was a first-rounder . . . Lions needed help at FS after William Graham was moved back to SS to challenge Demetrious Johnson . . . Wound up fifth on team with 70 tackles, 51 solos . . . Led Lions with five interceptions and defended 10 passes . . . Teamed with Johnson, who led with 112 tackles, 92 solos . . . Played cornerback at Iowa. He was college walk-on, but started four years . . . His 18 interceptions tied Iowa record held by Nile Kinnick, the 1939 Heisman Trophy winner . . . Born Dec. 30, 1962, in Kingston, Jamaica, and grew up in Brooklyn, N.Y.

KEITH DORNEY 29 6-5 285   Guard

Missed Weeks 2-5 with knee injury that required arthroscopic surgery. Returned with a vengeance in Week 6, but went out again in final game with groin injury . . . Another remarkable year in injury-plagued career . . . Teammates chose him to share offensive MVP honors with James Jones . . . Drafted in first round in 1979 out of Penn State to play tackle . . Named to All-Rookie team that year . . . Made Pro Bowl in 1982. Weight-room back injury cost him similar honor in 1983

...He played with broken toe in '85 and volunteered to move to RG when other teammates were injured...Offensive captain... Until last season he had been starter in 93 of his 94 games as a pro...Born Dec. 3, 1957, in Macungie, Pa.

GARRY JAMES 23 5-10 214   Running Back

Sorely needed outside threat after Billy Sims and Wilbert Montgomery were lost...Drafted in second round last year out of LSU, where he was fourth most productive career rusher in history. Also a great receiver in college with 50 catches as a senior...As NFL rookie he rushed 158 times for 680 yards and three TDs and caught 34 passes for 219 yards...Big play was 60-yard TD run vs. Pittsburgh in December...Born Sept. 4, 1963, in Gretna, La....Speedster was MVP in East-West Shrine Game following his LSU career.

JEFF CHADWICK 26 6-3 190   Wide Receiver

Home-state boy...Could be Detroit's Cris Collinsworth in controlled passing game... But has to get healthy...Was placed on injured reserve list before final game with Achilles injury...Also hurt in 1985. Broke collarbone...Has 4.5 speed, but was overlooked by scouts when he was timed at 4.75 as a college junior at Grand Valley State, where he set all sorts of school records...But Lion player personnel director Joe Bushofsky clocked him under 4.5 when Chadwick was a senior and the Lions signed him as a free agent in 1983 ...Last season he had 53 catches, one less than James Jones, and he gained 18.5 yards per catch and scored five TDs...Born Dec. 16, 1960, in Dearborn Heights, Mich.

KEITH FERGUSON 28 6-5 260   Defensive End

Acquired on waivers from San Diego on Nov. 21, 1985...Lions had lost Doug English and Martin Moss and desperately needed a defensive end...Ferguson started final four games of 1985 and retained job in 1986.. Named defensive MVP by Lion teammates last season...Led team with 9½ sacks and had 49 tackles, including 41 solos...Had fou of Lions' 11 sacks vs. Eagles in November... Played LB at Ohio State and started at right end for Chargers until he was cut... Lions use him at left end... Born April 3, 1959, in Miami... Was a fifth-round draft choice in 1981.

JIMMIE GILES 32 6-3 240   Tight End

Signed as free agent in middle of 1986 after being cut by Tampa Bay... Quickly replaced David Lewis, Lions' No. 1 draft pick in 1984 ... Lewis virtually disappeared from view except for some special teams sightings... Jeff Chadwick credited Giles for his increased production. "The free safety can't commit so early," said Chadwick, whose stats improved when Giles entered lineup after eight games... Bucs got Giles in trade with Houston in 1978, and he was four-time Pro Bowler ... Appeared to be slowing down dramatically in '85... Born Nov. 8, 1954, in Greenville, Miss.... Was Houston's third-round draft pick in 1977.

COACH DARRYL ROGERS: Has 12-20 record in two seasons with Lions, 7-9 in '85, 5-11 in '86...

Graduated from Fresno State, where he was nation's No. 2-ranked small-college pass receiver as a junior... A U.S. Marine... Had 129-84-7 record from 1965-84 as college head coach... Last two college teams were Michigan State and Arizona State... Took pride as rookie NFL coach in victories over Tom Landry, Don Shula, Bud Grant and Bill Walsh... Sixteenth Lions' head coach... Accustomed to taking over troubled programs. Michigan State was scarred by probation when he took over, and Arizona State was trying to recover from Frank Kush and went on probation after Rogers took over... Michigan State averaged 523 yards per game in 1978 to rewrite Big Ten record books for offense; Arizona State was nation's leading defense in 1982 with 228.9 yards per game... Born May 28, 1935, in Los Angeles.

GREATEST KICKER

Eddie Murray once spurned a tryout with the Vancouver Whitecaps of the North American Soccer League. It was a wise move. The NASL is dead, but Murray is still in business with the Lions.

He was born in Nova Scotia, raised in England and British Columbia and went to college at Tulane. A seventh-round draft choice in 1980, he is one of the most accurate kickers in history. Among kickers with 100 or more successful field goals, he ranks third with a .745 percentage (152 of 204), behind only Pittsburgh's Gary Anderson and Kansas City's Nick Lowery. He has also made 228 of 232 extra points.

INDIVIDUAL LION RECORDS

Rushing

Most Yards Game:	198	Bob Hoernschemeyer, vs N.Y. Yanks, 1950
Season:	1,437	Billy Sims, 1981
Career:	5,106	Billy Sims, 1980-84

Passing

Most TD Passes Game:	5	Gary Danielson, vs Minnesota, 1978
Season	26	Bobby Layne, 1951
Career:	118	Bobby Layne, 1950-58

Receiving

Most TD Passes Game:	4	Cloyce Box, vs Baltimore, 1950
Season:	15	Cloyce Box, 1952
Career:	35	Terry Barr, 1957-65

Scoring

Most Points Game:	24	Cloyce Box, vs Baltimore, 1950
Season:	128	Doak Walker, 1950
Career:	636	Errol Mann, 1969-76
Most TDs Game:	4	Cloyce Box, vs Baltimore, 1950
Season:	16	Billy Sims, 1980
Career:	47	Billy Sims, 1980-84

GREEN BAY PACKERS

TEAM DIRECTORY: Chairman: Dominic Olejiniczak; Pres.: Judge Robert Parins; Sec.: Peter Platten III; Assts. to Pres.: Bob Harlan, Tom Miller; Exec. Dir. Player Personnel: Tom Braatz; Dir. Pub. Rel.: Lee Remmel; Head Coach: Forrest Gregg. Home fields: Lambeau Field (56,926) and County Stadium, Milwaukee (55,976). Colors: Green and gold.

SCOUTING REPORT

OFFENSE: "We paid a dear price," admitted Forrest Gregg, whose team undertook a rebuilding program and dropped from 8-8 to 4-12. It was obvious that another change was needed, so the Packers went out and hired a real personnel specialist, Tom

All-purpose Walter Stanley catches 'em and returns 'em.

Braatz, who had been with the Falcons since 1965. He has his work cut out trying to put this offense back together.

The Packers had the worst rushing attack in the NFC, dead last, 14th out of 14 teams, with 100.9 yards per game. They were fifth in passing yardage (215.4 yards), but that's deceptive because they threw more passes than any team in the conference except for the 49ers. Only three times in the entire NFL (Indianapolis, St. Louis and Tampa Bay) scored fewer points.

Quarterback Randy Wright was called "the most improved player on the team" by coach Forrest Gregg. His 6.6 yards per throw was among the worst averages in the NFC, and he threw 23 interceptions. Better things will be expected with that experience.

The running game produced even less, a major disappointment for Gregg, too. But it got few opportunities with a team that was always trying to come from behind. Auburn fullback Brent Fullwood, the Packs' top pick, should be a help. Kenneth Davis (who had been suspended for his senior season at TCU) and Gary Ellerson failed to produce as much as expected, so Paul Ott Carruth and Gerry Ellis were starters.

There were also the devastating "distractions." James Lofton, the only Pro Bowler on the Packers, got into trouble with the law again and wound up being traded to the Raiders. He led the team with 64 catches and 840 yards despite missing the final game, and his departure only serves to accent the Packers' offensive woes. But at least the Packers have Phil Epps and Walter Stanley with Eddie Lee Ivery coming in on third downs.

DEFENSE: The defense didn't make anything good happen. It was last in the league in takeaways vs. giveaways, a minus 13. And it allowed the second-most points (418) in the NFC, better than only the Bucs.

The Packers will go to a 4-3 this season in the hope that the linemen are better than the linebackers. Alfonso Carreker, a first-round defensive end, never seemed comfortable on a three-man line. Maybe a change will help. Tim Harris, drafted in the fourth round out of Memphis State, is a player, but he needs some support whether he plays outside or the middle.

The secondary might be the most solid unit on the entire team, and that's even with the loss of Tim Lewis, who retired after a neck injury. Gregg contended that left cornerback Mark Lee should have gone to the Pro Bowl, and Tiger Greene was a positive force at strong safety with Ken Stills moving to free safety. Mossy Cade at the right corner was another player with problems off the field, but he played adequately.

PACKERS VETERAN ROSTER

HEAD COACH—Forrest Gregg. Assistant Coaches—Tom Coughlin, Dick Jauron, Virgil Knight, Dale Lindsay, Dick Modzelewski, Willie Peete, George Sefcik, Jerry Wampfler.

No.	Name	Pos.	Ht.	Wt.	NFL Exp.	College
4	Fusina, Chuck	QB	6-1	195	5	Penn State
10	Del Greco, Al	K	5-10	191	4	Auburn
11	Bosco, Robbie	QB	6-2	198	1	Brigham Young
13	Renner, Bill	P	6-0	198	2	Virginia Tech
16	Wright, Randy	QB	6-2	195	4	Wisconsin
18	Shield, Joe	QB	6-1	185	2	Trinity College
20	Berry, Ed	DB	5-10	183	2	Utah State
22	Lee, Mark	DB	5-11	188	8	Washington
23	Greene, George	DB	6-0	194	3	Western Carolina
24	Cade, Mossy	CB	6-1	198	3	Texas
28	Watts, Elbert	CB	6-1	205	2	Southern California
29	Stills, Ken	DB	5-10	186	3	Wisconsin
30	Carruth, Paul Ott	RB	6-1	220	2	Alabama
31	Ellis, Gerry	FB	5-11	235	8	Missouri
32	Simmons, John	CB-KR	5-11	192	7	SMU
33	Clark, Jessie	RB	6-0	228	5	Arkansas
36	Davis, Kenneth	RB	5-10	209	2	Texas Christian
37	Murphy, Mark	S	6-2	201	7	West Liberty
39	Parker, Freddie	RB	5-10	215	2	Mississippi Valley
40	Ivery, Eddie Lee	WR-HB	6-0	206	8	Georgia Tech
42	Ellerson, Gary	RB	5-11	219	3	Wisconsin
49	Greenwood, David	SS	6-3	210	3	Wisconsin
52	Weddington, Mike	LB	6-4	245	2	Oklahoma
53	Leopold, Bobby	LB	6-1	224	6	Notre Dame
55	Scott, Randy	LB	6-1	228	7	Alabama
56	Dent, Burnell	LB	6-1	236	2	Tulane
57	Moran, Rich	C-G	6-2	275	3	San Diego State
58	Cannon, Mark	C	6-3	270	4	Texas-Arlington
59	Anderson, John	LB	6-3	228	10	Michigan
65	Hallstrom, Ron	G	6-6	290	6	Iowa
67	Swanke, Karl	T-C	6-6	262	8	Boston College
69	Cherry, Bill	C-G	6-4	277	2	Middle Tennessee St.
70	Uecker, Keith	G	6-5	284	6	Auburn
72	Neville, Tom	T-G	6-5	306	2	Fresno State
73	Veingrad, Alan	T-G	6-5	277	2	East Texas State
74	Knight, Dan	T	6-5	280	2	San Diego State
75	Ruettgers, Ken	T	6-5	280	3	Southern California
76	Carreker, Alphonso	DE	6-6	271	4	Florida State
77	Feasel, Greg	T	6-7	301	2	Abilene Christian
79	Humphrey, Donnie	DE	6-3	295	4	Auburn
81	Ross, Dan	TE	6-4	240	8	Northeastern
82	Moffitt, Mike	TE	6-4	211	2	Fresno State
84	Franz, Nolan	WR	6-2	183	2	Tulane
85	Epps, Phillip	WR	5-10	165	5	Texas Christian
86	West, Ed	TE	6-1	243	4	Auburn
87	Stanley, Walter	WR-KR	5-9	179	3	Mesa College
89	Lewis, Mark	TE	6-2	237	3	Texas A&M
90	Johnson, Ezra	DE	6-4	264	11	Morris Brown
91	Noble, Brian	LB	6-3	252	3	Arizona State
92	Thomas, Ben	DE-NT	6-4	275	3	Auburn
93	Brown, Robert	DE	6-2	267	6	VPI
94	Martin, Charles	DT	6-4	282	4	Livingston
97	Harris, Timothy	LB	6-4	243	2	Memphis State
98	Moore, Brent	LB	6-5	242	2	Southern California
99	Dorsey, John	LB	6-2	243	4	Connecticut

TOP FIVE DRAFT CHOICES

Rd.	Name	Sel. No.	Pos.	Ht.	Wt.	College
1	Fullwood, Brent	4	RB	5-11	209	Auburn
2	Holland, Johnny	41	LB	6-2	221	Texas A&M
3	Croston, David	61	OT	6-5	280	Iowa
3	Stephen, Scott	69	LB	6-2	232	Arizona State
3	Neal, Frankie	71	WR	6-1	202	Ft. Hays State

Gregg only hopes a four-man line will create more pressure for a team that managed only 28 sacks.

KICKING GAME: A punting game would have helped a lot. Five punts were blocked, and the Packers averaged only 37.7 yards. Don Bracken and Bill Renner might get some competition in camp, but Gregg said he had no complaints about Al Del Greco's kicking. Maybe the addition of Willie Peete as special teams coordinator and backfield coach will help this unit. He comes from Kansas City. The return units are respectable thanks to Walter Stanley.

THE ROOKIES: Tom Braatz, the Packers' new personnel specialist, put together an impressive group, starting with Fullwood, who provides a lot of speed. Fullwood led Auburn and the SEC with 167 carries, 1,391 yards, an 8.3 average and 10 TDs. A half-dozen draft choices should make the team, including linebacker Johnny Holland of Texas A&M, tackle Dave Croston of Iowa, linebacker Scott Stephen of Arizona State, wide receiver Frankie Neal of Fort Hays State and sleeper Jeff Drost, an Iowa tackle who missed much of '86 with injuries.

OUTLOOK: Bleak. Gregg hoped the Packers would come up with at least two "immediate impact" players in the draft. Even then they won't be worth much this year. They are still at least a year away from making their presence felt. Gregg said, "We had a better team on injured reserve than we started." The injuries might have a positive impact on some young players who gained experience.

PACKER PROFILES

WALTER STANLEY 24 5-9 179   Receiver/Returner

Didn't catch a pass as rookie in 1985, but had 34 catches for gaudy 21.1-yard average last season... Drafted in fourth round as return specialist and receiving project. Had limited college experience in two seasons at Colorado as return specialist before transferring to Mesa College, where he did not play on intercollegiate level... A 55-yard kickoff return vs. Vikings was second-longest by the Packers last season. He returned 28 for a 20-yard average. Had 33 punt returns for 316 yards, 9.9 yards per try. Included was 83-yard return vs. Lions for TD... Amassed 1,617 yards in all-purpose yardage... Best

day as a receiver might have been five catches for 97 yards vs. Steelers in ninth game...Obviously was the most improved Packer in '86...Still runs imprecise pass routes, but watch out when he gets the ball...Born Nov. 5, 1962, in Chicago.

KEN RUETTGERS 25 6-5 280   Tackle

The seventh player chosen in the 1985 draft ...Appeared Packer scouts had overestimated his athletic ability, but hard work has helped him toward goals...Started only two games as a rookie, but moved into left tackle position last season...Was a captain at Southern California and could become a badly needed leader for Green Bay...Has distinction of wearing No. 75, which coach Forrest Gregg wore as a premier tackle... Needlepoint is a favorite hobby. Explain that one...He's trying to be more aggressive...Born Aug. 20, 1962, in Bakersfield, Cal.

MARK LEE 29 5-11 188   Cornerback

Nine interceptions at left corner were a career high in his seventh season. Only one interception shy of team record...Packers claim he's their best since Willie Buchanon...Came back from back surgery in '85...Only one interception came on tipped ball. Others were clean takeaways...Interceptions more impressive considering opponents were throwing at Mossy Cade, who was a disappointment (again)...Only bomb completed against Lee was 72-yard catch by Saints' Eric Martin when Lee fell in zone coverage...Allowed only three TD catches...Still needs work against run despite improvement... Played with groin injury vs. Redskins...Born March 20, 1958, in Hanford, Cal....Second-round draft choice in 1980.

MARK CANNON 25 6-3 270   Center

A lost season. Was signed late and suffered two knee injuries that knocked him off the roster...The Packers need him back, or their inside running game will continue to spin its wheels. He's counted on heavily...Was the team's success story of '85. He was an 11th-round draft choice out of Texas-Arlington in '84 and handled long snaps on special teams until Larry McCarren was forced to retire in '85 with an injury . . . Karl Swanke played center when Cannon got hurt last year. Swanke debuted at position in seventh game. He has played every position on offensive line in seven seasons as a Packer. He played five positions in one game in 1981, including tight end. But Cannon is the man the Packers want at center for the rest of the decade . . . Born June 14, 1962, in Austin, Tex.

ALPHONSO CARREKER 25 6-2 271   Defensive End

There was one golden moment in snowy Lambert Field in 1985 when Carreker had four sacks vs. Tampa Bay. There was hope at that moment he would provide the pass rush that was so sorely lacking. Alas, Carreker didn't get four sacks all of last season. He finished with only 3½ . . . A highly conspicuous No. 1 draft choice in '84, he had teammates grumbling that he isn't playing up to his ability or paycheck . . . Secretary of the Defense at Florida State had awesome sack totals. But Packers managed only 28 sacks last season, and Carreker is taking the blame . . . As Packer defensive coordinator Dick Modzelewski said, "He's not a rookie anymore." . . . Born May 25, 1962, in Columbus, Ohio.

CHARLES MARTIN 28 6-4 282   Nose Tackle

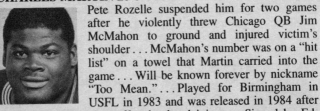

Pete Rozelle suspended him for two games after he violently threw Chicago QB Jim McMahon to ground and injured victim's shoulder . . . McMahon's number was on a "hit list" on a towel that Martin carried into the game . . . Will be known forever by nickname "Too Mean." . . . Played for Birmingham in USFL in 1983 and was released in 1984 after three games when he suffered a hand injury . . . Signed by Edmonton in CFL, but was released and joined Packers for $60,000 salary . . . Was nickel tackle for Packers in 1984 and became starter at nose in 1985 . . . Blocked field goal vs. Minnesota . . . Made Small College All-American in '81 and '82 at Livingston U. . . . Born Aug. 31, 1959, in Canton, Ga.

TIM HARRIS 23 6-4 243   Linebacker

In rookie season, he got eight of Packers' 28 sacks as left outside linebacker and defensive end... Got two of those sacks in finale vs. Giants... Gained 10 pounds last season... Packers might beef him up five or six more pounds if his speed isn't affected. That's because he is sometimes used as a down lineman... Played defensive end at Memphis State before being drafted in fourth round by Packers... Got a chance to play when John Anderson suffered a season-ending injury vs. Minnesota on Sept. 28. Harris debuted as starter vs. Cleveland on Oct. 19... "You can see the improvement in him game by game," said Dick Modzelewski... Born Sept. 10, 1964, in Birmingham, Ala.

RANDY WRIGHT 26 6-2 195   Quarterback

Is this guy good enough? Maybe not... Only second Packer to throw for 3,000 yards in a season. Lynn Dickey did it three times. Completed 263 out of 392 passes for 3,247 yards in '86... Also led NFC with 23 interceptions ... Blame a lot of them on his line... When line jelled late in year, he cut way down on interceptions... Took beating. Played with dislocated finger, sprained ankle and assorted aches and pains ... Coach Forrest Gregg called those "learning experience."... Robbie Bosco, third-round choice in '86, might get crack at job, but Wright won't go quietly... Born Jan. 12, 1961, in Austin, Tex.... A sixth-round choice out of Wisconsin in 1984 NFL draft and a ninth-round pick of Memphis in USFL draft.

PHILLIP EPPS 28 5-10 165   Wide Receiver

Season ended with ankle injury in 12th game vs. Bears... Has verged on being a great receiver for two seasons... Faster than James Lofton, he was brilliant sprinter at TCU before being drafted in 12th round in 1982... Had nine catches (for 99 yards) vs. Bears in third game last season, a career high... Wound up with personal-high 49 catches for 612 yards despite missing four games... Had been used on returns until last year . . . Became starter in 1985 by replacing John Jefferson. Importance increases again because of trade of Lofton to Raiders . . . Born Nov. 11, 1958, in Atlanta, Tex.

COACH FORREST GREGG: Picked as the successor to another legendary Packer player, Bart Starr . . . Agreed to five-year contract on Dec. 24, 1983, to become ninth head coach in team's history . . . Spent four years before that with the Bengals. Over '81 and '82 seasons Bengals went 19-6 and reached the Super Bowl (losing to the 49ers) . . . After two 8-8 years with Packers, Gregg went to management last year and asked whether team should be completely dismantled. With blessing of team president, Judge Robert J. Parins, he started discarding players and substituting younger personnel. The result was a 4-12 season, but Gregg was assured that he would be given more time to rebuild. Maybe new GM, Tom Braatz, will find some players for him . . . Coaches tough, aggressive style. Teams overly pugnacious at times . . . That's how he played. Named to nine Pro Bowls during 14-year career as an offensive lineman. Also won five league titles as a player . . . Battled cancer in late 70s . . . Born Oct. 18, 1933, in Birthright, Tex. . . . All-Southwest Conference tackle at SMU.

GREATEST KICKER

Don Chandler was supposedly giving up in frustration and packing to leave the Giants' camp as a rookie from Florida in 1956 when an assistant coach, Vince Lombardi, convinced him to keep trying. He remained 12 years in the NFL.

The first nine were with the Giants, who won six conference titles and a World Championship with him. But the Packers lay claim to him, too. Lombardi rescued him again in 1965 when Chandler's career hit the rocks and took him to Green Bay.

In Super Bowl II he had four field goals and three PATs in a 33-14 victory over the Raiders. Packer fans chose him over Don Hutson and Paul Hornung, kickers and offensive Hall of Famers, when it was time to elect a kicker for the all-time Green Bay team. He had 117 conversions, 48 FGs in 83 attempts and 261 points as a Packer. He also holds the Packer record for the longest punt, 90 yards vs. the 49ers in 1965.

INDIVIDUAL PACKER RECORDS

Rushing

Most Yards Game:	186	Jim Taylor, vs N.Y. Giants, 1961
Season:	1,474	Jim Taylor, 1962
Career:	8,207	Jim Taylor, 1958-66

Passing

Most TD Passes Game:	5	Cecil Isbell, vs Cleveland, 1942
	5	Don Horn, vs St. Louis, 1969
	5	Lynn Dickey, vs New Orleans, 1981
	5	Lynn Dickey, vs Houston, 1983
Season:	32	Lynn Dickey, 1983
Career:	152	Bart Starr 1956-71

Receiving

Most TD Passes Game:	4	Don Hutson, vs Detroit, 1945
Season:	17	Don Hutson, 1943
Career:	99	Don Hutson, 1935-45

Scoring

Most Points Game:	33	Paul Hornung, vs Baltimore, 1961
Season:	176	Paul Hornung, 1960
Career:	823	Don Hutson, 1935-45
Most TDs Game:	5	Paul Hornung, vs Baltimore, 1961
Season:	19	Jim Taylor, 1962
Career:	105	Don Hutson, 1935-45

LOS ANGELES RAMS

TEAM DIRECTORY: Pres.: Georgia Frontiere; VP-Finance: John Shaw; Dir. Operations: Dick Beam; Adm. Football Operations: Jack Faulkner; Dir. Player Personnel: John Math; Dir. Marketing: Pete Donovan; Dir. Pub. Rel. John Oswald; Head Coach: John Robinson. Home field: Anaheim Stadium (69,007). Colors: Royal blue, gold and white.

SCOUTING REPORT

OFFENSE: Hang on, Eric. Help is on the way. Eric Dickerson has singlehandedly taken the Rams' one-dimensional offense to the playoffs, then taken the blame when they get eliminated. It's unfair. Only five players have gained more than 1,800 yards, and Dickerson has done it three times, including 1,821 yards on 404 carries last year.

The Rams were third in rushing (2,457 yards) and dead last in passing (2,196 yards). So John Robinson finally bought Jim Everett, the third player drafted in 1986, for a very dear price from Houston. Everett started six games, including the NFC wild-card game, but he went only 3-3. The Rams and Everett still didn't seem comfortable with each other, so Robinson hired Ernie Zampese, an architect of the Chargers' passing attack.

"We're going to put in basically the passing game he has used at San Diego," said Robinson. "We'll try to combine what he has done with our running game, trying to mesh the two ideas."

Now, they need someone to catch the ball. Ron Brown has not quite lived up to his world class reputation, and Henry Ellard is not a complete answer at the other receiver position. Tight end is a bit shaky, too. Tony Hunter was on injured reserve for the final five games and was making a very slow comeback after a simple knee scope in the offseason.

The offensive line must adjust its thinking to protect Everett. The Rams beat the bushes for the likes of Mike Schad of Queens (Canada) and Tom Newberry of Wisconsin-LaCrosse last year to add depth to an excellent line with three Pro Bowlers (Dennis Harrah, Jackie Slater and Doug Smith). With a few more bodies (perhaps using those three '87 draft picks from the Bears for Doug Flutie) it could be interesting.

DEFENSE: The Rams are still looking for a pass-rusher and a nickel back. The defense was ranked fourth in the NFC (304.4 yards per game), but it didn't scare people. Gary Jeter has been the designated pass-rusher, but he's getting up in years.

Nobody in the NFL rushed for more than Eric Dickerson.

The Rams' sack total fell from 56 in 1985 to 39 last year. This is one reason the Rams spent their top draft pick on Winston-Salem defensive end Donald Evans.

Among the linebackers, Mike Wilcher's totals also dipped. He was no longer the force he had been in the past, and Karl Ekern, an anonymous sort, was chosen to go to the Pro Bowl instead. Kevin Greene was pushing Wilcher at times for the job and has been promised more playing time this year. An inside backer like Jim Collins (knee) is also tough to replace, and his absence was

RAMS VETERAN ROSTER

HEAD COACH—John Robinson. Assistant Coaches—Dick Coury, Artie Gigantino, Marv Goux, Gil Haskell, Hudson Houck, Steve Shafer, Fritz Shurmur, Norval Turner, Fred Whittingham, Ernie Zampese.

No.	Name	Pos.	Ht.	Wt.	NFL Exp.	College
89	Brown, Ron	WR	5-11	181	4	Arizona State
53	Busick, Steve	LB	6-4	227	8	Southern California
50	Collins, Jim	LB	6-2	230	7	Syracuse
72	Cox, Robert	T	6-5	260	1	UCLA
21	Cromwell, Nolan	S	6-1	200	11	Kansas
29	Dickerson, Eric	RB	6-3	220	5	SMU
8	Dils, Steve	QB	6-1	191	8	Stanford
71	Doss, Reggie	DE	6-4	263	10	Hampton Institute
55	Ekern, Carl	LB	6-3	222	11	San Jose State
80	Ellard, Henry	WR	5-11	175	5	Fresno State
11	Everett, Jim	QB	6-5	212	2	Purdue
63	Goebel, Hank	T	6-7	255	1	Cal State-Fullerton
25	Gray, Jerry	CB	6-0	185	3	Texas
91	Greene, Kevin	LB	6-3	238	3	Auburn
44	Guman, Mike	RB	6-2	218	8	Penn State
60	Harrah, Dennis	G	6-5	265	13	Miami
3	Hatcher, Dale	P	6-2	200	3	Clemson
81	Hill, David	TE	6-2	240	12	Texas A&I
83	House, Kevin	WR	6-1	185	8	Southern Illinois
87	Hunter, Tony	TE	6-4	237	5	Notre Dame
47	Irvin, LeRoy	CB	5-11	187	8	Kansas
59	Jerue, Mark	LB	6-3	232	5	Washington
77	Jeter, Gary	DE	6-4	260	11	Southern California
86	Johnson, Damone	TE	6-4	230	2	Cal Poly SLO
20	Johnson, Johnnie	S	6-1	183	8	Texas
1	Lansford, Mike	PK	6-0	183	6	Washington
45	Long, Darren	TE	6-3	240	2	Long Beach State
67	Love, Duval	G	6-3	263	3	UCLA
90	McDonald, Mike	LB	6-1	230	4	Southern California
69	Meisner, Greg	NT	6-3	253	7	Pittsburgh
12	Millen, Hugh	QB	6-5	215	1	Washington
98	Miller, Shawn	NT	6-4	255	4	Utah State
66	Newberry, Tom	G	6-1	279	2	Wis.-LaCrosse
22	Newsome, Vince	S	6-1	179	5	Washington
58	Owens, Mel	LB	6-2	224	7	Michigan
75	Pankey, Irv	T	6-4	267	8	Penn State
30	Redden, Barry	RB	5-10	205	6	Richmond
93	Reed, Doug	DE	6-3	262	4	San Diego State
97	Schad, Mike	G	6-5	270	1	Queens (Ontario)
84	Scott, Chuck	WR	6-2	202	2	Vanderbilt
78	Slater, Jackie	T	6-4	271	12	Jackson State
61	Slaton, Tony	C	6-4	265	4	Southern California
56	Smith, Doug	C	6-3	260	10	Bowling Green
49	Sutton, Mickey	CB	5-8	165	2	Montana
32	Tyrrell, Tim	RB	6-1	201	4	Northern Illinois
51	Vann, Norwood	LB	6-1	225	4	East Carolina
33	White, Charles	RB	5-10	190	7	Southern California
54	Wilcher, Mike	LB	6-3	240	5	North Carolina
99	Wright, Alvin	NT	6-2	285	2	Jacksonville St.
88	Young, Michael	WR	6-1	185	3	UCLA

TOP FIVE DRAFT CHOICES

Rd.	Name	Sel. No.	Pos.	Ht.	Wt.	College
2	Evans, Donald	47	DE	6-2	267	Winston-Salem
3	Hicks, Clifford	74	DB	5-10	183	Oregon
4	Bartlett, Doug	91	DT	6-2	250	Northern Illinois
4	Keim, Larry	109	LB	6-4	226	Texas A&M
5	Mersereau, Scott	136	DT	6-4	275	So. Connecticut

deeply felt.

In the secondary, Tim Fox finally called it a career although he had alternated with three other safeties last season. The starting defensive backs are all solid. Safety Nolan Cromwell is coming off a great season although he is 32, and both cornerbacks, Jerry Gray and LeRoy Irvin, were Pro Bowlers. Biggest loss here was Gary Green, who was injured, then cut.

KICKING GAME: Dale Hatcher had a bad year. His gross average dropped from 43.2 to 38.6 yards on 97 punts, a mind-boggling number for such a successful team. Mike Lansford was still effective, kicking 17-of-24 field goals, but the return specialists were uneven. Maybe Henry Ellard's late arrival was partly to blame on punt returns.

THE ROOKIES: Without a first-round draft pick because of the Everett trade, the Rams were forced to beat the bushes to come up with Evans. He was the first of five consecutive defensive selections. In the sixth round, the Rams got around to a tight end, Jon Embree of Colorado, whose blocking might help. It is a most unpromising rookie class.

OUTLOOK: Imagine the Chargers with an 1,800-yard rusher. Imagine the Rams with Dan Fouts in his prime. Now imagine what the Rams might become if Ernie Zampese can work his magic in L.A. The Rams should be fighting it out with the 49ers for quite some time for the western title.

RAM PROFILES

ERIC DICKERSON 26 6-3 220   **Running Back**

Fifth-best rushing performance in NFL history —404 carries (club record), 1,821 yards, 11 TDs, 4.5 average, 11 100-yard games. Also 205 yards receiving... Picked for Pro Bowl third time in the four years since he left SMU ... Only sour note was in playoffs when his fumbles led to the elimination of the Rams against Redskins. Same thing happened previous year against Chicago... Also led NFC with 15 fumbles in regular season... Forgive him. If Rams don't have him, they're nothing offensively... Said big thrill was his TD throw to David Hill that beat Atlanta... Set club career records for most rushes

(1,465), most yards (6,968) and most touchdowns (57)...Born Sept. 2, 1960, in Sealy, Tex....Was second pick in 1983 draft.

JIM EVERETT 24 6-5 212   Quarterback

After years of run, run, run, Rams gave G Kent Hill, DE William Fuller, first- and fifth-round draft choices in 1987 and a first-round draft choice in 1988 to Houston for Everett last September...Third player selected in 1985 draft behind Bo Jackson and Falcons' Tony Casillas...Outstanding at Purdue (572 of 965, 7,411 yards, 43 TDs, 33 interceptions)...Tremendous rookie pressure...He wound up as a starter, completing 73 of 147 for 1,108 yards, eight touchdowns, and had eight interceptions...Rams were still last in NFL in passing...With experience, Everett could be the answer to John Robinson's prayers...Born Jan. 3, 1963, in Albuquerque, N.M.

DOUG SMITH 30 6-3 260   Center

Selected to Pro Bowl for third straight year ...Remains anonymous...Excellent blocker for pass or run...Rams compare him to Rich Saul and Ken Iman...Has started at four different positions, left guard, right guard, right tackle, center...Overachiever who wasn't drafted out of Bowling Green...Born Nov. 25, 1956, in Columbus, Ohio...Has a degree in education and is working on a master's degree in exercise physiology at Cal State-Fullerton.

JERRY GRAY 25 6-0 185   Cornerback

Eight interceptions returned for 101 yards, 12.6 average...Finished season by going to Pro Bowl...A far cry from rookie season in 1985 when he played mainly on nickel defense and special teams. First-rounder out of Texas had no sacks until playoffs and 10 of his 15 tackles were on special teams...Retirement of four-time Pro Bowler Gary Green with neck injury hastened move from safety to corner...Tied for fifth in the NFL with his interceptions and led team in passes defensed ...Born Dec. 2, 1961, in Lubbock, Tex.

LEROY IRVIN 29 5-11 185   Cornerback

Made second trip to Pro Bowl... Trivia: Only player whose last name starts with an "I" to participate in the Pro Bowl... Six interceptions for 150 yards, 25.0 average... Second straight year with five interceptions and third straight year with an interception returned for a TD... That TD return was for 50 yards vs. Dallas... He also scored touchdowns by returning a blocked field goal 65 yards against the 49ers and by returning a recovered fumble 22 yards against the Bears... An outstanding punt-returner in first five years... Drafted in third round in 1980 out of Kansas... Born Sept. 15, 1957, in Fort Dix, N.J.

NOLAN CROMWELL 32 6-1 200   Safety

One of Rams' ancient safeties last year. Tim Fox was one year older, Johnnie Newsome was one year younger... Sometimes alternated quarters with Vince Newsome at SS... Intercepted 5 passes for 101 yards. Got 80 yards on longest return of his career for TD vs. Lions on Oct 19. "They told me the ref was catching me on the sideline," he kidded... Legendary career. QB at Kansas, he was drafted in second round in 1977... Has been a starter since 1979... Was free safety until 1985... Went to Pro Bowl four straight years, 1980-83... Born Jan. 30, 1955, in Smith Center, Kan.

TOM NEWBERRY 24 6-1 279   Guard

Rams spent first two 1986 draft picks on offensive linemen. Tackle Mike Schad from Canada spent year on injured reserve. Newberry, a second-rounder from Wisconsin-La Crosse, became permanent starter when Kent Hill, a five-time Pro Bowler, was traded to Houston... Rams' only 1986 draft choice to play at all... Strong, quick and smart... Eighth best shot-putter in world in 1985. Runs 40 in 4.68. Benches 460-plus pounds, squats 740-plus... Won four bouts by KO in tough-man contest. Graduated with degree in geography ... Pulls well... Played fullback in high school... Born Dec. 20, 1962, in Onalaska, Wis.

CARL EKERN 33 6-3 222   Linebacker

Defensive captain . . . Missed three weeks with ankle injury, but finally received Pro Bowl recognition in 10th season . . . Third in tackles on tough defense . . . Four consecutive seasons with more than 100 tackles for inside LB . . . Fifth-rounder out of San Jose State in 1978 waited five seasons before his first start. Knee injuries forced him to miss entire 1979 season and six games in 1982 . . . Player representative . . . Born May 27, 1954, in Richland, Wash.

JACKIE SLATER 33 6-4 271   Tackle

Captain and anchor of offensive line . . . Man in front of Eric Dickerson . . . Drafted in third round out of Jackson State in 1976 . . . Only Dennis Harrah has played more games among active Rams . . . Became a starter in 1979 . . . Named NFC Offensive Lineman of the Year by the NFC's defensive linemen and linebackers . . . Received game ball for his performance against Too Tall Jones . . . Made Pro Bowl for third time in four years . . . Harrah and Doug Smith were other Ram offensive linemen who went to Hawaii . . . Born May 27, 1954, in Jackson, Miss.

HENRY ELLARD 26 5-11 175   Wide Receiver

Tough holdout. Showed up in week eight . . . Rams stewed and considered trade although he was most dangerous player besides Dickerson . . . Still led team in receiving (34 catches, 447 yards, 4 TDs) and punt returns (14 for 127 yards, 9.1 average) . . . However, return production fell way off . . . Had entered season with 13.5-yard average and at least one TD every year . . . Holdout dropped him below '85 production as a receiver when he caught 54 passes for 811 yards, but if his '86 stats were projected for full season he might have had 78 catches, 1,022 yards . . . Drafted in second round in 1983 out of Fresno State . . . Went to Pro Bowl as punt-returner in 1984 . . . Born July 21, 1961, in Fresno, Cal.

COACH JOHN ROBINSON: Arrived from Southern Cal at same time Eric Dickerson arrived from SMU in 1983 . . . Rams were 2-7 in 1982, but since that duo showed up, L.A. has been 42-17 and appeared in the playoffs for four consecutive years . . . Robinson's coaching experience spans more than 25 years. After lettering at end for Oregon, he became assistant at that school from 1960-71. Also assisted at USC from 1972-74 before first excursion into NFL with Raiders in 1975 under John Madden, a boyhood friend . . . Succeeded John McKay at USC in 1976 and teams had 67-14-2 record in seven seasons . . . Coached Charles White and Marcus Allen at USC to prepare him for Dickerson . . . Installed one-back offense and 3-4 defense in '83 . . . Teams have lacked passing, a drawback if they fall behind. Also have rotten luck in playoffs, where turnovers and mistakes spoiled their chances . . . Went 10-6 in regular season last year, but lost on mistakes in NFC wild-card game while outgaining Redskins.

GREATEST KICKER

Bob Waterfield was a man of many talents. He was famous as a quarterback (still third on the Rams' all-time list with 11,893 yards passing) and as the husband of actress Jane Russell. But he was also a great punter and kicker.

He led the league four times in PATs (Cleveland Rams 1945, L.A. Rams 1946, '50, '52) and three times in field goals (1947, '49, '51). The one-time UCLA star played for the Rams from 1945 through 1952. He piled up a Ram-record 573 points on 13 TDs, 315 PATs and 60 FGs. He kicked five FGs in one game vs. Detroit in 1951.

As a punter, he had kicks of 88 yards in 1948 and 86 in 1947, still Ram records, and he averaged 44.6 yards on 39 punts in 1946, the third-best average for a Ram season. His 315 punts are the second most in the team's history. He coached the Rams from 1960-62.

INDIVIDUAL RAM RECORDS
Rushing

Most Yards Game:	248	Eric Dickerson, vs Dallas, 1985
Season:	2,105	Eric Dickerson, 1984
Career:	6,968	Eric Dickerson, 1983-86

Passing

Most TD Passes Game:	5	Bob Waterfield, vs N.Y. Bulldogs, 1949
	5	Norm Van Brocklin, vs Detroit, 1950
	5	Norm Van Brocklin, vs N.Y. Yanks, 1951
	5	Roman Gabriel, vs Cleveland, 1965
	5	Vince Ferragamo, vs New Orleans, 1980
	5	Vince Ferragamo, vs San Francisco, 1983
Season:	30	Vince Ferragamo, 1980
Career:	154	Roman Gabriel, 1962-72

Receiving

Most TD Passes Game:	4	Bob Shaw, vs Washington, 1949
	4	Elroy Hirsch, vs N.Y. Yanks, 1951
	4	Harold Jackson, vs Dallas, 1973
Season:	17	Elroy Hirsch, 1951
Career:	53	Elroy Hirsch, 1949-57

Scoring

Most Points Game:	24	Elroy Hirsch, vs N.Y. Yanks, 1951
	24	Bob Shaw, vs Washington, 1949
	24	Harold Jackson, vs Dallas, 1973
Season:	130	David Ray, 1973
Career:	573	Bob Waterfield, 1945-52
Most TDs Game:	4	Elroy Hirsch, vs N.Y. Yanks, 1951
	4	Bob Shaw, vs Washington, 1949
	4	Harold Jackson, vs Dallas, 1973
Season:	20	Eric Dickerson, 1983
Career:	57	Eric Dickerson, 1983-86

MINNESOTA VIKINGS

TEAM DIRECTORY: Pres.: Max Winter; Exec. VP/GM: Mike Lynn; Dir. Administration: Harley Peterson; Dir. Football Operations: Jerry Reichow; Dir. Pub. Rel.: Merrill Swanson; Head Coach: Jerry Burns. Home field: Hubert H. Humphrey Metrodome (63,000). Colors: Purple, white and gold.

Tommy Kramer was highest-rated NFL passer in '86.

SCOUTING REPORT

OFFENSE: Quarterback Tommy Kramer and a mistake-proof offense took the Vikings to their best record since 1980. Kramer finally made the Pro Bowl at the age of 31, in his 10th season in the NFL. He finished the season as the highest-rated passer in the league. And if age or injuries set in, the Vikings have a replacement, Wade Wilson.

In the meantime, Kramer and the Vikings seem to have a few good seasons left. There are two offensive linemen, center Dennis Swilley and guard Jim Hough, above 30, but the heart of the line is tackle Gary Zimmerman, who shunned the Giants and forced them to trade him to the Vikings on draft day in 1986.

Receiver Sammy White, a two-time Pro Bowler, didn't play last year and retired at the end of the season. But there were already able replacements. Anthony Carter and Leo Lewis both averaged more than 18 yards per catch, and Hassan Jones, a rookie, had more than 20 yards per catch. Tight end Steve Jordan and running back Darrin Nelson each had more than 50 catches. Little wonder that the Vikings gained 4,185 yards passing and only 1,738 rushing. Penn State running back D.J. Dozier, the Vikings top pick, should help the ground game.

Jerry Burns wasted no time in establishing himself as head coach. At the end of the season, he had 14 players who had not been with the club in 1985, and several of them were big contributors, including Zimmerman and Jones on offense.

DEFENSE: Watch out, Bears. Another defense is rising in the Central Division. Only one newcomer, free safety John Harris, a nine-year veteran acquired in a trade, started on defense. Most of the defensive starters are young and virtually every position has a young challenger—Gerald Robinson and Joe Phillips on the defensive line, Jesse Solomon at linebacker and David Evans and Neal Guggemos in the secondary.

The Vikings played an opportunistic style of football. They had 42 takeaways (40 by the defense) and lost the ball only 29 times on fumbles and interceptions. The Vikings scored 22 times (15 touchdowns and seven field goals) following the takeaways; the opposition scored only four TDs and four FGs. They allowed a total of only 273 points.

On the defensive line, three of the four starters (Tim Newton, Keith Millard and Chris Doleman) were in only their second season. They made life miserable for teams that tried to run, and the line accounted for 27 sacks. The old man on the line, Doug Martin, is only 30, and if he resembles his brother, the Giants'

VIKINGS VETERAN ROSTER

HEAD COACH—Jerry Burns. Assistant Coaches—Tom Batta, Pete Carroll, Monte Kiffin, John Michels, Floyd Peters, Dick Rehbein, Bob Schnelker, Marc Trestman, Paul Wiggin.

No.	Name	Pos.	Ht.	Wt.	NFL Exp.	College
46	Anderson, Alfred	RB	6-1	220	4	Baylor
58	Ashley, Walker Lee	LB	6-0	237	4	Penn State
21	Bess, Rufus	CB	5-9	189	9	South Carolina State
62	Boyd, Brent	G	6-3	280	7	UCLA
23	Brown, Ted	RB	5-10	212	9	North Carolina State
47	Browner, Joey	S	6-2	212	5	USC
81	Carter, Anthony	WR	5-11	175	3	Michigan
8	Coleman, Greg	P	6-0	184	11	Florida A&M
56	Doleman, Chris	LB	6-5	250	3	Pittsburgh
26	Evans, David	CB	6-0	178	2	Central Arkansas
—	Freeman, Steve	S	5-11	185	12	Mississippi State
41	Guggemos, Neal	S	6-0½	187	2	St. Thomas
80	Gustafson, Jim	WR	6-1	181	2	St. Thomas
44	Harris, John	S	6-2	198	10	Arizona State
82	Hilton, Carl	TE	6-3	232	2	Houston
30	Holt, Issiac	CB	6-1	197	3	Alcorn State
51	Hough, Jim	C-G	6-2	269	10	Utah State
99	Howard, David	LB	6-2	232	3	Cal-Long Beach
72	Huffman, David	T	6-6	284	8	Notre Dame
76	Irwin, Tim	T	6-7½	288	7	Tennessee
84	Jones, Hassan	WR	6-0	195	2	Florida State
83	Jordan, Steve	TE	6-3½	230	6	Brown
9	Kramer, Tommy	QB	6-2	205	11	Rice
39	Lee, Carl	DB	5-11½	187	5	Marshall
87	Lewis, Leo	WR	5-8	170	7	Missouri
63	Lowdermilk, Kirk	C	6-3	269	3	Ohio State
27	Lush, Mike	S	6-2	195	2	East Stroudsburg St.
71	MacDonald, Mike	G	6-4	267	3	Boston College
57	Martin, Chris	LB	6-2	239	5	Auburn
79	Martin, Doug	DE	6-3	270	8	Washington
75	Millard, Keith	DT	6-6	262	3	Washington State
86	Mularkey, Mike	TE	6-4	234	5	Florida
77	Mullaney, Mark	DE	6-6	248	13	Colorado State
1	Nelson, Chuck	K	5-11½	172	4	Washington
20	Nelson, Darrin	RB	5-9	183	6	Stanford
96	Newton, Tim	DT	6-0	287	3	Florida
91	Phillips, Joe	DT	6-4	278	2	SMU
88	Rhymes, Buster	WR	6-1½	218	3	Oklahoma
36	Rice, Allen	RB	5-10	204	4	Baylor
95	Robinson, Gerald	DE	6-3	256	2	Auburn
68	Rouse, Curtis	G	6-3	335	6	Tenn.-Chattanooga
78	Schippang, Gary	T	6-4	279	2	West Chester
53	Schuh, Jeff	LB	6-3	234	7	Minnesota
54	Solomon, Jesse	LB	6-0	235	8	Florida State
74	Stensrud, Mike	DT	6-5	280	9	Iowa State
55	Studwell, Scott	LB	6-2	230	11	Illinois
67	Swilley, Dennis	C	6-3	266	10	Texas A&M
66	Tausch, Terry	G	6-5	276	6	Texas
37	Teal, Willie	CB	5-10	192	8	Louisiana State
11	Wilson, Wade	QB	6-3	213	7	East Texas State
65	Zimmerman, Gary	T	6-6	280	2	Oregon

TOP FIVE DRAFT CHOICES

Rd.	Name	Sel. No.	Pos.	Ht.	Wt.	College
1	Dozier, D.J.	14	RB	6-1	210	Penn State
2	Berry, Ray	44	LB	6-2	227	Baylor
3	Thomas, Henry	72	DT	6-2	263	Louisiana State
4	Rutland, Reginald	100	DB	6-2	192	Georgia Tech
6	Richardson, Greg	156	WR	6-6	166	Alabama

George Martin, he can continue for five more years.

Middle linebacker Scott Studwell, 33, is the old man of the defense. And he'll be tough to replace when that day comes. But he is surrounded by more young starters, Chris Martin and David Howard.

And the secondary is just as young with the exception of Harris. There are cornerbacks Issiac Holt and Carl Lee, who have a total of six years' experience, and strong safety Joey Browner, a four-year vet.

Considering their age and ability, the Vikings' defense is going to be challenging the Bears before long.

KICKING GAME: Kicker Chuck Nelson missed only 6-of-28 field-goal attempts, and one of those was blocked. He was signed during a February kicker camp and made an immediate impact.

Punter Greg Coleman's average dropped slightly. But it was still respectable at 41.4 yards. And Rufus Bess was effective as both a punt and kickoff returner.

THE ROOKIES: The Vikings already have a good, young team, and Dozier fits their offensive scheme perfectly. He adds needed size to the backfield. Minnesota's next three choices went for defensive players, but they still had a couple left over to get Greg Richardson, the Alabama wide receiver/kick-returner who averaged 17.09 yards on 23 catches and 7.83 yards on 42 punt returns, and Montana quarterback Brent Pease, who will be given a shot at backing up Kramer.

OUTLOOK: The Vikings slipped up on folks last season. But don't expect them to go away very soon. They might have to replace some offensive players, but their defense will carry them through any tough times for a lot of seasons.

VIKING PROFILES

TOMMY KRAMER 32 6-2 205   Quarterback

After worst season of his career in 1985, last year Kramer was starter in Pro Bowl. First such trip in 10 NFL seasons... Highest QB rating in NFL at 92.6, barely nosing out Dolphin Dan Marino's 92.5... Completed 208 of 372 passes for 3,000 yards and 24 TDs (NFC high) with only 10 interceptions... Average gain of 8.06 yards per attempt also led NFC

. . . His 490 yards in OT loss vs. the Redskins was highest output by an NFC quarterback last year . . . First NFL QB to pass for over 450 yards twice in a career . . . Missed final week of season with elbow injury, and backup Wade Wilson had 361 yards vs. Saints . . . Rice grad was 27th player selected in 1977 draft . . . Became starter in '79 when Fran Tarkenton retired . . . Has had 3,000-yard seasons five times . . . Born March 7, 1955, in San Antonio, Tex.

ANTHONY CARTER 26 5-11 175   Wide Receiver

Had 38 catches for 686 yards . . . His seven TDs were tied for third best in NFC, and his 18.1 yards per catch was fifth best . . . Those stats were slight decline from first season with Vikings in 1985 . . . All-Big Ten three times at Michigan. Played for three years in USFL with Michigan and Oakland. USFL totals included 161 catches, 3,076 yards, 37 TDs . . . Vikings acquired NFL rights from Miami, which had made him the 334th player (twelfth round) chosen in the 1983 draft . . . Carter had five 100-yard games in 1985, only one in '86 . . . Born Sept. 17, 1960, in Riviera Beach, Fla., and lives in his home town in the offseason.

SCOTT STUDWELL 33 6-2 230   Linebacker

Rugged MLB led club in tackles for six consecutive years, but he was displaced by strong safety Joey Browner last season . . . Had 81 unassisted tackles, lowest total since 1979, but was second on team . . . Jesse Solomon of Florida was drafted in 12th round and served as his understudy . . . Studwell broke Dick Butkus' Illinois season record with 177 tackles as senior . . . Weighed 260 pounds and played tackle. Went late in draft (No. 250, ninth round) because speed was suspect until he trimmed down . . . Born Aug. 27, 1954, in Evansville, Ind.

STEVE JORDAN 26 6-3½ 230   Tight End

Led team with 58 catches and 859 yards receiving. Those stats were second only to Giants' Mark Bavaro among NFC tight ends . . . Had six TD catches while Bavaro had only four . . . Most receiving yardage by a Viking since Ahmad Rashad's 1,095 in 1980 . . . Selected to Pro Bowl for first time in five NFL seasons . . . Two 100-yard receiving games . . .

Proved that 1985 was no fluke. Had 68 catches (first time a Viking receiver had more than 60 catches since Joe Senser and Sammy White each did it in 1961) for 795 yards in '85 . . . Was seventh-round draft choice out of Brown in 1982 . . . Ivy Leaguer has degree in civil engineering . . . Born Jan. 10, 1961, in Phoenix, Ariz.

DOUG MARTIN 30 6-3 270   Defensive End

A copy of his big brother, George, who plays for the Giants. They opposed each other for first time last season. George had six tackles, Doug had three tackles, three assists with sack and defensed a pass . . . Named NFC Defensive Player of the Month for September . . . Second on Vikings with nine sacks (behind Keith Millard with 10½) . . . Forced three fumbles and recovered two . . . Ninth player chosen in 1980 draft . . . Attended Washington, where he was chosen Most Valuable Lineman in 1979 Sun Bowl . . . Born May 22, 1957, in Fairfield, Cal.

DARRIN NELSON 28 5-9 183   Running Back

Versatile back was ninth in NFC with 1,386 yards from scrimmage. Had 53 catches for 593 yards and three TDs and 191 carries for 793 yards and four TDs . . . Also returned three kicks for 105 yards . . . Arrived late in camp because of contract dispute, and Vikings reportedly considered trading him . . . While at Stanford, he became NCAA's all-time, all-purpose yardage leader: 4,033 rushing, 2,368 receiving, 484 returns . . . First running back and seventh player selected in 1982 draft . . . Became first rookie running back ever to start an opening game for Vikings . . . Born Jan. 2, 1959, in Sacramento, Cal.

JOEY BROWNER 27 6-2 212   Safety

Led Vikings in tackles (98), fumbles forced (3), fumbles recovered (4) . . . Returned interception 39 yards for touchdown . . . Went to Pro Bowl for second straight year. In '85, he was selected by John Robinson as special teamer in Pro Bowl. Last year, he went for his defensive credentials . . . Still excelled on specials with nine tackles . . . Two brothers also play in NFL. Ross plays for Cincinnati and Keith was traded to 49ers by Bucs in offseason . . . At Southern California he played strong safety as freshman, cornerback as sophomore and junior and free safety as senior . . . Became first defensive back ever selected by Vikings in the first round in '83 draft . . . Born May 15, 1960, in Warren, Ohio.

ISSIAC HOLT 24 6-1 197   Cornerback

Eight interceptions in second NFL season. Most interceptions by Viking since Paul Krause had 10 in 1975 . . . Came a long way in one year. Had one interception as rookie . . . Started only one game in 1985. Had eight tackles in that game, only 25 for season . . . Had 52 tackles last season . . . Fourth defensive back and 30th player chosen in '85 draft . . . Set NCAA I-AA record with 24 career interceptions at Alcorn State . . . Born Oct. 4, 1962, in Birmingham, Ala. . . . Nicknamed "Ike" in college.

GERALD ROBINSON 24 6-3-256   Defensive End

Third defensive end and 14th player selected in 1986 draft . . . One of the four first-round picks on Vikings' defensive line last season. Doug Martin (1980), Keith Millard (1984) and Chris Doleman (1985) were the others . . . Robinson played well at right end and was named NFC Player of the Week vs. the Bears on Oct. 19 for six solo tackles and 2½ assists . . . Next week he broke his right fibula vs. Cleveland. "Just when I was getting on a roll," he said . . . Finished season with 26 tackles, 12 solos, 3½ sacks. Also had 17 special-teams tackles . . . Born May 4, 1963, in Tuskegee, Ala . . . Youngest of 12 children . . . Led Auburn defense as an end.

GARY ZIMMERMAN 25 6-6 280   Tackle

Anchored offensive line at left tackle in first NFL season . . . Played two seasons in USFL with L.A. Express . . . Giants acquired his NFL rights in supplemental draft in 1984. Refused to play on East Coast when Express folded. Was acquired by Vikings for two second-round draft picks . . . David Huffman held off challenge for several weeks, but by season's end Zimmerman established himself... Has versatility to play tackle, center or guard. Handled long snaps for Express ... Voted Outstanding Offensive Lineman in Pac-10 as senior at Oregon in 1983... Born Dec. 13, 1961, in Fullerton, Cal.

COACH JERRY BURNS: Vikings' 9-7 record in 1986 was best since 9-7 in 1980... Burns was first Viking coach to have winning record in his first year. Norm Van Brocklin was 3-11 in '61, Bud Grant 3-8-3 in 1967 and Les Steckel 3-13 in 1984... Served as Vikings' assistant head coach and offensive coordinator since 1968 and got credit for devising short passing game and one-back offense... Played QB at Michigan... Upon graduation served as backfield coach for Hawaii in 1951 and at Whittier in '52... Coached a year of high-school ball in Detroit in 1954 before a 12-year stretch (1954-65) at Iowa (the last five years as head coach) as Hawkeyes won two Big Ten titles... Left for Green Bay for two years, then moved to Vikings... Jerry Reichow, director of Packer football operations, and Frank Gilliam, director of player personnel, played for Burns at Iowa... Born Jan. 24, 1927, in Detroit.

GREATEST KICKER

Kicking is a gypsy life, but when the Vikings find a kicker they like, they keep him. Punter Greg Coleman has been with the Vikings since 1978 and has gotten better and better. But he has a way to go before he matches Fred Cox's stay from 1963-77.

From his rookie season until 1973, Cox scored in 151 consecutive games, a string that still stands as an NFL record, and from 1968-70 he made field goals in 31 consecutive games, another NFL mark. In 1965, '69 and '70 he led the league in field goals.

He made 282 of 455 field goals, 519 of 538 PATs and scored 1,365 points. The second-highest scorer in team history is Bill Brown with only 456. Cox's most productive day was on Sept. 23, 1973, against the Bears when he made five of six field-goal attempts.

INDIVIDUAL VIKING RECORDS

Rushing

Most Yards Game:	200	Chuck Foreman, vs Philadelphia, 1976
Season:	1,155	Chuck Foreman, 1976
Career:	5,879	Chuck Foreman, 1973-79

Passing

Most TD Passes Game:	7	Joe Kapp, vs Baltimore, 1969
Season:	26	Tommy Kramer, 1981
Career	239	Francis Tarkenton, 1961-66, 1972-78

Receiving

Most TD Passes Game:	4	Ahmad Rashad, vs San Francisco, 1979
Season:	11	Jerry Reichow, 1961
Career:	50	Sammy White, 1976-85

Scoring

Most Points Game:	24	Chuck Foreman, vs Buffalo, 1975
	24	Ahmad Rashad, vs San Francisco, 1979
Season:	132	Chuck Foreman, 1975
Career:	1,365	Fred Cox, 1963-77
Most TDs Game:	4	Chuck Foreman, vs Buffalo, 1975
	4	Ahmad Rashad, vs San Francisco, 1979
Season:	22	Chuck Foreman, 1975
Career:	76	Bill Brown, 1962-74

NEW ORLEANS SAINTS

TEAM DIRECTORY: Owner: Tom Benson; Pres./GM: Jim Finks; VP-Administration: Jim Miller; Bus. Mgr./Controller: Bruce Broussard; Dir. Pub. Rel./Marketing: Greg Suit; Dir. Media Services; Rusty Kasmiersky; Head Coach: Jim Mora. Home field: Superdome (69,723). Colors: Old gold, black and white.

SCOUTING REPORT

OFFENSE: Injuries took a heavy toll. But the Saints need help even when they're healthy. Indeed, they had their most success when their quarterback, Bobby Hebert, was sidelined. After all

Rickey Jackson made fourth straight trip to Pro Bowl.

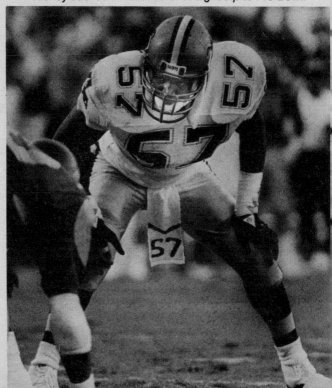

those years in the USFL and two seasons with the Saints, Hebert is still a mystery. He has a good arm, but the other quarterback, Dave Wilson, has a far superior head. Wilson took over and led the Saints to five victories in six games when Hebert got hurt in midseason.

The Saints survived other injuries, too. Tackle Jim Dombrowski and guard Ralph William were both injured, and their subs, Bill Contz and Chuck Commiskey, didn't kill the quarterback. Jim Erkenback, the offensive line coach, got some attention for that feat. He was signed to what amounts to a lifetime contract with the Cowboys, and Paul Boudreau, from Edmonton of the CFL, was added to the Saints' staff.

The Saints also were without Hokie Gajan, the fullback who was emerging as a real star for his blocking and running, and Barry Word, who was in jail for 4½ months for drug problems. The Saints are waiting to see how well both Gajan and Word turn out. In the meantime, they always have Rookie-of-the-Year Rueben Mayes, who was simply outstanding in earning a Pro Bowl assignment. Mayes underwent surgery on his Achilles after the season, but it's hard to imagine he might be any better. He enabled the Saints to outrush their opponents for only the second time in their history. They were fifth in the NFC with 129.6 yards per game.

Perhaps the weakest area is at the receivers, but GM Jim Finks always fills those positions last. The starters, Mike Jones and Eric Martin, were used mainly on timing patterns, partly to accommodate Wilson. And there is very little depth.

DEFENSE: It's amazing that the Saints allowed only 287 points, seventh in the NFL. There are 14 teams in the NFC, and 13 had a better pass defense than the Saints. New Orleans gave up 221.4 yards per game passing, and most of that yardage was blamed on the secondary. Reggie Sutton, on the reserved list all year because of a drug problem, will probably challenge veteran Johnnie Poe on the right corner. Dave Waymer had a surprising season on the left corner. The best of the defensive backs is Antonio Gibson, who was "stolen" from the USFL. He can run and hit with the big boys at strong safety. But the free safety, Frank Wattelet, is strictly an overachiever.

Nose tackle Tony Elliott, placed on injured reserve with a knee problem in December, creates uncertainty on the defensive line. He was a free agent and didn't work out although he lived in New Orleans. Expected to help out is No. 1 pick Shawn Knight, a 6-6, 288-pound defensive tackle from Brigham Young.

The linebacking corps could use some upgrading, too. Rickey

SAINTS VETERAN ROSTER

HEAD COACH—Jim Mora. Assistant Coaches—Paul Boudreau, Vic Fangio, Joe Marciano, Russell Paternostro, John Pease, Steve Sidwell, Jim Skipper, Carl Smith, Steve Walters.

No.	Name	Pos.	Ht.	Wt.	NFL Exp.	College
7	Andersen, Morten	K	6-2	205	7	Michigan State
96	Andrus, Sheldon	NT	6-1	271	1	Nicholls State
85	Brenner, Hoby	TE	6-4	245	7	Southern California
67	Brock, Stan	T	6-6	292	8	Colorado
75	Clark, Bruce	DE	6-3	274	6	Penn State
66	Commiskey, Chuck	G	6-4	290	2	Mississippi
70	Contz, Bill	T	6-5	270	5	Penn State
50	Del Rio, Jack	LB	6-4	238	3	Southern California
72	Dombrowski, Jim	T	6-5	289	2	Virginia
95	Dumbauld, Jonathan	NT	6-4	256	2	Kentucky
63	Edelman, Brad	G	6-6	270	6	Missouri
83	Edwards, Kelvin	WR	6-2	197	2	Liberty Baptist
99	Elliott, Tony	NT	6-2	275	6	North Texas State
43	Fowler, Bobby	FB	6-2	225	2	Louisiana Tech
46	Gajan, Hokie	FB	5-11	230	5	Louisiana State
97	Geathers, James	DE	6-7	290	4	Wichita State
27	Gibson, Antonio	SS	6-3	204	2	Cincinnati
77	Gilbert, Daren	T	6-6	295	3	Cal-Fullerton
88	Goodlow, Eugene	WR	6-2	186	5	Kansas State
37	Gray, Mel	RB	5-9	166	2	Purdue
10	Hansen, Brian	P	6-3	209	4	Sioux Falls
80	Harris, Herbert	WR	6-1	206	2	Lamar
92	Haynes, James	LB	6-2	233	4	Mississippi Valley
3	Hebert, Bobby	QB	6-4	214	3	Northwest Louisiana
61	Hilgenberg, Joel	C-G	6-3	252	4	Iowa
40	Hilliard, Dalton	RB	5-8	204	2	Louisiana State
57	Jackson, Rickey	LB	6-2	239	7	Pittsburgh
32	Jakes, Van	DB	6-0	190	2	Kent State
24	Johnson, Bobby	DB	6-0	187	5	Texas
53	Johnson, Vaughan	LB	6-3	235	2	North Carolina State
86	Jones, Mike	WR	5-11	183	5	Tennessee
23	Jordan, Buford	FB	6-0	223	2	McNeese State
55	Kohlbrand, Joe	LB	6-4	242	3	Miami
60	Korte, Steve	C	6-2	269	5	Arkansas
84	Martin, Eric	WR	6-1	207	3	Louisiana State
39	Maxie, Brett	DB	6-2	194	3	Texas Southern
36	Mayes, Rueben	RB	5-11	200	2	Washington State
43	McLemore, Dana	DB	5-10	183	6	Hawaii
51	Mills, Sam	LB	5-9½	220	2	Montclair State
25	Poe, Johnnie	CB	6-1	194	7	Missouri
68	Saindon, Pat	G	6-3	273	2	Vanderbilt
56	Swilling, Pat	LB	6-2	242	4	Georgia Tech
82	Tice, John	TE	6-5	249	5	Maryland
54	Toles, Alvin	LB	6-1	227	3	Tennessee
73	Warren, Frank	DE	6-4	290	7	Auburn
—	Waters, Mike	FB	6-2	230	2	San Diego State
49	Wattelet, Frank	FS	6-1	186	7	Kansas
44	Waymer, Dave	CB	6-1	188	8	Notre Dame
—	Weaver, Emanuel	NT	6-5	285	2	South Carolina
94	Wilks, Jim	DE	6-5	266	7	San Diego State
45	Williams, John	FB	5-11	205	3	Wisconsin
79	Williams, Ralph	G	6-3	298	5	Southern
18	Wilson, Dave	QB	6-3	211	6	Illinois

TOP FIVE DRAFT CHOICES

Rd.	Name	Sel. No.	Pos.	Ht.	Wt.	College
1	Knight, Shawn	11	DT	6-6	288	Brigham Young
2	Hill, Lonzell	40	WR	5-11	189	Washington
3	Adams, Michael	67	DB	5-10	195	Arkansas State
4	Trapilo, Steve	96	G	6-5	281	Boston College
5	Mack, Milton	123	DB	5-11	182	Alcorn State

Jackson is a Pro Bowler at the left outside position. But the two insider backers, Sam Mills and Alvin Toles, won starting jobs after the season began, and Pat Swilling might take over the right side from James Haynes. There are jobs there for the taking.

KICKING GAME: A funny thing happened to punter Brian Hansen in the middle of the season. He signed a new contract and his punting stats dropped dramatically. He still finished fourth in the NFC with a 42.7-yard gross and was third with a 36.6 net.

The kicker, Morten Andersen, was a Pro Bowler with an amazing season, and the return specialists, Eric Martin and Mel Gray, were also ranked high.

THE ROOKIES: The Saints tried to get some help for their pass defense by choosing Knight in the first round, then adding four defensive backs, Mike Adams of Arkansas State, Milton Mack of Alcorn A&M, Gene Atkins of Florida A&M and Toi Cook of Stanford. The other area they went for in a big way was receivers, with Washington's Lonzell Hill (43 catches, 721 yards, 8 TDs), Stanford's Thomas Henley and North Carolina Central's Robert Clark.

OUTLOOK: Finks is building this team. Give him enough time, and he'll get the people. In the meantime, Mora has created a good attitude among the players he has. If Hebert would just come through, the Saints could be a surprise.

SAINT PROFILES

RUEBEN MAYES 24 5-11 200   **Running Back**

NFL's Rookie of the Year... Didn't start until fifth game, but was No. 3 rusher in NFC with 286 carries for 1,353 yards. Trailed only Eric Dickerson and Joe Morris... All but 120 yards gained in final 12 games... Ankle injury in Week 8 vs. Jets held him to only four carries... His 4.7-yard average per carry was second best among NFC running backs... Elected to Pro Bowl. But instead of going to Hawaii, he underwent surgery on Achilles tendon on Dec. 23. Recovery on schedule... Selected with third-round pick acquired from Bucs in 1985 trade for David Greenwood... Held every rushing record at Washington State . . . Born June 16, 1963, in North Battleford, Saskatchewan . . . Gained 203 yards, 2 TDs on 28 carries vs. Dolphins on best day . . . Also had 17 catches.

RICKEY JACKSON 29 6-2 239   Linebacker

Fourth straight Pro Bowl appearance . . . Called best outside linebacker south of New Jersey . . . Led Saints in tackles (117 with 87 solos) and sacks (9) . . . Hard hitting forced five fumbles, another team high . . . Also good in coverage, defending 12 passes . . . Buddy of Giants' Lawrence Taylor . . . Played defensive end at Pitt and was overshadowed by Hugh Green's publicity . . . Plays left outside linebacker for Saints . . . Contract expired after last season . . . Born March 20, 1958, in Pahokee, Fla. . . . Tight end in high school.

TONY ELLIOTT 28 6-2 275   Nose Tackle

Inspirational story of guy who beat drugs . . . Waived before 1984 season when he appeared to be marginal player. Reactivated in November 1984 and started three of team's last four games that season . . . Started all 16 in 1985 and first 15 in 1986. Missed last game with minor knee injury . . . Somewhat erratic player . . . Finished season with 29 tackles and 3½ sacks . . . No veteran on Saints' roster can beat him out . . . Born April 23, 1959, in New York City and grew up in Bridgeport, Conn. . . . Has worked offseason in the Center for Study of Sport in Society at Northeastern University, with the focus on youth and drugs . . . Was a fifth-rounder out of North Texas State in 1982.

DAVE WAYMER 29 6-1 188   Cornerback

Takes chances and sometimes gets burned, but also had nine interceptions, including two against Green Bay and Atlanta . . . Led team for third straight year in interceptions, and last year's total was only one shy of Dave Whitsell's club record. No Saint had more than seven interceptions since 1967 . . . Not bad for a guy who was hurt in the preseason and replaced as a starter by Willie Tullis. But Tullis walked out without warning, skipped the second regular-season game and went home to Houston. So Waymer held the LCB spot again . . . Born July 1,

1958, in Brooklyn, N.Y., and starred at West Charlotte (N.C.) High School on the way to Notre Dame, where he obtained degree in economics . . . Was Saints' second-round choice in 1980 draft.

JIM DOMBROWSKI 23 6-6 289   Tackle

Sixth player and first offensive lineman taken in '86 draft . . . Had very short rookie season . . . Signed second week of training camp and didn't know assignments when season began. But Jim Mora used him as a starter anyway . . . Broke foot in third game. Played injured, but missed rest of season . . . But rehab program makes him candidate for regular duties this year . . . Was a consensus first-team All-American at Virginia, where he was voted by conference coaches as best ACC blocker for two years . . . Received bachelor's degree in biology in 1985 and played as grad student (exercise physiology) that fall en route to what he plans as a medical career in orthopedic surgery—with time out for pro football . . . Born Oct. 19, 1963, in Williamsville, N.Y.

SAM MILLS 28 5-8½ 220   Linebacker

Another of Jim Mora's USFL refugees . . . Shortest linebacker in NFL . . . Second on team with 92 tackles . . . Originally went to camp with Cleveland as a free agent, and Sam Rutigliano hated to cut him . . . Rutigliano's call to Philadelphia Stars' GM Carl Peterson landed Mills USFL job . . . Outstanding for three seasons (1983-85) under Mora in USFL. Was all-league twice . . . Comes out on passing situations, but very good against run . . . Credited for Eric Dickerson's 57-yard putdown (only four in second half) against Saints . . . Born June 3, 1959, in Neptune, N.J. . . . Attended Montclair State.

DAVE WILSON 28 6-3-211   Quarterback

Won't go away. Had shoulder surgery at end of '85 season and was expected to be backup . . . Replaced injured Bobby Hebert in third game and held job until he twisted knee in 16th game . . . Completed 189 of 342 for 2,353 yards and 10 TDs. Had 17 interceptions, which dragged down rating . . . On busiest day threw 43 passes and completed 24 vs. Rams on Nov. 23 . . . On most productive day had 273 yards vs. New England . . . On most accurate day hit 12 of 16 for 165 yards vs. 49ers on Nov. 2 . . . Contract ended last season, but he'll be back for seventh season . . . Attended Illinois and was supplemental draft choice in 1981 after losing eligibility . . . Born April 27, 1959, in Anaheim, Cal.

BOBBY HEBERT 27 6-4 215   Quarterback

Still a mystery despite that $1.3-million signing bonus and $3.5-million, five-year deal in 1985. Contract, which was result of pressure from Louisiana governor and local citizens, runs through 1989 if Saints don't go broke first . . . Last season was a fiasco. Started three games, then broke foot . . . Had best statistical day vs. Green Bay thanks to completions for 72 and 84 yards to Eric Martin . . . Was reactivated Nov. 8, but didn't play until final game when he replaced Dave Wilson. Turned into a horror show. By halftime Saints trailed Vikings, 30-3. Hebert threw four interceptions . . . Led Michigan Panthers to title in USFL's initial season (1983). Never matched those stats . . . Born Aug. 19, 1960, in Galliano, La. Graduated from Northwestern Louisiana State.

HOKIE GAJAN 27 5-11 226   Fullback

Looks ready to return after injuring knee in 10th game of 1985 and missing all of 1986 . . . Could make a big difference . . . A vicious pass-blocker who was beaten only one time for a sack in five seasons. That's against the best tackles and outside linebackers opponents could throw at him . . . Not a bad runner and receiver, either. Gained 615 yards and averaged six yards per carry in 1984. Also caught 35 passes that year. During career has 5.4-yard rushing average . . . Ironically, he got job because of injury in 1981. Saints were ready to cut him when he got in auto accident and was hospitalized. Broke ankle during recovery. Might say Saints kept him by accident. Might call it lucky break . . . Born Sept. 6, 1959, in Baton Rouge, La. . . . Attended Louisiana State.

MEL GRAY 26 5-9 175   **Running Back**

A gnat with blazing speed . . . Returned kickoff 101 yards for TD against 49ers on Sept. 21 and finished with 186 yards on three returns that day for club record . . . Averaged 27.9 yards on 31 returns for season . . . Was used to catch passes out of backfield late in season . . . Averaged 22.5 yards on his only two catches . . . Might be moved to wide receiver this year . . . Was a very big play man for L.A. Express of USFL . . . Was sprinter and leading rusher for Purdue . . . Attended Lafayette High in Williamsburg, Va., school that produced Lawrence Taylor . . . Also attended Coffeyville (Kan.) JC, which enrolled eventual Heisman Trophy winner Mike Rozier . . . Born March 16, 1961, in Williamsburg, Va.

COACH JIM MORA: Saints outscored opponents for only the second time in franchise history (288-287) after Mora moved from USFL . . . Most successful coach in that defunct league. Took Stars to USFL championship three times and won it twice . . . Tolerated no nonsense at New Orleans, a dramatic change from the Phillips' regime . . . Terrific organizer . . . Tight end at Occidental College, where he roomed with Congressman and Presidential candidate Jack Kemp . . . After graduation in 1957, he remained as coach at alma mater for seven years . . . Also coached defense at Stanford, Colorado and Washington . . . With Seattle Seahawks from 1978-81 and with Patriots in 1982 . . . Jumped at chance to be head coach in USFL. Stars were 16-4, 19-2 and 13-7-1 . . . Was among eight candidates interviewed by Jim Finks for Saints' job . . . Born May 24, 1935, in Glendale, Cal. . . . Earned a master's degree in education at USC.

GREATEST KICKER

Drafting a kicker is one of the biggest gambles in pro football. But the Saints won that gamble when they selected Morten Andersen, a Danish-born kicker from Michigan State, in the fourth round in 1982. Andersen went to the Pro Bowl the last two seasons with the best field-goal percentage in the NFC (31 of 35 in 1985 and 26 of 30 in 1986).

His career began with a sprained ankle on his opening kickoff, but he has made a nice recovery. He has made 97 of 121 field goals, a 80.2 percentage that makes him the most accurate kicker in NFL history. He also has made 134 of 137 PATs.

He holds club records for most consecutive games scoring (50, 1983-present), most consecutive games with FG (19), most consecutive FGs made (20) and most lifetime points (425).

INDIVIDUAL SAINT RECORDS
Rushing

Most Yards Game:	206	George Rogers, vs St. Louis, 1983
Season:	1,674	George Rogers, 1981
Career:	4,267	George Rogers, 1981-84

QB Dave Wilson aims to pick up where he left off in '86.

Passing

Most TD Passes Game:	6	Billy Kilmer, vs St. Louis, 1969
Season:	23	Archie Manning, 1980
Career:	155	Archie Manning, 1971-81

Receiving

Most TD Passes Game:	3	Dan Abramowicz, vs San Francisco, 1971
Season:	9	Henry Childs, 1977
Career:	37	Dan Abramowicz, 1967-72

Scoring

Most Points Game:	18	Walt Roberts, vs Philadelphia, 1967
	18	Dan Abramowicz, vs San Francisco, 1971
	18	Archie Manning, vs Chicago, 1977
	18	Chuck Muncie, vs San Francisco, 1979
	18	George Rogers, vs Los Angeles, 1981
	18	Wayne Wilson, vs Atlanta, 1982
Season:	120	Morten Andersen, 1985
Career:	425	Morten Andersen, 1982-86
Most TDs Game:	3	Walt Roberts, vs Philadelphia, 1967
	3	Dan Abramowicz, vs San Francisco, 1971
	3	Archie Manning, vs Chicago, 1977
	3	Chuck Muncie, vs San Francisco, 1979
	3	George Rogers, vs Los Angeles, 1981
	3	Wayne Wilson, vs Atlanta, 1982
Season:	13	George Rogers, 1981
Career:	37	Dan Abramowicz, 1967-72

NEW YORK GIANTS

TEAM DIRECTORY: Pres.: Wellington Mara; VP/Treasurer: Timothy Mara; VP/GM: George Young; Dir. Pro Personnel: Tom Boisture; Dir. Pub. Rel.: Ed Croke; Head Coach: Bill Parcells. Home field: Giants Stadium (76,891). Colors: Blue, red and white.

SCOUTING REPORT

OFFENSE: If the champion Giants had one great receiver, they would be awesome. Lionel Manuel has displayed some flashes, but he has been injured the past two seasons. Maybe he is the answer, but the Giants were taking no chances and drafted Michigan State speedster Mark Ingram in the first round. They are set at tight end with Zeke Mowatt and All-Pro Mark Bavaro.

Over the last three seasons, Phil Simms has been healthy, and he has proved just how good he can be. The Giants were only 11th in the NFC in passing yards (3,133), but they made the plays they had to make. When the team was trailing against San Francisco, Minnesota and even Denver in the Super Bowl, Simms did the job.

It helps Simms a lot now that everybody is keying on running back Joe Morris. He has proved his durability, and Bill Parcells has said that 2,000 yards is not out of the question. Maurice Carthon, one of the best blocking backs in the NFL, has been frustrated by not getting to carry the football. But the real key in the backfield this year might be George Adams, who was lost for all of '86 with a freakish groin injury. Adams can run and catch. He had 1,128 yards of all-purpose offense in 1985 as a rookie. But he must learn to block better if he wants to be in the same backfield as Morris.

The offensive line is probably the least appreciated group on the team. But Brad Benson, who went to the Pro Bowl last year, is no better than any other starters. He will face tough competition at tackle this year from William Roberts. And Damian Johnson might challenge at guard. The line was measured wrongly by 46 sacks last season. Parcells said he could cut that total in half if he told Simms to get rid of the ball. But that's not the Giants' style.

DEFENSE: Still the heart of the Giants, the defense was ranked second in the NFL right behind the Bears. Nobody ran on the Giants, who were first in rushing defense. They allowed only 80.3 yards per game while Chicago, the next-best team against

Mark Bavaro lets his catches and blocks do the talking.

the run, was giving up 91.4 yards. After a while, other teams stopped trying to run with the ball.

That's because everybody suspected the secondary could be had. When free safety Terry Kinard got hurt, the secondary lost its leader, and everybody else back there is only average. But the secondary benefitted from the pressure applied by the front seven. Most of the time it played things safe in a zone while Lawrence Taylor et al were terrorizing the quarterback.

Taylor's offseason rehabilitation was a key for the defense. He had the best season of his career to be only the second defensive player to be named NFL MVP. But in some games he wasn't the best linebacker on the field. Carl Banks, who plays on the opposite end, also became a dominant force, especially in the playoffs, and it was a miscarriage of justice that he didn't make the Pro Bowl.

KICKING GAME: The search for a kicker ended when the Giants signed Raul Allegre, the sixth kicker in two seasons. From inside the 40 he was deadly, and he wound up making 24-of-32 attempts overall. He was one of the major differences in the

GIANTS VETERAN ROSTER

HEAD COACH—Bill Parcells. Assistant Coaches—Bill Belichick, Romeo Crennel, Ron Ehrhardt, Len Fontes, Ray Handley, Fred Hoaglin, Pat Hodgson, Lamar Leachman, Johnny Parker, Mike Pope, Mike Sweatman.

No.	Name	Pos.	Ht.	Wt.	NFL Exp.	College
33	Adams, George	RB	6-1	225	2	Kentucky
2	Allegre, Raul	K	5-10	167	5	Texas
24	Anderson, Ottis	RB	6-2	225	9	Miami
67	Ard, Bill	G	6-3	270	7	Wake Forest
58	Banks, Carl	LB	6-4	235	4	Michigan State
89	Bavaro, Mark	TE	6-4	245	3	Notre Dame
60	Benson, Brad	T	6-3	270	10	Penn State
64	Burt, Jim	NT	6-1	260	7	Miami
53	Carson, Harry	LB	6-2	240	12	South Carolina St.
44	Carthon, Maurice	RB	6-1	225	3	Arkansas State
25	Collins, Mark	CB	5-10	190	2	Cal-Fullerton
39	Davis, Tyrone	CB	6-1	190	2	Clemson
77	Dorsey, Eric	DE	6-5	280	2	Notre Dame
28	Flynn, Tom	S	6-0	195	4	Pittsburgh
30	Galbreath, Tony	RB	6-0	228	12	Missouri
61	Godfrey, Chris	G	6-3	265	5	Michigan
54	Headen, Andy	LB	6-5	242	5	Clemson
48	Hill, Kenny	S	6-0	195	7	Yale
74	Howard, Erik	NT	6-4	268	2	Washington State
57	Hunt, Byron	LB	6-5	242	7	SMU
88	Johnson, Bobby	WR	5-11	171	4	Kansas
68	Johnson, Damian	T	6-5	290	2	Kansas State
52	Johnson, Thomas	LB	6-3	248	2	Ohio State
59	Johnston, Brian	C	6-3	275	2	North Carolina
51	Jones, Robbie	LB	6-2	230	4	Alabama
69	Jordan, David	G	6-6	276	4	Auburn
43	Kinard, Terry	S	6-1	200	5	Clemson
5	Landeta, Sean	P	6-0	200	3	Towson State
46	Lasker, Greg	S	6-0	200	2	Arkansas
86	Manuel, Lionel	WR	5-11	180	4	Pacific
70	Marshall, Leonard	DE	6-3	285	5	LSU
75	Martin, George	DE	6-4	255	13	Oregon
80	McConkey, Phil	WR	5-10	170	4	Navy
76	McGriff, Curtis	DE	6-5	276	7	Alabama
87	Miller, Solomon	WR	6-1	185	2	Utah State
20	Morris, Joe	RB	5-7	195	6	Syracuse
84	Mowatt, Zeke	TE	6-3	240	4	Florida State
63	Nelson, Karl	T	6-6	285	4	Iowa State
65	Oates, Bart	C	6-3	265	3	Brigham Young
34	Patterson, Elvis	CB	5-11	188	4	Kansas
55	Reasons, Gary	LB	6-4	234	4	NW Louisiana State
66	Roberts, William	T	6-5	280	3	Ohio State
81	Robinson, Stacy	WR	5-11	186	3	North Dakota State
22	Rouson, Lee	RB	6-1	222	4	Colorado
17	Rutledge, Jeff	QB	6-1	195	9	Alabama
78	Sally, Jerome	NT	6-3	270	6	Missouri
11	Simms, Phil	QB	6-3	214	9	Morehead State
56	Taylor, Lawrence	LB	6-3	243	7	North Carolina
73	Washington, John	DE	6-4	275	1	Oklahoma State
27	Welch, Herb	DB	5-11	180	3	UCLA
23	Williams, Perry	CB	6-2	203	4	North Carolina St.

TOP FIVE DRAFT CHOICES

Rd.	Name	Sel. No.	Pos.	Ht.	Wt.	College
1	Ingram, Mark	28	WR	5-11	188	Michigan State
2	White, Adrian	55	DB	6-0	200	Florida
3	Baker, Stephen	84	WR	5-7	160	Fresno State
4	Turner, Odessa	112	WR	6-3	205	NW Louisiana
5	O'Connor, Paul	140	G	6-3	274	Miami

Giants last season. But the Giants also possess the finest punter in the NFC, Sean Landeta, who led the NFC and went to the Pro Bowl. He averaged 44.8 yards. Coverage also improved. When Phil McConkey was brought back from Green Bay he provided a reliable return specialist, but the Giants still want a breakaway threat back there.

THE ROOKIES: The Giants used the draft to fill their needs for a fast receiver and find some secondary depth. They chose three receivers—Ingram, Stephen Baker of Fresno State and Odessa Turner of Northwestern Louisiana—in the first four rounds, and they selected defensive back Adrian White of Florida in the second round. It was an impressive group, considering the Giants chose last.

OUTLOOK: The Giants are going to be one of the three best teams in the NFC, but they might get a taste of humility when they play the Bears on the opening Monday night. And the Rams might threaten if they put together a pass offense. The Giants would be finished if they lost Simms, in the manner that the Bears lost Jim McMahon. And there are plenty of questions behind Morris. No, the Giants are not a dynasty.

GIANT PROFILES

PHIL SIMMS 30 6-3 214   Quarterback

Has had better stats, but never a better season, capped by his selection as MVP in Super Bowl XXI... Threw 22 touchdowns and completed 259 of 468 passes for 3,487 yards, second-highest yardage total in NFC... Coaches like to run, but he was clutch factor in key comebacks at Minnesota and San Francisco... Tied team record with four 300-yard passing games and went 27-for-38 for 388 yards and two TDs in regular-season comeback from 17-point deficit vs. 49ers... Years of frustrating injuries after he was first-rounder from Morehead State. Now has 48 straight starts, tops among active quarterbacks in NFC... Super Bowl was his greatest game, 22-for-25 for 268 yards and 3 TDs... Endorsements started on field in Pasadena with Disneyland commercial... Born Nov. 3, 1956, in Springfield, Ky.

JOE MORRIS 26 5-7 195   **Running Back**

After nasty training-camp holdout he got a new deal just an hour before regular-season opener, then proved he deserved it . . . Set club rushing record with 1,516 yards and scored 14 TDs despite missing camp and one game with allergic illness . . . Also had 21 catches for 233 yards and TD, but had highest percentage of drops on team . . . Eight games with more than 100 yards . . . Back-to-back 181-yard performances vs. Washington and Dallas . . . Selected to Pro Bowl for second straight year . . . Has overcome slow start after being second-rounder at Syracuse in 1982 behind Butch Woolfolk . . . Born Sept. 15, 1960, in Fort Bragg, N.C.

LAWRENCE TAYLOR 28 6-3 243   **Linebacker**

Erased the doubts after a subpar '85 season and offseason drug rehab . . . NFL's MVP, marking only second time that honor has gone to a defensive player . . . A unanimous starter in Pro Bowl, marking his sixth consecutive year in Hawaii . . . NFC Defensive Player of the Year . . . Didn't talk to press until season was in its final weeks . . . Let performance speak for him . . . Led NFL with 20½ sacks . . . Had 96 tackles, forced three fumbles . . . In divisional playoff vs. 49ers, ran interception back 34 yards for TD . . . No. 1 pick out of North Carolina in 1981 . . . Born Feb. 4, 1959, in Williamsburg, Va.

MARK BAVARO 24 6-4 245   **Tight End**

Finest tight end in NFC in only second season . . . Earned starting job in Pro Bowl . . . Hates nickname "Rambo" . . . Very strong, very silent . . . NFL Films could make highlight film of plays with him carrying tacklers down the field . . . Such a play sparked Giants' comeback vs. 49ers when he dragged three tacklers for 14 yards . . . Set team records for a tight end with 66 catches and 1,001 yards . . . Also a devastating blocker . . . Played with broken toe and broken jaw . . . Offseason program features self-inflicted punishment (getting strangled and punched in the stomach) to overcome fear . . . Led spartan life by staying in hotel all last year . . . Might be part of two-tight-end offense if Zeke Mowatt is 100 percent . . . Stolen in the '84 draft as fourth-round pick out of Notre Dame . . . Born April 28, 1963, in Winthrop, Mass.

CARL BANKS 25 6-4 235   Linebacker

He's the other bookend on Giants' defense... Played brilliantly opposite Lawrence Taylor, but didn't get recognition he deserved... In playoffs, he was described as "best defensive player on the field" by a Giant coach... Flashiest move was giving away T-shirts calling him "Killer" Banks. That nickname is apropos... Only third in sacks with 6½... Recovered two fumbles, and forced two... Chops down runners and led team with 120 tackles... No. 3 overall draft pick in 1984 out of Michigan State.... He's in final year of huge contract, one of the spoils of NFL-USFL war... Born Feb. 29, 1962, in Flint, Mich.

HARRY CARSON 33 6-2 240   Linebacker

Giants' No. 2 tackler with total of 118... The Gatorade Kid... Often disguises himself on sidelines (as doctor or security guard) before dumping bucket on Bill Parcells... Named to Pro Bowl for eighth time in nine years... Plugs middle against runs and has ability to play every down despite advancing years... Second oldest Giant after defensive end George Martin, who's also coming back this year... Season highlight was dumping bucket of popcorn on President Reagan at White House... Born Nov. 26, 1953, in Florence, S.C.... Fourth-round pick out of South Carolina State in 1976.

BRAD BENSON 31 6-3 270   Offensive Tackle

A guy the Giants wanted to replace for years made the Pro Bowl... A tribute to 77 consecutive starts and two highly visible TV performances against Dexter Manley of Washington... He also owes some success to the bloody bandage on his nose. He was a great sideline shot. Offseason nose job could destroy his charisma... Has played every position on offensive line... Now settled at left tackle, but he must fight off challenge by William Roberts in camp... Seems Benson has fought off challenges ever since he arrived as a free agent out of Penn State in 1977 after being cut as an eighth-rounder by New England... The Giants have several better linemen, but none as famous... Raises attack dogs, a fitting hobby... Born Nov. 25, 1955, in Altoona, Pa.

LEONARD MARSHALL 25 6-3 285   Defensive End

Dissatisfied with 12 sacks and 60 tackles... Underwent agility training to supplement the Giants' offseason program... Once famous for his girth, he now disdains the flabby guys like William Perry... Two sacks and a deflected pass in Super Bowl created havoc for Denver... Named to Pro Bowl for second time, a sign of respect from peers... He benefits from being on same side as Lawrence Taylor, but Taylor benefits from being with Marshall... Top game was against St. Louis when he had six tackles and two sacks... Former LSU star born Oct. 22, 1961, in Franklin, La.

JIM BURT 28 6-1 260   Nose Tackle

Only nose tackle in history to get a $100,000 advance for a book... He got famous when he went into the stands at Giants Stadium after winning NFC title... He is always in the middle of the defense and trouble... He was first guy to douse Bill Parcells back in 1985, and he doused a reporter last season... Odd things happen to him—like going fishing during Super Bowl week and catching a seagull instead of a fish... Missed time with a bad back, which threatened his career two years ago before he underwent enzyme treatments... Avid weight-lifter... One of Parcells' gym rats... So insecure as free-agent rookie out of Miami in 1981, he would hide on cut days... Nobody better against the run, but he will share time with second-year man Erik Howard, the strongest player on the team... Born June 7, 1959, in Buffalo.

PHIL McCONKEY 30 5-10 170   Wide Receiver

Don't count him out. He's not very big, and he's not very fast by today's standards. But he's all heart... The Giants thought they were rid of him last year when they drafted a bunch of receivers, so McConkey was cut and picked up by Green Bay. But Giants made trade to get him back after the fourth game... Mr. Enthusiasm... His career got off to very late start after serving obligatory hitch as helicopter pilot following graduation from Navy... Volunteers for everything... Not fancy as a return specialist, but he never makes mistakes...Caught 16 passes for 279 yards, and had two TD catches in playoffs, including Super Bowl ricochet out of Mark Bavaro's hands... Had 32 punt returns for 253 yards and 24 kickoff returns for 471 yards...Shared book: "Simms to McConkey."...A cult figure...Born Feb. 24, 1957, in Buffalo.

COACH BILL PARCELLS: Coach of the Year in fourth season as head coach of the Giants...No-nonsense personality. Refused White House invitation after Super Bowl XXI. Spurns speaking engagements and endorsements...Was wooed by Atlanta after Super Bowl although he had two more seasons on contract...Plays vital role in player selection...Cool relationship with GM George Young...Best buddies include Indiana coach Bobby Knight and Raider boss Al Davis... All-Missouri Valley linebacker at Wichita State and middle draft pick of Lions...Decided to coach instead of play...Was assistant at Wichita State, Army, Vanderbilt, Florida State and Texas Tech. Head coach at Air Force in 1978...Took season off in 1979 for family reasons...Joined Patriots as linebacker coach in 1980 and became Giants' defensive coordinator under Ray Perkins in 1981. When Perkins left, he took charge...Giants were 3-12-1 in first season, but in last three they have been 33-15. Went to playoffs three straight years and won Super Bowl last season...Born Aug. 22, 1941, in Englewood, N.J.

GREATEST KICKER

Dave Jennings arrived unannounced from St. Lawrence in 1974 and remained with the Giants through 1984. During all those years the Giants had only two winning records, but Jennings became a hero.

He holds the NFL record for 623 punts without having one blocked, no minor accomplishment considering his meager protection. Other punters had better averages, but he was a master at placing the ball precisely. He also had a knack for drawing roughing penalties. He was chosen MVP by his teammates in

1980 when he led the NFL with a 44.8 average, and he went to the Pro Bowl four times.

His punts with the Giants travelled 38,792 yards, then he moved to the Jets in 1985. Last season he set an NFL record for most punts in a career, 1,090. Sean Landeta is another great Giant punter, but it will be a few more years before he makes folks forget Jennings.

INDIVIDUAL GIANT RECORDS

Rushing

Most Yards Game:	218	Gene Roberts, vs Chi. Cardinals, 1950
Season:	1,516	Joe Morris, 1986
Career:	4,638	Alex Webster, 1955-64

Passing

Most TD Passes Game:	7	Y. A. Tittle, vs Washington, 1962
Season:	36	Y. A. Tittle, 1963
Career:	173	Charlie Conerly, 1948-61

Receiving

Most TD Passes Game:	4	Earnest Gray, vs St. Louis, 1980
Season:	13	Homer Jones, 1967
Career:	48	Kyle Rote, 1951-61

Scoring

Most Points Game:	24	Ron Johnson, vs Philadelphia, 1972
	24	Earnest Gray, vs St. Louis, 1980
Season:	127	Ali Haji-Sheikh, 1983
Career:	646	Pete Gogolak, 1966-74
Most TDs Game:	4	Ron Johnson, vs Philadelphia, 1972
	4	Earnest Gray, vs St. Louis, 1980
Season:	21	Joe Morris, 1985
Career:	78	Frank Gifford, 1952-60, 1962-64

PHILADELPHIA EAGLES

TEAM DIRECTORY: Owner: Norman Braman; Pres.: Harry Gamble; VP-Finance: Mimi Box; VP-Marketing: Decker Uhlhorn; Dir. Player Personnel: Joe Woolley; Dir. Communications: Ed Wisneski; Head Coach: Buddy Ryan. Home field: Veterans Stadium (73,484). Colors: Kelly green, white and silver.

SCOUTING REPORT

OFFENSE: If Buddy Ryan doesn't do something about his offensive line, somebody is going to be killed. And it might be his quarterback, Randall Cunningham. The Eagles gave up an NFL-

Randall Cunningham survived sacks and got respect.

record 104 sacks for 708 yards last year. To improve that statistic, Bill Walsh, an assistant coach with 27 years of pro experience, was hired to coach the offensive linemen. He spent the last four years with the Oilers' great linemen, so coming to the Eagles might be a rude adjustment.

Ryan blames part of last year's problems on all of the moves he made along the line. "And remember," he said, "we had backs getting beat, too, and quarterbacks who didn't get rid of the ball the way they should. I think we have some people here who are good offensive linemen. They just need to improve on techniques and become tougher."

Cunningham's survival should make him tougher. He got little respect last year, especially when he was shuttled out on third downs. He gained 540 yards rushing and lost 489 on 72 of those sacks. But when the Eagles cut Ron Jaworski rather than keep him around as a tutor, Cunningham became the main man at quarterback. He was one great receiver, Mike Quick, but the possible loss of Junior Tautalatasi, questionable for 1987 with a bad knee, would be another problem. Tautalatasi had 41 catches, the most by a rookie since Charlie Young's 55 in 1973.

But Ryan still believes the Eagles will rise or fall on running back Keith Byars and his sidekick, Anthony Toney. "Byars is the key," the coach said bluntly.

The problem is that Byars broke a bone in his left foot in preseason camp and required surgery that means he won't be available until September. And will he be at full speed?

DEFENSE: Ryan's style has started to make a difference. The Eagles had 36 takeaways and 53 sacks. The defense started slowly, then came on with a rush. Given time, Ryan will turn them into terrors.

Defensive lineman Reggie White was part of that slow start with only three of his 18 sacks in the first half of the season. But he's the backbone of the line. "He's the best I've ever seen," said Ryan. The Eagles tried to give White some help by drafting Miami tackle Jerome Brown in the first round.

In the secondary, the Eagles are counting on the return of All-Pro free safety Wes Hopkins, who injured his knee in the fourth game. The team still had 23 interceptions, the Eagles' most since 1981, and the young players will have a season under their belts. Ryan felt that Andre Waters should have been a Pro Bowler in his first season as a starter at strong safety. Elbert Foules, who started the last three games in 1987, will open at left cornerback instead of Evan Cooper, and Roynell Young will start on the right side.

EAGLES VETERAN ROSTER

HEAD COACH—Buddy Ryan. Assistant Coaches—Dave Atkins, Jeff Fisher, Dale Haupt, Ronnie Jones, Dan Neal, Wade Phillips, Ted Plumb, Doug Scovil, Bill Walsh.

No.	Name	Pos.	Ht.	Wt.	NFL Exp.	College
63	Baker, Ron	G	6-4	274	10	Oklahoma State
77	Black, Mike	T-G	6-4	290	2	Sacramento State
98	Brown, Greg	DE	6-5	265	7	Kansas State
41	Byars, Keith	RB	6-1	230	2	Ohio State
6	Cavanaugh, Matt	QB	6-2	212	10	Pittsburgh
71	Clarke, Ken	DT	6-2	275	10	Syracuse
50	Cobb, Garry	LB	6-2	230	9	Southern California
79	Conwell, Joe	T	6-5	275	2	North Carolina
21	Cooper, Evan	CB-PR	5-11	184	4	Michigan
45	Crawford, Charles	RB-KR	6-2	235	2	Oklahoma State
12	Cunningham, Randall	QB	6-4	192	3	Nevada-Las Vegas
84	Darby, Byron	TE	6-4	262	5	Southern California
78	Darwin, Matt	C	6-4	260	2	Texas A&M
67	Feehery, Gerry	C	6-2	270	5	Syracuse
29	Foules, Elbert	CB	5-11	185	5	Alcorn State
33	Frizzell, William	S	6-3	198	4	N. Carolina Central
86	Garrity, Gregg	WR-PR	5-10	169	5	Penn State
26	Haddix, Michael	FB	6-2	227	4	Mississippi State
62	Haden, Nick	G-C	6-2	270	2	Penn State
34	Hoage, Terry	S	6-3	199	4	Georgia
48	Hopkins, Wes	FS	6-1	212	5	Southern Methodist
81	Jackson, Kenny	WR	6-0	180	4	Penn State
53	Jiles, Dwayne	LB	6-4	242	3	Texas Tech
54	Johnson, Alonzo	LB	6-3	222	2	Florida
85	Johnson, Ron	WR	6-3	186	2	Long Beach State
59	Joyner, Seth	LB	6-2	241	2	Texas-El Paso
52	Kraynak, Rich	LB	6-1	230	5	Pittsburgh
65	Landsee, Bob	G-C	6-4	273	2	Wisconsin
58	Lee, Byron	LB	6-2	230	2	Ohio State
89	Little, Dave	TE	6-2	236	4	Middle Tennessee
8	McFadden, Paul	K	5-11	163	4	Youngstown State
74	Mitchell, Leonard	T	6-7	295	7	Houston
82	Quick, Mike	WR	6-2	190	6	North Carolina St.
66	Reeves, Ken	T-G	6-5	275	4	Texas A&M
55	Reichenbach, Mike	LB	6-2	238	4	East Stroudsburg
76	Schreiber, Adam	G-C	6-4	270	4	Texas
95	Schulz, Jody	LB	6-3	235	4	East Carolina
96	Simmons, Clyde	DT-DE	6-6	258	2	Western Carolina
68	Singletary, Reggie	G-T	6-3	272	2	North Carolina St.
83	Smith, Phil	WR	6-3	188	2	San Diego State
88	Spagnola, John	TE	6-4	242	8	Yale
93	Strauthers, Tom	DT-DE	6-4	264	5	Jackson State
37	Tautalatasi, Junior	RB	5-10	205	2	Washington State
10	Teltschik, John	P	6-2	215	2	Texas
25	Toney, Anthony	FB	6-0	227	2	Texas A&M
69	Tupper, Jeff	DE	6-5	269	2	Oklahoma
20	Waters, Andre	SS	5-11	185	4	Cheyney
92	White, Reggie	DE-DT	6-5	285	2	Tennessee
22	Wilson, Brenard	S	6-0	185	9	Vanderbilt
43	Young, Roynell	CB	6-1	185	8	Alcorn State

TOP FIVE DRAFT CHOICES

Rd.	Name	Sel. No.	Pos.	Ht.	Wt.	College
1	Brown, Jerome	9	DT	6-2	291	Miami
3	Tamburello, Ben	65	C	6-3	269	Auburn
4	Evans, Byron	93	LB	6-2	218	Arizona
5	Alexander, David	121	G	6-3	263	Tulsa
6	Moten, Ron	149	LB	6-1	227	Florida

Alonzo Johnson and Seth Joyner, picked by Ryan in last year's draft, will surround Mike Reichenbach in the linebacking corp. The year of experience should help. The Eagles had only 14 players on the final 45-man roster with more than three seasons of experience.

KICKING GAME: The Eagles were erratic. Even Paul McFadden missed kicks that could have made a difference in five losses. But he is still one of the most accurate kickers in his first two seasons, and he may get some relief if John Teltschik, picked up on waivers during the preseason, handles kickoffs. A blocked punt and a couple of punt returns for TDs hurt the Eagles, but they also blocked five field goals, two punts and a PAT. They're aggressive. Once again, all they need is experience.

THE ROOKIES: Ryan got a great lineman in Brown, an Outland Trophy finalist. The Eagles now have the makings of one of the finest defensive lines in the NFC. Center Ben Tamburello of Auburn, guard David Alexander of Tulsa and tackle Brian Williams of Central Michigan were scattered throughout the draft to bolster an offensive line that gave up an NFL-record 104 sacks.

OUTLOOK: Believe in Buddy Ryan. He has been a winner everywhere he coached. His players are developing discipline and toughness. Asked to pick the winner of the NFC East, every other coach went with the Giants. But Buddy was surrendering nothing. "I picked the Giants last year and they won the Super Bowl," he said. "So I'll pick the Eagles this year, and we'll win the Super Bowl." It's not that easy. But a few contenders will get their lumps from Philadelphia this year.

EAGLE PROFILES

RANDALL CUNNINGHAM 24 6-4 192   **Quarterback**

As Ron Jaworski limped into the sunset after his release during offseason, Cunningham became more apparent as heir in his third year ... Way he runs and shoots, he could have played basketball instead of football for Nevada-Las Vegas ... Was 18th in NFL in rushing with 540 yards on 66 carries. But still got battered for 72 sacks for minus 489 yards

... When he threw he completed 111 of 209 passes for 1,391 yards, eight TDs. Also threw seven interceptions... Used in third-and-long situations at start of year... A leading punter in college, Cunningham tried two. One was deflected and went 15 yards, the other went 39 yards... Buddy Ryan's opinion (only one that counts): "I think using him on third down, although a lot of people second-guessed that, really brought him along and helped him mature as a quarterback." ... On best day (vs. Raiders) he went 22-for-39 for 298 yards and three TDs with only one interception... Born March 27, 1963, in Santa Barbara, Cal.

KEITH BYARS 23 6-1 230   Running Back

Buddy Ryan was getting second-guessed when he chose Byars in round one. Many teams backed off after Byars fractured bone in right foot and struggled through senior year at Ohio State. Piece of bone was grafted from hip to foot. But he was able to carry the ball twice in Eagles' opener... Wound up with 577 yards on 177 carries. Only averaged 3.3 yards, but his total yards were most by any rookie in team's history. His 127 yards vs. St. Louis in December were second highest in a game by a rookie... Alas, he broke a bone in his left foot last spring and was expected to be out until September... Born Oct. 14, 1963, in Philadelphia.

MIKE QUICK 28 6-2 190   Wide Receiver

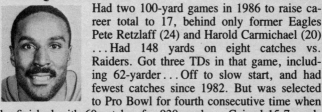

Had two 100-yard games in 1986 to raise career total to 17, behind only former Eagles Pete Retzlaff (24) and Harold Carmichael (20) ... Had 148 yards on eight catches vs. Raiders. Got three TDs in that game, including 62-yarder... Off to slow start, and had fewest catches since 1982. But was selected to Pro Bowl for fourth consecutive time when he finished with 60 catches for 939 yards... Gained 15.7 yards per catch... Seemed more effective with Randall Cunningham at QB... Teammates elected him Offensive MVP... Has to be helped with Kenny Jackson threatening opponents on opposite end... Leading receiver in North Carolina State history was No. 1 draft choice in 1982... Born May 14, 1959, in Hamlet, N.C.

ROYNELL YOUNG 29 6-1 185   Cornerback

Chosen defensive MVP by teammates... Career-high six interceptions to raise seven-year total to 20. Also defensed team-high 19 passes and forced three fumbles (against Dallas, Seattle, Raiders)... Hampered by injuries in '84 and '85, but when Wes Hopkins was hurt last year he took charge... First-round draft choice in 1980 out of Alcorn State ... Breeds cattle in Texas during offseason... Born Dec. 1, 1957, in New Orleans.

REGGIE WHITE 25 6-5 285   DE-DT

MVP in Pro Bowl with four sacks although NFC lost... First team on most All-NFC teams... Had 52 QB pressures, more than double what runnerup Greg Brown had in that category... Eighteen sacks ranked him third in NFC. Four-sack days vs. Cardinals and Raiders in November... Blocked field goals against Giants and Cardinals... Former Tennessee star also became USFL star with Memphis... An ordained Baptist minister, he is called "Minister of Defense"... Extremely active in charitable causes... Lombardi Award finalist at Tennessee... Born Dec. 19, 1961, in Chattanooga, Tenn.

MIKE REICHENBACH 25 6-2 238   Linebacker

Buddy Ryan saw something that others missed. A free agent in 1984 out of East Stroudsburg, Reichenbach was considered so-so performer when Ryan chose him to be the leader of the defense, the equivalent of Bears' Mike Singletary... Reichenbach tied for club lead with 129 tackles... Noted for intelligence. Majored in environmental science and worked for toxic waste disposal company in Delaware Valley... Got help last year from Garry Cobb, acquired from Lions for Wilbert Montgomery in 1985, and draft picks Alonzo Johnson in round two and Seth Joyner in round eight... Born Sept. 14, 1961, in Bethlehem, Pa.

ANDRE WATERS 25 5-11 185   Strong Safety

First season as a starter. Replaced Ray Ellis ... Free agent in '84, he was a backup and special-teams player for two years ... Tied middle linebacker Mike Reichenbach for club lead with 129 tackles. His 90 initial hits were only one fewer than Reichenbach had ... Contributed six of Eagles' 23 interceptions, tying Roynell Young for club lead ... Also forced three fumbles and recovered three fumbles ... No longer returned kickoffs ... Served in Army Reserve during summers of '81 and '82 while at Cheyney State ... Born March 10, 1962, in Belle Glade, Fla.

REGGIE SINGLETARY 23 6-3 272   Guard/Tackle

After being chosen to NFL's All-Rookie team last year, he'll be moved to offensive line this year ... That's where Eagles figure they need the most help, and he'll work at tackle with new offensive line coach Bill Walsh ... As a defensive lineman, he was a backup, but got a start as a rookie ... Was 315th player chosen in draft out of North Carolina State ... Might play a part in rebuilding of offensive line, but he'll struggle just to make team ... Born Jan. 17, 1964, in Whiteville, N.C.

ANTHONY TONEY 24 6-0 227   Fullback

After getting Keith Byars in round one, Buddy Ryan chose another back, Anthony Toney, of Texas A&M, in round two. He called them "those two big studs." ... They gave a glimpse of what he hoped for in December vs. St. Louis. While Byars got 127 yards, Toney got 74. It was best two-man rushing performance for Eagles since 1979 ... Toney's 4.1 average was the best on the team. He wound up with 69 carries for 285 yards ... Also developed as blocker ... Used to work as mailman in College Station, Tex. ... Wasn't used as receiver in college, but caught 13 passes for 177 yards last year ... Quickly moved ahead of Michael Haddix, a first-rounder in 1983 ... Born Sept. 23, 1962, in Salinas, Cal.

SETH JOYNER 22 6-2 241   **Linebacker**

After last season, Buddy Ryan put out the word that Joyner would replace Garry Cobb, 30, as a starter...Joyner, an eighth-rounder from Texas-El Paso, will presumably play left side, and Alonzo Johnson, a second-rounder last year, will start on right side...Of course, it's subject to change...Joyner is about 15 pounds heavier than Cobb, who was fourth on the team in tackles last year and had six sacks...Joyner had 42 tackles, two sacks, interception and forced fumble; Johnson had 71 tackles, one sack, three interceptions...Born Nov. 18, 1964, in Spring Valley, N.Y.

COACH BUDDY RYAN: Always entertaining, on and off the

field...Finished 5-10-1 with 20 new players on roster in first season with Eagles...Was an assistant coach on three Super Bowl teams: Bears (1985), Vikings (1976) and Jets (1968) ...Brilliant defensive coach who learned trade with Weeb Ewbank...Developed "46" defense for maximum pressure on the quarterback...Owns horse ranch in Kentucky, where he is able to relax...Eagles improved dramatically during course of '86 season. Biggest disappointment was loss to Bears in second game (13-10 in overtime)...Bears were team he left three days after Super Bowl XX...Radio show was prime-time hit in Philadelphia as he traded barbs with callers...Hard to imagine him as offensive guard at Oklahoma State. Easier to imagine him as a blitzing linebacker...Born Feb. 16, 1934, in Frederick, Okla.

GREATEST KICKER

Bobby Walston was mainly a receiver. But no one should overlook his contributions to the Eagles as a kicker. In 12 seasons from 1951 through 1962, he scored 881 points, 406 more than the team's next highest scorer, kicker Sam Baker. There were 365 extra points, 80 field goals and 46 TD catches.

His 25 points against the Redskins in 1954 stand as a team record. He was NFL Rookie of the Year in 1951 after arriving from Georgia. His 114 points in 1954 stood as the team record until Paul McFadden got 116 in 1984.

INDIVIDUAL EAGLE RECORDS

Rushing

Most Yards Game:	205	Steve Van Buren, vs Pittsburgh, 1949
Season:	1,512	Wilbert Montgomery, 1979
Career:	6,538	Wilbert Montgomery, 1977-84

Passing

Most TD Passes Game:	7	Adrian Burk, vs Washington, 1954
Season:	32	Sonny Jurgensen, 1961
Career:	167	Ron Jaworski, 1977-85

Receiving

Most TD Passes Game:	4	Joe Carter, vs Cincinnati, 1934
	4	Ben Hawkins, vs Pittsburgh, 1969
Season:	13	Tommy McDonald, 1960 and 1961
	13	Mike Quick, 1983
Career:	79	Harold Carmichael, 1971-83

Scoring

Most Points Game:	25	Bobby Walston, vs Washington, 1954
Season:	116	Paul McFadden, 1984
Career:	881	Bobby Walston, 1951-62
Most TDs Game:	4	Joe Carter, vs Cincinnati, 1934
	4	Clarence Peaks, vs St. Louis, 1958
	4	Tommy McDonald, vs N.Y. Giants, 1959
	4	Ben Hawkins, vs Pittsburgh, 1969
	4	Wilbert Montgomery, vs Washington, 1978
	4	Wilbert Montgomery, vs Washington, 1979
Season:	18	Steve Van Buren, 1945
Career:	79	Harold Carmichael, 1971-83

ST. LOUIS CARDINALS

TEAM DIRECTORY: Chairman: William Bidwill; VP-Administration: Curt Mosher; Dir. Pro Personnel: Larry Wilson; Dir. Pub. Rel.: Bob Rose; Head Coach: Gene Stallings. Home field: Busch Stadium (51,392). Colors: Cardinal red, white and black.

SCOUTING REPORT

OFFENSE: The Cardinals were pathetic. They scored the fewest points in the NFL (218) and ranked ahead of only Kansas City and Tampa Bay in offensive yardage (281.4 per game). Injuries were a major problem, and the team physician accused some

Stump Mitchell (Luis Sharpe blocking) averaged 4.6 yards.

players of dogging when they could have played. Loss of Roy Green for part of the season for foot surgery left receiving corps in turmoil, and J.T. Smith was the only vet receiver for several weeks.

While teammates were taking heat, Stump Mitchell earned a medal by gaining 800 yards rushing and 276 receiving, despite injuries. He became the Cardinals' main man when Ottis Anderson, apparently at the end of a fine career, was pawned off on the Giants.

The offensive line was badly manhandled a few times (seven sacks vs. Giants). But it showed some improvement over the previous season despite injuries and the presence of three rookies, Ray Brown, Gene Chilton and Derek Kennard, for part of the season.

Neil Lomax still takes most of the blame for the offensive woes. Entering his seventh year, Lomax had decent stats, and coach Gene Stallings said he "was throwing the ball real well. I'm satisfied with the way he's running the offense." However, Cliff Stoudt was a temporary replacement for Lomax. The Cards hope it's only a matter of time before No. 1 pick Kelly Stouffer of Colorado is ready to take over.

There are a lot of ifs. IF everybody is healthy, IF everybody wants to play, IF the scouts manage to come up with some good talent in the draft, the offense will be better. Stallings has his work cut out.

DEFENSE: St. Louis ranked first in the NFL in pass defense (164.8 yards per game) and fourth overall (304 yards). But they were 25th in rushing defense (139.2 yards) and 21st in scoring defense (351 points).

Stallings will make a major change to a 4-3 defense with Niko Noga in the middle between E.J. Junior and either Anthony Bell (first-rounder in '86) or Charlie Baker. Freddie Joe Nunn will add 20 pounds and play defensive end.

In the secondary, Stallings' area of special interest, there are excellent safeties in Leonard Smith and Lonnie Young. But there are questions at the corners. Stallings says Carl Carter "has a chance to be a good cornerback" in his second year. And after being shuttled between offense and defense, Cedric Mack and Wayne Smith will challenge for the other spot now that Lionel Washington has been traded away.

A major move on the defensive line might shift nose tackle David Galloway to end at least part of the time.

Questions remain on the line. The Cardinals don't know if Curtis Greer can come back from his second knee operation. And

CARDINALS VETERAN ROSTER

HEAD COACH—Gene Stallings. Assistant Coaches—Marv Braden, Tom Bresnahan, LeBaron Caruthers, Jim Johnson, Hank Kuhlmann, Leon McLaughlin, Mal Moore, Joe Pascale, Mel Renfro, Jim Shofner.

No.	Name	Pos.	Ht.	Wt.	NFL Exp.	College
16	Austin, Kent	QB	6-1	195	2	Mississippi
60	Baker, Al	DE	6-6	270	10	Colorado State
52	Baker, Charlie	LB	6-2	234	8	New Mexico
55	Bell, Anthony	LB	6-3	231	2	Michigan State
74	Bergold, Scott	DE	6-7	263	2	Wisconsin
62	Brown, Ray	T-G	6-5	257	2	Arkansas State
89	Boso, Cap	TE	6-3	224	2	Illinois
71	Bostic, Joe	G	6-3	268	9	Clemson
41	Carter, Carl	CB	5-11	180	2	Texas Tech
14	Cater, Greg	P	6-0	191	6	Tenn.-Chattanooga
58	Chilton, Gene	C	6-3	271	2	Texas
64	Clark, Randy	C	6-4	270	8	Northern Illinois
79	Clasby, Bob	DE	6-5	260	2	Notre Dame
66	Dawson, Doug	G	6-3	267	4	Texas
56	DiBernardo, Rick	LB	6-3	225	2	Notre Dame
35	Drain, Eric	FB	6-2	210	1	Missouri
73	Duda, Mark	NT	6-3	279	5	Maryland
31	Ferrell, Earl	FB	6-0	224	6	East Tennessee St.
65	Galloway, David	NT	6-3	279	6	Florida
81	Green, Roy	WR	6-0	195	9	Henderson State
75	Greer, Curtis	DE	6-4	258	8	Michigan
82	Holmes, Don	WR	5-10	180	2	Mesa College
78	Hughes, Van	DE	6-3	280	2	S.W. Texas St.
87	Johnson, Troy	WR	6-1	175	2	Southern
54	Junior, E. J.	LB	6-3	235	7	Alabama
70	Kennard, Derek	G	6-3	285	2	Nevada-Reno
10	Lee, John	K	5-11	182	2	UCLA
15	Lomax, Neil	QB	6-3	215	7	Portland State
47	Mack, Cedric	CB	6-0	194	5	Baylor
80	Marsh, Doug	TE	6-3	238	8	Michigan
76	Mays, Stafford	DE	6-2	255	8	Washington
30	Mitchell, Stump	HB	5-9	188	7	The Citadel
59	Monaco, Ron	LB	6-1	225	2	So. Carolina
38	Nelson, Lee	FS	5-10	185	11	Florida St.
57	Noga, Niko	LB	6-1	235	4	Hawaii
85	Novacek, Jay	TE	6-4	217	3	Wyoming
53	Nunn, Freddie Joe	LB	6-4	228	3	Mississippi
63	Robbins, Tootie	T	6-5	302	6	East Carolina
51	Ruether, Mike	C	6-4	275	2	Texas
39	Sargent, Broderick	FB	5-10	215	2	Baylor
11	Schubert, Eric	K	5-8	193	3	Pittsburgh
67	Sharpe, Luis	T	6-4	260	6	UCLA
36	Sikahema, Vai	HB-KR-PR	5-9	191	2	BYU
84	Smith, J.T.	WR	6-2	185	10	North Texas State
61	Smith, Lance	T	6-2	262	3	Louisiana State
45	Smith, Leonard	SS	5-11	202	5	McNeese State
44	Smith, Wayne	DB	6-0	170	6	Purdue
18	Stoudt, Cliff	QB	6-4	215	9	Youngstown State
86	Swanson, Eric	WR	5-11	186	2	Tennessee
83	Tilley, Pat	WR	5-10	178	12	Louisiana Tech
48	Washington, Lionel	DB	6-0	188	5	Tulane
24	Wolfley, Ron	FB	6-0	222	3	West Virginia
43	Young, Lonnie	S	6-1	182	3	Michigan State

TOP FIVE DRAFT CHOICES

Rd.	Name	Sel. No.	Pos.	Ht.	Wt.	College
1	Stouffer, Kelly	6	QB	6-3	214	Colorado State
2	McDonald, Tim	34	SS	6-3	205	Southern California
3	Awalt, Robert	62	TE	6-5	240	San Diego State
3	Scotts, Colin	70	DT	6-6	265	Hawaii
4	Saddler, Rod	90	DT	6-5	265	Texas A&M

Stallings might move Bob Clasby from end to tackle and David Galloway from tackle to end. Galloway certainly has the speed with five sacks from the nose last year. Al Baker, who had a team-high 10 sacks, will challenge at end, too.

KICKING GAME: The problem began with field position created by specials. Stallings has looked everywhere for a long snapper. "You can bet we'll have several in camp," he said. That's one of the biggest problems the Cardinals need to overcome. He blames a lot of special teams' woes on the lack of a long snapper. Danny Cater was last in the NFC in punting with a 37.2 average, and John Lee was a second-round bust who underwent knee surgery on Nov. 18. However, Vai Sikahema was a bright spot, leading the NFC with 12.1 yards and two TDs on punt returns and 22.9 yards on kickoff returns. Sikahema went to the Pro Bowl (where he had a nightmarish day) along with hitter Ron Wolfley.

THE ROOKIES: The Cardinals aired their disenchantment with Lomax by choosing Stouffer with the sixth pick in a good draft. Curiously, Stouffer ranked only eighth in passing in the Western Athletic Conference, averaging only 6.96 yards per attempt while throwing for 14 interceptions and seven TDs. But he is highly regarded by the scouts. St. Louis had the second-most picks in the draft with 15, and used nine for defense.

OUTLOOK: Last season Stallings found out what he has and doesn't have. This year he will try to fill some of those needs. But the Cardinals are not going to provide a threat for the Giants yet in the NFC East.

CARDINAL PROFILES

ROY GREEN 29 6-0 195   **Wide Receiver**

Tough times since record-breaking 1,555 yards receiving in '84 . . . Injuries took a toll and attitude was questioned. Only 693 yards in '85 because of toe and ankle injuries . . . Enrolled in weight program for first time in career before '86 season. But underwent surgery on Sept. 22 to remove calcium deposit in left ankle and was inactive for five weeks. Team doctor questioned whether surgery was necessary... When healthy, he looked like '84 all over... A 48-yard TD catch vs. Eagles was longest since '84... Still drew double coverage. That's how Saints snapped his string of 74 games with at least one reception. The streak went back to 1982 when he quit playing cornerback and became a fulltime receiver... Would not object to a trade... Born June 30, 1957, in Magnolia, Ark.... Fourth-rounder out of Henderson State in 1979.

NEIL LOMAX 28 6-3 215   Quarterback

Was supposed to be the NFL's next superstar in '84 after being a second-rounder in '81. But his inconsistency has been a problem, and opposing defenses question his courage under pressure... Completed 57 percent of his passes last year and had only 12 interceptions in 421 attempts. But passes averaged only 6.14 yards... Was replaced by Cliff Stoudt on Nov. 2 vs. Philadelphia after throwing for only 47 yards in first half. Streak of 52 consecutive starts (the longest among active players at the time) ended the following week vs. the 49ers... But he made a strong finish. In back-to-back games vs. Eagles and Giants, he completed 50 of 75 passes for 543 yards. And that's despite nine sacks by the Giants... Maybe a healthy Green can revive Lomax... Attended Portland State... Born Feb. 17, 1959, in Lake Oswego, Ore.

STUMP MITCHELL 28 5-9 188   Running Back

Out of Ottis Anderson's shadow. Anderson's trade to Giants might have been a coup for Cardinals, but Mitchell must produce... After 1,006 yards in 1985, he fell to 800 yards on 174 carries, but his 4.6 average was one of the best in league... Also became a favorite target for Lomax... Knee injury hampered him and caused missed time... Took some vicious hits and had to be helped off field a couple of times, but always came back... Gets $10,000 bonus every game he rushes for 100 yards. Missed bonus by a foot against Eagles... Redskin defensive end Dexter Manley offered him $5,000 to fumble. "I told him, 'You're a friend, but I can't do that,' " said Citadel product. "Dexter is crazy."... Easy to understand nickname. He's short, and his real name is Lyvonia Albert... Born March 15, 1959, in Kingsland, Ga.

LUIS SHARPE 27 6-4 260   Tackle

After disappointing '85 season, he came back strong. "I have a lot to prove," he said. "I feel I let a lot of people down.". . . Had played 44 games during 16-month stretch—16 in '84 with Cardinals, 12 with Memphis in ill-fated USFL, 16 more with Cardinals in '85. . . Played best football of his career near end of last season. . . Has string of 72 consecutive starts. . . Born June 16, 1960, in Havana, Cuba, and speaks fluent Spanish. . . One of four Cardinals from abroad. Others were Niko Noga (American Somoa), Vai Sikahema (Tonga) and John Lee (Korea). . . First-rounder out of UCLA in 1982.

J.T. SMITH 31 6-2 185   Wide Receiver/Returner

Simply amazing. Picked up as a free agent out of desperation in September 1985 and eclipsed everything he had done with the Chiefs. . . Was third-best receiver in NFC with 80 catches for 1,014 yards and six TDs. . . Had career-best game with 10 catches for 154 yards in November vs. 49ers. Also caught 10 for 131 yards vs. Eagles in December. Those were most catches by a Cardinal in a game since Ottis Anderson had 12 vs. Washington in 1984. . . Broke Roy Green's record for receptions. Caught four or more passes in 14 games. . . At least Vai Sikahema was able to take over returns, or he might have broken every multipurpose offensive record. . . A clutch man on third down, he gained seven first downs with catches against the 49ers. More amazing because he was so sick he was vomiting on sidelines during that game. . . Attended North Texas State. . . Born Oct. 29, 1955, in Leonard, Tex.

EARL FERRELL 29 6-0 224   Fullback

One of the few healthy Cardinals, he made up for his ailing teammates. . . Rushed 124 times for 548 yards and caught 56 passes for 434 yards. The 49ers' Roger Craig and Cowboys' Herschel Walker were only backs with more catches. . . He set career records for rushing attempts, rushing yards, catches and receiving yards. . . Also had career single-game records with 71 yards rushing vs. Buffalo and a couple of six-reception efforts. . . Season marked a dramatic comeback from '85 when he was suspended for the final five games because of drug involvement. That suspension snapped a string of 52 consecutive games... Also a better-than-average blocker... He has to stay out of trouble this year... Graduated from East Tennessee State... Born March 27, 1958, in South Boston, Va.

DAVID GALLOWAY 28 6-3 279　　　　　Nose Tackle

Missed first two games with a groin injury, but wound up with stats better than '85... Replaced Giants' Jim Burt as most underrated defensive tackle in the league... In 54 pro starts he has 34 sacks... Began commanding double-team respect midway through season ... A second-round draft pick in 1982, he could provide leadership for a team that badly needs some... He proved himself in difficult switch from 4-3 to 3-4 defense last year... Finalist for Lombardi Trophy at Florida in 1981... Born Feb. 16, 1959, in Brandon, Fla.

LONNIE YOUNG 24 6-1 182　　　　　　　Safety

Played very well when he wasn't hurt. Thigh bruise wrecked his second season. Started first eight games, then suffered deep thigh bruise vs. Redskins on Oct. 21. Did not play well again until last fourth of season when he came up with 10 tackles vs. Eagles and 11 vs. Giants in back-to-back games... Cardinals continue to be near bottom in interceptions, and he could provide some if he returns to rookie form... Surprise of '85. Was 325th of 336 players taken in draft. When Cardinals called his home at 2 AM, a Dallas scout was knocking on the door to sign Young to a free-agent contract. However, most teams were fooled by a poor 4.75 clocking in workouts at Michigan State. Was ill, but hid it from the scouts... Born July 18, 1963, in Flint, Mich.

LEONARD SMITH 26 5-11 202　　　　　　　Safety

A No. 1 draft choice out of McNeese State in 1983, he didn't make it as a cornerback but he's an outstanding strong safety... Led team in tackles and had five sacks... Best days were against Bills and Eagles. Sacked Jim Kelly twice and caused a fumble in loss to Buffalo and had 20 tackles, two sacks and a blocked field goal vs. Philadelphia in

December... Other big games were against Saints' Rueben Mayes and Giants' Mark Bavaro. Also had interception and 10 tackles vs. 49ers.... Played with protective cast on left hand after breaking metacarpal vs. Rams on Sept. 7.... Defensive captain along with E. J. Junior. Calls signals for secondary... Hobby is restoring classic cars... Born Sept. 2, 1960, in New Orleans.

E.J. JUNIOR 27 6-3 235   Linebacker

Will move outside, and Niko Nogo will be in middle of new 4-3... Last season marred by injuries. Severe ankle sprain limited him all year, cutting way back on productivity... After 106 tackles in '85, he had less than half that many last year. Missed Pro Bowl for first time in three years. After drug problems in '83, he became a team leader. Makes defensive calls for front seven and serves as captain... Involved in offseason trade rumors... His ability to cover receivers was seriously hampered. Had five of Cardinals' 13 interceptions in '85, most by a Cardinal linebacker since Leo Sanford in 1956. Defensing passes was a problem last year... Played shortstop and catcher for Alabama and was drafted by San Francisco Giants, but he came to St. Louis as the fourth player chosen in the '81 draft... Born Dec. 8, 1959, in Nashville, Tenn.

COACH GENE STALLINGS: Disciple of Bear Bryant and Tom Landry...

Inherited a team that was a far cry from the teams he coached in his 14 seasons with the Cowboys... Meetings with Landry's Cowboys were biggest disappointments in a dismal season... Team's .313 percentage was just a shade above the worst seasons in franchise history—.312 percentages in 1979, 1980 and 1985... A student of Bryant, first as an All-Southwest Conference receiver at Texas A&M, then as an assistant at Alabama... Later became head coach at Texas A&M and defeated Bryant's Crimson Tide in 1968 in the Cotton Bowl... When he was fired at Texas A&M after the 1971 season, Bryant urged him to take the Dallas job as coach of defensive backs instead of staying in college ranks ... Passed up chance to coach Birmingham in USFL, and finally got head-coaching post with Cardinals last season... Owner Billy Bidwill is standing behind him... Born March 2, 1935, in Paris, Tex.

GREATEST KICKER

Jim Bakken's most memorable afternoon was spent in Pittsburgh on Sept. 24, 1967, when he was sent in for nine field-goal attempts and came away with seven. Both numbers went into the NFL record book.

He spent 17 seasons with the Cardinals, 1962-78. Only quarterback Jim Hart played longer in St. Louis, and no Cardinal comes close to Bakken's 234 consecutive games. Not bad considering he kicked only one field goal over 50 yards. The one-time Wisconsin Badger made four Pro Bowl appearances. In a pinch in 1965, he even punted and averaged 42.2 yards on 26 tries.

Some of his best seasons were late in his career—1975 (19 of 24 FGs) and 1976 (20 of 27). He retired with 1,380 points.

INDIVIDUAL CARDINAL RECORDS

Rushing

Most Yards Game:	203	John David Crow, vs Pittsburgh, 1960
Season:	1,605	Ottis Anderson, 1979
Career:	7,999	Ottis Anderson, 1979-86

Passing

Most TD Passes Game:	6	Jim Hardy, vs Baltimore, 1950
	6	Charley Johnson, vs Cleveland, 1965
	6	Charley Johnson, vs New Orleans, 1969
Season:	28	Charley Johnson, 1963
	28	Neil Lomax, 1984
Career:	205	Jim Hart, 1966-82

Receiving

Most TD Passes Game:	5	Bob Shaw, vs Baltimore, 1950
Season:	15	Sonny Randle, 1960
Career:	60	Sonny Randle, 1959-66

Scoring

Most Points Game:	40	Ernie Nevers, vs Chicago, 1929
Season:	117	Jim Bakken, 1967
	117	Neil O'Donoghue, 1984
Career:	1,380	Jim Bakken, 1962-78
Most TDs Game:	6	Ernie Nevers, vs Chicago, 1929
Season:	17	John David Crow, 1962
Career:	60	Sonny Randle, 1959-66

SAN FRANCISCO 49ERS

TEAM DIRECTORY: Owner: Edward J. DeBartola Jr.; Pres./ Head Coach: Bill Walsh; Administrative VP-GM: John McVay; Dir. Publicity: Jerry Walker. Home field: Candlestick Park (61,499). Colors: 49er gold and scarlet.

SCOUTING REPORT

OFFENSE: The problem barely shows. You can't see it in the statistics that had the 49ers ranked first in passing in the NFC with 256 yards per game. But the offensive line got old all at once, and there are not enough replacements to patch the holes. It doesn't help, either, that tight end Russ Francis has all those years. He spent the offseason wrestling and announcing.

But the 49ers survived last year despite the age and despite a series of disabling injuries. Joe Montana was on the injured reserve list from weeks 2-9 and Jeff Kemp missed weeks 8-11. An insurance this season, the 49ers traded for Tampa Bay quarterback Steve Young. In one game against Green Bay at midseason, San Francisco was able to muster only 39 uniformed players and started third-string quarterback Mike Moroski. But the 49ers still won the West, and Montana was still the NFC's second-ranked passer.

In the backfield, Joe Cribbs joined Roger Craig, and together

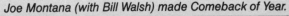

Joe Montana (with Bill Walsh) made Comeback of Year.

they combined for 1,420 yards rushing and 970 yards passing. When there was a crisis, an injury to Cribbs, Wendell Tyler was brought back. But the 49ers got by.

Jerry Rice dispelled all notions that the 49ers are only a dink passing team with his 18.3-yard average on an NFC-high 86 catches. Dwight Clark had only 61 catches, and everybody accused him of slowing down. But he was probably only being compared to Rice.

Aside from the offensive line, the 49ers have few weaknesses, and they constantly tried to improve through trades during the offseason. No. 1 pick Harris Barton, a tackle from North Carolina, will add some depth.

DEFENSE: The defense began rebuilding before last season. It was as effective as the offense, winding up fifth in the NFC. The defense was better than it rated because teams were forced to pass when they fell behind. And the 49 takeaways tied the Chiefs for the NFL lead.

That performance was more remarkable because it was achieved with major contributions from four rookies. Don Griffin and Tim McKyer combined for nine interceptions as the starting cornerbacks, Charles Haley had 12 sacks and forced four fumbles, and Larry Roberts played some defensive end.

During the offseason, defensive coordinator George Seifert tried to strengthen his linebacking corp, which has depended on finesse instead of brute power for too long. It made a bid for the Cardinals' E.J. Junior, then finally succeeded in getting Keith Browner, a former starter, from Tampa Bay.

The 49ers were well padded in the secondary with the kids backed up by vet safeties Carlton Williamson (who led the team in tackles) and Ronnie Lott (who had 10 interceptions and 14 passes defensed).

And there are no complaints on the defensive line with nose tackles Michael Carter and Manu Tuiasosopo and ends Dwaine Board, Jeff Stover, Roberts and Haley.

KICKING GAME: Ray Wersching's percentage dropped, but six of his 10 misses were from outside of 40 yards. At 37, he is probably near the end. Max Runager is not a great punter, but adequate. He puts a high percentage inside the 20. In addition to his defensive duties, Griffin was second in punt returns with a 9.9 average.

THE ROOKIES: After watching the Giants batter his offensive line, Walsh went for Barton in the first round and guard Jeff

49ERS VETERAN ROSTER

HEAD COACH—Bill Walsh. Assistant Coaches—Jerry Attaway, Norb Hecker, Sherman Lewis, Bobb McKitrick, Bill McPherson, Ray Rhodes, George Seifert, Fred von Appen.

No.	Name	Pos.	Ht.	Wt.	NFL Exp.	College
4	Runager, Max	P	6-1	189	8	South Carolina
8	Young, Steve	QB	6-2	200	3	Brigham Young
14	Wersching, Ray	PK	5-11	215	14	California
15	Moroski, Mike	QB	6-4	200	8	California-Davis
16	Montana, Joe	QB	6-2	195	8	Notre Dame
20	Nixon, Tory	CB	5-11	186	2	San Diego State
22	McKyer, Tim	CB	6-0	174	1	Texas-Arlington
26	Tyler, Wendell	RB	5-10	207	9	UCLA
27	Williamson, Carlton	S	6-0	204	6	Pittsburgh
28	Cribbs, Joe	RB	5-11	190	6	Auburn
29	Griffin, Don	CB	6-0	176	1	Middle Tennessee St.
30	Ring, Bill	FB	5-10	205	6	Brigham Young
33	Craig, Roger	FB	6-0	224	4	Nebraska
42	Lott, Ronnie	S	6-0	200	6	Southern California
44	Rathman, Tom	FB	6-1	232	1	Nebraska
46	Holmoe, Tom	S	6-2	195	3	Brigham Young
49	Fuller, Jeff	S-LB	6-2	216	3	Texas &M
50	Ellison, Riki	LB	6-2	225	4	Southern California
51	Cross, Randy	G	6-3	265	11	UCLA
53	McColl, Milt	LB	6-6	230	6	Stanford
54	Ferrari, Ron	LB	6-0	215	5	Illinois
55	Fahnhorst, Jim	LB	6-4	230	3	Minnesota
56	Quillan, Fred	C	6-5	266	9	Oregon
58	Turner, Keena	LB	6-2	222	7	Purdue
62	McIntyre, Guy	G	6-3	264	3	Georgia
64	Durrette, Michael	G	6-4	280	1	West Virginia
65	Rogers, Doug	DE	6-5	280	4	Stanford
68	Ayers, John	G	6-5	265	10	West Texas State
69	Collie, Bruce	T-G	6-6	275	2	Texas-Arlington
71	Fahnhorst, Keith	T	6-6	273	13	Minnesota
72	Stover, Jeff	DE	6-5	275	5	Oregon
74	Wallace, Steve	T	6-5	276	1	Auburn
76	Board, Dwaine	DE	6-5	248	7	North Carolina A&T
77	Paris, Wm. "Bubba"	T	6-6	299	4	Michigan
78	Tuiasosopo, Manu	NT	6-3	262	8	UCLA
80	Rice, Jerry	WR	6-2	200	2	Miss. Valley State
81	Francis, Russ	TE	6-6	242	11	Oregon
83	Crawford, D.	WR-KR	5-10	185	1	Memphis State
84	Margerum, Ken	WR	6-0	180	5	Stanford
86	Frank, John	TE	6-3	225	3	Ohio State
87	Clark, Dwight	WR	6-4	215	8	Clemson
91	Roberts, Larry	DE	6-3	264	1	Alabama
94	Haley, Charles	DE	6-5	230	1	James Madison
95	Carter, Michael	NT	6-2	285	3	Southern Methodist
99	Walter, Michael	LB	6-3	238	4	Oregon
—	Browner, Keith	LB	6-5	240	3	Southern California

TOP FIVE DRAFT CHOICES

Rd.	Name	Sel. No.	Pos.	Ht.	Wt.	College
1	Barton, Harris	22	OT	6-4	283	North Carolina
1	Flagler, Terrence	25	RB	5-11	199	Clemson
2	Bregel, Jeff	37	G	6-4	281	Southern California
5	Jokisch, Paul	134	WR	6-7	230	Michigan
6	White, Bob	162	LB	6-3	254	Penn State

Bregel in round three. Barton is a versatile player who can work at any position. In the second round, the 49ers got Terrence Flagler of Clemson, a successor to the departed Wendell Tyler. Flagler averaged 121.7 yards per game, most of it on 180 carries for 1,176 yards. And just in case Young is not the man who eventually replaces Montana, Walsh picked up one of those Stanford quarterbacks, John Paye, who was overlooked because of shoulder surgery.

OUTLOOK: The 49ers will be a playoff contender for a long time. They have to rejuvenate their offensive line soon. But Bill Walsh will find a way.

49ER PROFILES

JOE MONTANA 31 6-2 195   **Quarterback**

Showed true grit in '86. Injured back in '85, and wrenched it again in first game of '86. Underwent disk surgery and was not expected back until this season. Returned in Week 10 after 55 days ... Finished season rated second among NFC quarterbacks with 191 completions, 307 attempts, 2,236 yards, 8 TDs, 9 interceptions ... QB rating was worst of his career, but it's all relative ... Received concussion in first half against Giants in playoffs when Jim Burt levelled him with clean hit ... Failed to be elected to Pro Bowl for first time in four years ... Two-time Super Bowl MVP (XVI,XIX) ... Born June 11, 1956, in New Eagle, Pa. ... Notre Dame alumnus was 82nd pick in 1979 draft.

STEVE YOUNG 25 6-2 200   **Quarterback**

It was academic Bucs wouldn't carry him on payroll after signing Vinny Testaverde ... Ranked last among qualifying NFC quarterbacks with 65.5 rating. Bucs ranked last in NFC in passing, 165.1 yards per game ... Young completed 195 of 363 passes for 2,282 yards, eight TDs. But he threw 13 interceptions and was sacked 47 times for 326 yards ... Not far behind Eagles' Randall Cunningham with 425 yards and five TDs on 74 carries ... Neither the L.A. Express of USFL nor Bucs won with him. He gets blame. It's obviously not all his fault, but he was getting paid more than anybody else on the team (six-year, $4.8-million deal)... Mormon born Oct. 11, 1961, in Salt Lake City, Utah... Most accurate passer in NCAA history at BYU... Throws left-handed; plays golf and shoots basketball right-handed.

JERRY RICE 24 6-2 200 — Wide Receiver

Led NFL with 1,570 yards and 15 touchdowns receiving. Led NFC with 86 catches... Was Sports Illustrated's Player of the Year and started in Pro Bowl... Great day: 12 catches for 204 yards vs. Redskins... Was 16th player and third receiver drafted in 1985 out of Mississippi Valley State... His '86 yardage was third most in an NFL season. Only Charley Hennigan of Houston in 1961 (1,746) and Lance Alworth of San Diego in 1965 (1,602) had more receiving yards... Only five players have had more TD catches in a season... Born Oct. 13, 1962, in Starkville, Miss.... Haunted by fumble just before he was going to score in playoffs vs. Giants... Turnover was turning point.

ROGER CRAIG 27 6-0 224 — Fullback

Led all NFL backs with 81 catches. Good for 624 yards... Ranked eighth in NFC in rushing with 204 carries for 830 yards... His 292 career catches are club record for a back, surpassing Ken Willard's 273 from 1965-73 ... Caught 12 passes against Giants to tie a team record, but gained only 75 yards on those catches... In only four seasons has 5,996 yards from scrimmage... Drafted in round two in 1983 after playing behind Jarvis Redwine and Mike Rozier at Nebraska... Born July 10, 1960, in Preston, Miss.

JOE CRIBBS 29 5-11 190 — Running Back

Acquired in trade with Buffalo during '86 training camp. By first game Cribbs was listed at top of depth chart... A second-round Buffalo pick out of Auburn in 1980, Cribbs had three huge seasons (1980, '81, '83) with Bills before jumping to Birmingham of USFL in 1984... After two seasons in the USFL, he returned to the Bills on Oct. 13, 1985, demanding a trade . . . In first season with 49ers, he had 152 carries for 590 yards and five TDs and 35 catches for 346 yards . . . Hurting part of the year, so Bill Walsh re-signed Wendell Tyler for stretch run . . . Best game was Week 15 when he carried 23 times for 107 yards and two TDs vs. Patriots . . . Born Jan. 5, 1958, in Sulligent, Ala.

DWIGHT CLARK 30 6-4 215   Wide Receiver

Joe Montana's good buddy had 61 catches (10th in NFC) for 794 yards (13th in NFC) . . . Has caught a pass in 104 regular-season games . . . It was seventh 50-catch season, a feat surpassed by only Seattle's Steve Largent . . . But whispers say he's slowing down, and 49ers are looking at other receivers . . . Has played every game (121) since coming from Clemson as 10th-round pick in '79 . . . Awesome career stats: 482 catches, 6,460 yards, 43 TDs . . . Born Jan. 8, 1957, in Kinston, N.C.

RUSS FRANCIS 34 6-6 242   Tight End

Just keeps rolling along . . . Caught 41 passes for 505 yards, a 12.3 average . . . Number of catches match his best performance during his first six seasons in the NFL at New England. The 41 are second only to 1985 season when he caught 44 . . . Maybe the time off keeps him going . . . Didn't play football in senior year at Oregon and retired for 1981 season when he got tired of playing in New England and forced trade to 49ers . . . Born April 3, 1953, in Seattle.

JEFF STOVER 29 6-5 275   Defensive End

Played everywhere on defensive line . . . And sometimes played nowhere . . . His 11 sacks were second only to Charles Haley's 12. In last two seasons, he has 21 sacks . . . Started 11 games in '85 before knee injury . . . When John Harty went on injured reserve Oct. 24, 1986, he started some games at left end . . . Great success story . . . Did not play football in college at Oregon. Tossed hammer and shot-put instead . . . Was working as carpenter when former 49er Leon Donohue suggested tryout . . . Had not played football since 1975, but was signed to contract in 1982 . . . In spite of having no real position of his own, he was third in tackles among defensive linemen with 37 . . . Also defensed two passes . . . Born May 22, 1958, in Corning, Cal.

DON GRIFFIN 23 6-0 176   Cornerback

Replaced injured Eric Wright at right corner . . . Tough role for rookie drafted way down in sixth round out of Middle Tennessee State . . . Wright went to Pro Bowl in '84, but he injured hamstring at end of '85 season and never got untracked last year . . . Griffin played safety in college, but made smooth transition . . . Named NFC Defensive Rookie of Year by NFLPA . . . Defensed 18 passes and was fourth on team with 72 tackles . . . Also returned punts and ranked second in NFC. Had 38 for 377 yards, a 9.9 average. Took one back 76 yards for a TD vs. Atlanta . . . Had four kick returns for 82 yards vs. Minnesota. . . . Kid brother of Bengal defensive back James Griffin . . . Born March 17, 1964, in Pelham, Ga.

TIM McKYER 23 6-0 174   Cornerback

Replaced great Ronnie Lott, who moved to free safety . . . Lott led NFC with 10 interceptions and went to Pro Bowl for fifth time at his new position . . . McKyer didn't do so badly, either . . . Was tied for seventh in NFC with six interceptions and returned one 21 yards for a touchdown . . . Also led team with 23 passes defensed . . . Taken in third round out of Texas-Arlington . . . Stats in first pro season were more impressive than any he had in college . . . Had one punt return and one kickoff return last year . . . Born Sept. 5, 1963, in Orlando, Fla.

CHARLES HALEY 23 6-5 230   Defensive End

Rookie led 49ers with 12 sacks. Tied with Giants' Leonard Marshall for fifth place in NFC. Trailed only Lawrence Taylor of Giants, Dexter Manley of Washington, Reggie White of Philadelphia and Jim Jeffcoat of Dallas . . . From James Madison, which also spawned great Washington receiver Gary Clark . . . Drafted in fifth round (96th player chosen).

Bill Walsh thought nobody else knew about Haley, but Bill Parcells would have snatched him with Giants' next pick ... Linebacker in college ... Had 59 tackles, three forced fumbles, an interception and three defensed passes for 49ers ... Born Jan. 6, 1964, in Gladys, Va.

COACH BILL WALSH: His true genius is not his Super Bowl  victories XVI, XIX. It is keeping the 49ers at the top of the NFC West for so long ... Led team to 10-5-1 record and into playoffs for fifth time in six seasons ... Finds kids to fill holes ... His 76 victories are most ever by a 49er coach. Buck Shaw held the record with 72 ... Overall record is 76-53-1 in regular season ... Tennis fanatic ... Played end offensively and defensively at San Jose State ... Had two-year hitch in the Army ... Was assistant for Raiders and Bengals. When Bengals snubbed him as head coach, he went to Chargers as offensive coordinator in 1977 ... Spent next two years with Stanford as head coach and had 17-7 record ... Finally got pro job he wanted in 1979 ... Almost quit in 1982 because of "burnout." ... The 49ers were 2-14 team when he got them ... Soft-spoken erudite man known for creativity ... Born Nov. 30, 1931, in Los Angeles.

GREATEST KICKER

More than two decades since his departure, Tommy Davis' name still fills the 49ers' record book. From his debut in 1959 through the 13th game of 1965, he made every PAT, a string of 234 that still stands as a league record. Not even Ray Wersching matched that string.

He also was a long-distance kicker. On Oct. 17, 1965, he made two field goals from 53 yards at Los Angeles. He also had another from 50 yards later that season against the Rams. It was the LSU product's best season, 17 of 27 for a .630 percentage.

In 1962, Davis had three spectacular punts—82 yards against Minnesota on Sept. 30; 79 yards at Chicago on Oct. 14; 81 yards at St. Louis on Nov. 25. He went to Pro Bowl in 1963 and 1964, and his 44.68-yard career punting average is third best in NFL history behind Indianapolis' Rohn Stark and Washington's Sammy Baugh.

INDIVIDUAL 49ER RECORDS
Rushing

Most Yards Game:	194	Delvin Williams, vs St. Louis, 1976
Season:	1,262	Wendell Tyler, 1984
Career:	7,344	Joe Perry, 1948-60, 1963

Passing

Most TD Passes Game:	5	Frank Albert, vs Cleveland (AAC), 1949
	5	John Brodie, vs Minnesota, 1965
	5	Steve Spurrier, vs Chicago, 1972
	5	Joe Montana, vs Atlanta, 1985
Season:	30	John Brodie, 1965
Career:	214	John Brodie, 1957-73

Receiving

Most TD Passes Game:	3	Alyn Beals, vs Brooklyn (AAC), 1948
	3	Alyn Beals, vs Chicago (AAC), 1949
	3	Gordy Soltau, vs Los Angeles, 1951
	3	Bernie Casey, vs Minnesota, 1962
	3	Dave Parks, vs Baltimore, 1965
	3	Gene Washington, vs San Diego, 1972
	3	Jerry Rice, vs Indianapolis, 1986
	3	Jerry Rice, vs St. Louis, 1986
Season:	15	Jerry Rice, 1986
Career:	59	Gene Washington, 1969-76

Scoring

Most Points Game:	26	Gordy Soltau, vs Los Angeles, 1951
Season:	126	Ray Wersching, 1983
Career:	896	Ray Wersching, 1977-86
Most TDs Game:	4	Bill Kilmer, vs Minnesota, 1961
Season:	16	Jerry Rice, 1986
Career:	61	Ken Willard, 1965-73

TAMPA BAY BUCCANEERS

TEAM DIRECTORY: Owner/Chairman: Hugh Culverhouse; VP: Joy Culverhouse; VP/Head Coach: Ray Perkins; Dir. Administration: Jim McVay; Dir. Player Personnel: Jerry Angelo; Dir. Pub. Rel.: Rick Odioso. Home field: Tampa Stadium (74,317). Colors: Florida orange, white and red.

SCOUTING REPORT

OFFENSE: Ray Perkins' methods are familiar. His first player with the Giants was a quarterback, Phil Simms. His first player with the Bucs is Vinny Testaverde. Perkins will tear apart a losing team, right to the foundation. He'll get rid of anybody he doesn't want and anybody who doesn't want him. He'll step back, tear it apart again. And again. Until, finally, he gets to the playoffs. During the building years he'd rather have overachieving free agents than underachieving veterans. He'll make a few trades for vital needs, but most of the players will be draft choices. And in the end, they will be his players and his team.

Running back James Wilder is his kind of player, a winner who happens to play for a losing team. The offense will be built around Wilder and Testaverde and a few more good men. He has already gotten rid of his star lineman, Sean Farrell, for an edge in the draft. Running back Ron Springs is gone, too. And Steve Young has been dispatched with his million-dollar contract to San Francisco.

But the Bucs will take time to rebuild. Nathan Wonsley, a free agent who would fit beautifully in Perkins' new two-back scheme, is trying to come back from a broken neck. There are no wide receivers worth mentioning except Gerald Carter, who started 15 games and caught 42 passes. Ron Heller, who started at Penn State next to Farrell, is the best lineman left, but the rest of the line is not impressive. Maybe Marvin Powell has a year left and can be Farrell's replacement, but he's coming off knee surgery. The tight end is a free agent, Calvin Magee, and Perkins wants him to lose 39 pounds, down to 240. If Magee succeeds, he could be a real asset.

Perkins made one early addition, center Dan Turk from the Steelers. More will soon follow.

DEFENSE: This area is a lot worse than the offense—14th against passing, 14th against rushing, 14th in the NFC. Pathetic. While the offense was gaining 272.6 yards per game and scoring 239 points, the defense was allowing 473 points and 395.8 yards.

Vinny Testaverde will try to prove the price is right.

The best of the lot can be found on the defensive line. David Logan had a couple of great seasons, but at 240 pounds he is beginning to slip from the beating he took. And it's not as easy for him without Lee Roy Selmon at his side. Ron Holmes is desperately trying to live up to his status as a No. 1 draft pick and

BUCCANEERS VETERAN ROSTER

HEAD COACH—Ray Perkins. Assistant Coaches—Larry Beightol, John Bobo, Bill Clay, Sylvester Croom, Mike DuBose, Doug Graber, Kent Johnston, Joe Kines, Herb Paterra, Rodney Stokes, Marc Trestman, Richard Williamson.

No.	Name	Pos.	Ht.	Wt.	NFL Exp.	College
82	Bell, Jerry	TE	6-5	230	6	Arizona State
38	Bligen, Dennis	RB	5-11	215	4	St. John's
34	Boatner, Mack	RB	6-0	220	2	Southeast Louisiana
52	Brantley, Scot	LB	6-1	230	8	Florida
78	Cannon, John	DE	6-5	260	6	William & Mary
87	Carter, Gerald	WR	6-1	190	8	Texas A&M
23	Castille, Jeremiah	DB	5-10	175	5	Alabama
31	Curry, Craig	DB	6-1	190	4	Texas
58	Davis, Jeff	LB	6-0	230	6	Clemson
17	DeBerg, Steve	QB	6-3	210	11	San Jose State
85	Dunn, K.D.	TE	6-3	235	3	Clemson
26	Easmon, Ricky	DB	5-10	160	3	Florida
95	Faulkner, Chris	TE	6-4	250	3	Florida
35	Franklin, Pat	RB	6-1	230	2	Southwest Texas St.
81	Freeman, Phil	WR	5-11	185	3	Arizona
36	Futrell, Bobby	DB	5-11	190	2	Elizabeth City St.
5	Garcia, Frank	P	6-0	210	5	Tucson
83	Gillespie, Willie	WR	5-9	170	2	Tennessee-Chattanooga
4	Gonzalez, Leon	WR	5-11	165	2	Bethune Cookman
92	Goode, Conrad	OT	6-6	285	3	Missouri
60	Grimes, Randy	C	6-4	270	5	Baylor
84	Harris, Leonard	WR	5-8	155	2	Texas Tech
89	Heflin, Vince	WR	6-0	185	6	Central St. (Ohio)
73	Heller, Ron	OT	6-6	280	4	Penn State
90	Holmes, Ron	DE	6-4	255	3	Washington
25	Howard, Bobby	RB	6-0	210	2	Indiana
1	Igwebuike, Donald	PK	5-9	185	3	Clemson
22	Jones, Rod	DB	6-0	175	2	Southern Methodist
75	Kellin, Kevin	DE	6-6	265	2	Minnesota
—	Kemp, Bobby	S	6-0	191	7	Cal-Fullerton
98	Keys, Tyrone	DE	6-7	270	5	Mississippi State
76	Logan, David	NT	6-2	250	9	Pittsburgh
77	Maarleveld, J.D.	OT	6-6	300	2	Maryland
86	Magee, Calvin	TE	6-3	240	3	Southern
68	Mallory, Rick	G	6-2	265	3	Washington
21	McKeever, Vito	DB	6-0	180	2	Florida
59	Murphy, Kevin	LB	6-2	230	2	Oklahoma
71	Nelson, Bob	NT-DE	6-3	265	2	Miami
74	Powell, Marvin	OT	6-5	270	11	Southern California
54	Randle, Ervin	LB	6-1	250	3	Baylor
64	Robinson, Greg	OT	6-5	285	2	Sacramento State
41	Swoope, Craig	DB	6-1	200	2	Illinois
72	Taylor, Rob	OT	6-6	290	2	Northwestern
—	Turk, Dan	C	6-4	270	2	Wisconsin
56	Walker, Jackie	LB	6-5	245	2	Jackson State
37	Walker, Kevin	DB	5-11	180	2	East Carolina
27	Walker, Quentin	RB	6-0	205	2	Virginia
10	Walls, Herkie	WR	5-8	160	4	Texas
51	Washington, Chris	LB	6-4	230	4	Iowa State
32	Wilder, James	RB	6-3	225	7	Missouri
80	Williams, David	WR	6-3	190	2	Illinois
46	Wonsley, Nathan	RB	5-10	190	2	Mississippi
66	Yarno, George	G	6-2	265	8	Washington State
8						

TOP FIVE DRAFT CHOICES

Rd.	Name	Sel. No.	Pos.	Ht.	Wt.	College
1	Testaverde, Vinny	1	QB	6-5	218	Miami
2	Reynolds, Ricky	36	CB	6-0	181	Washington State
2	Winston, Moss	50	LB	6-3	240	Miami
2	Smith, Don	51	RB	6-0	195	Mississippi State
3	Carrier, Mark	57	WR	6-0	181	Nicholls State

replace Selmon. He has begun lifting weights, but it will take time. And John Cannon, who was sidelined with a broken bone in his leg, and Bob Nelson shared the other end.

The inside linebackers are Scot Brantley and Jeff Davis, but they get little help. Keith Browner was a starter a year ago, but he was traded. Maybe he'll be replaced by Jackie Walker, whose strength is rushing the passer and sticking to basics. Chris Washington is the right outside linebacker, but he's average.

Only two defensive backs, Craig Swoope at strong safety and Rod Jones at the right corner, both '86 draft picks, are likely to make any impact. Ivory Sully, who was replaced by Swoope, is gone. And Bobby Kemp, a rather notorious hitter when he played for the Bengals, might get a shot at left corner.

KICKING GAME: Donald Igwebuike made 17-of-24 field goals. He replaced a boyhood buddy from Nigeria, Obed Ariri, at Clemson, then replaced him again at Tampa Bay. He'll stick around. But Danny Garcia, 40.1 gross and 32.7 net, might not be good enough for a replay as punter. Many tried returns, and failed. Fifteen different Bucs are included in the kickoff-return stats, and together they only averaged 17.4 yards.

THE ROOKIES: Perkins wasted no time in starting his rebuilding program from the ground up. He collected 20 picks, by far the most of any team in the draft. And he divided them evenly, 10 offense, nine defense, one for punter Greg Davis of The Citadel. He opened the draft with Testaverde, a potential franchise quarterback, and closed it with Don Shula's son, Mike, who played for Perkins at Alabama. The Bucs could wind up with more than a dozen rookies on their roster.

OUTLOOK: Bleak. Come back in two years and see what happens. It will get uglier before it gets pretty.

BUCCANEER PROFILES

VINNY TESTAVERDE 23 6-5 218   Quarterback

Received $8.2-million, six-year contract, including $2-million signing bonus, on April 3. When Bo Jackson spurned chance at similar deal last year to play baseball, owner Hugh Culverhouse decided to take no chances on draft day . . . Led Miami Hurricanes to 21-3 record as starter . . . Heisman Trophy winner in '86 when he threw for 2,557 yards and

26 TDs...Over career threw for 6,058 yards with 48 TDs and 25 interceptions...Miami challenged for national title, but Testaverde threw five interceptions in Fiesta Bowl loss to Penn State ...Steve Young became expendable moment Testaverde signed...Born Nov. 13, 1963, in Brooklyn, N.Y.

JAMES WILDER 29 6-3 225   Running Back

Ran 190 times for 704 yards and two TDs. Caught 43 passes for 326 yards and one TD ...Fifteenth in NFC in total yards from scrimmage...Hurts tacklers...Also an excellent blocker...Slowed down early when he suffered a painful bruised sternum on Sept. 14. Didn't have a 100-yard game until week eight. In first seven games he had only 73 carries for 232 yards for no touchdowns and 18 catches for 178 yards and one touchdown. Came on strong when healthy... Stats still far below team-record 1,544 yards rushing in 1984, when he made only Pro Bowl appearance, and 1,300 yards in 1985...Was second-round pick in 1981 after setting all-time rushing records at Missouri...Born May 12, 1958, in Sikeston, Mo.

GERALD CARTER 30 6-1 190   Wide Receiver

Old man of the receiving corps. Theo Bell retired before '86 season and Kevin House, Bucs' all-time leading receiver, was cut in purge before seventh game...Finished with 42 catches for 640 yards last season... Drafted in ninth round out of Texas A&M in 1980. Cut in camp and signed with Jets, who waived him after three games. Re-signed with Bucs in December. Wild rookie year...Caught total of 11 passes in 1981 and 1982, then hit stride...Started every game in 1985 ...Born June 19, 1957, in Bryan, Tex.

CALVIN MAGEE 24 6-3 240   Tight End

When the Bucs' four-time Pro Bowler Jimmie Giles (296 catches, 4,447 yards) was cut before the seventh game, Magee became starter ...Had seven catches for 67 yards in first six games and wound up as Bucs' leading receiver with 45 for 564 yards for season, placing him with best tight ends in conference...All the more impressive since he'd ballooned to

278 pounds in offseason ... As rookie free agent out of Southern in 1985, he had 26 catches, mainly at U-back after injury to Jerry Bell ... Scored TD on very first pro play, one-yard catch vs. Bears ... Huge hands, good power ... Born April 23, 1963, in New Orleans.

GEORGE YARNO 30 6-2 265   Guard

Called "smallest tackle in NFC" when he started there out of necessity in 1985. Moved to left guard in 1986 and started all 16 games ... A free agent in 1979 from Washington State, where he was an All Pac-10 defensive lineman ... First played offensive line in Challenge Bowl for coach John McKay after senior season. Volunteered when injury left team in bind ... Makes most of ability ... Played two back-to-back seasons. Was with Bucs in fall of '83, Denver Gold of USFL in spring of '84, Gold in spring of '85 and Bucs in fall of '85 ... Born Aug. 12, 1957, in Spokane, Wash.

DAVID LOGAN 30 6-2 250   Nose Tackle

Only defensive lineman to start every game in '86 ... String of consecutive starts now at 105 games, going back to Sept. 20, 1980 ... Sadly enough, never made Pro Bowl although he deserved to go several times. Might be slipping a bit now ... Led team with 19 QB pressures in 1986. Had 60 tackles, seven tackles for loss, two fumbles caused and two recovered ... Small, but quick ... A 12th-round draft choice out of Pitt in 1979 ... Missed rookie year with hyperxtended knee ... Born Oct. 25, 1956, in Pittsburgh.

ROD JONES 23 6-0 175   Cornerback

No other defensive back started more than 12 games. He started all 16 ... Led team with 14 passes defensed, but had only one interception on right corner ... Fourth on team with 80 tackles ... Was learning on the job ... Was 25th player drafted last year ... Blazing speed. Nicknamed "K.O." at SMU for his hitting ability ... Won two NCAA track titles— 400 meters in 1984 and 1600-meter relay team in 1986 ... Talented cartoonist ... Born March 31, 1964, in Dallas.

JEFF DAVIS 27 6-0 230   Linebacker

Created a bit of havoc for a sad defense by causing six fumbles . . . Led team in tackles for third straight season (136) at right inside linebacker . . . Started every game for last three seasons . . . Overcomes lack of height, which left him ignored by scouts . . . Clemson All-American was drafted in fifth round in 1981 . . . Got degree in 1984 in industrial management . . . Operates travel agency . . . Born Jan. 26, 1960, in Greensboro, N.C.

RON HOLMES 24 6-4 255   Defensive End

First-rounder in 1985 . . . Had very difficult assignment of replacing six-time Pro Bowler Lee Roy Selmon as a rookie . . . Looked more comfortable at right end in 1986 . . . Missed three starts in first half of the season with knee injury and Bob Nelson filled in . . . Had only one sack in second half of season and finished with 2½. But led team with 23 QB hurries and had six tackles for loss . . . Still credits Selmon for much of his success, dating back to college days at Washington, where a scout gave him films of Selmon to study . . . Born Aug. 26, 1963, in Ft. Benning, Ga.

COACH RAY PERKINS: Another Bear Bryant disciple . . .

Loves offense . . . Was All-American receiver at Alabama, playing with Joe Namath, Steve Sloan and Ken Stabler . . . Played five seasons with Colts . . . Began coaching at Mississippi State in 1973 . . . Worked as assistant to Chuck Fairbanks with Patriots from 1974-77 and to Don Coryell with Chargers in 1978 . . . Took Giants' top job the following year and led team to playoffs in '81 for first time in 18 years . . . Resigned abruptly when offered job as Bryant's successor at Alabama in 1983 . . . Went to three bowl games and won them all in four years at Alabama. Resigned abruptly again to return to NFL . . . Title is coach and vice president-football operations . . . A doer . . . Some kids marry high-school sweethearts, he married his high-school teacher back in Petal, Miss. . . . Hobby is golf . . . Admits "I'm not a miracle worker." . . . Born Nov. 6, 1941, in Mount Olive, Miss.

GREATEST KICKER

Frank Garcia wins by default. He's the only Buc in history to have led the NFC in a statistical category. His glorious moment came in 1983 when he had a 42.2-yard average on 95 punts. He should have won an award for guts in 1985 when he punted despite a stress fracture in his plant leg and averaged 42.0 yards on 77 punts.

An Arizona product, he made a tour before reaching the Bucs as a free agent in 1983. He had unsuccessful tryouts with Atlanta, San Diego, Green Bay and Tampa Bay. He was also cut by Seattle after one game and by the Chicago Blitz of the USFL. With the Bucs he has 319 punts for 13,179 yards, a 41.3 average. He has had at least one 60-yard punt in each of his four seasons.

INDIVIDUAL BUCCANEER RECORDS

Rushing

Most Yards Game:	219	James Wilder, vs Minnesota, 1983
Season:	1,544	James Wilder, 1984
Career:	4,882	James Wilder, 1981-86

Passing

Most TD Passes Game:	4	Steve DeBerg, vs Miami, 1985
	4	Doug Williams, vs Minnesota, 1980
	4	Doug Williams, vs Detroit, 1981
	4	Jack Thompson, vs Houston, 1983
Season:	20	Doug Williams, 1980
Career:	73	Doug Williams, 1978-82

Receiving

Most TD Passes Game:	4	Jimmie Giles, vs Miami, 1985
Season:	9	Kevin House, 1981
Career:	34	Jimmie Giles, 1978-86

Scoring

Most Points Game:	24	Jimmie Giles, vs Miami, 1985
Season:	96	Donald Igwebuike, 1985
Career:	240	James Wilder, 1981-86
Most TDs Game:	4	Jimmie Giles, vs Miami, 1985
Season:	13	James Wilder, 1984
Career:	40	James Wilder, 1981-86

WASHINGTON REDSKINS

TEAM DIRECTORY: Chairman: Jack Kent Cooke; Exec. VP: John Kent Cooke; GM: Bobby Beathard; Dir. Player Personnel: Dick Daniels; Dir Media Rel.: John C. Konoza; Head Coach: Joe Gibbs. Home field: Robert F. Kennedy Stadium (55,750). Colors: Burgundy and gold.

SCOUTING REPORT

OFFENSE: Jay Schroeder's 1986 appearance marked the ninth time in 13 years that the Redskins have sent a quarterback to the Pro Bowl. In one year, Schroeder has become the focus of a new airborne offense that ranked third in yardage (5,601) and fourth

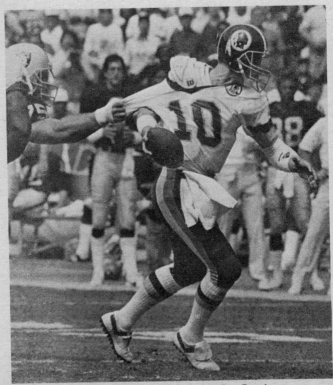

Jay Schroeder went on a tear in Pro Bowl year.

in points (368) in the NFC.

Washington averaged only 108.3 yards per game rushing, but it passed for 241.8 yards. It proved time after time it could come from behind. And Schroeder was the reason.

But the offense is not without problems. Anthony Jones' knee injury left the Redskins without a spare tight end, and Bobby Beathard chided the offensive line at the end of last season, calling it "just average." R.C. Thielemann, 32, and Russ Grimm might be pushed at the guard positions. Raleigh McKenzie might be the one who moves into the starting lineup.

The running game should have been better with George Rogers, Kelvin Bryant and Keith Griffin. It ranked 13th in the NFC, and the Redskins were outrushed by their opponents (1,732 yards to 1,805). The Redskins were always a team that ran to win. But last season they ran only 45.4 percent of the time and threw 54.6 percent. It was the first time since 1981 that they threw more than they ran.

Dan Henning's return from Atlanta might have a positive effect on the offense. He will have the joy of working with the receivers, Art Monk and Gary Clark, and he will have input into the game plan. Monk suggested last year that the Redskins had become "stereotyped." Henning can provide a respected dissenting opinion for Joe Gibbs.

DEFENSE: Washington ranked next to last in the NFC in defense, yielding 331.1 yards per game. And most of the yardage was against the pass.

The defense also ranked 13th in takeaways, ahead of only St. Louis. It had only 19 interceptions and nine fumble recoveries. There is obviously a lot of room for improvement.

The starting linebackers—Rich Milot, Neal Olkewicz and Monte Coleman—all joined the Redskins in 1979, and they were all born in 1957. It's time to look for replacements. Mel Kaufman's Achilles injury last season cast a dark shadow over the linebacking corps and left it without depth.

The secondary has needs, too. Darrell Green is an exciting left cornerback, but Gibbs kept looking for the right man at the right corner all last year. At least, Gibbs was able to find his man at strong safety, Crushin' Kansan Alvin Walton. But free safety Curtis Jordan, 33, is among the oldest Redskins and probably nearing the end. Nebraska's Brian Davis, the Redskins' top pick, will be a welcome addition.

The only truly solid area of the defense is the line. Dexter Manley had 18 sacks, right behind Lawrence Taylor, but he had trouble getting to the quarterback late in the year and eventually

REDSKINS VETERAN ROSTER

HEAD COACH—Joe Gibbs. Assistant Coaches—Chuck Banker, Don Breaux, Joe Bugel, Joe Diange, Dan Henning, Bill Hickman, Larry Peccatiello, Richie Petitbon, Jerry Rhome, Dan Riley, Charley Taylor, Torgy Torgeson.

No.	Name	Pos.	Ht.	Wt.	NFL Exp.	College
4	Atkinson, Jess	K	5-9	168	3	Maryland
26	Badanjek, Rick	RB	5-8	218	2	Maryland
53	Bostic, Jeff	C	6-2	260	8	Clemson
23	Bowles, Todd	S	6-2	203	2	Temple
29	Branch, Reggie	RB	5-11	227	3	East Carolina
24	Bryant, Kelvin	RB	6-2	195	2	North Carolina
58	Burks, Shawn	LB	6-1	230	2	LSU
65	Butz, Dave	DT	6-7	295	15	Purdue
—	Caldwell, Ravin	LB	6-3	229	1	Arkansas
84	Clark, Gary	WR	5-9	175	3	James Madison
48	Coffey, Ken	S	6-0	198	4	SW Texas State
51	Coleman, Monte	LB	6-2	230	9	Central Arkansas
—	Copeland, Anthony	LB	6-2	250	1	Louisville
12	Cox, Steve	P	6-4	195	7	Arkansas
56	Daniels, Calvin	LB	6-3	241	6	North Carolina
32	Dean, Vernon	CB	5-11	178	6	San Diego State
86	Didier, Clint	TE	6-5	240	6	Portland State
—	Fells, Kenny	RB	6-0	190	1	Henderson State
—	Frain, Todd	TE	6-2	235	1	Nebraska
30	Garner, Dwight	RB	5-8	183	2	California
—	Gouveia, Kurt	LB	6-1	227	1	Brigham Young
77	Grant, Darryl	DT	6-1	275	7	Rice
28	Green, Darrell	CB	5-8	170	5	Texas A&I
35	Griffin, Keith	RB	5-8	185	4	Miami
68	Grimm, Russ	G	6-3	275	7	Pittsburgh
78	Hamel, Dean	DT	6-3	275	3	Tulsa
64	Hamilton, Steve	DE-DT	6-4	255	3	East Carolina
88	Holloway, Derek	WR	5-7	166	2	Arkansas
66	Jacoby, Joe	T	6-7	305	7	Louisville
31	Jenkins, Ken	RB-KR	5-8	185	5	Bucknell
82	Jones, Anthony	TE	6-3	248	4	Wichita State
22	Jordan, Curtis	FS	6-2	205	11	Texas Tech
55	Kaufman, Mel	LB	6-2	218	6	Cal Poly-SLO
74	Koch, Markus	DE	6-5	275	2	Boise State
54	Krakoski, Joe	LB	6-1	224	1	Washington
72	Manley, Dexter	DE	6-3	257	7	Oklahoma State
71	Mann, Charles	DE	6-6	270	5	Nevada-Reno
73	May, Mark	T	6-6	295	7	Pittsburgh
63	McKenzie, Raleigh	G	6-2	262	3	Tennessee
60	McQuaid, Dan	T	6-7	278	3	Nevada-Las Vegas
57	Milot, Rich	LB	6-4	237	9	Penn State
81	Monk, Art	WR	6-3	209	8	Syracuse
41	Morrison, Tim	CB	6-1	195	2	North Carolina
52	Olkewicz, Neal	LB	6-0	230	9	Maryland
87	Orr, Terry	TE	6-3	227	2	Texas
38	Rogers, George	RB	6-2	225	7	South Carolina
—	Rosen, Jeff	G	6-3	274	1	Delaware
11	Rypien, Mark	QB	6-4	234	1	Washington State
46	Sanders, Ricky	RB	5-11	180	2	SW Texas State
10	Schroeder, Jay	QB	6-4	215	4	UCLA
69	Thielemann, R.C.	G	6-4	262	11	Arkansas
76	Tilton, Ron	G	6-4	250	2	Tulane
89	Verdin, Clarence	WR-KR	5-8	160	2	Southwest Louisiana
40	Walton, Alvin	S	6-0	180	2	Kansas
85	Warren, Don	TE	6-4	242	9	San Diego State
45	Wilburn, Barry	CB	6-3	186	3	Mississippi
47	Williams, Doug	QB	6-4	220	7	Grambling
80	Yarber, Eric	WR-KR	5-8	156	2	Idaho
—	Zendejas, Max	K	5-11	184	2	Arizona

TOP FIVE DRAFT CHOICES

Rd.	Name	Sel. No.	Pos.	Ht.	Wt.	College
2	Davis, Brian	30	CB	6-2	190	Nebraska
2	Kleine, Wally	48	OT	6-9	274	Notre Dame
5	Smith, Tim	117	RB	5-11	216	Texas Tech
6	Gage, Steve	144	DB	6-3	210	Tulsa
6	Simmons, Ed	164	OT	6-5	275	E. Washington

checked into an alcohol rehab program. The line also had occa-
sional trouble against the run, especially in the first half of the
season. It gave up 128.9 yards per game and 4.4 yards per carry
in the first eight games, but only 96.5 and 3.4 in the next eight.

KICKING GAME: Jess Atkinson appeared like an angel late in
the year after Mark Moseley faded away and Max Zendejas was
hurt. Atkinson was a perfect 6-for-6 on field goals in the
playoffs, but he has a spotty past. The Redskins must take a very
hard look at the kickers they bring to camp. Zendejas will get
another try, but at least one Redskin joyfully proclaimed "no
mas" when Zendejas left.

Punting is no problem with Steve Cox, and he can also handle
kickoffs and long field goals. If he could kick short, the Redskins
would have no kicking problem. Returns are adequate, too.

THE ROOKIES: The Redskins had only 11 picks and they
didn't have a first-rounder. They got around to Davis on the 30th
pick, starting a run on secondary players. Then they chose tackle
Wally Kleine of Notre Dame on the 48th pick. But the Redskins
can't expect much help from this draft. At least Kleine has ties to
Washington. His father is a Texas oilman, and he is buddies with
VP George Bush.

OUTLOOK: Teams that are 13th in rushing offense and 13th in
overall defense don't usually go very far in the NFC. The Redskins got to the NFC title game last year, but they have to improve defensively if they want to repeat that success. Joe Gibbs
cannot pull the playoffs out of his hat every year, but he is good
and has an ability to adapt to his personnel better than any other
coach in the conference.

REDSKIN PROFILES

JAY SCHROEDER 26 6-4 215　　　　　　　　**Quarterback**

Had a Pro Bowl year...Led NFC in yards
(4,109), attempts (541) and completions (276)
and was second in average gain (7.6) and TD
passes (22). However, also threw 22
interceptions...Has 19-6 record since replacing Joe Theismann in 11th game of 1985...
Redskins became big-play, come-from-behind
team with him. In two-minute drills over last

two seasons he has five TDs, eight field goals made, two field goals missed . . . Has not been sacked in seven of his 25 games . . . Remarkable success for one full season. Started only one game at UCLA and got only as far as Class A in aborted baseball career after being picked in third round of '84 NFL draft. Only quarterbacks chosen ahead of him were Boomer Esiason and Rick McIvor . . . Born June 28, 1961, in Palisades, Cal.

GEORGE ROGERS 28 6-2 225   Running Back

Led NFL in TDs (18 regular season, one playoffs) and gained 1,203 yards on 303 carries. Fourth 1,000-yard season as pro. Others were with Saints in 1981 and 1983 and Redskins in 1985 . . . Drove Joe Gibbs crazy with fumbles in '85, but is currently working on string of 118 carries without a fumble . . . Since being first pick of '81 draft out of South Carolina, he has produced 6,563 yards. Only Walter Payton, Eric Dickerson and Tony Dorsett had more over that span. . . . Born Dec. 8, 1958, in Duluth, Ga.

KELVIN BRYANT 26 6-2 195   Running Back

Set club record with 13 catches against Giants . . . Played 10 games, but had 707 yards (449 on 43 catches; 258 on 69 carries) . . . Great USFL pickup. Drafted by Redskins out of North Carolina in seventh round of 1983 draft, he played three seasons in USFL and won two titles with Philadelphia and Baltimore Stars . . . Had six straight 1,000-yard rushing years (three in college, three with USFL), but he was more dangerous catching passes for Washington . . . Missed six games after injuring knee and ankle vs. Raiders on Sept. 14 . . . Born Sept. 26, 1960, in Tarboro, N.C.

DEXTER MANLEY 28 6-3 257   Defensive End

Loves to talk . . . Stirred up excitement by skipping practice . . . Blamed absence on a hangover and underwent alcohol treatment before '86 season . . . Angry at not making Pro Bowl in '85, he got there in '86 . . . Only Lawrence Taylor of the Giants had more sacks. Manley was tied with Philadelphia's Reggie White for second-most sacks (18) . . .

Real trouble getting to quarterbacks late in season...Former Oklahoma State player was embarrassed twice on national TV by Giants' Brad Benson...Holds NFL's official record with 64 sacks since official records were kept in 1982. Has 1½ more than Jets' Mark Gastineau...Born Feb. 2, 1959, in Houston.

DARRELL GREEN 27 5-8 170   Cornerback

Five interceptions in regular season and one in the playoffs. Also nine pass deflections and two forced fumbles...Made Pro Bowl for second straight year...Also helped out on punt returns...Called "MX," he has great speed...Resilient when beaten...Missed first start in four seasons...Won NFL's Fastest Man Contest in 1986...Lived up to that reputation when he came across the field and caught Eric Dickerson from behind to save a touchdown against the Rams in the playoffs...Born Feb. 15, 1960, in Houston...Attended Texas A&I...A first-round pick in 1983.

ART MONK 29 6-3 209   Wide Receiver

First Redskin to have three straight 1,000-yard seasons and also first to have three straight 70-catch seasons. Has a catch in 66 straight games. Five 100-yard games in 1986 give him total of 26 for career...Made third straight Pro Bowl...Still the Redskins' deep threat ...Quiet and unassuming, much like former Syracuse teammate Joe Morris of the Giants ...Addition of Ricky Sanders and maturity of Gary Clark last year will take heat off Monk...NFL's most productive receiver over last three years in yards (3,666) and catches (270)...Born Dec. 5, 1957, in White Plains, N.Y.

DAVE BUTZ 37 6-7 295   Defensive Tackle

Contemplated retirement, but Redskins want him back..."The biggest man I ever saw," said Giants' defensive line coach Fred Hoaglin. "His head is as big as a pumpkin." And his shoes are 7EEEEEEE...Oldest Redskin —14 years in league...Feet are quicker than expected, and he's a wide detour if a runner wants to go around him...Leading vote-getter among defensive linemen for Redskins' 50th anniversary team . . . Played in 200th NFL game, including playoffs . . . Led linemen with 91 tackles and added six sacks, 12 QB hurries and three pass deflections . . . Contract expired Feb. 1, but Redskins made qualifying offer . . . Born June 23, 1950, in Lafayette, Ala. . . . Played at Purdue and was first-round pick by St. Louis in 1973 draft . . . Came to Washington in draft deal in '75 . . . Nephew of Earl Butz, former Secretary of Agriculture.

GARY CLARK 25 5-9 175   Wide Receiver

Redskins always have more than one big receiver . . . Clark had 1,265 yards, 97 more than Art Monk, despite ankle injury that prevented a catch in the final two games . . . Set club record with 241 yards vs. Giants . . . Had nine catches for 35 yards or more . . . No pair of receivers on any team have had more catches than Clark and Monk for two straight years. They combined for 163 in '85 and 147 in '86. Former James Madison player was born May 1, 1962, in Dublin, Va.

RUSS GRIMM 28 6-3 275   Guard

An original Hog. Others still with Redskins are Joe Jacoby, Jeff Bostic, Mark May. R.C. Thielemann came later . . . Elected to Pro Bowl for fourth time . . . In balloting by fans for the Redskins' 50th anniversary tream, Jacoby, Bostic and Grimm were top three vote-getters for offensive linemen . . . Line allowed only 28 sacks last season . . . Born May 2, 1959, in Scottsdale, Pa. . . . Third-round pick out of Pittsburgh in 1981.

NEAL OLKEWICZ 30 6-0 230   Linebacker

Came into NFL with Rich Milot and Monte Coleman in 1979. Olkewicz was a free agent out of Maryland and Milot and Coleman were lightly regarded draft picks. But they combined over the years for 326 games, 2,359 tackles, 54 sacks and 27 interceptions . . . Olkewicz is still going strong, although he is far from fitting the L.T. mold . . . Led team for third time with 183 tackles and added 24 tackles in playoffs . . .

Good against the run, but also had 10 QB hurries and two sacks ... Born Jan. 30, 1957, in Phoenixville, Pa.

COACH JOE GIBBS: First among active coaches in winning percentage (.710) ... Remarkable 71-29, including three division titles, two conference titles and one Super Bowl crown (XVII) ... Last year's 12-4 record was good for playoffs again, but Redskins lost in NFC championship game ... Three of last year's losses were to Giants ... Rarely stops working. When he does, he's usually giving speech for one of his religious or charitable causes or jogging ... Also hunts, water skis and plays racquetball. Was national racquetball champion in 35-and-over group in 1976 ... Played tight end for Don Coryell at San Diego State, which won 27 of 31 games ... Coached offense for Bill Peterson's high-scoring Florida State teams ... Also assisted John McKay at Southern Cal and Frank Broyles at Arkansas ... Coached in NFL with Coryell at St. Louis and San Diego and with McKay at Tampa Bay ... Joined Redskins in 1981 and got off to 0-5 start ... Then turned it all around ... Born Nov. 25, 1940, in Mocksville, N.C.

GREATEST KICKER

Sorry, Mark Moseley. Sammy Baugh is the easy winner. Baugh was the best at everything he did with the Redskins from 1937 through 1952. He was not only one of the great quarterbacks (22,085 yards and 187 TD passes), he was an outstanding defensive back (31 interceptions).

And as a punter he led the league for four straight years, 1940-43. He had the first- and third-best punting averages in history—51.4 in 1940 and 48.73 in 1941. His career average, 45.1, is second-best in history.

In 1942, when the Bears took an early lead in a title game, Baugh's 85-yard quick kick got the Redskins rolling toward a 14-6 victory. His 14 punts vs. the Eagles in 1939 ties the NFL record for most in a game and his 59.4-yard average on five punts vs. the Lions in 1940 is among the highest of all time.

INDIVIDUAL REDSKIN RECORDS

Rushing

Most Yards Game:	206	George Rogers, vs St. Louis, 1985
Season:	1,347	John Riggins, 1983
Career:	7,472	John Riggins, 1976-79, 1981-85

Passing

Most TD Passes Game:	6	Sam Baugh, vs Brooklyn, 1943
	6	Sam Baugh, vs St. Louis, 1947
Season:	31	Sonny Jurgensen, 1967
Career:	187	Sammy Baugh, 1937-52

Receiving

Most TD Passes Game:	3	Hugh Taylor (5 times)
	3	Jerry Smith, vs Los Angeles, 1967
	3	Jerry Smith, vs Dallas, 1969
	3	Hal Crisler (once)
	3	Joe Walton (once)
	3	Pat Richter, vs Chicago, 1968
	3	Larry Brown, vs Philadelphia, 1973
	3	Jean Fugett, vs San Francisco, 1976
	3	Alvin Garrett, vs Lions, 1982
	3	Art Monk, vs Indianapolis, 1984
Season:	12	Hugh Taylor, 1952
	12	Charley Taylor, 1966
	12	Jerry Smith, 1967
Career:	79	Charley Taylor, 1964-77

Scoring

Most Points Game:	24	Dick James, vs Dallas, 1961
	24	Larry Brown, vs Philadelphia, 1973
Season:	161	Mark Moseley, 1983
	144	John Riggins, 1983
Career:	1,176	Mark Moseley, 1974-85
Most TDs Game:	4	Dick James, vs Dallas, 1961
	4	Larry Brown, vs Philadelphia, 1973
Season:	24	John Riggins, 1983
Career:	90	Charley Taylor, 1964-77

Art Monk gets set for another 1,000-yard campaign.

OFFICIAL 1986 NFL STATISTICS

(Compiled by Elias Sports Bureau)

RUSHING

TOP TEN RUSHERS

	Att	Yards	Avg	Long	T
Dickerson, Eric, Rams	404	1821	4.5	t42	1
Morris, Joe, Giants	341	1516	4.4	54	1
Warner, Curt, Sea.	319	1481	4.6	t60	1
Mayes, Rueben, N.O.	286	1353	4.7	50	
Payton, Walter, Chi.	321	1333	4.2	41	
Riggs, Gerald, Atl.	343	1327	3.9	31	
Rogers, George, Wash.	303	1203	4.0	42	1
Brooks, James, Cin.	205	1087	5.3	t56	
Jackson, Earnest, Pitt.	216	910	4.2	31	
Jones, James, Det.	252	903	3.6	39	

NFC - INDIVIDUAL RUSHERS

	Att	Yards	Avg	Long	T
Dickerson, Eric, Rams	404	1821	4.5	t42	1
Morris, Joe, Giants	341	1516	4.4	54	1
Mayes, Rueben, N.O.	286	1353	4.7	50	
Payton, Walter, Chi.	321	1333	4.2	41	
Riggs, Gerald, Atl.	343	1327	3.9	31	
Rogers, George, Wash.	303	1203	4.0	42	1
Jones, James, Det.	252	903	3.6	39	
Craig, Roger, S.F.	204	830	4.1	25	
Mitchell, Stump, St.L.	174	800	4.6	44	
Nelson, Darrin, Minn.	191	793	4.2	42	
Dorsett, Tony, Dall.	184	748	4.1	33	
Walker, Herschel, Dall.	151	737	4.9	t84	1
Wilder, James, T.B.	190	704	3.7	t45	
James, Garry, Det.	159	688	4.3	t60	
Cribbs, Joe, S.F.	152	590	3.9	19	
Byars, Keith, Phil.	177	577	3.3	32	

t = touchdown
Leader based on most yards gained

Bears' Walter Payton has missed only one game in 12 years.

	Att	Yards	Avg	Long	TD
Ferrell, Earl, St.L.	124	548	4.4	25	0
Cunningham, Randall, Phil. ...	66	540	8.2	20	5
Davis, Kenneth, G.B.	114	519	4.6	50	0
Redden, Barry, Rams	110	467	4.2	t41	4
Hilliard, Dalton, N.O.	121	425	3.5	36	5
Young, Steve, T.B.	74	425	5.7	31	5
Anderson, Alfred, Minn.	83	347	4.2	29	2
Ellis, Gerry, G.B.	84	345	4.1	24	2
Wonsley, Nathan, T.B.	73	339	4.6	t59	3
Carruth, Paul, G.B.	81	308	3.8	42	2
Archer, David, Atl.	52	298	5.7	22	0
Ellerson, Gary, G.B.	90	287	3.2	18	3
Springs, Ron, T.B.	74	285	3.9	40	0
Toney, Anthony, Phil.	69	285	4.1	43	1
Austin, Cliff, Atl.	62	280	4.5	22	1
Haddix, Michael, Phil.	79	276	3.5	18	0
Suhey, Matt, Chi.	84	270	3.2	17	2
Carthon, Maurice, Giants	72	260	3.6	12	0
Bryant, Kelvin, Wash.	69	258	3.7	t22	4
Pelluer, Steve, Dall.	41	255	6.2	21	1
Brown, Ted, Minn.	63	251	4.0	60	4
Anderson, Ottis, St.L.-Giants	75	237	3.2	16	3
Sanders, Thomas, Chi.	27	224	8.3	t75	5
Thomas, Calvin, Chi.	56	224	4.0	23	0
Rice, Allen, Minn.	73	220	3.0	19	2
Stamps, Sylvester, Atl.	30	220	7.3	48	0
Andrews, William, Atl.	52	214	4.1	13	1
Jordan, Buford, N.O.	68	207	3.0	10	1
Griffin, Keith, Wash.	62	197	3.2	12	0
Rouson, Lee, Giants	54	179	3.3	t21	2
Tautalatasi, Junior, Phil. ...	51	163	3.2	50	0
McMahon, Jim, Chi.	22	152	6.9	23	1
Lomax, Neil, St.L.	35	148	4.2	18	1
Anderson, Neal, Chi.	35	146	4.2	23	0
Rathman, Tom, S.F.	33	138	4.2	t29	1
Tyler, Wendell, S.F.	31	127	4.1	14	0
White, Charles, Rams	22	126	5.7	19	0
Tomczak, Mike, Chi.	23	117	5.1	16	3
Howard, Bobby, T.B.	30	110	3.7	16	1
Newsome, Tim, Dall.	34	110	3.2	13	2
Gentry, Dennis, Chi.	11	103	9.4	29	1
Crawford, Charles, Phil.	28	88	3.1	15	1
Gault, Willie, Chi.	8	79	9.9	33	0
Harmon, Derrick, S.F.	27	77	2.9	15	1
Moore, Alvin, Det.	19	73	3.8	18	0
Rice, Jerry, S.F.	10	72	7.2	18	1
Simms, Phil, Giants	43	72	1.7	18	1
Dixon, Floyd, Atl.	11	67	6.1	23	0
Bligen, Dennis, Jets	20	65	3.3	10	1

	Att	Yards	Avg	Long	TD
Sikahema, Vai, St.L.	16	62	3.9	23	0
Galbreath, Tony, Giants	16	61	3.8	10	0
Collier, Reggie, Dall.	6	53	8.8	21	0
Stoudt, Cliff, St.L.	7	53	7.6	17	0
Kemp, Jeff, S.F.	15	49	3.3	12	0
Kramer, Tommy, Minn.	23	48	2.1	13	1
Schroeder, Jay, Wash.	36	47	1.3	20	1
Coleman, Greg, Minn.	2	46	23.0	30	0
Everett, Jim, Rams	16	46	2.9	14	1
Hipple, Eric, Det.	16	46	2.9	13	0
Cherry, Tony, S.F.	11	42	3.8	10	0
Clark, Jessie, G.B.	18	41	2.3	9	0
Wright, Randy, G.B.	18	41	2.3	18	1
Montana, Joe, S.F.	17	38	2.2	17	0
Flutie, Doug, Chi.	9	36	4.0	19	1
Jaworski, Ron, Phil.	13	33	2.5	10	0
Fuller, Steve, Chi.	8	30	3.8	10	0
Gray, Mel, N.O.	6	29	4.8	11	0
Johnson, Bobby, Giants	2	28	14.0	22	0
Monk, Art, Wash.	4	27	6.8	21	0
Cavanaugh, Matt, Phil.	9	26	2.9	11	0
Ferguson, Joe, Det.	5	25	5.0	14	0
Ivery, Eddie Lee, G.B.	4	25	6.3	15	0
Johnson, Billy, Atl.	6	25	4.2	10	0
Manuel, Lionel, Giants	1	25	25.0	25	0
Hunter, Herman, Det.	3	22	7.3	18	0
Moroski, Mike, S.F.	6	22	3.7	12	1
Williams, Scott, Det.	13	22	1.7	5	2
Whisenhunt, Ken, Atl.	1	20	20.0	20	0
Clack, Darryl, Dall.	4	19	4.8	8	0
Rutledge, Jeff, Giants	3	19	6.3	18	0
Stanley, Walter, G.B.	1	19	19.0	19	0
Wilson, Dave, N.O.	14	19	1.4	14	1
Wilson, Wayne, Minn.-N.O.	10	19	1.9	6	0
Wolfley, Ron, St.L.	8	19	2.4	8	0
Epps, Phillip, G.B.	4	18	4.5	20	0
Williams, Keith, Atl.	3	18	6.0	8	0
Del Rio, Jack, N.O.	1	16	16.0	16	0
White, Danny, Dall.	8	16	2.0	10	1
Hebert, Bobby, N.O.	5	14	2.8	7	0
Jones, Hassan, Minn.	1	14	14.0	14	0
Carter, Anthony, Minn.	1	12	12.0	12	0
Matthews, Aubrey, Atl.	1	12	12.0	12	0
Schonert, Turk, Atl.	11	12	1.1	7	1
Fusina, Chuck, G.B.	7	11	1.6	6	0
Sherrard, Mike, Dall.	2	11	5.5	8	0
Cosbie, Doug, Dall.	1	9	9.0	9	0
Wilson, Wade, Minn.	13	9	0.7	13	1
Clark, Bret, Atl.	2	8	4.0	6	0

	Att	Yards	Avg	Long	TD
Waters, Mike, Phil.	5	8	1.6	5	0
Campbell, Scott, Atl.........	1	7	7.0	7	0
Franklin, Pat, T.B.	7	7	1.0	4	0
Jones, Joey, Atl.	1	7	7.0	7	0
Bailey, Stacey, Atl.	1	6	6.0	6	0
Edwards, Kelvin, N.O.	1	6	6.0	6	0
Jackson, Kenny, Phil.	1	6	6.0	6	0
Lavette, Robert, Dall.	10	6	0.6	5	0
Brown, Ron, Rams	4	5	1.3	11	0
Dils, Steve, Rams	10	5	0.5	5	0
Fowler, Todd, Dall.	6	5	0.8	2	0
House, Kevin, T.B.	2	5	2.5	4	0
Marsh, Doug, St.L.	1	5	5.0	5	0
Ring, Bill, S.F.	3	4	1.3	4	0
Allen, Greg, T.B.	1	3	3.0	3	0
Baker, Tony, Atl.	1	3	3.0	3	0
Bartkowski, Steve, Rams	6	3	0.5	7	0
Carpenter, Rob, Rams	2	3	1.5	3	0
Miller, Solomon, Giants	1	3	3.0	3	0
Guman, Mike, Rams	2	2	1.0	3	0
DeBerg, Steve, T.B.	2	1	0.5	t1	1
Hostetler, Jeff, Giants	1	1	1.0	1	0
Austin, Kent, St.L.	1	0	0.0	0	0
Ferragamo, Vince, G.B.	1	0	0.0	0	0
Hansen, Brian, N.O.	1	0	0.0	0	0
Long, Chuck, Det.	2	0	0.0	0	0
Renner, Bill, G.B.	1	0	0.0	0	0
Swanke, Karl, G.B.	1	0	0.0	0	0
Teltschik, John, Phil.	1	0	0.0	0	0
Perry, William, Chi.	1	-1	-1.0	-1	0
Frank, John, S.F.	1	-3	-3.0	-3	0
Green, Roy, St.L.	2	-4	-2.0	1	0
Carter, Gerald, T.B.	1	-5	-5.0	-5	0
Hunter, Tony, Rams	1	-6	-6.0	-6	0
Black, Mike, Det.	1	-8	-8.0	-8	0
Garcia, Frank, T.B.	1	-11	-11.0	-11	0
Buford, Maury, Chi.	1	-13	-13.0	-13	0
Ellard, Henry, Rams	1	-15	-15.0	-15	0
Lewis, Leo, Minn.	3	-16	-5.3	-2	0

AFC – INDIVIDUAL RUSHERS

Warner, Curt, Sea.	319	1481	4.6	t60	13
Brooks, James, Cin.	205	1087	5.3	t56	5
Jackson, Earnest, Pitt.	216	910	4.2	31	5
Abercrombie, Walter, Pitt. ...	214	877	4.1	t38	6
McNeil, Freeman, Jets	214	856	4.0	40	5

	Att	Yards	Avg	Long	TD
Hampton, Lorenzo, Mia.	186	830	4.5	t54	9
Winder, Sammy, Den.	240	789	3.3	31	9
Allen, Marcus, Raiders	208	759	3.6	t28	5
Mack, Kevin, Clev.	174	665	3.8	20	10
Rozier, Mike, Hou.	199	662	3.3	t19	4
Riddick, Robb, Buff.	150	632	4.2	t41	4
McMillan, Randy, Ind.	189	609	3.2	28	3
Hector, Johnny, Jets	164	605	3.7	41	8
Williams, John L., Sea.	129	538	4.2	36	0
McCallum, Napoleon, Raiders ..	142	536	3.8	18	1
Dickey, Curtis, Clev.	135	523	3.9	47	6
Kinnebrew, Larry, Cin.	131	519	4.0	39	8
Pruitt, Mike, K.C.	139	448	3.2	16	2
Anderson, Gary, S.D.	127	442	3.5	17	1
James, Craig, N.E.	154	427	2.8	16	4
Collins, Tony, N.E.	156	412	2.6	17	3
Wilson, Stanley, Cin.	68	379	5.6	t58	8
Bell, Greg, Buff.	90	377	4.2	42	4
Adams, Curtis, S.D.	118	366	3.1	22	4
Willhite, Gerald, Den.	85	365	4.3	42	5
Bentley, Albert, Ind.	73	351	4.8	t70	3
Spencer, Tim, S.D.	99	350	3.5	23	6
Davenport, Ron, Mia.	75	314	4.2	35	0
Green, Boyce, K.C.	90	314	3.5	27	3
Heard, Herman, K.C.	71	295	4.2	40	2
Byner, Earnest, Clev.	94	277	2.9	37	2
Elway, John, Den.	52	257	4.9	24	1
Moriarty, Larry, Hou.-K.C. ...	90	252	2.8	11	1
Hawkins, Frank, Raiders	58	245	4.2	15	0
Smith, Jeff, K.C.	54	238	4.4	t32	3
Gill, Owen, Ind.	53	228	4.3	18	1
Johnson, Bill, Cin.	39	226	5.8	34	0
Pinkett, Allen, Hou.	77	225	2.9	14	2
James, Lionel, S.D.	51	224	4.4	24	0
Wallace, Ray, Hou.	52	218	4.2	19	3
Wonsley, George, Ind.	60	214	3.6	46	1
Nathan, Tony, Mia.	27	203	7.5	20	0
Kelly, Jim, Buff.	41	199	4.9	20	0
McGee, Buford, S.D.	63	187	3.0	20	7
Harmon, Ronnie, Buff.	54	172	3.2	38	0
Tatupu, Mosi, N.E.	71	172	2.4	13	1
Eason, Tony, N.E.	35	170	4.9	26	0
Erenberg, Rich, Pitt.	42	170	4.0	17	1
Bennett, Woody, Mia.	36	162	4.5	16	0
Moon, Warren, Hou.	42	157	3.7	19	2
Byrum, Carl, Buff.	38	156	4.1	18	0
Morris, Randall, Sea.	19	149	7.8	t49	1
Givins, Earnest, Hou.	9	148	16.4	t43	1
Esiason, Boomer, Cin.	44	146	3.3	23	1

	Att	Yards	Avg	Long	TD
Sewell, Steve, Den.	23	123	5.3	15	1
Krieg, Dave, Sea.	35	122	3.5	19	1
Paige, Tony, Jets	47	109	2.3	9	2
Malone, Mark, Pitt.	31	107	3.5	45	5
Fontenot, Herman, Clev.	25	105	4.2	16	1
Moore, Ricky, Buff.	33	104	3.2	14	1
Lang, Gene, Den.	29	94	3.2	14	1
Hayes, Jeff, Cin.	3	92	30.7	t61	1
Pollard, Frank, Pitt.	24	86	3.6	12	0
Banks, Chuck, Hou.	29	80	2.8	9	0
Fryar, Irving, N.E.	4	80	20.0	31	0
Blackledge, Todd, K.C.	23	60	2.6	14	0
Weathers, Robert, N.E.	21	58	2.8	t16	1
Woolfolk, Butch, Hou.	23	57	2.5	15	0
Jennings, Stanford, Cin.	16	54	3.4	10	1
Strachan, Steve, Raiders	18	53	2.9	10	0
Hilger, Rusty, Raiders	6	48	8.0	16	0
Plunkett, Jim, Raiders	12	47	3.9	11	0
O'Brien, Ken, Jets	17	46	2.7	11	0
Wilson, Marc, Raiders	14	45	3.2	13	0
Everett, Major, Clev.	12	43	3.6	8	0
Dupard, Reggie, N.E.	15	39	2.6	11	0
Clayton, Mark, Mia.	2	33	16.5	22	0
Brown, Eddie, Cin.	8	32	4.0	17	0
Hughes, David, Pitt.	14	32	2.3	8	0
Mueller, Vance, Raiders	13	30	2.3	8	0
Ryan, Pat, Jets	8	28	3.5	18	0
Barber, Marion, Jets	11	27	2.5	8	0
Williams, Dokie, Raiders	3	27	9.0	19	0
Grogan, Steve, N.E.	9	23	2.6	10	1
Kubiak, Gary, Den.	6	22	3.7	10	0
Trudeau, Jack, Ind.	13	21	1.6	8	1
Hogeboom, Gary, Ind.	10	20	2.0	6	1
Kiel, Blair, Ind.	3	20	6.7	9	0
Reeder, Dan, Pitt.	6	20	3.3	6	0
Kosar, Bernie, Clev.	24	19	0.8	17	0
Carter, Joe, Mia.	4	18	4.5	9	0
Wilkins, Gary, Buff.	3	18	6.0	11	0
Bell, Ken, Den.	9	17	1.9	12	0
Holt, Harry, Clev.	1	16	16.0	t16	1
Johnson, Vance, Den.	5	15	3.0	6	0
Bouza, Matt, Ind.	1	12	12.0	12	0
Luck, Oliver, Hou.	2	12	6.0	8	0
McNeil, Gerald, Clev.	1	12	12.0	12	0
Sanders, Chuck, Pitt.	4	12	3.0	13	0
Capers, Wayne, Ind.	1	11	11.0	11	0
Lane, Eric, Sea.	6	11	1.8	4	0
Brister, Bubby, Pitt.	6	10	1.7	9	0
King, Bruce, Buff.	4	10	2.5	7	0

	Att	Yards	Avg	Long	TD
McGee, Tim, Cin.	4	10	2.5	8	0
Gilbert, Gale, Sea.	3	8	2.7	12	0
Ellis, Craig, Mia.	3	6	2.0	2	0
Herrmann, Mark, S.D.	2	6	3.0	6	0
Jackson, Mark, Den.	2	6	3.0	5	0
Brooks, Bill, Ind.	4	5	1.3	12	0
Faaola, Nuu, Jets	3	5	1.7	2	0
Flick, Tom, S.D.	6	5	0.8	7	1
Hawthorne, Greg, N.E.	1	5	5.0	5	0
Gaynor, Doug, Cin.	1	4	4.0	4	0
Edwards, Stan, Hou.	1	3	3.0	3	0
Boddie, Tony, Den.	1	2	2.0	2	0
Franklin, Byron, Sea.	1	2	2.0	2	0
Seitz, Warren, Pitt.	3	2	0.7	2	0
Townsell, JoJo, Jets	1	2	2.0	2	0
Oliver, Hubert, Hou.	1	1	1.0	1	0
Slaughter, Webster, Clev.	1	1	1.0	1	0
Guy, Ray, Raiders	1	0	0.0	0	0
Horan, Mike, Den.	1	0	0.0	0	0
Jennings, Dave, Jets	1	0	0.0	0	0
Kenney, Bill, K.C.	18	0	0.0	9	0
Kidd, John, Buff.	1	0	0.0	0	0
Pagel, Mike, Clev.	2	0	0.0	0	0
Reich, Frank, Buff.	1	0	0.0	0	0
Starring, Stephen, N.E.	1	0	0.0	0	0
Strock, Don, Mia.	1	0	0.0	0	0
Mathison, Bruce, S.D.	1	−1	−1.0	−1	0
Mobley, Orson, Den.	1	−1	−1.0	−1	0
Paige, Stephone, K.C.	2	−2	−1.0	12	0
Fouts, Dan, S.D.	4	−3	−0.8	0	0
Lipps, Louis, Pitt.	4	−3	−0.8	8	0
Marino, Dan, Mia.	12	−3	−0.3	13	0
Toon, Al, Jets	2	−3	−1.5	2	0
Broughton, Walter, Buff.	1	−6	−6.0	−6	0
Ramsey, Tom, N.E.	1	−6	−6.0	−6	0
Jones, Cedric, N.E.	1	−7	−7.0	−7	0
Reed, Andre, Buff.	3	−8	−2.7	4	0
Roby, Reggie, Mia.	2	−8	−4.0	0	0
Duper, Mark, Mia.	1	−10	−10.0	−10	0
Edmonds, Bobby Joe, Sea.	1	−11	−11.0	−11	0
Langhorne, Reggie, Clev.	1	−11	−11.0	−11	0
Norman, Chris, Den.	1	−11	−11.0	−11	0
Sohn, Kurt, Jets	2	−11	−5.5	−3	0
Collinsworth, Cris, Cin.	2	−16	−8.0	−6	0

PASSING

TOP TEN PASSERS

	Att	Comp	Pct Comp	Yds
Kramer, Tommy, Minn.	372	208	55.9	3000
Marino, Dan, Mia.	623	378	60.7	4746
Krieg, Dave, Sea.	375	225	60.0	2921
Eason, Tony, N.E.	448	276	61.6	3328
Esiason, Boomer, Cin.	469	273	58.2	3959
O'Brien, Ken, Jets	482	300	62.2	3690
Kosar, Bernie, Clev.	531	310	58.4	3854
Kelly, Jim, Buff.	480	285	59.4	3593
Plunkett, Jim, Raiders	252	133	52.8	1986
Montana, Joe, S.F.	307	191	62.2	2236

AFC − INDIVIDUAL QUALIFIERS

	Att	Comp	Pct Comp	Yds
Marino, Dan, Mia.	623	378	60.7	4746
Krieg, Dave, Sea.	375	225	60.0	2921
Eason, Tony, N.E.	448	276	61.6	3328
Esiason, Boomer, Cin.	469	273	58.2	3959
O'Brien, Ken, Jets	482	300	62.2	3690
Kosar, Bernie, Clev.	531	310	58.4	3854
Kelly, Jim, Buff.	480	285	59.4	3593
Plunkett, Jim, Raiders	252	133	52.8	1986
Elway, John, Den.	504	280	55.6	3485
Fouts, Dan, S.D.	430	252	58.6	3031
Kenney, Bill, K.C.	308	161	52.3	1922
Wilson, Marc, Raiders	240	129	53.8	1721
Malone, Mark, Pitt.	425	216	50.8	2444
Moon, Warren, Hou.	488	256	52.5	3489
Trudeau, Jack, Ind.	417	204	48.9	2225

AFC − NON-QUALIFIERS

	Att	Comp	Pct	Yds
Strock, Don, Mia.	20	14	70.0	152
Grogan, Steve, N.E.	102	62	60.8	976
Kiel, Blair, Ind.	25	11	44.0	236
Ryan, Pat, Jets	55	34	61.8	342
Hogeboom, Gary, Ind.	144	85	59.0	1154
Gilbert, Gale, Sea.	76	42	55.3	485
Hilger, Rusty, Raiders	38	19	50.0	266
Blackledge, Todd, K.C.	211	96	45.5	1200
Herrmann, Mark, S.D.	97	51	52.6	627
Kubiak, Gary, Den.	38	23	60.5	249

t = Touchdown
Leader based on rating points, minimum 224 attempts

Avg Gain	TD	Pct TD	Long	Int	Pct Int	Rating Points
8.06	24	6.5	t76	10	2.7	92.6
7.62	44	7.1	t85	23	3.7	92.5
7.79	21	5.6	t72	11	2.9	91.0
7.43	19	4.2	49	10	2.2	89.2
8.44	24	5.1	57	17	3.6	87.7
7.66	25	5.2	t83	20	4.1	85.8
7.26	17	3.2	t72	10	1.9	83.8
7.49	22	4.6	t84	17	3.5	83.3
7.88	14	5.6	t81	9	3.6	82.5
7.28	8	2.6	48	9	2.9	80.7

Avg Gain	TD	Pct TD	Long	Int	Pct Int	Rating Points
7.62	44	7.1	t85	23	3.7	92.5
7.79	21	5.6	t72	11	2.9	91.0
7.43	19	4.2	49	10	2.2	89.2
8.44	24	5.1	57	17	3.6	87.7
7.66	25	5.2	t83	20	4.1	85.8
7.26	17	3.2	t72	10	1.9	83.8
7.49	22	4.6	t84	17	3.5	83.3
7.88	14	5.6	t81	9	3.6	82.5
6.91	19	3.8	53	13	2.6	79.0
7.05	16	3.7	t65	22	5.1	71.4
6.24	13	4.2	53	11	3.6	70.8
7.17	12	5.0	t57	15	6.3	67.4
5.75	15	3.5	48	18	4.2	62.5
7.15	13	2.7	t81	26	5.3	62.3
5.34	8	1.9	t84	18	4.3	53.5

Avg Gain	TD	Pct TD	Long	Int	Pct Int	Rating Points
7.60	2	10.0	21	0	0.0	125.4
9.57	9	8.8	t69	2	2.0	113.8
9.44	2	8.0	50	0	0.0	104.8
6.22	2	3.6	36	1	1.8	84.1
8.01	6	4.2	60	6	4.2	81.2
6.38	3	3.9	t38	3	3.9	71.4
7.00	1	2.6	54	1	2.6	70.7
5.69	10	4.7	t70	6	2.8	67.6
6.46	2	2.1	28	3	3.1	66.8
6.55	1	2.6	26	3	7.9	55.7

	Att	Comp	Pct Comp	Yds
Anderson, Ken, Cin.	23	11	47.8	171
Luck, Oliver, Hou.	60	31	51.7	341
Brister, Bubby, Pitt.	60	21	35.0	291
Flick, Tom, S.D.	73	33	45.2	361
Reich, Frank, Buff.	19	9	47.4	104
(Fewer than 10 attempts)				
Anderson, Gary, S.D.	1	1	100.0	4
Bentley, Albert, Ind.	0	0	---	0
Brennan, Brian, Clev.	1	1	100.0	35
Brooks, James, Cin.	1	0	0.0	0
Fontenot, Herman, Clev.	1	1	100.0	46
Gaynor, Doug, Cin.	3	3	100.0	30
Givins, Earnest, Hou.	2	0	0.0	0
Gossett, Jeff, Clev.	2	1	50.0	30
Green, Boyce, K.C.	1	0	0.0	0
Holohan, Pete, S.D.	2	1	50.0	21
James, Craig, N.E.	4	1	25.0	10
Jensen, Jim, Mia.	2	0	0.0	0
Johnson, Vance, Den.	1	0	0.0	0
Kreider, Steve, Cin.	1	0	0.0	0
Largent, Steve, Sea.	1	1	100.0	18
Marshall, Henry, K.C.	1	0	0.0	0
McGee, Buford, S.D.	1	1	100.0	1
Morris, Randall, Sea.	1	0	0.0	0
Newsome, Harry, Pitt.	2	1	50.0	12
Norman, Chris, Den.	1	1	100.0	43
Pagel, Mike, Clev.	3	2	66.7	53
Ramsey, Tom, N.E.	3	1	33.3	7
Rozier, Mike, Hou.	1	1	100.0	13
Sewell, Steve, Den.	1	1	100.0	23
Willhite, Gerald, Den.	4	1	25.0	11

NFC - INDIVIDUAL QUALIFIERS

	Att	Comp	Pct Comp	Yds
Kramer, Tommy, Minn.	372	208	55.9	3000
Montana, Joe, S.F.	307	191	62.2	2236
Hipple, Eric, Det.	305	192	63.0	1919
Simms, Phil, Giants	468	259	55.3	3487
Lomax, Neil, St.L.	421	240	57.0	2583
Schroeder, Jay, Wash.	541	276	51.0	4109
Archer, David, Atl.	294	150	51.0	2007
Jaworski, Ron, Phil.	245	128	52.2	1405
Pelluer, Steve, Dall.	378	215	56.9	2727
Wright, Randy, G.B.	492	263	53.5	3247
Wilson, Dave, N.O.	342	189	55.3	2353
Young, Steve, T.B.	363	195	53.7	2282

Avg Gain	TD	Pct TD	Long	Int	Pct Int	Rating Points
7.43	1	4.3	43	2	8.7	51.2
5.68	1	1.7	27	5	8.3	39.7
4.85	0	0.0	58	2	3.3	37.6
4.95	2	2.7	26	8	11.0	29.9
5.47	0	0.0	37	2	10.5	24.8
4.00	1	100.0	t4	0	0.0	122.9
----	0	---	0	0	---	0.0
35.00	0	0.0	35	0	0.0	118.8
0.00	0	0.0	0	0	0.0	39.6
46.00	1	100.0	t46	0	0.0	158.3
10.00	0	0.0	16	0	0.0	108.3
0.00	0	0.0	0	0	0.0	39.6
15.00	0	0.0	30	1	50.0	56.3
0.00	0	0.0	0	1	100.0	0.0
10.50	0	0.0	21	0	0.0	87.5
2.50	1	25.0	t10	1	25.0	39.6
0.00	0	0.0	0	0	0.0	39.6
0.00	0	0.0	0	0	0.0	39.6
0.00	0	0.0	0	1	100.0	0.0
18.00	0	0.0	18	0	0.0	118.8
0.00	0	0.0	0	0	0.0	39.6
1.00	0	0.0	1	0	0.0	79.2
0.00	0	0.0	0	0	0.0	39.6
6.00	1	50.0	t12	0	0.0	108.3
43.00	1	100.0	t43	0	0.0	158.3
17.67	0	0.0	45	0	0.0	109.7
2.33	0	0.0	7	0	0.0	42.4
13.00	0	0.0	13	0	0.0	118.8
23.00	1	100.0	t23	0	0.0	158.3
2.75	0	0.0	11	0	0.0	39.6
8.06	24	6.5	t76	10	2.7	92.6
7.28	8	2.6	48	9	2.9	80.7
6.29	9	3.0	46	11	3.6	75.6
7.45	21	4.5	49	22	4.7	74.6
6.14	13	3.1	t48	12	2.9	73.6
7.60	22	4.1	t71	22	4.1	72.9
6.83	10	3.4	65	9	3.1	71.6
5.73	8	3.3	56	6	2.4	70.2
7.21	8	2.1	t84	17	4.5	67.9
6.60	17	3.5	62	23	4.7	66.2
6.88	10	2.9	t63	17	5.0	65.8
6.29	8	2.2	46	13	3.6	65.5

NFC — NON-QUALIFIERS

	Att	Comp	Pct Comp	Yds
White, Danny, Dall.	153	95	62.1	1157
Kemp, Jeff, S.F.	200	119	59.5	1554
Wilson, Wade, Minn.	143	80	55.9	1165
Flutie, Doug, Chi.	46	23	50.0	361
Cunningham, Randall, Phil. ...	209	111	53.1	1391
Moroski, Mike, S.F.	73	42	57.5	493
Schonert, Turk, Atl.	154	95	61.7	1032
Everett, Jim, Rams	147	73	49.7	1018
Long, Chuck, Det.	40	21	52.5	247
Ferguson, Joe, Det.	155	73	47.1	941
Fusina, Chuck, G.B.	32	19	59.4	178
McMahon, Jim, Chi.	150	77	51.3	995
Fuller, Steve, Chi.	64	34	53.1	451
Dils, Steve, Rams	129	59	45.7	693
Bartkowski, Steve, Rams	126	61	48.4	654
Ferragamo, Vince, G.B.	40	23	57.5	283
Collier, Reggie, Dall.	15	8	53.3	96
Cavanaugh, Matt, Phil.	58	28	48.3	397
Stoudt, Cliff, St.L.	91	52	57.1	542
Tomczak, Mike, Chi.	151	74	49.0	1105
DeBerg, Steve, T.B.	96	50	52.1	610
Hebert, Bobby, N.O.	79	41	51.9	498
(Fewer than 10 attempts)				
Anderson, Alfred, Minn.	2	1	50.0	17
Arapostathis, Evan, St.L.	1	0	0.0	0
Bono, Steve, Minn.	1	1	100.0	3
Byars, Keith, Phil.	2	1	50.0	55
Campbell, Scott, Pitt.-Atl. ..	7	1	14.3	7
Dickerson, Eric, Rams	1	1	100.0	15
Galbreath, Tony, Giants	1	0	0.0	0
Hilliard, Dalton, N.O.	3	1	33.3	29
House, Kevin, Rams	0	0	---	0
Lofton, James, G.B.	1	0	0.0	0
Mitchell, Stump, St.L.	3	1	33.3	15
Payton, Walter, Chi.	4	0	0.0	0
Renfro, Mike, Dall.	1	1	100.0	23
Rice, Allen, Minn.	1	0	0.0	0
Rice, Jerry, S.F.	2	1	50.0	16
Riggs, Gerald, Atl.	1	0	0.0	0
Rutledge, Jeff, Giants	3	1	33.3	13
Wattelet, Frank, N.O.	1	1	100.0	13
Williams, Doug, Wash.	1	0	0.0	0

Avg Gain	TD	Pct TD	Long	Int	Pct Int	Rating Points
7.56	12	7.8	63	5	3.3	97.9
7.77	11	5.5	t66	8	4.0	85.7
8.15	7	4.9	39	5	3.5	84.4
7.85	3	6.5	t58	2	4.3	80.1
6.66	8	3.8	t75	7	3.3	72.9
6.75	2	2.7	52	3	4.1	70.2
6.70	4	2.6	41	8	5.2	68.4
6.93	8	5.4	t60	8	5.4	67.8
6.18	2	5.0	t34	2	5.0	67.4
6.07	7	4.5	73	7	4.5	62.9
5.56	0	0.0	42	1	3.1	61.7
6.63	5	3.3	t58	8	5.3	61.4
7.05	2	3.1	t50	4	6.3	60.1
5.37	4	3.1	t65	4	3.1	60.0
5.19	2	1.6	42	3	2.4	59.4
7.08	1	2.5	50	3	7.5	56.6
6.40	1	6.7	27	2	13.3	55.8
6.84	2	3.4	49	4	6.9	53.6
5.96	3	3.3	t24	7	7.7	53.5
7.32	2	1.3	85	10	6.6	50.2
6.35	5	5.2	45	12	12.5	49.7
6.30	2	2.5	84	8	10.1	40.5
8.50	0	0.0	17	0	0.0	79.2
0.00	0	0.0	0	0	0.0	39.6
3.00	0	0.0	3	0	0.0	79.2
27.50	1	50.0	t55	0	0.0	135.4
1.00	0	0.0	7	0	0.0	39.6
15.00	1	100.0	t15	0	0.0	158.3
0.00	0	0.0	0	0	0.0	39.6
9.67	1	33.3	t29	0	0.0	109.7
----	0	---	0	0	---	0.0
0.00	0	0.0	0	0	0.0	39.6
5.00	1	33.3	t15	0	0.0	90.3
0.00	0	0.0	0	1	25.0	0.0
23.00	0	0.0	23	0	0.0	118.8
0.00	0	0.0	0	0	0.0	39.6
8.00	0	0.0	16	0	0.0	77.1
0.00	0	0.0	0	0	0.0	39.6
4.33	1	33.3	t13	0	0.0	87.5
13.00	0	0.0	13	0	0.0	118.8
0.00	0	0.0	0	0	0.0	39.6

TOP TEN PASS RECEIVERS

	No	Yards	Avg	Long	TD
Christensen, Todd, Raiders ...	95	1153	12.1	35	8
Rice, Jerry, S.F.	86	1570	18.3	t66	15
Toon, Al, Jets	85	1176	13.8	t62	8
Morgan, Stanley, N.E.	84	1491	17.8	t44	10
Craig, Roger, S.F.	81	624	7.7	48	0
Smith, J.T., St.L.	80	1014	12.7	45	6
Anderson, Gary, S.D.	80	871	10.9	t65	8
Collins, Tony, N.E.	77	684	8.9	49	5
Walker, Herschel, Dall.	76	837	11.0	t84	2
Clark, Gary, Wash.	74	1265	17.1	55	7

TOP TEN RECEIVERS BY YARDS

	Yards	No	Avg	Long	TD
Rice, Jerry, S.F.	1570	86	18.3	t66	15
Morgan, Stanley, N.E.	1491	84	17.8	t44	10
Duper, Mark, Mia.	1313	67	19.6	t85	11
Clark, Gary, Wash.	1265	74	17.1	55	7
Toon, Al, Jets	1176	85	13.8	t62	8
Christensen, Todd, Raiders ...	1153	95	12.1	35	8
Clayton, Mark, Mia.	1150	60	19.2	t68	10
Brooks, Bill, Ind.	1131	65	17.4	t84	8
Hill, Drew, Hou.	1112	65	17.1	t81	5
Largent, Steve, Sea.	1070	70	15.3	t38	9

TOP TEN INTERCEPTORS

	No	Yards	Avg	Long	TD
Lott, Ronnie, S.F.	10	134	13.4	t57	1
Cherry, Deron, K.C.	9	150	16.7	49	0
Waymer, Dave, N.O.	9	48	5.3	17	0
Lee, Mark, G.B.	9	33	3.7	11	0
Gray, Jerry, Rams	8	101	12.6	28	0
Lippett, Ronnie, N.E.	8	76	9.5	43	0
Holt, Issiac, Minn.	8	54	6.8	27	0
McElroy, Vann, Raiders	7	105	15.0	28	0
Breeden, Louis, Cin.	7	72	10.3	t36	1
Richardson, Mike, Chi.	7	69	9.9	32	0

TOP TEN KICKOFF RETURNERS

	No	Yards	Avg	Long	TD
Gentry, Dennis, Chi.	20	576	28.8	t91	1
Gray, Mel, N.O.	31	866	27.9	t101	1
Sanchez, Lupe, Pitt.	25	591	23.6	64	0
McGee, Tim, Cin.	43	1007	23.4	94	0
Humphery, Bobby, Jets	28	655	23.4	t96	1
Bell, Ken, Den.	23	531	23.1	42	0
Sikahema, Vai, St.L.	37	847	22.9	44	0
Lang, Gene, Den.	21	480	22.9	42	0
Bess, Rufus, Minn.	31	705	22.7	43	0
Edmonds, Bobby Joe, Sea.	34	764	22.5	46	0

TOP TEN PUNT RETURNERS

	No	FC	Yards	Avg	Long	TD
Edmonds, Bobby Joe, Sea.	34	14	419	12.3	t75	1
Sikahema, Vai, St.L.	43	16	522	12.1	t71	2
Willhite, Gerald, Den.	42	8	468	11.1	t70	1
Fryar, Irving, N.E.	35	10	366	10.5	t59	1
Griffin, Don, S.F.	38	18	377	9.9	t76	1
Mandley, Pete, Det.	43	9	420	9.8	t81	1
Jenkins, Ken, Wash.	28	11	270	9.6	39	0
Stanley, Walter, G.B.	33	7	316	9.6	t83	1
Martin, Eric, N.O.	24	9	227	9.5	39	0
Anderson, Gary, S.D.	25	10	227	9.1	30	0

TOP TEN LEADERS – SACKS

	No
Taylor, Lawrence, Giants	20.5
Manley, Dexter, Wash. ...	18.5
White, Reggie, Phil.	18.0
Jones, Sean, Raiders	15.5
Smith, Bruce, Buff.	15.0
Williams, Lee, S.D.	15.0
Jeffcoat, Jim, Dall.	14.0
Jones, Rulon, Den.	13.5
O'Neal, Leslie, S.D.	12.5
Haley, Charles, S.F.	12.0
Marshall, Leonard, Giants	12.0
Green, Jacob, Sea.	12.0
Willis, Keith, Pitt.	12.0

TOP TEN PUNTERS

	No	Yards	Long	Avg
Stark, Rohn, Ind.	76	3432	63	45.2
Landeta, Sean, Giants	79	3539	61	44.8
Roby, Reggie, Mia.	56	2476	73	44.2
Donnelly, Rick, Atl.	78	3421	71	43.9
Cox, Steve, Wash.	75	3271	58	43.6
Hansen, Brian, N.O.	81	3456	66	42.7
Camarillo, Rich, N.E.	89	3746	64	42.1
Mojsiejenko, Ralf, S.D.	72	3026	62	42.0
Teltschik, John, Phil.	108	4493	62	41.6
Runager, Max, S.F.	83	3450	62	41.6

TOP TEN SCORERS - NON-KICKERS

	TD	TDR	TDP	TDM	PTS
Rogers, George, Wash.	18	18	0	0	108
Rice, Jerry, S.F.	16	1	15	0	96
Morris, Joe, Giants	15	14	1	0	90
Walker, Herschel, Dall.	14	12	2	0	84
Winder, Sammy, Den.	14	9	5	0	84
Warner, Curt, Sea.	13	13	0	0	78
Hampton, Lorenzo, Mia.	12	9	3	0	72
Walker, Wesley, Jets	12	0	12	0	72
Dickerson, Eric, Rams	11	11	0	0	66
Duper, Mark, Mia.	11	0	11	0	66
Paige, Stephone, K.C.	11	0	11	0	66
Payton, Walter, Chi.	11	8	3	0	66

Total Punts	TB	Blk	Opp Ret	Ret Yds	In 20	Net Avg
76	5	0	48	502	22	37.2
79	11	0	41	386	24	37.1
56	9	0	23	200	13	37.4
79	9	1	47	477	19	35.0
75	16	0	36	220	21	36.4
82	11	1	37	234	17	36.6
92	7	3	60	565	16	33.1
74	11	2	42	368	15	32.9
109	10	1	62	631	20	33.6
85	8	2	49	373	23	34.3

TOP TEN SCORERS - KICKERS

	XP	XPA	FG	FGA	PTS
Franklin, Tony, N.E.	44	45	32	41	140
Butler, Kevin, Chi.	36	37	28	41	120
Wersching, Ray, S.F.	41	42	25	35	116
Nelson, Chuck, Minn.	44	47	22	28	110
Andersen, Morten, N.O.	30	30	26	30	108
Johnson, Norm, Sea.	42	42	22	35	108
Allegre, Raul, Giants	33	33	24	32	105
Karlis, Rich, Den.	44	45	20	28	104
Breech, Jim, Cin.	50	51	17	32	101
Lowery, Nick, K.C.	43	43	19	26	100

NFL STANDINGS
1921-1986

1921

	W	L	T	Pct.
Chicago Staleys	10	1	1	.909
Buffalo All-Americans	9	1	2	.900
Akron, Ohio, Pros	7	2	1	.778
Green Bay Packers	6	2	2	.750
Canton, Ohio, Bulldogs	4	3	3	.571
Dayton Triangles	4	3	1	.571
Rock Island Independents	5	4	1	.556
Chicago Cardinals	2	3	2	.400
Cleveland Indians	2	6	0	.250
Rochester Jeffersons	2	6	0	.250
Detroit Heralds	1	7	1	.125
Columbus Panhandles	0	6	0	.000
Cincinnati Celts	0	8	0	.000

1922

	W	L	T	Pct.
Canton, Ohio, Bulldogs	10	0	2	1.000
Chicago Bears	9	3	0	.750
Chicago Cardinals	8	3	0	.727
Toledo Maroons	5	2	2	.714
Rock Island Independents	4	2	1	.667
Dayton Triangles	4	3	1	.571
Green Bay Packers	4	3	3	.571
Racine, Wis., Legion	5	4	1	.556
Akron, Ohio, Pros	3	4	2	.429
Buffalo All-Americans	3	4	1	.429
Milwaukee Badgers	2	4	3	.333
Marion, O., Oorang Indians	2	6	0	.250
Minneapolis Marines	1	3	0	.250
Evansville Crimson Giants	0	2	0	.000
Louisville Brecks	0	3	0	.000
Rochester Jeffersons	0	3	1	.000
Hammond, Ind., Pros	0	4	1	.000
Columbus Panhandles	0	7	0	.000

1923

	W	L	T	Pct.
Canton, Ohio, Bulldogs	11	0	1	1.000
Chicago Bears	9	2	1	.818
Green Bay Packers	7	2	1	.778
Milwaukee Badgers	7	2	3	.778
Cleveland Indians	3	1	3	.750
Chicago Cardinals	8	4	0	.667
Duluth Kelleys	4	3	0	.571
Buffalo All-Americans	5	4	3	.556
Columbus Tigers	5	4	1	.556
Racine, Wis., Legion	4	4	2	.500
Toledo Maroons	2	3	2	.400
Rock Island Independents	2	3	3	.400

Minneapolis Marines	2	5	2	.286
St. Louis All-Stars	1	4	2	.200
Hammond, Ind., Pros	1	5	1	.167
Dayton Triangles	1	6	1	.143
Akron, Ohio, Indians	1	6	0	.143
Marion, O., Oorang Indians	1	10	0	.091
Rochester Jeffersons	0	2	0	.000
Louisville Brecks	0	3	0	.000

1924

	W	L	T	Pct.
Cleveland Bulldogs	7	1	1	.875
Chicago Bears	6	1	4	.857
Frankford Yellowjackets	11	2	1	.846
Duluth Kelleys	5	1	0	.833
Rock Island Independents	6	2	2	.750
Green Bay Packers	8	4	0	.667
Buffalo Bisons	6	4	0	.600
Racine, Wis., Legion	4	3	3	.571
Chicago Cardinals	5	4	1	.556
Columbus Tigers	4	4	0	.500
Hammond, Ind., Pros	2	2	1	.500
Milwaukee Badgers	5	8	0	.385
Dayton Triangles	2	7	0	.222
Kansas City Cowboys	2	7	0	.222
Akron, Ohio, Indians	1	6	0	.143
Kenosha, Wis., Maroons	0	5	1	.000
Minneapolis Marines	0	6	0	.000
Rochester Jeffersons	0	7	0	.000

1925

	W	L	T	Pct.
Chicago Cardinals	11	2	1	.846
Pottsville, Pa., Maroons	10	2	0	.833
Detroit Panthers	8	2	2	.800
New York Giants	8	4	0	.667
Akron, Ohio, Indians	4	2	2	.667
Frankford Yellowjackets	13	7	0	.650
Chicago Bears	9	5	3	.643
Rock Island Independents	5	3	3	.625
Green Bay Packers	8	5	0	.615
Providence Steamroller	6	5	1	.545
Canton, Ohio, Bulldogs	4	4	0	.500
Cleveland Bulldogs	5	8	1	.385
Kansas City Cowboys	2	5	1	.286
Hammond, Ind., Pros	1	3	0	.250
Buffalo Bisons	1	6	2	.143
Duluth Kelleys	0	3	0	.000
Rochester Jeffersons	0	6	1	.000
Milwaukee Badgers	0	6	0	.000
Dayton Triangles	0	7	1	.000
Columbus Tigers	0	9	0	.000

1926

	W	L	T	Pct.
Frankford Yellowjackets	14	1	1	.933
Chicago Bears	12	1	3	.923
Pottsville, Pa., Maroons	10	2	1	.833
Kansas City Cowboys	8	3	1	.727
Green Bay Packers	7	3	3	.700
Los Angeles Buccaneers	6	3	1	.667
New York Giants	8	4	1	.667
Duluth Eskimos	6	5	2	.545
Buffalo Rangers	4	4	2	.500
Chicago Cardinals	5	6	1	.455
Providence Steamroller	5	7	0	.417
Detroit Panthers	4	6	2	.400
Hartford Blues	3	7	0	.300
Brooklyn Lions	3	8	0	.273
Milwaukee Badgers	2	7	0	.222
Akron, Ohio, Indians	1	4	3	.200
Dayton Triangles	1	4	1	.200
Racine, Wis., Legion	1	4	0	.200
Columbus Tigers	1	6	0	.143
Canton, Ohio, Bulldogs	1	9	3	.100
Hammond, Ind., Pros	0	4	0	.000
Louisville Colonels	0	4	0	.000

1927

	W	L	T	Pct.
New York Giants	11	1	1	.917
Green Bay Packers	7	2	1	.778
Chicago Bears	9	3	2	.750
Cleveland Bulldogs	8	4	1	.667
Providence Steamroller	8	5	1	.615
New York Yankees	7	8	1	.467
Frankford Yellowjackets	6	9	3	.400
Pottsville, Pa., Maroons	5	8	0	.385
Chicago Cardinals	3	7	1	.300
Dayton Triangles	1	6	1	.143
Duluth Eskimos	1	8	0	.111
Buffalo Bisons	0	5	0	.000

1928

	W	L	T	Pct.
Providence Steamroller	8	1	2	.889
Frankford Yellowjackets	11	3	2	.786
Detroit Wolverines	7	2	1	.778
Green Bay Packers	6	4	3	.600
Chicago Bears	7	5	1	.583
New York Giants	4	7	2	.364
New York Yankees	4	8	1	.333
Pottsville, Pa., Maroons	2	8	0	.200
Chicago Cardinals	1	5	0	.167
Dayton Triangles	0	7	0	.000

1929

	W	L	T	Pct.
Green Bay Packers	12	0	1	1.000
New York Giants	13	1	1	.929
Frankford Yellowjackets	9	4	5	.692
Chicago Cardinals	6	6	1	.500
Boston Bulldogs	4	4	0	.500
Orange, N.J., Tornadoes	3	4	4	.429
Stapleton Stapes	3	4	3	.429
Providence Steamroller	4	6	2	.400
Chicago Bears	4	9	2	.308
Buffalo Bisons	1	7	1	.125
Minneapolis Red Jackets	1	9	0	.100
Dayton Triangles	0	6	0	.000

1930

	W	L	T	Pct.
Green Bay Packers	10	3	1	.769
New York Giants	13	4	0	.765
Chicago Bears	9	4	1	.692
Brooklyn Dodgers	7	4	1	.636
Providence Steamroller	6	4	1	.600
Stapleton Stapes	5	5	2	.500
Chicago Cardinals	5	6	2	.455
Portsmouth, O., Spartans	5	6	3	.455
Frankford Yellowjackets	4	14	1	.222
Minneapolis Red Jackets	1	7	1	.125
Newark Tornadoes	1	10	1	.091

1931

	W	L	T	Pct.
Green Bay Packers	12	2	0	.857
Portsmouth, O., Spartans	11	3	0	.786
Chicago Bears	8	5	0	.615
Chicago Cardinals	5	4	0	.556
New York Giants	7	6	1	.538
Providence Steamroller	4	4	3	.500
Stapleton Stapes	4	6	1	.400
Cleveland Indians	2	8	0	.200
Brooklyn Dodgers	2	12	0	.143
Frankford Yellowjackets	1	6	1	.143

1932

	W	L	T	Pct.
Chicago Bears	7	1	6	.875
Green Bay Packers	10	3	1	.769
Portsmouth, O., Spartans	6	2	4	.750
Boston Braves	4	4	2	.500
New York Giants	4	6	2	.400
Brooklyn Dodgers	3	9	0	.250
Chicago Cardinals	2	6	2	.250
Stapleton Stapes	2	7	3	.222

1933

EASTERN DIVISION

	W	L	T	Pct.	Pts.	OP
N.Y. Giants	11	3	0	.786	244	101
Brooklyn	5	4	1	.556	93	54
Boston	5	5	2	.500	103	97
Philadelphia	3	5	1	.375	77	158
Pittsburgh	3	6	2	.333	67	208

WESTERN DIVISION

	W	L	T	Pct.	Pts.	OP
Chi. Bears	10	2	1	.833	133	82
Portsmouth	6	5	0	.545	128	87
Green Bay	5	7	1	.417	170	107
Cincinnati	3	6	1	.333	38	110
Chi. Cardinals	1	9	1	.100	52	101

NFL Championship: Chicago Bears 23, N.Y. Giants 21

1934

EASTERN DIVISION	W	L	T	Pct.	Pts.	OP
N.Y. Giants	8	5	0	.615	147	107
Boston	6	6	0	.500	107	94
Brooklyn	4	7	0	.364	61	153
Philadelphia	4	7	0	.364	127	85
Pittsburgh	2	10	0	.167	51	206

WESTERN DIVISION	W	L	T	Pct.	Pts.	OP
Chi. Bears	13	0	0	1.000	286	86
Detroit	10	3	0	.769	238	59
Green Bay	7	6	0	.538	156	112
Chi. Cardinals	5	6	0	.455	80	84
St. Louis	1	2	0	.333	27	61
Cincinnati	0	8	0	.000	10	243

NFL Championship: N.Y. Giants 30, Chicago Bears 13

1935

EASTERN DIVISION	W	L	T	Pct.	Pts.	OP
N.Y. Giants	9	3	0	.750	180	96
Brooklyn	5	6	1	.455	90	141
Pittsburgh	4	8	0	.333	100	209
Boston	2	8	1	.200	65	123
Philadelphia	2	9	0	.182	60	179

WESTERN DIVISION	W	L	T	Pct.	Pts.	OP
Detroit	7	3	2	.700	191	111
Green Bay	8	4	0	.667	181	96
Chi. Bears	6	4	2	.600	192	106
Chi. Cardinals	6	4	2	.600	99	97

NFL Championship: Detroit 26, N.Y. Giants 7
One game between Boston and Philadelphia was canceled.

1936

EASTERN DIVISION	W	L	T	Pct.	Pts.	OP
Boston	7	5	0	.583	149	110
Pittsburgh	6	6	0	.500	98	187
N.Y. Giants	5	6	1	.455	115	163
Brooklyn	3	8	1	.273	92	161
Philadelphia	1	11	0	.083	51	206

WESTERN DIVISION	W	L	T	Pct.	Pts.	OP
Green Bay	10	1	1	.909	248	118
Chi. Bears	9	3	0	.750	222	94
Detroit	8	4	0	.667	235	102
Chi. Cardinals	3	8	1	.273	74	143

NFL Championship: Green Bay 21, Boston 6

1937

EASTERN DIVISION	W	L	T	Pct.	Pts.	OP
Washington	8	3	0	.727	195	120
N.Y. Giants	6	3	2	.667	128	109
Pittsburgh	4	7	0	.364	122	145
Brooklyn	3	7	1	.300	82	174
Philadelphia	2	8	1	.200	86	177

WESTERN DIVISION	W	L	T	Pct.	Pts.	OP
Chi. Bears	9	1	1	.900	201	100
Green Bay	7	4	0	.636	220	122
Detroit	7	4	0	.636	180	105
Chi. Cardinals	5	5	1	.500	135	165
Cleveland	1	10	0	.091	75	207

NFL Championship: Washington 28, Chicago Bears 21

1938

EASTERN DIVISION	W	L	T	Pct.	Pts.	OP
N.Y Giants	8	2	1	.800	194	79
Washington	6	3	2	.667	148	154
Brooklyn	4	4	3	.500	131	161
Philadelphia	5	6	0	.455	154	164
Pittsburgh	2	9	0	.182	79	169

WESTERN DIVISION	W	L	T	Pct.	Pts.	OP
Green Bay	8	3	0	.727	223	118
Detroit	7	4	0	.636	119	108
Chi. Bears	6	5	0	.545	194	148
Cleveland	4	7	0	.364	131	215
Chi. Cardinals	2	9	0	.182	111	168

NFL Championship: N.Y. Giants 23, Green Bay 17

1939

EASTERN DIVISION	W	L	T	Pct.	Pts.	OP
N.Y. Giants	9	1	1	.900	168	85
Washington	8	2	1	.800	242	94
Brooklyn	4	6	1	.400	108	219
Philadelphia	1	9	1	.100	105	200
Pittsburgh	1	9	1	.100	114	216

WESTERN DIVISION	W	L	T	Pct.	Pts.	OP
Green Bay	9	2	0	.818	233	153
Chi. Bears	8	3	0	.727	298	157
Detroit	6	5	0	.545	145	150
Cleveland	5	5	1	.500	195	164
Chi. Cardinals	1	10	0	.091	84	254

NFL Championship: Green Bay 27, N.Y. Giants 0

1940

EASTERN DIVISION	W	L	T	Pct.	Pts.	OP	WESTERN DIVISION	W	L	T	Pct.	Pts.	OP
Washington	9	2	0	.818	245	142	Chi. Bears	8	3	0	.727	238	152
Brooklyn	8	3	0	.727	186	120	Green Bay	6	4	1	.600	238	155
N.Y. Giants	6	4	1	.600	131	133	Detroit	5	5	1	.500	138	153
Pittsburgh	2	7	2	.222	60	178	Cleveland	4	6	1	.400	171	191
Philadelphia	1	10	0	.091	111	211	Chi. Cardinals	2	7	2	.222	139	222

NFL Championship: Chicago Bears 73, Washington 0

1941

EASTERN DIVISION	W	L	T	Pct.	Pts.	OP	WESTERN DIVISION	W	L	T	Pct.	Pts.	OP
N.Y. Giants	8	3	0	.727	238	114	Chi. Bears	10	1	0	.909	396	147
Brooklyn	7	4	0	.636	158	127	Green Bay	10	1	0	.909	258	120
Washington	6	5	0	.545	176	174	Detroit	4	6	1	.400	121	195
Philadelphia	2	8	1	.200	119	218	Chi. Cardinals	3	7	1	.300	127	197
Pittsburgh	1	9	1	.100	103	276	Cleveland	2	9	0	.182	116	244

Western Division playoff: Chicago Bears 33, Green Bay 14
NFL Championship: Chicago Bears 37, N.Y. Giants 9

1942

EASTERN DIVISION	W	L	T	Pct.	Pts.	OP	WESTERN DIVISION	W	L	T	Pct.	Pts.	OP
Washington	10	1	0	.909	227	102	Chi. Bears	11	0	0	1.000	376	84
Pittsburgh	7	4	0	.636	167	119	Green Bay	8	2	1	.800	300	215
N.Y. Giants	5	5	1	.500	155	139	Cleveland	5	6	0	.455	150	207
Brooklyn	3	8	0	.273	100	168	Chi. Cardinals	3	8	0	.273	98	209
Philadelphia	2	9	0	.182	134	239	Detroit	0	11	0	.000	38	263

NFL Championship: Washington 14, Chicago Bears 6

1943

EASTERN DIVISION	W	L	T	Pct.	Pts.	OP	WESTERN DIVISION	W	L	T	Pct.	Pts.	OP
Washington	6	3	1	.667	229	137	Chi. Bears	8	1	1	.889	303	157
N.Y. Giants	6	3	1	.667	197	170	Green Bay	7	2	1	.778	264	172
Phil-Pitt	5	4	1	.556	225	230	Detroit	3	6	1	.333	178	218
Brooklyn	2	8	0	.200	65	234	Chi. Cardinals	0	10	0	.000	95	238

Eastern Division playoff: Washington 28, N.Y. Giants 0
NFL Championship: Chicago Bears 41, Washington 21

1944

EASTERN DIVISION	W	L	T	Pct.	Pts.	OP	WESTERN DIVISION	W	L	T	Pct.	Pts.	OP
N.Y. Giants	8	1	1	.889	206	75	Green Bay	8	2	0	.800	238	141
Philadelphia	7	1	2	.875	267	131	Chi. Bears	6	3	1	.667	258	172
Washington	6	3	1	.667	169	180	Detroit	6	3	1	.667	216	151
Boston	2	8	0	.200	82	233	Cleveland	4	6	0	.400	188	224
Brooklyn	0	10	0	.000	69	166	Card-Pitt	0	10	0	.000	108	328

NFL Championship: Green Bay 14, N.Y. Giants 7

1945

EASTERN DIVISION	W	L	T	Pct.	Pts.	OP	WESTERN DIVISION	W	L	T	Pct.	Pts.	OP
Washington	8	2	0	.800	209	121	Cleveland	9	1	0	.900	244	136
Philadelphia	7	3	0	.700	272	133	Detroit	7	3	0	.700	195	194
N.Y. Giants	3	6	1	.333	179	198	Green Bay	6	4	0	.600	258	173
Boston	3	6	1	.333	123	211	Chi. Bears	3	7	0	.300	192	235
Pittsburgh	2	8	0	.200	79	220	Chi. Cardinals	1	9	0	.100	98	228

NFL Championship: Cleveland 15, Washington 14

1946

EASTERN DIVISION	W	L	T	Pct.	Pts.	OP
N.Y. Giants	7	3	1	.700	236	162
Philadelphia	6	5	0	.545	231	220
Washington	5	5	1	.500	171	191
Pittsburgh	5	5	1	.500	136	117
Boston	2	8	1	.200	189	273

WESTERN DIVISION	W	L	T	Pct.	Pts.	OP
Chi. Bears	8	2	1	.800	289	193
Los Angeles	6	4	1	.600	277	257
Green Bay	6	5	0	.545	148	158
Chi. Cardinals	6	5	0	.545	260	198
Detroit	1	10	0	.091	142	310

NFL Championship: Chicago Bears 24, N.Y. Giants 14

1947

EASTERN DIVISION	W	L	T	Pct.	Pts.	OP
Philadelphia	8	4	0	.667	308	242
Pittsburgh	8	4	0	.667	240	259
Boston	4	7	1	.364	168	256
Washington	4	8	0	.333	295	367
N.Y. Giants	2	8	2	.200	190	309

WESTERN DIVISION	W	L	T	Pct.	Pts.	OP
Chi. Cardinals	9	3	0	.750	306	231
Chi. Bears	8	4	0	.667	363	241
Green Bay	6	5	1	.545	274	210
Los Angeles	6	6	0	.500	259	214
Detroit	3	9	0	.250	231	305

Eastern Division playoff: Philadelphia 21, Pittsburgh 0
NFL Championship: Chicago Cardinals 28, Philadelphia 21

1948

EASTERN DIVISION	W	L	T	Pct.	Pts.	OP
Philadelphia	9	2	1	.818	376	156
Washington	7	5	0	.583	291	287
N.Y. Giants	4	8	0	.333	297	388
Pittsburgh	4	8	0	.333	200	243
Boston	3	9	0	.250	174	372

WESTERN DIVISION	W	L	T	Pct.	Pts.	OP
Chi. Cardinals	11	1	0	.917	395	226
Chi. Bears	10	2	0	.833	375	151
Los Angeles	6	5	1	.545	327	269
Green Bay	3	9	0	.250	154	290
Detroit	2	10	0	.167	200	407

NFL Championship: Philadelphia 7, Chicago Cardinals 0

1949

EASTERN DIVISION	W	L	T	Pct.	Pts.	OP
Philadelphia	11	1	0	.917	364	134
Pittsburgh	6	5	1	.545	224	214
N.Y. Giants	6	6	0	.500	287	298
Washington	4	7	1	.364	268	339
N.Y. Bulldogs	1	10	1	.091	153	368

WESTERN DIVISION	W	L	T	Pct.	Pts.	OP
Los Angeles	8	2	2	.800	360	239
Chi. Bears	9	3	0	.750	332	218
Chi. Cardinals	6	5	1	.545	360	301
Detroit	4	8	0	.333	237	259
Green Bay	2	10	0	.167	114	329

NFL Championship: Philadelphia 14, Los Angeles 0

1950

AMERICAN CONFERENCE	W	L	T	Pct.	Pts.	OP
Cleveland	10	2	0	.833	310	144
N.Y. Giants	10	2	0	.833	268	150
Philadelphia	6	6	0	.500	254	141
Pittsburgh	6	6	0	.500	180	195
Chi. Cardinals	5	7	0	.417	233	287
Washington	3	9	0	.250	232	326

NATIONAL CONFERENCE	W	L	T	Pct.	Pts.	OP
Los Angeles	9	3	0	.750	466	309
Chi. Bears	9	3	0	.750	279	207
N.Y. Yanks	7	5	0	.583	366	367
Detroit	6	6	0	.500	321	285
Green Bay	3	9	0	.250	244	406
San Francisco	3	9	0	.250	213	300
Baltimore	1	11	0	.083	213	462

American Conference playoff: Cleveland 8, N.Y. Giants 3
National Conference playoff: Los Angeles 24, Chicago Bears 14
NFL Championship: Cleveland 30, Los Angeles 28

1951

AMERICAN CONFERENCE	W	L	T	Pct.	Pts.	OP
Cleveland	11	1	0	.917	331	152
N.Y. Giants	9	2	1	.818	254	161
Washington	5	7	0	.417	183	296
Pittsburgh	4	7	1	.364	183	235
Philadelphia	4	8	0	.333	234	264
Chi. Cardinals	3	9	0	.250	210	287

NATIONAL CONFERENCE	W	L	T	Pct.	Pts.	OP
Los Angeles	8	4	0	.667	392	261
Detroit	7	4	1	.636	336	259
San Francisco	7	4	1	.636	255	205
Chi. Bears	7	5	0	.583	286	282
Green Bay	3	9	0	.250	254	375
N.Y. Yanks	1	9	2	.100	241	382

NFL Championship: Los Angeles 24, Cleveland 17

1952

AMERICAN CONFERENCE

	W	L	T	Pct.	Pts.	OP
Cleveland	8	4	0	.667	310	213
N.Y. Giants	7	5	0	.583	234	231
Philadelphia	7	5	0	.583	252	271
Pittsburgh	5	7	0	.417	300	273
Chi. Cardinals	4	8	0	.333	172	221
Washington	4	8	0	.333	240	287

NATIONAL CONFERENCE

	W	L	T	Pct.	Pts.	OP
Detroit	9	3	0	.750	344	192
Los Angeles	9	3	0	.750	349	234
San Francisco	7	5	0	.583	285	221
Green Bay	6	6	0	.500	295	312
Chi. Bears	5	7	0	.417	245	326
Dallas	1	11	0	.083	182	427

National Conference playoff: Detroit 31, Los Angeles 21
NFL Championship: Detroit 17, Cleveland 7

1953

EASTERN CONFERENCE

	W	L	T	Pct.	Pts.	OP
Cleveland	11	1	0	.917	348	162
Philadelphia	7	4	1	.636	352	215
Washington	6	5	1	.545	208	215
Pittsburgh	6	6	0	.500	211	263
N.Y. Giants	3	9	0	.250	179	277
Chi. Cardinals	1	10	1	.091	190	337

WESTERN CONFERENCE

	W	L	T	Pct.	Pts.	OP
Detroit	10	2	0	.833	271	205
San Francisco	9	3	0	.750	372	237
Los Angeles	8	3	1	.727	366	236
Chi. Bears	3	8	1	.273	218	262
Baltimore	3	9	0	.250	182	350
Green Bay	2	9	1	.182	200	338

NFL Championship: Detroit 17, Cleveland 16

1954

EASTERN CONFERENCE

	W	L	T	Pct.	Pts.	OP
Cleveland	9	3	0	.750	336	162
Philadelphia	7	4	1	.636	284	230
N.Y. Giants	7	5	0	.583	293	184
Pittsburgh	5	7	0	.417	219	263
Washington	3	9	0	.250	207	432
Chi. Cardinals	2	10	0	.167	183	347

WESTERN CONFERENCE

	W	L	T	Pct.	Pts.	OP
Detroit	9	2	1	.818	337	189
Chi. Bears	8	4	0	.667	301	279
San Francisco	7	4	1	.636	313	251
Los Angeles	6	5	1	.545	314	285
Green Bay	4	8	0	.333	234	251
Baltimore	3	9	0	.250	131	279

NFL Championship: Cleveland 56, Detroit 10

1955

EASTERN CONFERENCE

	W	L	T	Pct.	Pts.	OP
Cleveland	9	2	1	.818	349	218
Washington	8	4	0	.667	246	222
N.Y. Giants	6	5	1	.545	267	223
Chi. Cardinals	4	7	1	.364	224	252
Philadelphia	4	7	1	.364	248	231
Pittsburgh	4	8	0	.333	195	285

WESTERN CONFERENCE

	W	L	T	Pct.	Pts.	OP
Los Angeles	8	3	1	.727	260	231
Chi. Bears	8	4	0	.667	294	251
Green Bay	6	6	0	.500	258	276
Baltimore	5	6	1	.455	214	239
San Francisco	4	8	0	.333	216	298
Detroit	3	9	0	.250	230	275

NFL Championship: Cleveland 38, Los Angeles 14

1956

EASTERN CONFERENCE

	W	L	T	Pct.	Pts.	OP
N.Y. Giants	8	3	1	.727	264	197
Chi. Cardinals	7	5	0	.583	240	182
Washington	6	6	0	.500	183	225
Cleveland	5	7	0	.417	167	177
Pittsburgh	5	7	0	.417	217	250
Philadelphia	3	8	1	.273	143	215

WESTERN CONFERENCE

	W	L	T	Pct.	Pts.	OP
Chi. Bears	9	2	1	.818	363	246
Detroit	9	3	0	.750	300	188
San Francisco	5	6	1	.455	233	284
Baltimore	5	7	0	.417	270	322
Green Bay	4	8	0	.333	264	342
Los Angeles	4	8	0	.333	291	307

NFL Championship: N.Y. Giants 47, Chicago Bears 7

1957

EASTERN CONFERENCE	W	L	T	Pct.	Pts.	OP	WESTERN CONFERENCE	W	L	T	Pct.	Pts.	OP
Cleveland	9	2	1	.818	269	172	Detroit	8	4	0	.667	251	231
N.Y. Giants	7	5	0	.583	254	211	San Francisco	8	4	0	.667	260	264
Pittsburgh	6	6	0	.500	161	178	Baltimore	7	5	0	.583	303	235
Washington	5	6	1	.455	251	230	Los Angeles	6	6	0	.500	307	278
Philadelphia	4	8	0	.333	173	230	Chi. Bears	5	7	0	.417	203	211
Chi. Cardinals	3	9	0	.250	200	299	Green Bay	3	9	0	.250	218	311

Western Conference playoff: Detroit 31, San Francisco 27
NFL Championship: Detroit 59, Cleveland 14

1958

EASTERN CONFERENCE	W	L	T	Pct.	Pts.	OP	WESTERN CONFERENCE	W	L	T	Pct.	Pts.	OP
N.Y. Giants	9	3	0	.750	246	183	Baltimore	9	3	0	.750	381	203
Cleveland	9	3	0	.750	302	217	Chi. Bears	8	4	0	.667	298	230
Pittsburgh	7	4	1	.636	261	230	Los Angeles	8	4	0	.667	344	278
Washington	4	7	1	.364	214	268	San Francisco	6	6	0	.500	257	324
Chi. Cardinals	2	9	1	.182	261	356	Detroit	4	7	1	.364	261	276
Philadelphia	2	9	1	.182	235	306	Green Bay	1	10	1	.091	193	382

Eastern Conference playoff: N.Y. Giants 10, Cleveland 0
NFL Championship: Baltimore 23, N.Y. Giants 17, sudden-death overtime

1959

EASTERN CONFERENCE	W	L	T	Pct.	Pts.	OP	WESTERN CONFERENCE	W	L	T	Pct.	Pts.	OP
N.Y. Giants	10	2	0	.833	284	170	Baltimore	9	3	0	.750	374	251
Cleveland	7	5	0	.583	270	214	Chi. Bears	8	4	0	.667	252	196
Philadelphia	7	5	0	.583	268	278	Green Bay	7	5	0	.583	248	246
Pittsburgh	6	5	1	.545	257	216	San Francisco	7	5	0	.583	255	237
Washington	3	9	0	.250	185	350	Detroit	3	8	1	.273	203	275
Chi. Cardinals	2	10	0	.167	234	324	Los Angeles	2	10	0	.167	242	315

NFL Championship: Baltimore 31, N.Y. Giants 16

1960 AFL

EASTERN DIVISION	W	L	T	Pct.	Pts.	OP	WESTERN DIVISION	W	L	T	Pct.	Pts.	OP
Houston	10	4	0	.714	379	285	L.A. Chargers	10	4	0	.714	373	336
N.Y. Titans	7	7	0	.500	382	399	Dall. Texans	8	6	0	.571	362	253
Buffalo	5	8	1	.385	296	303	Oakland	6	8	0	.429	319	388
Boston	5	9	0	.357	286	349	Denver	4	9	1	.308	309	393

AFL Championship: Houston 24, L.A. Chargers 16

1960 NFL

EASTERN CONFERENCE	W	L	T	Pct.	Pts.	OP	WESTERN CONFERENCE	W	L	T	Pct.	Pts.	OP
Philadelphia	10	2	0	.833	321	246	Green Bay	8	4	0	.667	332	209
Cleveland	8	3	1	.727	362	217	Detroit	7	5	0	.583	239	212
N.Y. Giants	6	4	2	.600	271	261	San Francisco	7	5	0	.583	208	205
St. Louis	6	5	1	.545	288	230	Baltimore	6	6	0	.500	288	234
Pittsburgh	5	6	1	.455	240	275	Chicago	5	6	1	.455	194	299
Washington	1	9	2	.100	178	309	L.A. Rams	4	7	1	.364	265	297
							Dall. Cowboys	0	11	1	.000	177	369

NFL Championship: Philadelphia 17, Green Bay 13

1961 AFL

EASTERN DIVISION	W	L	T	Pct.	Pts.	OP
Houston	10	3	1	.769	513	242
Boston	9	4	1	.692	413	313
N.Y. Titans	7	7	0	.500	301	390
Buffalo	6	8	0	.429	294	342

WESTERN DIVISION	W	L	T	Pct.	Pts.	OP
San Diego	12	2	0	.857	396	219
Dall. Texans	6	8	0	.429	334	343
Denver	3	11	0	.214	251	432
Oakland	2	12	0	.143	237	458

AFL Championship: Houston 10, San Diego 3

1961 NFL

EASTERN CONFERENCE	W	L	T	Pct.	Pts.	OP
N.Y. Giants	10	3	1	.769	368	220
Philadelphia	10	4	0	.714	361	297
Cleveland	8	5	1	.615	319	270
St. Louis	7	7	0	.500	279	267
Pittsburgh	6	8	0	.429	295	287
Dall. Cowboys	4	9	1	.308	236	380
Washington	1	12	1	.077	174	392

WESTERN CONFERENCE	W	L	T	Pct.	Pts.	OP
Green Bay	11	3	0	.786	391	223
Detroit	8	5	1	.615	270	258
Baltimore	8	6	0	.571	302	307
Chicago	8	6	0	.571	326	302
San Francisco	7	6	1	.538	346	272
Los Angeles	4	10	0	.286	263	333
Minnesota	3	11	0	.214	285	407

NFL Championship: Green Bay 37, N.Y. Giants 0

1962 AFL

EASTERN DIVISION	W	L	T	Pct.	Pts.	OP
Houston	11	3	0	.786	387	270
Boston	9	4	1	.692	346	295
Buffalo	7	6	1	.538	309	272
N.Y. Titans	5	9	0	.357	278	423

WESTERN DIVISION	W	L	T	Pct.	Pts.	OP
Dall. Texans	11	3	0	.786	389	233
Denver	7	7	0	.500	353	334
San Diego	4	10	0	.286	314	392
Oakland	1	13	0	.071	213	370

AFL Championship: Dallas Texans 20, Houston 17, sudden-death overtime

1962 NFL

EASTERN CONFERENCE	W	L	T	Pct.	Pts.	OP
N.Y. Giants	12	2	0	.857	398	283
Pittsburgh	9	5	0	.643	312	363
Cleveland	7	6	1	.538	291	257
Washington	5	7	2	.417	305	376
Dall. Cowboys	5	8	1	.385	398	402
St. Louis	4	9	1	.308	287	361
Philadelphia	3	10	1	.231	282	356

WESTERN CONFERENCE	W	L	T	Pct.	Pts.	OP
Green Bay	13	1	0	.929	415	148
Detroit	11	3	0	.786	315	177
Chicago	9	5	0	.643	321	287
Baltimore	7	7	0	.500	293	288
San Francisco	6	8	0	.429	282	331
Minnesota	2	11	1	.154	254	410
Los Angeles	1	12	1	.077	220	334

NFL Championship: Green Bay 16, N.Y. Giants 7

1963 AFL

EASTERN DIVISION	W	L	T	Pct.	Pts.	OP
Boston	7	6	1	.538	317	257
Buffalo	7	6	1	.538	304	291
Houston	6	8	0	.429	302	372
N.Y. Jets	5	8	1	.385	249	399

WESTERN DIVISION	W	L	T	Pct.	Pts.	OP
San Diego	11	3	0	.786	399	255
Oakland	10	4	0	.714	363	282
Kansas City	5	7	2	.417	347	263
Denver	2	11	1	.154	301	473

Eastern Division playoff: Boston 26, Buffalo 8
AFL Championship: San Diego 51, Boston 10

1963 NFL

EASTERN CONFERENCE	W	L	T	Pct.	Pts.	OP
N.Y. Giants	11	3	0	.786	448	280
Cleveland	10	4	0	.714	343	262
St. Louis	9	5	0	.643	341	283
Pittsburgh	7	4	3	.636	321	295
Dallas	4	10	0	.286	305	378
Washington	3	11	0	.214	279	398
Philadelphia	2	10	2	.167	242	381

WESTERN CONFERENCE	W	L	T	Pct.	Pts.	OP
Chicago	11	1	2	.917	301	144
Green Bay	11	2	1	.846	369	206
Baltimore	8	6	0	.571	316	285
Detroit	5	8	1	.385	326	265
Minnesota	5	8	1	.385	309	390
Los Angeles	5	9	0	.357	210	350
San Francisco	2	12	0	.143	198	391

NFL Championship: Chicago 14, N.Y. Giants 10

1964 AFL

EASTERN DIVISION

	W	L	T	Pct.	Pts.	OP
Buffalo	12	2	0	.857	400	242
Boston	10	3	1	.769	365	297
N.Y. Jets	5	8	1	.385	278	315
Houston	4	10	0	.286	310	355

WESTERN DIVISION

	W	L	T	Pct.	Pts.	OP
San Diego	8	5	1	.615	341	300
Kansas City	7	7	0	.500	366	306
Oakland	5	7	2	.417	303	350
Denver	2	11	1	.154	240	438

AFL Championship: Buffalo 20, San Diego 7

1964 NFL

EASTERN CONFERENCE

	W	L	T	Pct.	Pts.	OP
Cleveland	10	3	1	.769	415	293
St. Louis	9	3	2	.750	357	331
Philadelphia	6	8	0	.429	312	313
Washington	6	8	0	.429	307	305
Dallas	5	8	1	.385	250	289
Pittsburgh	5	9	0	.357	253	315
N.Y. Giants	2	10	2	.167	241	399

WESTERN CONFERENCE

	W	L	T	Pct.	Pts.	OP
Baltimore	12	2	0	.857	428	225
Green Bay	8	5	1	.615	342	245
Minnesota	8	5	1	.615	355	296
Detroit	7	5	2	.583	280	260
Los Angeles	5	7	2	.417	283	339
Chicago	5	9	0	.357	260	379
San Francisco	4	10	0	.286	236	330

NFL Championship: Cleveland 27, Baltimore 0

1965 AFL

EASTERN DIVISION

	W	L	T	Pct.	Pts.	OP
Buffalo	10	3	1	.769	313	226
N.Y. Jets	5	8	1	.385	285	303
Boston	4	8	2	.333	244	302
Houston	4	10	0	.286	298	429

WESTERN DIVISION

	W	L	T	Pct.	Pts.	OP
San Diego	9	2	3	.818	340	227
Oakland	8	5	1	.615	298	239
Kansas City	7	5	2	.583	322	285
Denver	4	10	0	.286	303	392

AFL Championship: Buffalo 23, San Diego 0

1965 NFL

EASTERN CONFERENCE

	W	L	T	Pct.	Pts.	OP
Cleveland	11	3	0	.786	363	325
Dallas	7	7	0	.500	325	280
N.Y. Giants	7	7	0	.500	270	338
Washington	6	8	0	.429	257	301
Philadelphia	5	9	0	.357	363	359
St. Louis	5	9	0	.357	296	309
Pittsburgh	2	12	0	.143	202	397

WESTERN CONFERENCE

	W	L	T	Pct.	Pts.	OP
Green Bay	10	3	1	.769	316	224
Baltimore	10	3	1	.769	389	284
Chicago	9	5	0	.643	409	275
San Francisco	7	6	1	.538	421	402
Minnesota	7	7	0	.500	383	403
Detroit	6	7	1	.462	257	295
Los Angeles	4	10	0	.286	269	328

Western Conference playoff: Green Bay 13, Baltimore 10, sudden-death overtime

NFL Championship: Green Bay 23, Cleveland 12

1966 AFL

EASTERN DIVISION

	W	L	T	Pct.	Pts.	OP
Buffalo	9	4	1	.692	358	255
Boston	8	4	2	.667	315	283
N.Y. Jets	6	6	2	.500	322	312
Houston	3	11	0	.214	335	396
Miami	3	11	0	.214	213	362

WESTERN DIVISION

	W	L	T	Pct.	Pts.	OP
Kansas City	11	2	1	.846	448	276
Oakland	8	5	1	.615	315	288
San Diego	7	6	1	.538	335	284
Denver	4	10	0	.286	196	381

AFL Championship: Kansas City 31, Buffalo 7

1966 NFL

EASTERN CONFERENCE

	W	L	T	Pct.	Pts.	OP
Dallas	10	3	1	.769	445	239
Cleveland	9	5	0	.643	403	259
Philadelphia	9	5	0	.643	326	340
St. Louis	8	5	1	.615	264	265
Washington	7	7	0	.500	351	355
Pittsburgh	5	8	1	.385	316	347
Atlanta	3	11	0	.214	204	437
N.Y. Giants	1	12	1	.077	263	501

WESTERN CONFERENCE

	W	L	T	Pct.	Pts.	OP
Green Bay	12	2	0	.857	335	163
Baltimore	9	5	0	.643	314	226
Los Angeles	8	6	0	.571	289	212
San Francisco	6	6	2	.500	320	325
Chicago	5	7	2	.417	234	272
Detroit	4	9	1	.308	206	317
Minnesota	4	9	1	.308	292	304

NFL Championship: Green Bay 34, Dallas 27

Super Bowl I: Green Bay (NFL) 35, Kansas City (AFL) 10

1967 AFL

EASTERN DIVISION

	W	L	T	Pct.	Pts.	OP
Houston	9	4	1	.692	258	199
N.Y. Jets	8	5	1	.615	371	329
Buffalo	4	10	0	.286	237	285
Miami	4	10	0	.286	219	407
Boston	3	10	1	.231	280	389

WESTERN DIVISION

	W	L	T	Pct.	Pts.	OP
Oakland	13	1	0	.929	468	238
Kansas City	9	5	0	.643	408	254
San Diego	8	5	1	.615	360	352
Denver	3	11	0	.214	256	409

AFL Championship: Oakland 40, Houston 7

1967 NFL

EASTERN CONFERENCE
Capitol Division

	W	L	T	Pct.	Pts.	OP
Dallas	9	5	0	.643	342	268
Philadelphia	6	7	1	.462	351	409
Washington	5	6	3	.455	347	353
New Orleans	3	11	0	.214	233	379

WESTERN CONFERENCE
Coastal Division

	W	L	T	Pct.	Pts.	OP
Los Angeles	11	1	2	.917	398	196
Baltimore	11	1	2	.917	394	198
San Francisco	7	7	0	.500	273	337
Atlanta	1	12	1	.077	175	422

Century Division

	W	L	T	Pct.	Pts.	OP
Cleveland	9	5	0	.643	334	297
N.Y. Giants	7	7	0	.500	369	379
St. Louis	6	7	1	.462	333	356
Pittsburgh	4	9	1	.308	281	320

Central Division

	W	L	T	Pct.	Pts.	OP
Green Bay	9	4	1	.692	332	209
Chicago	7	6	1	.538	239	218
Detroit	5	7	2	.417	260	259
Minnesota	3	8	3	.273	233	294

Conference Championships: Dallas 52, Cleveland 14; Green Bay 28, Los Angeles 7
NFL Championship: Green Bay 21, Dallas 17
Super Bowl II: Green Bay (NFL) 33, Oakland (AFL) 14

1968 AFL

EASTERN DIVISION

	W	L	T	Pct.	Pts.	OP
N.Y. Jets	11	3	0	.786	419	280
Houston	7	7	0	.500	303	248
Miami	5	8	1	.385	276	355
Boston	4	10	0	.286	229	406
Buffalo	1	12	1	.077	199	367

WESTERN DIVISION

	W	L	T	Pct.	Pts.	OP
Oakland	12	2	0	.857	453	233
Kansas City	12	2	0	.857	371	170
San Diego	9	5	0	.643	382	310
Denver	5	9	0	.357	255	404
Cincinnati	3	11	0	.214	215	329

Western Division playoff: Oakland 41, Kansas City 6
AFL Championship: N.Y. Jets 27, Oakland 23

1968 NFL

EASTERN CONFERENCE
Capitol Division

	W	L	T	Pct.	Pts.	OP
Dallas	12	2	0	.857	431	186
N.Y. Giants	7	7	0	.500	294	325
Washington	5	9	0	.357	249	358
Philadelphia	2	12	0	.143	202	351

WESTERN CONFERENCE
Coastal Division

	W	L	T	Pct.	Pts.	OP
Baltimore	13	1	0	.929	402	144
Los Angeles	10	3	1	.769	312	200
San Francisco	7	6	1	.538	303	310
Atlanta	2	12	0	.143	170	389

Century Division

	W	L	T	Pct.	Pts.	OP
Cleveland	10	4	0	.714	394	273
St. Louis	9	4	1	.692	325	289
New Orleans	4	9	1	.308	246	327
Pittsburgh	2	11	1	.154	244	397

Central Division

	W	L	T	Pct.	Pts.	OP
Minnesota	8	6	0	.571	282	242
Chicago	7	7	0	.500	250	333
Green Bay	6	7	1	.462	281	227
Detroit	4	8	2	.333	207	241

Conference Championships: Cleveland 31, Dallas 20; Baltimore 24, Minnesota 14
NFL Championship: Baltimore 34, Cleveland 0
Super Bowl III: N.Y. Jets (AFL) 16, Baltimore (NFL) 7

1969 AFL

EASTERN DIVISION

	W	L	T	Pct.	Pts.	OP
N.Y. Jets	10	4	0	.714	353	269
Houston	6	6	2	.500	278	279
Boston	4	10	0	.286	266	316
Buffalo	4	10	0	.286	230	359
Miami	3	10	1	.231	233	332

WESTERN DIVISION

	W	L	T	Pct.	Pts.	OP
Oakland	12	1	1	.923	377	242
Kansas City	11	3	0	.786	359	177
San Diego	8	6	0	.571	288	276
Denver	5	8	1	.385	297	344
Cincinnati	4	9	1	.308	280	367

Divisional playoffs: Kansas City 13, N.Y. Jets 6; Oakland 56, Houston 7
AFL Championship: Kansas City 17, Oakland 7

1969 NFL

EASTERN CONFERENCE

Capitol Division

	W	L	T	Pct.	Pts.	OP
Dallas	11	2	1	.846	369	223
Washington	7	5	2	.583	307	319
New Orleans	5	9	0	.357	311	393
Philadelphia	4	9	1	.308	279	377

Century Division

	W	L	T	Pct.	Pts.	OP
Cleveland	10	3	1	.769	351	300
N.Y. Giants	6	8	0	.429	264	298
St. Louis	4	9	1	.308	314	389
Pittsburgh	1	13	0	.071	218	404

WESTERN CONFERENCE

Coastal Division

	W	L	T	Pct.	Pts.	OP
Los Angeles	11	3	0	.786	320	243
Baltimore	8	5	1	.615	279	268
Atlanta	6	8	0	.429	276	268
San Francisco	4	8	2	.333	277	319

Central Division

	W	L	T	Pct.	Pts.	OP
Minnesota	12	2	0	.857	379	133
Detroit	9	4	1	.692	259	188
Green Bay	8	6	0	.571	269	221
Chicago	1	13	0	.071	210	339

Conference Championships: Cleveland 38, Dallas 14; Minnesota 23, Los Angeles 20
NFL Championship: Minnesota 27, Cleveland 7
Super Bowl IV: Kansas City (AFL) 23, Minnesota (NFL) 7

1970

AMERICAN CONFERENCE

Eastern Division

	W	L	T	Pct.	Pts.	OP
Baltimore	11	2	1	.846	321	234
Miami*	10	4	0	.714	297	228
N.Y. Jets	4	10	0	.286	255	286
Buffalo	3	10	1	.231	204	337
Boston	2	12	0	.143	149	361

Central Division

	W	L	T	Pct.	Pts.	OP
Cincinnati	8	6	0	.571	312	255
Cleveland	7	7	0	.500	286	265
Pittsburgh	5	9	0	.357	210	272
Houston	3	10	1	.231	217	352

Western Division

	W	L	T	Pct.	Pts.	OP
Oakland	8	4	2	.667	300	293
Kansas City	7	5	2	.583	272	244
San Diego	5	6	3	.455	282	278
Denver	5	8	1	.385	253	264

NATIONAL CONFERENCE

Eastern Division

	W	L	T	Pct.	Pts.	OP
Dallas	10	4	0	.714	299	221
N.Y. Giants	9	5	0	.643	301	270
St. Louis	8	5	1	.615	325	228
Washington	6	8	0	.429	297	314
Philadelphia	3	10	1	.231	241	332

Central Division

	W	L	T	Pct.	Pts.	OP
Minnesota	12	2	0	.857	335	143
Detroit*	10	4	0	.714	347	202
Chicago	6	8	0	.429	256	261
Green Bay	6	8	0	.429	196	293

Western Division

	W	L	T	Pct.	Pts.	OP
San Francisco	10	3	1	.769	352	267
Los Angeles	9	4	1	.692	325	202
Atlanta	4	8	2	.333	206	261
New Orleans	2	11	1	.154	172	347

*Wild Card qualifier for playoffs
Divisional playoffs: Baltimore 17, Cincinnati 0; Oakland 21, Miami 14
AFC Championship: Baltimore 27, Oakland 17
Divisional playoffs: Dallas 5, Detroit 0; San Francisco 17, Minnesota 14
NFC Championship: Dallas 17, San Francisco 10
Super Bowl V: Baltimore (AFC) 16, Dallas (NFC) 13

1971

AMERICAN CONFERENCE
Eastern Division

	W	L	T	Pct.	Pts.	OP
Miami	10	3	1	.769	315	174
Baltimore*	10	4	0	.714	313	140
New England	6	8	0	.429	238	325
N.Y. Jets	6	8	0	.429	212	299
Buffalo	1	13	0	.071	184	394

Central Division

	W	L	T	Pct.	Pts.	OP
Cleveland	9	5	0	.643	285	273
Pittsburgh	6	8	0	.429	246	292
Houston	4	9	1	.308	251	330
Cincinnati	4	10	0	.286	284	265

Western Division

	W	L	T	Pct.	Pts.	OP
Kansas City	10	3	1	.769	302	208
Oakland	8	4	2	.667	344	278
San Diego	6	8	0	.429	311	341
Denver	4	9	1	.308	203	275

NATIONAL CONFERENCE
Eastern Division

	W	L	T	Pct.	Pts.	OP
Dallas	11	3	0	.786	406	222
Washington*	9	4	1	.692	276	190
Philadelphia	6	7	1	.462	221	302
St. Louis	4	9	1	.308	231	279
N.Y. Giants	4	10	0	.286	228	362

Central Division

	W	L	T	Pct.	Pts.	OP
Minnesota	11	3	0	.786	245	139
Detroit	7	6	1	.538	341	286
Chicago	6	8	0	.429	185	276
Green Bay	4	8	2	.333	274	298

Western Division

	W	L	T	Pct.	Pts.	OP
San Francisco	9	5	0	.643	300	216
Los Angeles	8	5	1	.615	313	260
Atlanta	7	6	1	.538	274	277
New Orleans	4	8	2	.333	266	347

*Wild Card qualifier for playoffs

Divisional playoffs: Miami 27, Kansas City 24, sudden-death overtime; Baltimore 20, Cleveland 3

AFC Championship: Miami 21, Baltimore 0

Divisional playoffs: Dallas 20, Minnesota 12; San Francisco 24, Washington 20

NFC Championship: Dallas 14, San Francisco 3

Super Bowl VI: Dallas (NFC) 24, Miami (AFC) 3

1972

AMERICAN CONFERENCE
Eastern Division

	W	L	T	Pct.	Pts.	OP
Miami	14	0	0	1.000	385	171
N.Y. Jets	7	7	0	.500	367	324
Baltimore	5	9	0	.357	235	252
Buffalo	4	9	1	.321	257	377
New England	3	11	0	.214	192	446

Central Division

	W	L	T	Pct.	Pts.	OP
Pittsburgh	11	3	0	.786	343	175
Cleveland*	10	4	0	.714	268	249
Cincinnati	8	6	0	.571	299	229
Houston	1	13	0	.071	164	380

Western Division

	W	L	T	Pct.	Pts.	OP
Oakland	10	3	1	.750	365	248
Kansas City	8	6	0	.571	287	254
Denver	5	9	0	.357	325	350
San Diego	4	9	1	.321	264	344

NATIONAL CONFERENCE
Eastern Division

	W	L	T	Pct.	Pts.	OP
Washington	11	3	0	.786	336	218
Dallas*	10	4	0	.714	319	240
N.Y. Giants	8	6	0	.571	331	247
St. Louis	4	9	1	.321	193	303
Philadelphia	2	11	1	.179	145	352

Central Division

	W	L	T	Pct.	Pts.	OP
Green Bay	10	4	0	.714	304	226
Detroit	8	5	1	.607	339	290
Minnesota	7	7	0	.500	301	252
Chicago	4	9	1	.321	225	275

Western Division

	W	L	T	Pct.	Pts.	OP
San Francisco	8	5	1	.607	353	249
Atlanta	7	7	0	.500	269	274
Los Angeles	6	7	1	.464	291	286
New Orleans	2	11	1	.179	215	361

*Wild Card qualifier for playoffs

Divisional playoffs: Pittsburgh 13, Oakland 7; Miami 20, Cleveland 14

AFC Championship: Miami 21, Pittsburgh 17

Divisional playoffs: Dallas 30, San Francisco 28; Washington 16, Green Bay 3

NFC Championship: Washington 26, Dallas 3

Super Bowl VII: Miami (AFC) 14, Washington (NFC) 7

1973

AMERICAN CONFERENCE

Eastern Division

	W	L	T	Pct.	Pts.	OP
Miami	12	2	0	.857	343	150
Buffalo	9	5	0	.643	259	230
New England	5	9	0	.357	258	300
Baltimore	4	10	0	.286	226	341
N.Y. Jets	4	10	0	.286	240	306

Central Division

	W	L	T	Pct.	Pts.	OP
Cincinnati	10	4	0	.714	286	231
Pittsburgh*	10	4	0	.714	347	210
Cleveland	7	5	2	.571	234	255
Houston	1	13	0	.071	199	447

Western Division

	W	L	T	Pct.	Pts.	OP
Oakland	9	4	1	.679	292	175
Denver	7	5	2	.571	354	296
Kansas City	7	5	2	.571	231	192
San Diego	2	11	1	.179	188	386

NATIONAL CONFERENCE

Eastern Division

	W	L	T	Pct.	Pts.	OP
Dallas	10	4	0	.714	382	203
Washington*	10	4	0	.714	325	198
Philadelphia	5	8	1	.393	310	393
St. Louis	4	9	1	.321	286	365
N.Y. Giants	2	11	1	.179	226	362

Central Division

	W	L	T	Pct.	Pts.	OP
Minnesota	12	2	0	.857	296	168
Detroit	6	7	1	.464	271	247
Green Bay	5	7	2	.429	202	259
Chicago	3	11	0	.214	195	334

Western Division

	W	L	T	Pct.	Pts.	OP
Los Angeles	12	2	0	.857	388	178
Atlanta	9	5	0	.643	318	224
New Orleans	5	9	0	.357	163	312
San Francisco	5	9	0	.357	262	319

*Wild Card qualifier for playoffs
Divisional playoffs: Oakland 33, Pittsburgh 14; Miami 34, Cincinnati 16
AFC Championship: Miami 27, Oakland 10
Divisional playoffs: Minnesota 27, Washington 20; Dallas 27, Los Angeles 16
NFC Championship: Minnesota 27, Dallas 10
Super Bowl VIII: Miami (AFC) 24, Minnesota (NFC) 7

1974

AMERICAN CONFERENCE

Eastern Division

	W	L	T	Pct.	Pts.	OP
Miami	11	3	0	.786	327	216
Buffalo*	9	5	0	.643	264	244
New England	7	7	0	.500	348	289
N.Y. Jets	7	7	0	.500	279	300
Baltimore	2	12	0	.143	190	329

Central Division

	W	L	T	Pct.	Pts.	OP
Pittsburgh	10	3	1	.750	305	189
Cincinnati	7	7	0	.500	283	259
Houston	7	7	0	.500	236	282
Cleveland	4	10	0	.286	251	344

Western Division

	W	L	T	Pct.	Pts.	OP
Oakland	12	2	0	.857	355	228
Denver	7	6	1	.536	302	294
Kansas City	5	9	0	.357	233	293
San Diego	5	9	0	.357	212	285

NATIONAL CONFERENCE

Eastern Division

	W	L	T	Pct.	Pts.	OP
St. Louis	10	4	0	.714	285	218
Washington*	10	4	0	.714	320	196
Dallas	8	6	0	.571	297	235
Philadelphia	7	7	0	.500	242	217
N.Y. Giants	2	12	0	.143	195	299

Central Division

	W	L	T	Pct.	Pts.	OP
Minnesota	10	4	0	.714	310	195
Detroit	7	7	0	.500	256	270
Green Bay	6	8	0	.429	210	206
Chicago	4	10	0	.286	152	279

Western Division

	W	L	T	Pct.	Pts.	OP
Los Angeles	10	4	0	.714	263	181
San Francisco	6	8	0	.429	226	236
New Orleans	5	9	0	.357	166	263
Atlanta	3	11	0	.214	111	271

*Wild Card qualifier for playoffs
Divisional playoffs: Oakland 28, Miami 26; Pittsburgh 32, Buffalo 14
AFC Championship: Pittsburgh 24, Oakland 13
Divisional playoffs: Minnesota 30, St. Louis 14; Los Angeles 19, Washington 10
NFC Championship: Minnesota 14, Los Angeles 10
Super Bowl IX: Pittsburgh (AFC) 16, Minnesota (NFC) 6

1975

AMERICAN CONFERENCE

Eastern Division

	W	L	T	Pct.	Pts.	OP
Baltimore	10	4	0	.714	395	269
Miami	10	4	0	.714	357	222
Buffalo	8	6	0	.571	420	355
New England	3	11	0	.214	258	358
N.Y. Jets	3	11	0	.214	258	433

Central Division

	W	L	T	Pct.	Pts.	OP
Pittsburgh	12	2	0	.857	373	162
Cincinnati*	11	3	0	.786	340	246
Houston	10	4	0	.714	293	226
Cleveland	3	11	0	.214	218	372

Western Division

	W	L	T	Pct.	Pts.	OP
Oakland	11	3	0	.786	375	255
Denver	6	8	0	.429	254	307
Kansas City	5	9	0	.357	282	341
San Diego	2	12	0	.143	189	345

NATIONAL CONFERENCE

Eastern Division

	W	L	T	Pct.	Pts.	OP
St. Louis	11	3	0	.786	356	276
Dallas*	10	4	0	.714	350	268
Washington	8	6	0	.571	325	276
N.Y. Giants	5	9	0	.357	216	306
Philadelphia	4	10	0	.286	225	302

Central Division

	W	L	T	Pct.	Pts.	OP
Minnesota	12	2	0	.857	377	180
Detroit	7	7	0	.500	245	262
Chicago	4	10	0	.286	191	379
Green Bay	4	10	0	.286	226	285

Western Division

	W	L	T	Pct.	Pts.	OP
Los Angeles	12	2	0	.857	312	135
San Francisco	5	9	0	.357	255	286
Atlanta	4	10	0	.286	240	289
New Orleans	2	12	0	.143	165	360

*Wild Card qualifier for playoffs

Divisional playoffs: Pittsburgh 28, Baltimore 10; Oakland 31, Cincinnati 28
AFC Championship: Pittsburgh 16, Oakland 10
Divisional playoffs: Los Angeles 35, St. Louis 23; Dallas 17, Minnesota 14
NFC Championship: Dallas 37, Los Angeles 7
Super Bowl X: Pittsburgh (AFC) 21, Dallas (NFC) 17

1976

AMERICAN CONFERENCE

Eastern Division

	W	L	T	Pct.	Pts.	OP
Baltimore	11	3	0	.786	417	246
New England*	11	3	0	.786	376	236
Miami	6	8	0	.429	263	264
N.Y. Jets	3	11	0	.214	169	383
Buffalo	2	12	0	.143	245	363

Central Division

	W	L	T	Pct.	Pts.	OP
Pittsburgh	10	4	0	.714	342	138
Cincinnati	10	4	0	.714	335	210
Cleveland	9	5	0	.643	267	287
Houston	5	9	0	.357	222	273

Western Division

	W	L	T	Pct.	Pts.	OP
Oakland	13	1	0	.929	350	237
Denver	9	5	0	.643	315	206
San Diego	6	8	0	.429	248	285
Kansas City	5	9	0	.357	290	376
Tampa Bay	0	14	0	.000	125	412

NATIONAL CONFERENCE

Eastern Division

	W	L	T	Pct.	Pts.	OP
Dallas	11	3	0	.786	296	194
Washington*	10	4	0	.714	291	217
St. Louis	10	4	0	.714	309	267
Philadelphia	4	10	0	.286	165	286
N.Y. Giants	3	11	0	.214	170	250

Central Division

	W	L	T	Pct.	Pts.	OP
Minnesota	11	2	1	.821	305	176
Chicago	7	7	0	.500	253	216
Detroit	6	8	0	.429	262	220
Green Bay	5	9	0	.357	218	299

Western Division

	W	L	T	Pct.	Pts.	OP
Los Angeles	10	3	1	.750	351	190
San Francisco	8	6	0	.571	270	190
Atlanta	4	10	0	.286	172	312
New Orleans	4	10	0	.286	253	346
Seattle	2	12	0	.143	229	429

*Wild Card qualifier for playoffs

Divisional playoffs: Oakland 24, New England 21; Pittsburgh 40, Baltimore 14
AFC Championship: Oakland 24, Pittsburgh 7
Divisional playoffs: Minnesota 35, Washington 20; Los Angeles 14, Dallas 12
NFC Championship: Minnesota 24, Los Angeles 13
Super Bowl XI: Oakland (AFC) 32, Minnesota (NFC) 14

1977

AMERICAN CONFERENCE

Eastern Division

	W	L	T	Pct.	Pts.	OP
Baltimore	10	4	0	.714	295	221
Miami	10	4	0	.714	313	197
New England	9	5	0	.643	278	217
N.Y. Jets	3	11	0	.214	191	300
Buffalo	3	11	0	.214	160	313

Central Division

	W	L	T	Pct.	Pts.	OP
Pittsburgh	9	5	0	.643	283	243
Houston	8	6	0	.571	299	230
Cincinnati	8	6	0	.571	238	235
Cleveland	6	8	0	.429	269	267

Western Division

	W	L	T	Pct.	Pts.	OP
Denver	12	2	0	.857	274	148
Oakland*	11	3	0	.786	351	230
San Diego	7	7	0	.500	222	205
Seattle	5	9	0	.357	282	373
Kansas City	2	12	0	.143	225	349

NATIONAL CONFERENCE

Eastern Division

	W	L	T	Pct.	Pts.	OP
Dallas	12	2	0	.857	345	212
Washington	9	5	0	.643	196	189
St. Louis	7	7	0	.500	272	287
Philadelphia	5	9	0	.357	220	207
N.Y. Giants	5	9	0	.357	181	265

Central Division

	W	L	T	Pct.	Pts.	OP
Minnesota	9	5	0	.643	231	227
Chicago*	9	5	0	.643	255	253
Detroit	6	8	0	.429	183	252
Green Bay	4	10	0	.286	134	219
Tampa Bay	2	12	0	.143	103	223

Western Division

	W	L	T	Pct.	Pts.	OP
Los Angeles	10	4	0	.714	302	146
Atlanta	7	7	0	.500	179	129
San Francisco	5	9	0	.357	220	260
New Orleans	3	11	0	.214	232	336

*Wild Card qualifier for playoffs

Divisional playoffs: Denver 34, Pittsburgh 21; Oakland 37, Baltimore 31, sudden-death overtime

AFC Championship: Denver 20, Oakland 17

Divisional playoffs: Dallas 37, Chicago 7; Minnesota 14, Los Angeles 7

NFC Championship: Dallas 23, Minnesota 6

Super Bowl XII: Dallas (NFC) 27, Denver (AFC) 10

1978

AMERICAN CONFERENCE

Eastern Division

	W	L	T	Pct.	Pts.	OP
New England	11	5	0	.688	358	286
Miami*	11	5	0	.688	372	254
N.Y. Jets	8	8	0	.500	359	364
Buffalo	5	11	0	.313	302	354
Baltimore	5	11	0	.313	239	421

Central Division

	W	L	T	Pct.	Pts.	OP
Pittsburgh	14	2	0	.875	356	195
Houston*	10	6	0	.625	283	298
Cleveland	8	8	0	.500	334	356
Cincinnati	4	12	0	.250	252	284

Western Division

	W	L	T	Pct.	Pts.	OP
Denver	10	6	0	.625	282	198
Oakland	9	7	0	.563	311	283
Seattle	9	7	0	.563	345	358
San Diego	9	7	0	.563	355	309
Kansas City	4	12	0	.250	243	327

NATIONAL CONFERENCE

Eastern Division

	W	L	T	Pct.	Pts.	OP
Dallas	12	4	0	.750	384	208
Philadelphia*	9	7	0	.563	270	250
Washington	8	8	0	.500	273	283
St. Louis	6	10	0	.375	248	296
N.Y. Giants	6	10	0	.375	264	298

Central Division

	W	L	T	Pct.	Pts.	OP
Minnesota	8	7	1	.531	294	306
Green Bay	8	7	1	.531	249	269
Detroit	7	9	0	.438	290	300
Chicago	7	9	0	.438	253	274
Tampa Bay	5	11	0	.313	241	259

Western Division

	W	L	T	Pct.	Pts.	OP
Los Angeles	12	4	0	.750	316	245
Atlanta*	9	7	0	.563	240	290
New Orleans	7	9	0	.438	281	298
San Francisco	2	14	0	.125	219	350

*Wild Card qualifier for playoffs

First-round playoff: Houston 17, Miami 9

Divisional playoffs: Houston 31, New England 14; Pittsburgh 33, Denver 10

AFC Championship: Pittsburgh 34, Houston 5

First-round playoff: Atlanta 14, Philadelphia 13

Divisional playoffs: Dallas 27, Atlanta 20; Los Angeles 34, Minnesota 10

NFC Championship: Dallas 28, Los Angeles 0

Super Bowl XIII: Pittsburgh (AFC) 35, Dallas (NFC) 31

1979

AMERICAN CONFERENCE

Eastern Division

	W	L	T	Pct.	Pts.	OP
Miami	10	6	0	.625	341	257
New England	9	7	0	.563	411	326
N.Y. Jets	8	8	0	.500	337	383
Buffalo	7	9	0	.438	268	279
Baltimore	5	11	0	.313	271	351

Central Division

	W	L	T	Pct.	Pts.	OP
Pittsburgh	12	4	0	.750	416	262
Houston*	11	5	0	.688	362	331
Cleveland	9	7	0	.563	359	352
Cincinnati	4	12	0	.250	337	421

Western Division

	W	L	T	Pct.	Pts.	OP
San Diego	12	4	0	.750	411	246
Denver*	10	6	0	.625	289	262
Seattle	9	7	0	.563	378	372
Oakland	9	7	0	.563	365	337
Kansas City	7	9	0	.438	238	262

NATIONAL CONFERENCE

Eastern Division

	W	L	T	Pct.	Pts.	OP
Dallas	11	5	0	.688	371	313
Philadelphia*	11	5	0	.688	339	282
Washington	10	6	0	.625	348	295
N.Y. Giants	6	10	0	.375	237	323
St. Louis	5	11	0	.313	307	358

Central Division

	W	L	T	Pct.	Pts.	OP
Tampa Bay	10	6	0	.625	273	237
Chicago*	10	6	0	.625	306	249
Minnesota	7	9	0	.438	259	337
Green Bay	5	11	0	.313	246	316
Detroit	2	14	0	.125	219	365

Western Division

	W	L	T	Pct.	Pts.	OP
Los Angeles	9	7	0	.563	323	309
New Orleans	8	8	0	.500	370	360
Atlanta	6	10	0	.375	300	388
San Francisco	2	14	0	.125	308	416

Wild Card qualifier for playoffs
First-round playoff: Houston 13, Denver 7
Divisional playoffs: Houston 17, San Diego 14; Pittsburgh 34, Miami 14
AFC Championship: Pittsburgh 27, Houston 13
First-round playoff: Philadelphia 27, Chicago 17
Divisional playoffs: Tampa Bay 24, Philadelphia 17; Los Angeles 21, Dallas 19
NFC Championship: Los Angeles 9, Tampa Bay 0
Super Bowl XIV: Pittsburgh (AFC) 31, Los Angeles (NFC) 19

1980

AMERICAN CONFERENCE

Eastern Division

	W	L	T	Pct.	Pts.	OP
Buffalo	11	5	0	.688	320	260
New England	10	6	0	.625	441	325
Miami	8	8	0	.500	266	305
Baltimore	7	9	0	.438	355	387
N.Y. Jets	4	12	0	.250	302	395

Central Division

	W	L	T	Pct.	Pts.	OP
Cleveland	11	5	0	.688	357	310
Houston*	11	5	0	.688	295	251
Pittsburgh	9	7	0	.563	352	313
Cincinnati	6	10	0	.375	244	312

Western Division

	W	L	T	Pct.	Pts.	OP
San Diego	11	5	0	.688	418	327
Oakland*	11	5	0	.688	364	306
Kansas City	8	8	0	.500	319	336
Denver	8	8	0	.500	310	323
Seattle	4	12	0	.250	291	408

NATIONAL CONFERENCE

Eastern Division

	W	L	T	Pct.	Pts.	OP
Philadelphia	12	4	0	.750	384	222
Dallas*	12	4	0	.750	454	311
Washington	6	10	0	.375	261	293
St. Louis	5	11	0	.313	299	350
N.Y. Giants	4	12	0	.250	249	425

Central Division

	W	L	T	Pct.	Pts.	OP
Minnesota	9	7	0	.563	317	308
Detroit	9	7	0	.563	334	272
Chicago	7	9	0	.437	304	264
Tampa Bay	5	10	1	.343	271	341
Green Bay	5	10	1	.343	231	371

Western Division

	W	L	T	Pct.	Pts.	OP
Atlanta	12	4	0	.750	405	272
Los Angeles*	11	5	0	.688	424	289
San Francisco	6	10	0	.375	320	415
New Orleans	1	15	0	.063	291	487

Wild Card qualifier for playoffs
First-round playoff: Oakland 27, Houston 7
Divisional playoffs: San Diego 20, Buffalo 14; Oakland 14, Cleveland 12
AFC Championship: Oakland 34, San Diego 27
First-round playoff: Dallas 34, Los Angeles 13
Divisional playoffs: Philadelphia 31, Minnesota 16; Dallas 30, Atlanta 27
NFC Championship: Philadelphia 20, Dallas 7
Super Bowl XV: Oakland (AFC) 27, Philadelphia (NFC) 10

1981

AMERICAN CONFERENCE

Eastern Division

	W	L	T	Pct.	Pts.	OP
Miami	11	4	1	.719	345	275
N.Y. Jets*	10	5	1	.656	355	287
Buffalo*	10	6	0	.625	311	276
Baltimore	2	14	0	.125	259	533
New England	2	14	0	.125	322	370

Central Division

	W	L	T	Pct.	Pts.	OP
Cincinnati	12	4	0	.750	421	304
Pittsburgh	8	8	0	.500	356	297
Houston	7	9	0	.438	281	355
Cleveland	5	11	0	.313	276	375

Western Division

	W	L	T	Pct.	Pts.	OP
San Diego	10	6	0	.625	478	390
Denver	10	6	0	.625	321	289
Kansas City	9	7	0	.563	343	290
Oakland	7	9	0	.438	273	343
Seattle	6	10	0	.375	322	388

NATIONAL CONFERENCE

Eastern Division

	W	L	T	Pct.	Pts.	OP
Dallas	12	4	0	.750	367	277
Philadelphia*	10	6	0	.625	368	221
N.Y. Giants*	9	7	0	.563	295	257
Washington	8	8	0	.500	347	349
St. Louis	7	9	0	.438	315	408

Central Division

	W	L	T	Pct.	Pts.	OP
Tampa Bay	9	7	0	.563	315	268
Detroit	8	8	0	.500	397	322
Green Bay	8	8	0	.500	324	361
Minnesota	7	9	0	.438	325	369
Chicago	6	10	0	.375	253	324

Western Division

	W	L	T	Pct.	Pts.	OP
San Francisco	13	3	0	.813	357	250
Atlanta	7	9	0	.438	426	355
Los Angeles	6	10	0	.375	303	351
New Orleans	4	12	0	.250	207	378

*Wild card qualifier for playoffs
First-round playoff: Buffalo 31, N.Y. Jets 27
Divisional playoffs: San Diego 41, Miami 38 (OT); Cincinnati 28, Buffalo 21
AFC Championship: Cincinnati 27, San Diego 7
First-round playoff: N.Y. Giants 27, Philadelphia 21
Divisional playoffs: Dallas 38, Tampa Bay 0; San Francisco 38, N.Y. Giants 24
NFC Championship: San Francisco 28, Dallas 27
Super Bowl XVI: San Francisco (NFC) 26, Cincinnati (AFC) 21

*1982

AMERICAN CONFERENCE

	W	L	T	Pct.	Pts.	OP
L.A. Raiders	8	1	0	.889	260	200
Miami	7	2	0	.778	198	131
Cincinnati	7	2	0	.778	232	177
Pittsburgh	6	3	0	.667	204	146
San Diego	6	3	0	.667	288	221
N.Y. Jets	6	3	0	.667	245	166
New England	5	4	0	.556	143	157
Cleveland	4	5	0	.444	140	182
Buffalo	4	5	0	.444	150	154
Seattle	4	5	0	.444	127	147
Kansas City	3	6	0	.333	176	184
Denver	2	7	0	.222	148	226
Houston	1	8	0	.111	136	245
Baltimore	0	8	1	.063	113	236

NATIONAL CONFERENCE

	W	L	T	Pct.	Pts.	OP
Washington	8	1	0	.889	190	128
Dallas	6	3	0	.667	226	145
Green Bay	5	3	1	.611	226	169
Minnesota	5	4	0	.556	187	198
Atlanta	5	4	0	.556	183	199
St. Louis	5	4	0	.556	135	170
Tampa Bay	5	4	0	.556	158	178
Detroit	4	5	0	.444	181	176
New Orleans	4	5	0	.444	129	160
N.Y. Giants	4	5	0	.444	164	160
San Francisco	3	6	0	.333	209	206
Chicago	3	6	0	.333	141	174
Philadelphia	3	6	0	.333	191	195
L.A. Rams	2	7	0	.222	200	250

*Top eight teams in each Conference qualified for playoffs under format necessitated by strike-shortened season

First-round playoffs: Miami 28, New England 13; L.A. Raiders 27, Cleveland 10; N.Y. Jets 44, Cincinnati 17; San Diego 31, Pittsburgh 28
Second-round playoffs: N.Y. Jets 17, L.A. Raiders 14; Miami 34, San Diego 13
AFC Championship: Miami 14, N.Y. Jets 0
First-round playoffs: Green Bay 41, St. Louis 16; Washington 31, Detroit 7; Minnesota 30, Atlanta 24; Dallas 30, Tampa Bay 17
Second-round playoffs: Washington 21, Minnesota 7; Dallas 37, Green Bay 26
NFC Championship: Washington 31, Dallas 17
Super Bowl XVII: Washington 27, Miami 17

1983

AMERICAN CONFERENCE

Eastern Division

	W	L	T	Pct.	Pts.	OP
Miami	12	4	0	.750	389	250
New England	8	8	0	.500	274	289
Buffalo	8	8	0	.500	283	351
Baltimore	7	9	0	.438	264	354
N.Y. Jets	7	9	0	.438	313	331

Central Division

	W	L	T	Pct.	Pts.	OP
Pittsburgh	10	6	0	.625	355	303
Cleveland	9	7	0	.562	356	342
Cincinnati	7	9	0	.438	346	302
Houston	2	14	0	.125	288	460

Western Division

	W	L	T	Pct.	Pts.	OP
L.A. Raiders	12	4	0	.750	442	338
Seattle*	9	7	0	.562	403	397
Denver*	9	7	0	.562	302	327
San Diego	6	10	0	.375	358	462
Kansas City	6	10	0	.375	386	367

NATIONAL CONFERENCE

Eastern Division

	W	L	T	Pct.	Pts.	OP
Washington	14	2	0	.875	541	332
Dallas*	12	4	0	.750	479	360
St. Louis	8	7	1	.531	374	428
Philadelphia	5	11	0	.313	233	322
N.Y. Giants	3	12	1	.219	267	347

Central Division

	W	L	T	Pct.	Pts.	OP
Detroit	9	7	0	.562	347	286
Green Bay	8	8	0	.500	429	439
Chicago	8	8	0	.500	311	301
Minnesota	8	8	0	.500	316	348
Tampa Bay	2	14	0	.125	241	380

Western Division

	W	L	T	Pct.	Pts.	OP
San Francisco	10	6	0	.625	432	293
L.A. Rams*	9	7	0	.562	361	344
New Orleans	8	8	0	.500	319	337
Atlanta	7	9	0	.438	370	389

*Wild card qualifier for playoffs
First-round playoff: Seattle 31, Denver 7
Divisional playoffs: Seattle 27, Miami 20; L.A. Raiders 38, Pittsburgh 10
AFC Championship: L.A. Raiders 30, Seattle 14
First-round playoff: L.A. Rams 24, Dallas 17
Divisional playoffs: San Francisco 24, Detroit 23; Washington 51, L.A. Rams 7
NFC Championship: Washington 24, San Francisco 21
Super Bowl XVIII: L.A. Raiders 38, Washington 9

1984

NATIONAL CONFERENCE

Eastern Division

	W	L	T	Pct.	Pts.	OP
Washington	11	5	0	.688	426	310
N.Y. Giants*	9	7	0	.563	299	301
St. Louis	9	7	0	.563	423	345
Dallas	9	7	0	.563	308	308
Philadelphia	6	9	1	.406	278	320

Central Division

	W	L	T	Pct.	Pts.	OP
Chicago	10	6	0	.625	325	248
Green Bay	8	8	0	.500	390	309
Tampa Bay	6	10	0	.375	335	380
Detroit	4	11	1	.281	283	408
Minnesota	3	13	0	.188	276	484

Western Division

	W	L	T	Pct.	Pts.	OP
San Francisco	15	1	0	.939	475	227
L.A. Rams*	10	6	0	.625	346	316
New Orleans	7	9	0	.438	298	361
Atlanta	4	12	0	.250	281	382

AMERICAN CONFERENCE

Eastern Division

	W	L	T	Pct.	Pts.	OP
Miami	14	2	0	.875	513	298
New England	9	7	0	.563	362	352
N.Y. Jets	7	9	0	.438	332	364
Indianapolis	4	12	0	.250	239	414
Buffalo	2	14	0	.125	250	454

Central Division

	W	L	T	Pct.	Pts.	OP
Pittsburgh	9	7	0	.563	387	310
Cincinnati	8	8	0	.500	339	339
Cleveland	5	11	0	.313	250	297
Houston	3	13	0	.188	240	437

Western Division

	W	L	T	Pct.	Pts.	OP
Denver	13	3	0	.813	353	241
Seattle*	12	4	0	.750	418	282
L.A. Raiders*	11	5	0	.688	368	278
Kansas City	8	8	0	.500	314	324
San Diego	7	9	0	.438	394	413

*Wild card qualifier for playoffs
Wild Card Game: N.Y. Giants 16, L.A. Rams 13
NFC Divisional playoffs: San Francisco 21, N.Y. Giants 10; Chicago 23, Washington 19
NFC Championship: San Francisco 23, Chicago 0
Wild Card Game: Seattle 13, L.A. Raiders 7
AFC Divisional playoffs: Miami 31, Seattle 10; Pittsburgh 24, Denver 17
AFC Championship: Miami 45, Pittsburgh 28
Super Bowl XIX: San Francisco 38, Miami 16

1985

AMERICAN CONFERENCE

Eastern Division

	W	L	T	Pct.	Pts.	OP
Miami	12	4	0	.750	428	320
N.Y. Jets	11	5	0	.688	393	264
New England	11	5	0	.688	362	290
Indianapolis	5	11	0	.313	320	386
Buffalo	2	14	0	.125	200	381

CENTRAL DIVISION

	W	L	T	Pct.	Pts.	OP
Cleveland	8	8	0	.500	287	294
Cincinnati	7	9	0	.438	441	437
Pittsburgh	7	9	0	.438	379	355
Houston	5	11	0	.313	284	412

WESTERN DIVISION

	W	L	T	Pct.	Pts.	OP
L.A. Raiders	12	4	0	.750	354	308
Denver	11	5	0	.688	380	329
Seattle	8	8	0	.500	349	303
San Diego	8	8	0	.500	467	435
Kansas City	6	10	0	.375	327	360

NATIONAL CONFERENCE

Eastern Division

	W	L	T	Pct.	Pts.	OP
Dallas	10	6	0	.625	357	333
N.Y. Giants	10	6	0	.625	399	283
Washington	10	6	0	.625	298	313
Philadelphia	7	9	0	.438	286	310
St. Louis	5	11	0	.313	279	415

CENTRAL DIVISION

	W	L	T	Pct.	Pts.	OP
Chicago	15	1	0	.938	456	198
Green Bay	8	8	0	.500	337	355
Minnesota	7	9	0	.438	346	359
Detroit	7	9	0	.438	307	366
Tampa Bay	2	14	0	.125	294	448

WESTERN DIVISION

	W	L	T	Pct.	Pts.	OP
L.A. Rams	11	5	0	.688	340	287
San Francisco	10	6	0	.625	411	263
New Orleans	5	11	0	.313	294	401
Atlanta	4	12	0	.250	282	452

Wild Card Game: New England 26, N.Y. Jets 14
AFC Divisional playoffs: Miami 24, Cleveland 21; New England 27, L.A. Raiders 20
AFC Championship: New England 31, Miami 14
Wild Card Game: N.Y. Giants 17, San Francisco 3
NFC Divisional playoffs: L.A. Rams 20, Dallas 0; Chicago 21, N.Y. Giants 0
NFC Championship: Chicago 24, L.A. Rams 0
Super Bowl XX: Chicago 46, New England 10

1986

AMERICAN CONFERENCE

Eastern Division

	W	L	T	Pct.	Pts.	OP
N.Y. Giants	14	2	0	.875	371	236
Washington	12	4	0	.750	368	296
Dallas	7	9	0	.438	346	337
Philadelphia	5	10	1	.344	256	312
St. Louis	4	11	1	.281	218	351

Central Division

	W	L	T	Pct.	Pts.	OP
Chicago	14	2	0	.875	352	187
Minnesota	9	7	0	.563	398	273
Detroit	5	11	0	.313	277	326
Green Bay	4	12	0	.250	254	418
Tampa Bay	2	14	0	.125	239	473

Western Division

	W	L	T	Pct.	Pts.	OP
San Francisco	10	5	1	.656	374	247
L.A. Rams	10	6	0	.625	309	267
Atlanta	7	8	1	.469	280	280
New Orleans	7	9	0	.438	288	287

NATIONAL CONFERENCE

Eastern Division

	W	L	T	Pct.	Pts.	OP
New England	11	5	0	.688	412	307
N.Y. Jets	10	6	0	.625	364	386
Miami	8	8	0	.500	430	405
Buffalo	4	12	0	.250	287	348
Indianapolis	3	13	0	.188	229	400

Central Division

	W	L	T	Pct.	Pts.	OP
Cleveland	12	4	0	.750	391	310
Cincinnati	10	6	0	.625	409	394
Pittsburgh	6	10	0	.375	307	336
Houston	5	11	0	.313	274	329

Western Division

	W	L	T	Pct.	Pts.	OP
Denver	11	5	0	.688	378	327
Kansas City	10	6	0	.625	358	326
Seattle	10	6	0	.625	366	293
L.A. Raiders	8	8	0	.500	323	346
San Diego	4	12	0	.250	335	396

NFC Wild Card Game: Washington 19, L.A. Rams 7
NFC Divisional playoffs: Washington 27, Chicago 13; N.Y. Giants 49, San Francisco 3
NFC Championship: N.Y. Giants 17, Washington 0
AFC Wild Card Game: N.Y. Jets 35, Kansas City 15
AFC Divisional playoffs: Cleveland 23, N.Y. Jets 20 (2 OT); Denver 22, New England 17
AFC Championship: Denver 23, Cleveland 20 (OT)
Super Bowl XXI: N.Y. Giants 39, Denver 20

The down side of Super Bowl XXI for John Elway.

1987 NFL DRAFT

Player	Order No.	Pos.	College	Club	Round
Adams, David	309	RB	Arizona	Indianapolis	12
Adams, Mike	67	DB	Arkansas State	New Orleans	3
Adickes, John	154	C	Baylor	Chicago	6
Agee, Tommie	119	RB	Auburn	Seattle	5
Alexander, David	121	G	Tulsa	Philadelphia	5
Alvord, Steve	201	DT	Washington	St. Louis	8
Anderson, Anthony	256	DB	Grambling	San Diego	10
Anthony, Terrence	236	DB	Iowa State	Atlanta	9
Armentrout, Joe	224	RB	Wisconsin	Tampa Bay	9
Armstrong, Bruce	23	T	Louisville	New England	1
Armstrong, Scott	318	LB	Florida	Dallas	12
Atkins, Gene	179	DB	Florida A&M	New Orleans	7
Awalt, Robert	62	TE	San Diego State	St. Louis	3
Baker, Stephen	83	WR	Fresno State	New York Giants	3
Ball, Jerry	63	NT	Southern Methodist	Detroit	3
Ballard, Howard	283	T	Alabama A&M	Buffalo	11
Banks, Robert	176	DT	Notre Dame	Houston	7
Banks, Roy	114	WR	Eastern Illinois	Indianapolis	5
Barbay, Roland	184	NT	Louisiana State	Seattle	7
Bartalo, Steve	143	RB	Colorado State	Tampa Bay	6
Bartlett, Doug	91	NT	Northern Illinois	Los Angeles Rams	4
Barton, Harris	22	T	North Carolina	San Francisco	1
Beasley, Derrick	102	DB	Winston-Salem	New England	4
Bell, Leonard	76	DB	Indiana	Cincinnati	3
Bellini, Mark	170	WR	Brigham Young	Indianapolis	7
Bennett, Cornelius	2	LB	Alabama	Indianapolis	1
Bernstine, Rod	24	TE	Texas A&M	San Diego	1
Berry, Ray	44	LB	Baylor	Minnesota	2
Berthusen, Bill	321	DT	Iowa State	New York Giants	12
Beuerlein, Steve	110	QB	Notre Dame	Los Angeles Raiders	4
Blount, Alvin	235	RB	Maryland	Dallas	9
Bosa, John	16	DE	Boston College	Miami	1
Braggs, Stephen	165	DB	Texas	Cleveland	6
Brandon, David	60	LB	Memphis State	Buffalo	3
Braxton, Tyrone	334	DB	North Dakota State	Denver	12
Bregel, Jeff	37	G	Southern California	San Francisco	2
Brewton, Larry	303	DB	Temple	Cleveland	11
Brock, Louis	53	DB	Southern California	San Diego	2
Brooks, Michael	86	LB	Louisiana State	Denver	3
Brown, Jerome	9	DT	Miami	Philadelphia	1
Brown, Laron	304	WR	Texas	Washington	11
Brown, Raynard	259	WR	South Carolina	Detroit	10
Brown, Ron	204	LB	Southern California	San Diego	8
Brown, Tom	182	RB	Pittsburgh	Miami	7
Bruno, John	126	P	Penn State	St. Louis	5
Bryan, Steve	120	DE	Oklahoma	Chicago	5
Buchanan, Charles	205	DE	Tennessee State	Pittsburgh	8
Buck, Jason	17	DE	Brigham Young	Cincinnati	1
Bullitt, Steve	220	LB	Texas A&M	Cleveland	8
Burse, Tony	324	RB	Middle Tennessee	Seattle	12
Calhoun, Rick	230	RB	Cal State-Fullerton	Detroit	9
Carberry, Paul	260	DT	Oregon State	Philadelphia	10
Carlson, Cody	64	QB	Baylor	Houston	3
Carrier, Mark	57	WR	Nicholls State	Tampa Bay	3
Caston, Toby	159	LB	Louisiana State	Houston	6

Colts made Alabama LB Cornelius Bennett No. 2 overall.

Auburn RB Brent Fullwood was Packers' top pick.

Player	Order No.	Pos.	College	Club	Round
Chapura, Dick	277	DT	Missouri	Chicago	10
Clark, Louis	270	WR	Mississippi State	Seattle	10
Clark, Robert	263	WR	N. Carolina Central	New Orleans	10
Clay, John	15	T	Missouri	Los Angeles Raiders	1
Clemons, Michael	218	RB	William & Mary	Kansas City	8
Clinkscales, Joey	233	WR	Tennessee	Pittsburgh	9
Conlan, Shane	8	LB	Penn State	Buffalo	1
Conlin, Chris	132	T	Penn State	Miami	5
Cook, Toi	207	DB	Stanford	New Orleans	8
Cooper, Scott	308	DT	Kearney State	Tampa Bay	12
Croston, Dave	61	T	Iowa	Green Bay	3
Davis, Brian	30	DB	Nebraska	Washington	2
Davis, Elgin	330	RB	Central Florida	New England	12
Davis, Greg	246	P	Citadel	Tampa Bay	9
Davis, John	287	G	Georgia Tech	Houston	11
Davis, Wayne	229	LB	Alabama	St. Louis	9
De Line, Steve	189	K	Colorado State	San Francisco	7
Dennis, Mark	212	T	Illinois	Miami	8
Dixon, Randy	85	T	Pittsburgh	Indianapolis	4
Dove, Wes	312	DE	Syracuse	Seattle	12
Dozier, D.J.	14	RB	Penn State	Minnesota	1
Drost, Jeff	198	DT	Iowa	Green Bay	8
Duncan, Curtis	258	WR	Northwestern	Houston	10
Dusbabek, Mark	105	LB	Minnesota	Houston	4
Eccles, Scott	238	TE	Eastern New Mexico	Los Angeles Raiders	9
Elam, Onzy	75	LB	Tennessee State	New York Jets	3
Ellis, Jim	273	LB	Boise State	Los Angeles Raiders	10
Embree, Jon	166	TE	Colorado	Los Angeles Rams	6
Emery, Larry	320	RB	Wisconsin	Atlanta	12
Evans, Bryon	93	LB	Arizona	Philadelphia	4
Evans, Donald	47	DE	Winston-Salem	Los Angeles Rams	2
Evans, James	271	RB	Southern U.	Kansas City	10
Everett, Thomas	94	DB	Baylor	Pittsburgh	4
Faucette, Chuck	279	LB	Maryland	New York Giants	10
Fenney, Rick	211	RB	Washington	Minnesota	8
Flagler, Terrence	25	RB	Clemson	San Francisco	1
Flowers, Kenny	31	RB	Clemson	Atlanta	2
Francis, Ron	39	DB	Baylor	Dallas	2
Freeman, Lorenzo	89	DT	Pittsburgh	Green Bay	4
Fullwood, Brent	4	RB	Auburn	Green Bay	1
Gage, Steve	144	DB	Tulsa	Washington	6
Gambol, Chris	58	T	Iowa	Indianapolis	3
Gannon, Rich	98	QB	Delaware	New England	4
Garalczyk, Mark	146	DT	Western Michigan	St. Louis	6
Garza, Sammy	216	QB	Texas-El Paso	Seattle	8
Gay, Everett	124	WR	Texas	Dallas	5
Gesek, John	265	G	Cal State-Sacramento	Los Angeles Raiders	10
Gibson, Dennis	203	LB	Iowa State	Detroit	8
Gibson, Tom	116	DE	Northern Arizona	New England	5
Goebel, Joe	284	C	UCLA	San Diego	11
Gogan, Kevin	206	T	Washington	Dallas	8
Goode, Chris	253	DB	Alabama	Indianapolis	10
Gordon, Alex	42	LB	Cincinnati	New York Jets	2
Gordon, Sonny	157	DB	Ohio State	Cincinnati	6
Graf, Rick	43	LB	Wisconsin	Miami	2
Graham, Don	84	LB	Penn State	Tampa Bay	4
Grayson, Dave	217	LB	Fresno State	San Francisco	8
Greenwood, Marcus	310	RB	UCLA	San Diego	12
Hall, Delton	38	DB	Clemson	Pittsburgh	2
Hall, Ron	87	TE	Hawaii	Tampa Bay	4
Ham, Tracy	240	RB	Georgia Southern	Los Angeles Rams	9
Harbaugh, Jim	26	QB	Michigan	Chicago	1

Lions grabbed Washington DE Reggie Rogers.

Penn State LB Shane Conlan landed with the Bills.

Player	Order No.	Pos.	College	Club	Round
Harris, Archie	193	T	William & Mary	Chicago	7
Harris, Gregg	228	G	Wake Forest	Green Bay	9
Harris, William	195	TE	Bishop, Tex.	St. Louis	7
Harrison, Rob	254	DB	Cal State-Sacramento	Los Angeles Raiders	10
Heimuli, Lakei	249	RB	Brigham Young	Chicago	9
Henley, Thomas	152	WR	Stanford	New Orleans	6
Hicks, Cliff	74	DB	Oregon	Los Angeles Rams	3
Highsmith, Alonzo	3	RB	Miami	Houston	1
Hill, Bruce	106	WR	Arizona State	Tampa Bay	4
Hill, Lonzell	40	WR	Washington	New Orleans	2
Hitchcock, Ray	331	C	Minnesota	Washington	12
Hoge, Merril	261	RB	Idaho State	Pittsburgh	10
Holifield, John	328	RB	West Virginia	Cincinnati	12
Holland, Jamie	173	WR	Ohio State	San Diego	7
Holland, Johnny	41	LB	Texas A&M	Green Bay	2
Holmes, Bruce	325	LB	Minnesota	Kansas City	12
Horne, Greg	139	P	Arkansas	Cincinnati	5
Howard, Todd	73	LB	Texas A&M	Kansas City	3
Hudson, Doug	186	QB	Nicholls State	Kansas City	7
Hunter, Eddie	196	RB	Virginia Tech	New York Jets	8
Ingram, Mark	28	WR	Michigan State	New York Giants	1
Jackson, Bo	183	RB	Auburn	Los Angeles Raiders	7
Jackson, Kirby	129	DB	Mississippi State	New York Jets	5
Jaeger, Jeff	82	K	Washington	Cleveland	3
James, Michel	202	WR	Washington State	Houston	8
Jarostchuk, Ilia	127	LB	New Hampshire	St. Louis	5
Jarvis, Curt	169	NT	Alabama	Tampa Bay	7
Jefferson, Norman	335	DB	Louisiana State	Green Bay	12
Jeffires, Haywood	20	WR	North Carolina State	Houston	1
Jeffries, Eric	333	DB	Texas	Chicago	12
Jenkins, Alfred	248	RB	Arizona	Washington	9
Jessie, Tim	305	RB	Auburn	Chicago	11
Johnson, M.L.	243	LB	Hawaii	Seattle	9
Johnson, Tim	141	NT	Penn State	Pittsburgh	6
Johnson, Walter	46	LB	Louisiana Tech	Houston	2
Johnson, Will	138	LB	N.E. Louisiana	Chicago	5
Jokisch, Paul	134	WR	Michigan	San Francisco	5
Jones, Dale	262	LB	Tennessee	Dallas	10
Jones, Leonard	239	DB	Texas Tech	Minnesota	9
Jones, Nelson	115	DB	North Carolina State	San Diego	5
Jones, Rod	223	TE	Washington	New York Giants	8
Jordan, Tim	107	LB	Wisconsin	New England	4
Junkin, Mike	5	LB	Duke	Cleveland	1
Karsatos, Jim	322	QB	Ohio State	Miami	12
Kelley, Chris	178	TE	Akron	Pittsburgh	7
Kelm, Larry	108	LB	Texas A&M	Los Angeles Rams	4
Kiser, Paul	153	G	Wake Forest	Atlanta	6
Kleine, Wally	48	T	Notre Dame	Washington	2
Knight, Shawn	11	DT	Brigham Young	New Orleans	1
Lambiotte, Ken	232	QB	William & Mary	Philadelphia	9
Leach, Scott	234	LB	Ohio State	New Orleans	9
Lee, Gary	315	WR	Georgia Tech	Detroit	12
Leiker, Tony	172	DT	Stanford	Green Bay	7
Lewis, Sid	268	DB	Penn State	New York Jets	10
Lloyd, Greg	150	LB	Fort Valley State	Pittsburgh	6
Lockett, Charles	66	WR	Cal State-Long Beach	Pittsburgh	3
Lockett, Danny	148	LB	Arizona	Detroit	6
Logan, Marc	130	RB	Kentucky	Cincinnati	5
MacEsker, Joe	199	T	Texas-El Paso	San Diego	8
Mack, Milton	123	DB	Alcorn State	New Orleans	5
Majkowski, Don	255	QB	Virginia	Green Bay	10
Mann, Terence	293	NT	Southern Methodist	Miami	11

Seattle drafted Pitt DE Tony Woods as linebacker.

Brigham Young DE Jason Buck joins the Bengals.

Player	Order No.	Pos.	College	Club	Round
Manoa, Tim	80	RB	Penn State	Cleveland	3
Marshall, Warren	167	RB	James Madison	Denver	6
Marshall, Willie	145	WR	Temple	Green Bay	6
Martin, Kelvin	95	WR	Boston College	Dallas	4
Martin, Tracy	161	WR	North Dakota	New York Jets	6
Mataele, Stan	197	NT	Arizona	Tampa Bay	8
Mayes, Tony	137	DB	Kentucky	Tampa Bay	5
McClendon, Skip	77	DE	Arizona State	Cincinnati	3
McCluskey, David	269	RB	Georgia	Cincinnati	10
McDonald, Tim	34	DB	Southern California	St. Louis	2
McGrail, Joe	311	DT	Delaware	Buffalo	12
McKeller, Keith	227	TE	Jacksonville State	Buffalo	9
McLean, Ron	241	DE	Cal State-Fullerton	New York Jets	9
McLemore, Chris	288	RB	Arizona	Los Angeles Raiders	11
Mersereau, Scott	136	DT	Southern Connecticut	Los Angeles Rams	5
Mesner, Bruce	209	DE	Maryland	Buffalo	8
Migliazzo, Paul	221	LB	Oklahoma	Chicago	8
Miller, Chris	13	QB	Oregon	Atlanta	1
Miller, Chuckie	200	DB	UCLA	Indianapolis	8
Mitchell, Roland	33	DB	Texas Tech	Buffalo	2
Moore, Mark	104	DB	Oklahoma State	Seattle	4
Morgan, Dan	222	G	Penn State	Denver	8
Morris, Ron	54	WR	Southern Methodist	Chicago	2
Morse, Bobby	316	RB	Michigan State	Philadelphia	12
Moss, Winston	50	LB	Miami	Tampa Bay	2
Moten, Ron	149	LB	Florida	Philadelphia	6
Mraz, Mark	125	DE	Utah State	Atlanta	5
Mueller, Jamie	78	RB	Benedictine	Buffalo	3
Munford, Marc	111	LB	Nebraska	Denver	4
Nattiel, Ricky	27	WR	Florida	Denver	1
Neal, Frankie	71	WR	Fort Hays (Kan.)	Green Bay	3
Neal, Tommy	306	RB	Maryland	Denver	11
Neighbors, Wes	231	C	Alabama	Houston	9
Nicholas, Calvin	301	WR	Grambling	San Francisco	11
Nichols, Gerald	187	NT	Florida State	New York Jets	7
Nickerson, Hardy	122	LB	California	Pittsburgh	5
Noonan, Danny	12	DT	Nebraska	Dallas	1
O'Connor, Paul	140	G	Miami	New York Giants	5
Odomes, Nathaniel	29	DB	Wisconsin	Buffalo	2
Okoye, Christian	35	RB	Azusa Pacific	Kansas City	2
Oliver, Darryl	297	RB	Miami	Seattle	11
Onosai, Joe	151	G	Hawaii	Dallas	6
Ontko, Bob	247	LB	Penn State	Indianapolis	9
Oswald, Paul	289	C	Kansas	Pittsburgh	11
Palmer, Paul	19	RB	Temple	Kansas City	1
Parker, Stan	225	G	Nebraska	New York Giants	9
Paye, John	275	QB	Stanford	San Francisco	10
Pease, Brent	295	QB	Montana	Minnesota	11
Peat, Todd	285	G	Northern Illinois	St. Louis	11
Peoples, Tim	174	DB	Washington	St. Louis	7
Perry, Mario	294	TE	Mississippi	Los Angeles Raiders	11
Perryman, Bob	79	RB	Michigan	New England	3
Pidgeon, Tim	237	LB	Syracuse	Miami	9
Pike, Chris	158	DT	Tulsa	Philadelphia	6
Plummer, Bruce	250	DB	Mississippi State	Denver	9
Porter, Kerry	171	RB	Washington State	Buffalo	7
Raddatz, Craig	242	LB	Wisconsin	Cincinnati	9
Rakoczy, Gregg	32	C	Miami	Cleveland	2
Ransdell, Bill	327	QB	Kentucky	New York Jets	12
Reese, Jerry	264	TE	Illinois	Atlanta	10
Reid, Michael	181	LB	Wisconsin	Atlanta	7
Reveiz, Carlos	302	K	Tennessee	New England	11

Player	Order No.	Pos.	College	Club	Round
Reynolds, Ricky	36	DB	Washington State	Tampa Bay	2
Reynosa, Jim	281	DE	Arizona State	Indianapolis	11
Rice, Mike	214	P	Montana	New York Jets	8
Richardson, Craig	298	WR	Eastern Washington	Kansas City	11
Richardson, Greg	156	WR	Alabama	Minnesota	6
Richardson, Tim	160	RB	Pacific	New York Giants	6
Riesenberg, Doug	168	T	California	New York Giants	6
Riggs, Jim	103	TE	Clemson	Cincinnati	4
Riley, Bob	267	T	Indiana	Minnesota	10
Rivers, Garland	92	DB	Michigan	Detroit	4
Roberts, Steve	299	DE	Washington	Denver	11
Robinson, Freddie	142	DB	Alabama	Indianapolis	6
Rodriguez, Ruben	131	P	Arizona	Seattle	5
Rogers, Reggie	7	DE	Washington	Detroit	1
Rolling, Henry	135	LB	Nevada-Reno	Tampa Bay	5
Rutland, Reggie	100	DB	Georgia Tech	Minnesota	4
Saddler, Rod	90	DT	Texas A&M	St. Louis	4
Saleaumua, Dan	175	DT	Arizona State	Detroit	7
Schwedes, Scott	56	WR	Syracuse	Miami	2
Scott, Patrick	282	WR	Grambling	Green Bay	11
Scotts, Colin	70	DT	Hawaii	St. Louis	3
Seals, Leon	109	DE	Jackson State	Buffalo	4
Sellers, Lance	155	LB	Boise State	Miami	6
Shelley, Elbert	292	DB	Arkansas State	Atlanta	11
Shelley, Jonathan	245	DB	Mississippi	San Francisco	9
Shula, Mike	313	QB	Alabama	Tampa Bay	12
Simmonds, Mike	252	G	Indiana State	Detroit	10
Simmons, Ed	164	T	Eastern Washington	Washington	6
Siverling, Brian	286	TE	Penn State	Detroit	11
Smith, Al	147	LB	Utah State	Houston	6
Smith, Bill	191	P	Mississippi	Green Bay	7
Smith, David	272	LB	Northern Arizona	Los Angeles Rams	10
Smith, Don	51	RB	Mississippi State	Tampa Bay	2
Smith, Sean	101	DE	Grambling	Chicago	4
Smith, Steve	81	RB	Penn State	Los Angeles Raiders	3
Smith, Timmy	117	RB	Texas Tech	Washington	5
Sorrells, Tyrone	319	G	Georgia Tech	New Orleans	12
Stark, Chad	329	RB	North Dakota State	New York Giants	12
Stephen, Scott	69	LB	Arizona State	Green Bay	3
Stewart, Michael	213	DB	Fresno State	Los Angeles Rams	8
Stokes, Fred	332	DE	Georgia Southern	Los Angeles Rams	12
Stouffer, Kelly	6	QB	Colorado State	St. Louis	1
Stradford, Troy	99	RB	Boston College	Miami	4
Strozier, Wilbur	194	TE	Georgia	Denver	7
Swarn, George	118	RB	Miami (Ohio)	St. Louis	5
Swayne, Harry	190	DE	Rutgers	Tampa Bay	7
Sweeney, Kevin	180	QB	Fresno State	Dallas	7
Taliaferro, Curtis	208	LB	Virginia Tech	Atlanta	8
Tamburello, Ben	65	C	Auburn	Philadelphia	3
Taylor, Bobby	266	DB	Wisconsin	Miami	10
Taylor, Gene	163	WR	Fresno State	New England	6
Taylor, Kitrick	128	WR	Washington State	Kansas City	5
Taylor, Reggie	280	RB	Cincinnati	Tampa Bay	11
Tennell, Derek	185	TE	UCLA	Seattle	7
Testaverde, Vinny	1	QB	Miami	Tampa Bay	1
Thatcher, Chris	188	G	Lafayette	Cincinnati	7
Thomas, Eric	49	DB	Tulane	Cincinnati	2
Thomas, Henry	72	NT	Louisiana State	Minnesota	3
Thomas, Johnny	192	DB	Baylor	Washington	7
Tillman, Spencer	133	RB	Oklahoma	Houston	5
Timmer, Kirk	300	LB	Montana State	New York Jets	11
Trapilo, Steve	96	G	Boston College	New Orleans	4

Raiders tagged Missouri OT John Clay as first pick.

Temple RB Paul Palmer will carry for the Chiefs.

Player	Order No.	Pos.	College	Club	Round
Turner, Odessa	112	WR	N.W. Louisiana	New York Giants	4
Valentine, Ira	314	RB	Texas A&M	Houston	12
Van Dyke, Ralph	97	T	Southern Illinois	Atlanta	4
Vaughn, Clarence	219	DB	Northern Illinois	Washington	8
Vick, Roger	21	RB	Texas A&M	New York Jets	1
Villa, Danny	113	T	Arizona State	New England	5
Vlasic, Mark	88	QB	Iowa	San Diego	4
Walter, Dave	307	QB	Michigan Tech	New York Giants	11
Ward, Jeff	291	K	Texas	Dallas	11
Warne, Jim	296	T	Arizona State	Cincinnati	11
Watts, Randy	244	DE	Catawba	Kansas City	9
Wells, Arthur	290	TE	Grambling	New Orleans	11
White, Adrian	55	DB	Florida	New York Giants	2
White, Bob	162	LB	Penn State	San Francisco	6
Wilcher, Thomas	226	RB	Michigan	San Diego	9
Wilcots, Solomon	215	DB	Colorado	Cincinnati	8
Wilkerson, Bruce	52	T	Tennessee	Los Angeles Raiders	2
Wilkinson, Rafe	278	LB	Richmond	Denver	10
Williams, Alonzo	326	RB	Mesa, Colo.	Los Angeles Rams	12
Williams, Brian	177	T	Central Michigan	Philadelphia	7
Williams, Joel	210	TE	Notre Dame	Miami	8
Williams, Keith	323	DT	Florida	Minnesota	12
Wilson, Karl	59	DE	Louisiana State	San Diego	3
Wilson, Ted	274	WR	Central Florida	Washington	10
Winters, Frank	276	C	Western Illinois	Cleveland	10
Woods, Tony	18	LB	Pittsburgh	Seattle	1
Woodson, Rod	10	DB	Purdue	Pittsburgh	1
Wright, Charles	257	DB	Tulsa	St. Louis	10
Wright, Dana	251	RB	Findlay	New York Giants	9
Wyman, Dave	45	LB	Stanford	Seattle	2
Young, Theo	317	TE	Arkansas	Pittsburgh	12
Zimmerman, Jeff	68	G	Florida	Dallas	3

1987
NFL SCHEDULE

*NIGHT GAME

SUNDAY, SEPT. 13
Atlanta at Tampa Bay
Cincinnati at Indianapolis
Cleveland at New Orleans
Dallas at St. Louis
Detroit at Minnesota
Los Angeles Raiders at Green Bay
Los Angeles Rams at Houston
Miami at New England
New York Jets at Buffalo
Philadelphia at Washington *WIN*
San Diego at Kansas City
San Francisco at Pittsburgh
Seattle at Denver

MONDAY, SEPT. 14
*New York Giants at Chicago

SUNDAY, SEPT. 20
Dallas at New York Giants
Denver vs. Green Bay
at Milwaukee
Detroit at Los Angeles Raiders
Houston at Buffalo
Kansas City at Seattle
Miami at Indianapolis
Minnesota at Los Angeles Rams
New Orleans at Philadelphia
Pittsburgh at Cleveland
St. Louis at San Diego
San Francisco at Cincinnati
Tampa Bay at Chicago
Washington at Atlanta *LOSS*

MONDAY, SEPT. 21
*New England at New York Jets

SUNDAY, SEPT. 27
Atlanta at New Orleans
Buffalo at Dallas
Chicago at Detroit
Cincinnati at Los Angeles Rams
Green Bay at Tampa Bay
Indianapolis at St. Louis
Los Angeles Raiders at Houston
Minnesota at Kansas City
New York Jets at Pittsburgh
New York Giants at Miami

New England at Washington
Philadelphia at San Francisco
Seattle at San Diego

MONDAY, SEPT. 28
*Denver at Cleveland

SUNDAY, OCT. 4
Chicago at Philadelphia
Cleveland at New England
Dallas at New York Jets
Green Bay at Minnesota
Houston at Denver
Indianapolis at Buffalo
Kansas City at L.A. Raiders
L.A. Rams at New Orleans
Miami at Seattle
Pittsburgh at Atlanta
St. Louis at Washington *WIN*
San Diego at Cincinnati
Tampa Bay at Detroit

MONDAY, OCT. 5
*San Francisco at N.Y. Giants

SUNDAY, OCT. 11
Atlanta at San Francisco
Buffalo at New England
Cincinnati at Seattle
Detroit at Green Bay
Houston at Cleveland
Kansas City at Miami
Minnesota at Chicago
New Orleans at St. Louis
New York Jets at Indianapolis
Philadelphia at Dallas
Pittsburgh at Los Angeles Rams
San Diego at Tampa Bay
Washington at New York Giants *WIN*

MONDAY, OCT. 12
*Los Angeles Raiders at Denver

SUNDAY, OCT. 18
Cleveland at Cincinnati
Denver at Kansas City
Indianapolis at Pittsburgh

Los Angeles Rams at Atlanta
Miami at New York Jets
New England at Houston
New Orleans at Chicago
New York Giants at Buffalo
Philadelphia at Green Bay
St. Louis at San Francisco
San Diego at Los Angeles Raiders
Seattle at Detroit
Tampa Bay at Minnesota

MONDAY, OCT. 19
*Washington at Dallas *WIN*

SUNDAY, OCT. 25
Atlanta at Houston
Buffalo at Miami
Chicago at Tampa Bay
Cincinnati at Pittsburgh
Dallas at Philadelphia
Denver at Minnesota
Green Bay at Detroit
Kansas City at San Diego
New England at Indianapolis
New York Jets at Washington *WIN*
St. Louis at New York Giants
San Francisco at New Orleans
Seattle at Los Angeles Raiders

MONDAY, OCT. 26
*Los Angeles Rams at Cleveland

SUNDAY, NOV. 1
Cleveland at San Diego
Detroit at Denver
Houston at Cincinnati
Indianapolis at New York Jets
Kansas City at Chicago
L.A. Raiders at New England
Minnesota at Seattle
New Orleans at Atlanta
Philadelphia at St. Louis
Pittsburgh at Miami
San Francisco at L.A. Rams
Tampa Bay vs. Green Bay
  at Milwaukee
Washington at Buffalo *WIN*

MONDAY, NOV. 2
*New York Giants at Dallas

SUNDAY, NOV. 8
Atlanta at Cleveland
Chicago at Green Bay
Dallas at Detroit
Denver at Buffalo
Houston at San Francisco
Los Angeles Raiders at Minnesota
Miami at Cincinnati

New Orleans at L.A. Rams
Pittsburgh at Kansas City
San Diego at Indianapolis
Tampa Bay at St. Louis
Washington at Philadelphia *LOSS*
*New England at New York Giants

MONDAY, NOV. 9
*Seattle at New York Jets

SUNDAY, NOV. 15
Buffalo at Cleveland
Cincinnati at Atlanta
Dallas at New England
Detroit at Washington *Win*
Green Bay at Seattle
Houston at Pittsburgh
Indianapolis at Miami
Los Angeles Rams at St. Louis
Minnesota at Tampa Bay
New Orleans at San Francisco
New York Giants at Philadelphia
New York Jets at Kansas City
*L.A. Raiders at San Diego

MONDAY, NOV. 16
*Chicago at Denver

SUNDAY, NOV. 22
Atlanta at Minnesota
Buffalo at New York Jets
Cleveland at Houston
Detroit at Chicago
Denver at Los Angeles Raiders
Green Bay at Kansas City
Indianapolis at New England
New York Giants at New Orleans
Pittsburgh at Cincinnati
St. Louis at Philadelphia
San Diego at Seattle
San Francisco at Tampa Bay
*Miami at Dallas

MONDAY, NOV. 23
*Los Angeles Rams at Washington 7 *LOSS*

THURSDAY, NOV. 26
Kansas City at Detroit
Minnesota at Dallas

SUNDAY, NOV. 29
Cincinnati at New York Jets
Denver at San Diego
Green Bay at Chicago
Houston at Indianapolis
Miami at Buffalo
New Orleans at Pittsburgh
New York Giants at Washington 7 WIN

Philadelphia at New England
St. Louis at Atlanta
Tampa Bay at Los Angeles Rams
*Cleveland at San Francisco

MONDAY, NOV. 30
*Los Angeles Raiders at Seattle

SUNDAY. DEC. 6
Atlanta at Dallas
Buffalo at Los Angeles Raiders
Indianapolis at Cleveland
Kansas City at Cincinnati
Los Angeles Rams at Detroit
New England at Denver
Philadelphia at New York Giants
San Diego at Houston
San Francisco at Green Bay
Seattle at Pittsburgh
Tampa Bay at New Orleans
Washington at St. Louis
*Chicago at Minnesota

MONDAY, DEC. 7
*New York Jets at Miami

SUNDAY, DEC. 13
Atlanta at Los Angeles Rams
Buffalo at Indianapolis
Cincinnati at Cleveland
Dallas at Washington
Detroit at Tampa Bay
Houston at New Orleans
L.A. Raiders at Kansas City
Miami at Philadelphia
Minnesota vs. Green Bay
  at Milwaukee
New York Giants at St. Louis
New York Jets at New England
Pittsburgh at San Diego
*Denver at Seattle

MONDAY, DEC. 14
*Chicago at San Francisco

SATURDAY, DEC. 19
Green Bay at New York Giants
Kansas City at Denver

SUNDAY, DEC. 20
Cleveland at Los Angeles Raiders
Indianapolis at San Diego
Minnesota at Detroit
New England at Buffalo
New Orleans at Cincinnati
Philadelphia at New York Jets
Pittsburgh at Houston
St. Louis at Tampa Bay

San Francisco at Atlanta
Seattle at Chicago
*Washington at Miami

MONDAY, DEC. 21
*Dallas at Los Angeles Rams

SATURDAY, DEC. 26
Cleveland at Pittsburgh
Washington at Minnesota

SUNDAY, DEC. 27
Buffalo at Philadelphia
Chicago at Los Angeles Raiders
Cincinnati at Houston
Detroit at Atlanta
Green Bay at New Orleans
New York Jets at New York Giants
St. Louis at Dallas
San Diego at Denver
Seattle at Kansas City
Tampa Bay at Indianapolis
*L.A. Rams at San Francisco

MONDAY, DEC. 28
*New England at Miami

Nationally Televised Games

(Also carried on CBS Radio Network)

REGULAR SEASON

Monday, Sept. 14—New York Giants at Chicago (night, ABC)
Monday, Sept. 21—New England at New York Jets (night, ABC)
Monday, Sept. 28—Denver at Cleveland (night, ABC)
Monday, Oct. 5—San Francisco at New York Giants (night, ABC)
Monday, Oct. 12—Los Angeles Raiders at Denver (night, ABC)
Monday, Oct. 19—Washington at Dallas (night, ABC)
Monday, Oct. 26—Los Angeles Rams at Cleveland (night, ABC)
Monday, Nov. 2—New York Giants at Dallas (night, ABC)
Sunday, Nov. 8—New England at New York Giants (night, ESPN)
Monday, Nov. 9—Seattle at New York Jets (night, ABC)
Sunday, Nov. 15—Los Angeles Raiders at San Diego (night, ESPN)
Monday, Nov. 16—Chicago at Denver (night, ABC)
Sunday, Nov. 22—Miami at Dallas (night, ESPN)
Monday, Nov. 23—Los Angeles Rams at Washington (night, ABC)
Thursday, Nov. 26—(Thanksgiving) Kansas City at Detroit (day, NBC)
                    Minnesota at Dallas (day, CBS)
Sunday, Nov. 29—Cleveland at San Francisco (night, ESPN)
Monday, Nov. 30—Los Angeles Raiders at Seattle (night, ABC)
Sunday, Dec. 6—Chicago at Minnesota (night, ESPN)
Monday, Dec. 7—New York Jets at Miami (night, ABC)
Sunday, Dec. 13—Denver at Seattle (night, ESPN)
Monday, Dec. 14—Chicago at San Francisco (night, ABC)
Saturday, Dec. 19—Green Bay at New York Giants (day, CBS)
                    Kansas City at Denver (day, NBC)
Sunday, Dec. 20—Washington at Miami (night, ESPN)
Monday, Dec. 21—Dallas at Los Angeles Rams (night, ABC)
Saturday, Dec. 26—Cleveland at Pittsburgh (day, NBC)
                    Washington at Minnesota (day, CBS)
Sunday, Dec. 27—Los Angeles Rams at San Francisco (night, ESPN)
Monday, Dec. 28—New England at Miami (night, ABC)

POSTSEASON

Sunday, Jan. 3—AFC and NFC First—Round Playoffs (NBC and CBS)
Saturday, Jan. 9—AFC and NFC Divisional Playoffs (NBC and CBS)
Sunday, Jan. 10—AFC and NFC Divisional Playoffs (NBC and CBS)
Sunday, Jan. 17—AFC and NFC Championship Games (NBC and CBS)
Sunday, Jan. 31—Super Bowl XXII at San Diego Jack Murphy Stadium (ABC)
Sunday, Feb. 7—AFC-NFC Pro Bowl at Honolulu, Hawaii (ESPN)

Revised and updated with over 75 all
new sports records and photographs!

THE ILLUSTRATED
SPORTS RECORD BOOK
Zander Hollander and David Schulz

Here in a single book are more than 350
all-time sports records with stories and
photos so vivid it's like "being there." All the
sports classics are here: Babe Ruth, Wilt
Chamberlain, Muhammad Ali ... plus the
stories of such active stars as Dwight Gooden
and Wayne Gretzky. This is the authoritative
book on what the great records are, and
who set them—an engrossing, fun-filled
reference guide filled with anecdotes of
hundreds of renowned athletes whose
remarkable records remain as fresh as when
they were set.
